CW00672586

The Neuroscience of Adolescence

As scientific inquiry and public interest in the adolescent brain grow, so too does the need for an accessible textbook that communicates the growing research on this topic. *The Neuroscience of Adolescence* is a comprehensive educational tool for developmental cognitive neuroscience students at all levels as it details the varying elements that shape the adolescent brain. Historical notions of adolescence have focused on the significant hormonal changes that occur as one transitions from childhood to adolescence, but new research has revealed a more nuanced picture that helps inform our understanding of how the brain functions across the lifespan. By emphasizing the biological and neurobiological changes that occur during adolescence, this book gives students a holistic understanding of this developmental window and uniquely discusses the policy implications of neuroscience research for the lives of young people today.

Adriana Galván is an Associate Professor of Psychology at University of California, Los Angeles (UCLA), where she is also the Jeffrey Wenzel Term Chair in Behavioral Neuroscience and the director of the Developmental Neuroscience Laboratory. Galván's research focuses on adolescent brain development and has informed public policy on teenage driving, sleep, and juvenile justice. She received the American Psychological Association (APA) Early Career Distinguished Scientific Contribution Award, the APA Boyd McCandless Early Career Award, the William T. Grant Scholars Award and the Cognitive Neuroscience Society Young Investigator Award, and serves as a Network Scholar for the MacArthur Foundation Research Network on Law and Neuroscience. Her research has been funded by the National Science Foundation, the MacArthur Foundation, the National Institutes of Health, the Jacobs Foundation, and the William T. Grant Foundation. She regularly teaches a popular UCLA undergraduate course on the developing brain.

Cambridge Fundamentals of Neuroscience in Psychology

Developed in response to a growing need to make neuroscience accessible to students and other non-specialist readers, the *Cambridge Fundamentals of Neuroscience in Psychology* series provides brief introductions to key areas of neuroscience research across major domains of psychology. Written by experts in cognitive, social, affective, developmental, clinical, and applied neuroscience, these books will serve as ideal primers for students and other readers seeking an entry point to the challenging world of neuroscience.

Forthcoming Titles in the Series:

The Neuroscience of Intelligence, by Richard J. Haier
The Neuroscience of Expertise, by Merim Bilalić
Cognitive Neuroscience of Memory, by Scott D. Slotnick
The Neuroscience of Aging, by Angela Gutchess
The Neuroscience of Addiction, by Francesca Filbey

The Neuroscience of Adolescence

Adriana Galván
University of California, Los Angeles

CAMBRIDGE
UNIVERSITY PRESS

CAMBRIDGE
UNIVERSITY PRESS

University Printing House, Cambridge CB2 8BS, United Kingdom

One Liberty Plaza, 20th Floor, New York, NY 10006, USA

477 Williamstown Road, Port Melbourne, VIC 3207, Australia

314-321, 3rd Floor, Plot 3, Splendor Forum, Jasola District Centre, New Delhi - 110025, India

79 Anson Road, #06-04/06, Singapore 079906

Cambridge University Press is part of the University of Cambridge.

It furthers the University's mission by disseminating knowledge in the pursuit of education, learning and research at the highest international levels of excellence.

www.cambridge.org
Information on this title: www.cambridge.org/9781107461857
DOI: 10.1017/9781316106143

© Adriana Galv ´an 2017

This publication is in copyright. Subject to statutory exception and to the provisions of relevant collective licensing agreements, no reproduction of any part may take place without the written permission of Cambridge University Press.

First published 2017

A catalogue record for this publication is available from the British Library

Library of Congress Cataloging in Publication data
Names: Galvaán, Adriana, 1979– author.
Title: The neuroscience of adolescence / Adriana Galván.
Description: Cambridge, United Kingdom ; New York, NY : Cambridge University Press, 2017 | Includes bibliographical references.
Identifiers: LCCN 2016048271| ISBN 9781107089921 (hardback) | ISBN 9781107461857 (paperback)
Subjects: | MESH: Mental Processes – physiology | Adolescent – physiology | Brain – physiology | Puberty – physiology | Adolescent Development – physiology
Classification: LCC RJ503.7.A36 | NLMWL 337 | DDC 616.800835 – dc23
LC record available at https://lccn.loc.gov/2016048271

ISBN 978-1-107-08992-1 Hardback
ISBN 978-1-107-46185-7 Paperback

Cambridge University Press has no responsibility for the persistence or accuracy of URLs for external or third-party internet websites referred to in this publication, and does not guarantee that any content on such websites is, or will remain, accurate or appropriate.

To the past and current students of Psych 161 at UCLA

To my parents and sisters, t.k.m.

To my future adolescents, Gustavo and Lucia

To my inspiring husband Bill

Contents

The color plate section can be found between pp. 206 and 207

Figures

Preface

The explosion of research on the adolescent brain in recent years has triggered enthusiastic media attention on this topic. Popular outlets such as *Time*, *The Wall Street Journal*, *National Geographic*, and *The New Yorker* have all featured research on the adolescent brain. The rationale for writing this book is twofold. First, this book will fill a growing need in the area of developmental cognitive neuroscience. Although there are numerous textbooks on cognitive neuroscience and a couple of popular textbooks on adolescent psychology, there is currently no single textbook that merges these two disciplines together from a developmental cognitive neuroscience perspective. As scientific inquiry and public interest in the adolescent brain has grown, so too has the need for a comprehensive and accessible textbook that communicates extant neuroscience research on this topic. This book was motivated by my own frustration at failing to find a suitable textbook for an upper-division undergraduate course on the developing adolescent brain. The goal is for the book to serve as an educational tool for developmental cognitive neuroscience students and trainees at all levels. Second, the book will describe the multi-faceted elements that shape the adolescent brain. Historical notions of the adolescent have focused on the significant hormonal changes that occur as individuals transition from childhood to adolescence. However, new research using cutting-edge technology to visualize the healthy human brain presents a more nuanced picture of adolescence. Tools such as structural and functional magnetic resonance imaging (sMRI and fMRI) have informed our understanding of how the brain functions across the lifespan. By emphasizing both biological and neurobiological changes that occur during adolescence, this book will introduce readers to a more holistic understanding of this important developmental window.

Woven into empirical data and research approaches are the latest neurobiological and psychological models that have been proposed to explain adolescent behavior. The general premise of these models is that the brain regions we rely on for decision-making and judgment develop along different developmental trajectories: the motivational and emotional systems outpace maturation of the prefrontal cortex, which is important for regulating behavior and goal-planning. The book describes these models in detail and then provides the most up-to-date take on their relevance, utility, and limitations.

An innovative aspect of this book is that it was written with an eye toward the policy implications of research on the adolescent brain. These themes are woven through the chapters and then described in greater detail in Chapter 8 on policy. The main topics discussed are the role of adolescent neuroscience on the juvenile justice system, teenage driving, teenage sleep, and health decisions.

How to Use this Book

The book is intended to introduce an academic audience, with some background in developmental psychology, cognitive neuroscience, and/or neuroimaging, to the burgeoning field of developmental cognitive neuroscience in general and the adolescent brain in particular.

The book is organized by cognitive domains. Each chapter discusses the development of a particular construct, such as social processing or cognition during adolescence. Particular brain regions tend to be implicated in particular constructs (the prefrontal cortex, for instance, is considered the most important hub of high cognition), so each chapter focuses on the relevant brain region(s). However, this is not intended to imply that there is a one-to-one correspondence between one brain region and one cognitive domain. The brain works as an entire network, so even brain regions that are not explicitly mentioned in particular chapters may play a role in supporting the construct of interest. As such, there is reference to other chapters within each chapter but it is written so that the book can be used flexibly and not necessarily taught in sequential order.

Each chapter ends with a bulleted list of major themes in the chapter, a set of review questions to help guide comprehension, and a list of suggested further readings. There are too many great articles to list so only a select few, usually review papers, are listed. Sprinkled throughout the chapter you will find images of concepts or data from the empirical research reviewed in the chapter. Space constraints limit our ability to include all the important data figures that are germane to the central themes, so students are encouraged to read the original articles.

The final chapter on policy aims to introduce students to the important strides adolescent brain research has made in informing public policy and legal sanctions related to adolescent development. It is by no means an exhaustive inventory of adolescent policy but is simply meant to be a primer of this important topic.

CHAPTER ONE

What Is Adolescence?

Learning Objectives

- What is adolescence?
- What is the history of adolescence?
- What are the current theories of adolescent brain development?
- What is the "function" of adolescence?
- A roadmap for using this book.

1.1 Introduction

Adolescence is an exciting time in life when individuals are more excitable, volatile, and exploratory than they will ever be. It is when children begin the long journey toward independence that is central to becoming well-adjusted adults. The term "adolescence" stems from the Latin *adolescere*, which means "to grow up" or "to grow to maturity" (Slee, Campbell, and Spears, 2012). Across the world and across different species, adolescence serves an important function: it is the time when individuals move from a state of dependence on caregivers to one of relative independence. This transition period lends itself to many changes that include physical growth and biological development, increasing cognitive sophistication, and changes in psychosocial skills. It is therefore no surprise that adolescents become more self-aware, capable of appreciating abstract concepts, interested in new ideas, and passionate leaders of causes they believe in.

Although adolescence has long been recognized as an important transitional period in our society, it has recently drawn more attention from policymakers and scholars. Adolescence is now a forefront topic of health reports (UN, 2011), advocacy documents (UN, 2012), and publications in academic journals. There is also worldwide attention to adolescents and their health, illustrated by several recent United Nations initiatives (Ki-moon, 2013). Together, this focus on adolescence has encouraged a lively discourse on how to treat, protect, and support youth. This book will focus on the role of brain and physical development on these important topics as they relate to adolescent well-being. We will also explore how the advent of brain imaging tools gave us the ability to peek into the adolescent brain to determine how its development contributes to characteristic adolescent behaviors.

1.2 Periods of Development

Development is the study of change across the lifespan. Patterns of developmental change begin at conception and continue through until death. These include physical, neural, physiological, and behavioral changes that all occur in distinct ways depending on the period of development. Some of these changes are biologically driven, which means they are caused by genes or physiology, and some are environmentally driven, meaning they are influenced by things in the person's environment, including parents, siblings, peers, and neighborhoods; most changes are the product of the interactions between biology and environment.

Although developmental psychologists and developmental cognitive neuroscientists who study adolescence mainly focus on individuals who are adolescents, they appreciate that understanding the developmental periods that precede and follow adolescence is equally important. In general, there are three developmental periods: childhood, adolescence, and adulthood.

1.2.1 Childhood

Childhood is comprised of the prenatal period, infancy, early childhood, and late childhood. The **prenatal period** is the development that occurs from the point of conception until birth. In humans, this period lasts approximately 9 months and is a time of significant growth: the organism morphs from a single cell to one complete with all the organs it will ever have in its lifetime. During this time, there is complete dependence on the mother for nutrients. **Infancy** encompasses the period from birth through approximately 18 months of age. Many important psychological activities and much physical learning occur during this time and there is extreme dependence on adult caregivers. Infants engage in active sensorimotor coordination, gross motor skill learning (e.g. walking), language learning, and intense social engagement, particularly between parent and child. **Early childhood** is the developmental period that follows the end of infancy and extends through about 5–6 years of age (approximately when a child enrolls in kindergarten). During this time, there is a focus on becoming more self-sufficient, as children begin to spend many hours playing alone and with peers. It is also during this time that they begin more complex language and reading skills. **Middle and late childhood** is the developmental period that extends from about kindergarten to right before adolescence (10 or 11 years of age). Significant academic learning occurs during this time, as children become more engaged in the fundamental skills of reading, writing, and arithmetic. Self-regulation of behavior increases during this time.

1.2.2 Adolescence

Given all the learning, skill emergence, and social interactions that occur prior to adolescence, childhood sets up adolescents with a rich developmental history. The combination of genetic background and childhood developmental history contributes to the course of adolescent development and associated brain development during this time. This is important to remember as we learn about the changes that occur during adolescence. Adolescent researchers face a daunting task in deciding how to define the "adolescent" group in their research studies. Most scientists have identified adolescence as "the gradual period of transition from childhood to adulthood" (Spear, 2000). Some neuroscience studies on human adolescents define adolescence by age, grade level, or pubertal status.

The exact timing of adolescence is not as clear-cut as that of childhood because its definition encompasses multiple factors, a topic we will return to later in this chapter. The age range of adolescence also varies with cultural and historical circumstances. In the United States, adolescence begins at approximately 11 to 13 years of age and ends in the late teenage years (approximately 18–19 years of age). **Early adolescence** typically encompasses the period from the middle school years and includes most of the pubertal development that characterizes the early part of adolescence (reviewed in greater detail in Chapter 2). **Late adolescence** refers approximately to the period after the majority of the pubertal transition. Significant psychosocial and cognitive changes occur during this time, including increases in orientation toward peers, romantic interests, and identity exploration, as well as more sophisticated cognitive abilities, including abstract thought, future planning and goal setting, and career exploration.

1.2.3 Adulthood

Similar to childhood and adolescence, adulthood is a heterogenous period of development that is not characterized by any one behavior or

Box 1.1 Adolescent Population Worldwide

- In 2015, the 3.1 billion people under the age of 25 represent about 42 percent of the world's total population.
- Africa, Asia and Latin America and the Caribbean are home to 90 percent of the world's young people: 1.7 billion youth aged 0–14 years old and 1.1 billion aged 15–24 years old.
- The number of young people are projected to grow to 3.4 billion by 2050.

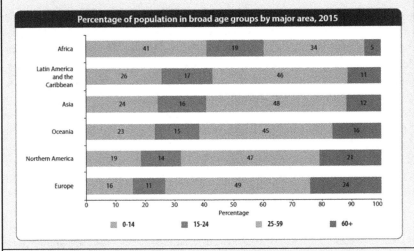

Source: United Nations, Department of Economic and Social Affairs, Population Division (2015). World Population Prospects 2015 – Data Booklet (ST/ESA/SER.A/377)

developmental milestone. It is the period of development that spans the greatest number of years as it includes early, middle, and late adulthood. **Early adulthood** (sometimes referred to as emerging adulthood: Arnett, 2011) refers to the late adolescent years and early 20s and lasts through the mid-30s. This period of life is very important in establishing complete financial and personal independence and is often when individuals attend college away from home as well as focus on career development. There is also a high prevalence of marriage in the late 20s. **Middle adulthood** begins at approximately 35 to 40 years of age and ends at some point between approximately 55 and 65 years of age. This period is when most child-rearing occurs, as individuals in this age group tend to have children undergoing childhood or adolescence. **Late adulthood** is the developmental period that lasts from approximately 65 years of age until death. In the United States, the average life expectancy is 77.4 and 82.2 for males and females, respectively.

1.3 Adolescence: A Historical Perspective

Behaviors that typically emerge during adolescence have been noted throughout history: Aristotle (384–322 BC) observed that "youth are heated by Nature as drunken man by wine." Socrates characterized youth as inclined to "contradict their parents" and "tyrannize their teachers" (attributed to Socrates by Plato, and cited in Lazarus, 1963). However, before 1904 adolescence was not recognized as a unique period of development. This may be hard to imagine today because teenagers, or adolescents, constitute such an important role in our society. G. Stanley Hall was a psychologist who is often credited with being the first to acknowledge adolescence as an important period of human development that he referred to as a period of "storm and stress" (1904). This phrase was taken from the German *Sturm und Drang* movement, and comprised three key aspects: conflict with parents, mood disruptions, and risky behavior. Hall noted that this is characteristic of most adolescents, biologically based, and influenced by culture (Arnett, 2011). Psychoanalytic theorists, especially Anna Freud (1946, 1958, 1968), strongly endorsed Hall's proposed model of adolescence and attributed these characteristic behaviors to the hormonal changes of puberty, believing that they introduced significant distress for the adolescent. Similarly, Sigmund Freud, and later his daughter Anna Freud, believed that the surge in hormones leads to psychological conflict in ways that affect adolescent behavior. Erik Erikson's theory was centered on the idea that pubertal changes, in conjunction with pressures from society, lead to an identity crisis that forces the adolescent to examine and define who she is.

In contrast, Margaret Mead (1928) and Ruth Benedict (1934) believed that adolescence is a culturally defined experience. They led fellow anthropologists in countering the universality of storm and stress in adolescence by drawing on multiple examples in non-Western cultures in which the characteristic adolescent behavior was not observed (Mead, 1928). They argued that, based on their treatment of young people, societies create their own culture surrounding the period of adolescence: societies that treat adolescence as a troubling period of life that must simply be tolerated until it passes experience stressful and tumultuous adolescent periods while societies that celebrate adolescence exhibit a relaxed and unflustered adolescent experience. Although most contemporary adolescent theorists no longer attribute adolescent behavior to "storm and stress" they do acknowledge its relevance to understanding behavioral changes during adolescence.

1.4 Adolescence across the Globe and across Species

Adolescent-related behaviors are observed world-wide, across different cultures (Schlegel, 2001) and species (Spear, 2000). Rodents in the developmental period that is equivalent to human adolescence, immediately prior to and following sexual maturation, exhibit behavioral changes that are similar to those commonly observed in human adolescents. These behaviors include increased peer-directed social interactions (Douglas, Varlinskaya, and Spear, 2004), occasional increases in fighting with parents (Csikszentmihalyi, Larson, and Prescott, 1977), increases in novelty-seeking, sensation-seeking, and risk-taking (Laviola, Macri, Morley-Fletcher, and Adriani, 2003), increased consummatory behavior (Friemel, Spanagel, and Schneider, 2010), and greater per occasion alcohol use (Doremus-Fitzwater, Varlinskaya, and Spear, 2010). The increased proclivity toward drug use that is observed in human adolescents is also observed in adolescent rats (Brenhouse and Andersen, 2008; Torres, Tejeda, Natividad, and O'Dell, 2008) and nonhuman primates (Nelson et al., 2009). These data suggest that some of the characteristic adolescent behaviors observed in humans may be embedded in an evolutionary history that has adapted in ways to facilitate behaviors that are important in the developing organism. Indeed, rapid progress is being achieved across laboratories in studies with animals and with human adolescents showing that neural changes in systems that underlie motivational, affective, and behavioral regulation influence the processing of and responding to events in the environment in ways that bias behavior.

Across different cultures and societies, adolescence is recognized as a distinct developmental period in which children begin to transition into adulthood. This typically occurs by the adoption of increasingly "adult-like" behaviors such as getting married, moving away from the family, and/or bearing children. However, anthropologists note that the extent to which adolescence is acknowledged and the way each society characterizes the transition from childhood to adulthood varies greatly by culture. In some traditional societies public ceremonies are used to commemorate the transition from child to adult social status. In contrast, modern industrialized societies rarely publicly acknowledge adolescence, in part because there are several developmental milestones (that occur at different ages) that are considered critical to the transition from child to adult, including completion of secondary schooling, age of legal status, getting a job, getting married, or becoming a parent.

1.5 Theoretical Models of Adolescent Brain Development

What is the general construction of the brain? Developmental psychologists and neuroscientists have pondered over this question for decades. Long gone are the outdated debates about "nature versus nurture," as we can now all agree that the brain is a product of both a genetic or biological outline and the environment. However, it is still fascinating that the brain gets constructed in ways that are both similar across humans (for instance, the general anatomy of the brain is similar across individuals) and yet different at the same time (everyone's brain processes information slightly differently). The developmental psychologist Esther Thelen devoted her career to addressing this question: How do we make more from something less? How does a walking and talking toddler emerge from a helpless infant? Read about her dynamic systems theory in Box 1.2.

What is the general construction of the adolescent brain? This section introduces the prevailing neurobiological models of adolescence. As with every period of development, applying theoretical perspectives to empirical research helps researchers gain a better understanding about the behaviors and changes often observed during adolescence. Although they differ slightly in their focus, these models tend to highlight the differences in maturation rates of brain systems implicated in emotion, social, and reward processing from those that are important for regulation of behavior. These different systems have sometimes been referred to as "hot" and "cold" systems, respectively. The hot system generally refers to regions that are responsive to affective events in the organism's environment, including fears, desires, pleasure, and reflexes. In contrast, the cold system generally refers to regions that are implicated in cognition and goal-planning, and are less engaged during emotional reactivity. Each of these models is illustrated in Figure 1.1 (Casey, 2015).

1.5.1 Dual Systems Model (Figure 1.1a)

Steinberg and colleagues (2008) describe adolescent behavior in the domains of sensation-seeking and risky decisions in terms of a dual

Box 1.2 Dynamic Systems Theory

Esther Thelen, a renowned developmental psychologist, viewed development as a change within a complex dynamic system. This framework posits that developing organisms are complex systems composed of very many individual elements embedded within, and open to, a complex environment that can exhibit coherent behavior (Smith and Thelen, 2003). For instance, applied to brain development specifically, this theory would suggest that the brain (the complex system) is composed of individual brain regions (individual elements) that can work together to produce an output. Furthermore, these regions (and thus the complex system overall) develop and change through a process called "self-organization" which refers to the changes that occur after repeated experience and because of organic, naturally occurring development. In this sense, brain development occurs both as an unfolding of normative development (informed by a genetic blueprint, as in the case of puberty) and because of the brain's response to the environment. Smith and Thelan go on to say that development, therefore, can be thought of as a "series of evolving and dissolving patterns of varying dynamic stability, rather than an inevitable march towards maturity." This is an important concept because it encompasses many of the themes we will review in this book: plasticity (the ability to change), normative biological development (puberty), evolving patterns (change based on the environment), dissolving patterns (pruning of neural connections that cease being useful), and maturity (and the challenge to define it). They provide an example that nicely illustrates this point: infant crawling. They write, "Crawling is a coherent behaviour that infants use to locomote when they have sufficient strength and coordination to assume a hands-and-knees posture, but are not balanced and strong enough to walk upright. Crawling is a stable behaviour for several months. But when infants learn to walk, the crawling pattern becomes destablilized by the patterns of standing and walking. There is no 'programme' for crawling assembled in the genes or wired in the nervous system. It self-organizes as a solution to a problem (move across the room), later to be replaced by a more efficient solution."

systems model. According to this model, risky decision-making in adolescence is the product of the interaction of two neurobiological systems: the socioemotional system, comprised of limbic regions including the amygdala, ventral striatum, orbitofrontal cortex, and medial prefrontal cortex, and the cognitive control system, comprised of the lateral prefrontal and parietal cortices. Around the time of puberty, the

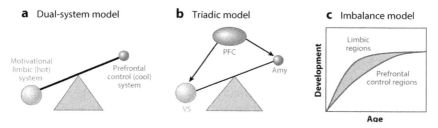

a Dual-system model   **b** Triadic model   **c** Imbalance model

Figure 1.1 An illustration of the three prevailing models of adolescent behavior.

surge in dopaminergic activity within the socioemotional system leads to increases in sensation-seeking and risky decision-making, outpacing the development (and engagement of) the cognitive control system. This temporal gap leads to heightened vulnerability to these behaviors during adolescence (Steinberg, 2010).

1.5.2 Triadic Model (Figure 1.1b)

Ernst and colleagues (Ernst, Pine, and Hardin, 2006) proposed the *Triadic Model* of motivated behavior. This model attributes the determinants of motivated behavior to three functional neural systems, the prefrontal cortex, the striatum, and the amygdala, and focuses on how the maturational timing of each region contributes to age-related differences in motivated behavior as people mature (Ernst, 2014). The prefrontal cortex is implicated in the regulation aspect of motivated behavior. The striatum is implicated in the motivation aspects of the model and the amygdala is implicated in the emotion components of behavior. Together, these three nodes, and the constructs they are associated with, serve to coordinate the calculation of whether to approach (engage in) or avoid a particular behavior and the regulation of that calculation. This model has been used to describe typical adolescent behaviors, including cognitive impulsivity, risk-seeking, emotional intensity, and social orientation.

1.5.3 Imbalance Model (Figure 1.1c)

The imbalance model was developed by Casey and colleagues (Casey, Getz, and Galván, 2008). This model emerged from empirical studies that examined the developmental transition from childhood through adolescence and into adulthood and translation across species (nonhuman primate and rodent) (Casey, 2015). According to this model, developmental changes in the neurochemical, structural, and functional composition of the brain proceed on distinct timelines, such that some brain regions exhibit the changes earlier in development than other brain regions. This leads to an imbalance of how these regions bias behavior because of differential engagement across different stages of development. For instance, it has been used to explain nonlinear changes in behavior during adolescence because regions implicated in reward (e.g. striatum) exhibit greater engagement, in terms of striatal activation and behavioral bias toward reward, relative to regions critical for behavioral regulation (e.g. prefrontal cortex). Importantly, unlike models that focus on specific brain regions, the Imbalance Model aims to attribute adolescent behavior to the coordinated integration of multiple brain circuits (Casey, Galván, and Somerville, 2015). This model focuses on the dynamic neurochemical, connectivity, and functional interactions across development in circuits that are essential for self-control.

1.5.4 Social Information Processing Model

This model, proposed by Nelson and colleagues, is similar to the other models of adolescent development (Nelson, Lieibenluft, McClure, and Pine, 2005). An added twist is that it describes risk-taking behavior in terms of an overactive affective node, including normative adolescent changes in the limbic system, due to a surge of gonadal hormone levels at puberty.

1.5.5 Fuzzy Trace Theory

Reyna and colleagues (Reyna and Farley, 2006) have applied fuzzy trace theory (FTT) as an explanatory framework for adolescent risk behavior. FTT posits that sophisticated "judgment and decision making is based on simple mental representations of choice ('fuzzy' memory traces) as opposed to more detailed, quantitative representations (verbatim memory traces)" (Rivers, Reyna, and Mills, 2008). According to FTT, decision-making becomes less computational and more intuitive as development proceeds. Earlier in development (in adolescence) risky decision-making involves precise calculations (e.g. does the exact amount of fun or money I will gain outweigh the exact amount of risk involved in achieving the fun or money?) whereas adults shift to a "fuzzier" calculation that simply ranks the options (e.g. ranking the potential rewards against the risk involved to get the reward). Fuzzy trace theory has been used to explain a myriad of real-world adolescent decision-making.

As you can see, these models are very similar in the message they send: the contribution of different brain regions to behavior is biased toward greater emotional reactivity and reward-driven behaviors during adolescence. This is clearly a simplistic account and none of the authors of these models believes the adolescent brain or adolescent behavior is that simple. However, the models were created as a response to the growing neuroscientific evidence suggesting that important brain regions evince unique activation profiles during adolescence. With increasing sophistication in neuroscience tools has come a more nuanced view of the neural computations that occur during adolescence. Now that we have the ability to measure how brain regions communicate with one another, these models are being refined to consider how interconnections within and across brain systems also contribute to characteristic adolescent behavior (Casey et al., 2015; Galván, 2014). Adolescent brain experts are also working to determine the important role that environmental context and developmental history play in shaping the adolescent brain (Crone and Dahl, 2012; Pfeifer and Allen, 2012). In a recent model, Crone and Dahl proposed that the adolescent brain is primed for flexibility because of its plasticity, a topic we will return to in Chapter 4. As illustrated in Figure 1.2, the integrative model they outline puts pubertal changes and both positive and negative outcomes front and center. In other words, in addition to incorporating the neurodevelopmental changes that occur in adolescence, they highlight the inputs to and outputs of this mixture of factors that all coalesce during this developmental window.

1.6 What is the Function of Adolescence?

At no other time in life are individuals healthier, stronger, or more passionate than during adolescence (Dahl, 2004). They are also, arguably, the most reckless, impulsive, and stubborn. This puzzle has led theorists to consider whether there is a particular "function" of adolescence. Most have come to the general conclusion that the main function of adolescence is to establish independence. The well-known developmental psychologist Erik Erikson noted that "adolescence is a time when young people set the pattern for their future lives" while Alice Schlegel concluded that "the function of adolescence across cultures is to prepare children for their adult reproductive careers, similar to higher primates" (Schlegel, 2001).

One important aspect of preparing for adulthood is establishing independence from the family unit and caregiver. In nonhuman animals, this

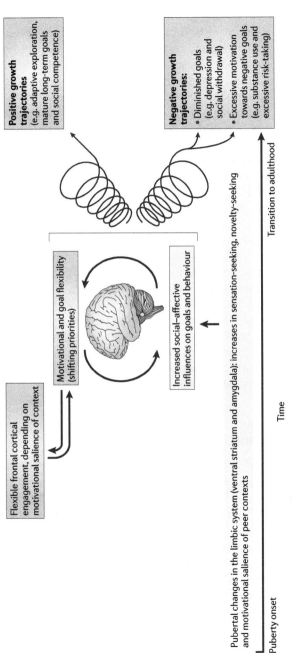

Figure 1.2 A proposed model of adolescent development by Crone and Dahl (2012). The model illustrates the role of puberty in initiating changes in social and affective processing (yellow boxes), which in turn interact with changes in cognitive control and social cognitive development (blue boxes). These interactions contribute to flexibility in the engagement of frontal cortical systems in adolescents that depends on the motivational salience of the context. These tendencies can lead to both positive and negative outcomes. ACC, anterior cingulate cortex; DLPFC, dorsolateral prefrontal cortex; mPFC, medial PFC; TPJ, temporoparietal junction.

autonomy typically involves leaving the home troop to seek out new sexual mates, food resources, and sleeping burrows or trees. Humans, on the other hand, vary greatly in the extent to which they "leave" the family unit. Some adolescents stay close to home even after they have legally become adults whereas others move far from their families and only visit them occasionally. The very definition of "independence" varies across generations, adolescents, parents, and societies. The end of adolescence in most societies is marked by when an individual is "mature enough" to be trusted with certain responsibilities, including driving a vehicle, having legal sexual relations, serving in the armed forces or on a jury, purchasing, selling, and drinking alcohol, voting, finishing certain levels of education, marriage, and renting a car. But even the age at which these rights and privileges are granted varies within a single nation or culture. In most cases, how the standard legal age limits were determined seems rather arbitrary and inconsistent across the various activities that require an age restriction. For instance, youth can hold employment in many US states at the age of 14 but are not legally allowed to drive, vote, and buy alcohol until the ages of 16, 18, and 21 years, respectively. They can fight in wars and serve in the armed forces at age 18 but cannot rent a car until age 25. We will return to this topic in Chapter 8 when we review the role of adolescent brain research on public policy and the juvenile justice system.

By some standards, individuals transition from adolescence into adulthood when they are either married or financially independent, or both. In previous generations, these events typically coincided with graduation from college. The median age of marriage was 20.3 for females and 22.8 for males in 1950. Figure 1.3 illustrates how this pattern has changed over time. Since the late 1980s, youth have remained more financially dependent on their parents for longer and are marrying later. In 2015, the median age of marriage jumped to 27.6 for females and 29.5 for males. One reason for this trend is that there has been an increase in the number of people (particularly women) who are attending college or university. In fall 2014, 17.3 million students enrolled in American colleges and universities, a 31% increase from 13.2 million in 2000 (nces.ed.gov, 2016). In 1970, 42.3% of the college-attending population were women; today, women make up 56.8% of the college population (nces.ed.gov, 2016). This increase makes individuals more dependent on parents or government loans for financial support, particularly as the costs of college continue to rise steadily. Adjusting for inflation and represented in current dollars, the average total cost of college in 1976–77 including

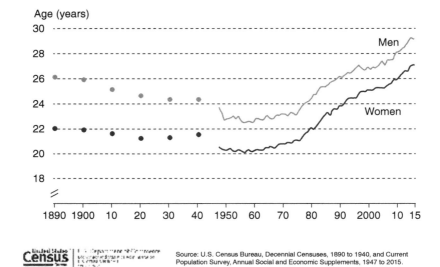

Figure 1.3 US Census data indicate that median age of first marriage is steadily rising across generations in both men and women.

tuition, fees, and room and board was $7,146 for a public university and $14,686 for private institutions; for the 2012–13 academic year the costs were $15,022 and $39,173 for public and private nonprofit institutions, respectively (US Department of Education, 2015). The economic crisis in 2008 further contributed to continued financial dependence on parents, as college graduates struggled to find jobs and moved back home. A 2011 Pew Research Center analysis of US Census data reported that 39% of adults ages 18 to 34 said they either lived with their parents or had moved back in at some point in recent years. Among 18 to 24 year olds, 53% said they lived at home or had moved in temporarily, compared with 41% among adults ages 25 to 29, and 17% among those aged 30 to 34, and 60% reported being financially linked to their parents (Pew Research Center, 2012).

The delayed emotional and financial dependence undoubtedly contributes to the protracted transition from adolescence into young adulthood. As we will read about in later chapters, neuroscience research suggests that the brain continues to mature through the mid-20s. Whether and how the delayed dependence on caregivers influences brain development is a topic we will revisit in Chapter 4 when we discuss plasticity of the brain.

1.6.1 How Does the Brain Facilitate Independence?

An increased proclivity toward exploration, willingness to take risks, and seeking out potential mates and new adventures is at the very core of transitioning from a state of dependence on caregivers to one of relative independence (Galván, 2013b). Brain development that occurs during adolescence is critically important in facilitating these behaviors. Greater engagement of reward circuitry involved in motivated behavior during adolescence plays a role in why adolescents are more likely to take risks, and enjoy doing it, than adults or children. Less engagement of the regions that might make one pause before taking a risk also leads to more choices that involve risk. In addition to the many social factors that contribute to changes in adolescent behavior, including peer influence, risk availability, and personality traits, changes in the brain regions we rely on to make decisions also contribute to the greater propensity to engage in independence-seeking behaviors. In later chapters, we will delve more deeply into the specific brain systems that underlie these adaptive behavioral changes.

1.7 Human Brain Development: An Overview

Throughout this book we will discuss the specific changes that occur in the brain during adolescence but it is worth reviewing a few basic facts about the human brain and its development. Human brain development is a prolonged process compared to nonhuman animals. The developmental periods of early childhood and adolescence in particular exhibit protracted development in the human species as compared with most other species (Thompson and Nelson, 2001). One reason for this might be that the human brain undergoes a lengthier maturation process in order to generate the relatively complex cortex that humans possess. Our brains function by transmitting information through nerve cells, called **neurons**. The human brain has a greater number of neurons than any other animal. To give one example: whereas the average honeybee brain has 950,000 neurons (Menzel and Giurfa, 2001), humans have approximately 100 billion neurons (Shepherd, 1998)! Surprisingly, humans do not have the heaviest brains; killer whales actually have the heaviest brains at 5,620 grams on average, compared to approximately 1300–1400 grams on average for the human brain. Many of the additional neurons humans have are located in the surface of the brain, the cerebral cortex. As such, a greater proportion of the human brain (77%) is made up of the cerebral cortex compared to other animals; by comparison only 31% of the rat brain is the cerebral cortex. The total surface area of the cerebral cortex is 2,500 cm^2 (2.5 m^2) in humans and only 6 cm^2 in the rat (Nieuwenhuys, Donkelaar, and Nicholson, 1998).

One prevailing theory is that the elongation of human brain development and the significantly greater number of neurons in the cortex contribute to our higher cognitive ability and enhanced capacity for learning. Large longitudinal studies that used neuroimaging techniques to quantify the size and volume of the human brain have shown that developmental changes are observed in cortical development throughout young adulthood (e.g. Giedd et al., 2015). By the time an individual reaches adolescence, the majority of basic anatomical structural development has occurred. In fact, the size of the brain is pretty stable after approximately age 5 (Casey, Giedd, and Thomas, 2000). However, brain changes that occur during adolescence and early adulthood involve subtle refinement of regions that are most responsive to the environment.

1.7.1 Interactive Specialization Framework

As we will read about throughout this book, different brain regions are "specialists" in different cognitive domains. Although all regions work together, the prefrontal cortex is generally considered the primary regulation area while the striatum is mostly responsible for processing reward and pleasure. A fundamental question in developmental neuroscience is how different brain regions develop their specificity. If they all start off relatively unspecified in function, how is it that they acquire expertise? According to Mark Johnson, a prominent developmental psychologist, the answer lies in the *Interactive Specialization* framework (Johnson, 2011). Two key ideas underlie this framework. The first is the idea that neural change in some cortical regions occurs as regions interact and compete with each other. From this perspective, some cortical regions begin with poorly defined and broad functionality, and consequently are partially activated in a wide range of different tasks. Over the course of development, these regions become more selective in what they respond to, as based on activity-dependent interactions between regions. For instance, a region that was originally activated by a wide variety of visual objects may come to respond only (or mostly) to the human face. The second notion central to Interactive Specialization is that brain development involves a process of organizing patterns of interregional interactions. In other words, how any one region develops is largely based on the ongoing development of the regions around it. The onset of new behavioral competencies during infancy will therefore be associated with changes in activity over several regions (networks), and not just with the onset of activity in one or more additional region(s) (Johnson, 2011).

1.8 The Importance of Understanding Adolescent Brain Development

Why are scientists interested in studying adolescent brain development? One reason is that it helps answer questions from inquiring parents about why their teenagers do and say the things they do and say. Perhaps more importantly, understanding the neurobiology of this period of life provides the opportunity to study intriguing developmental questions that cannot be answered with children and adult populations alone. By including adolescents in neurodevelopmental studies, scientists can obtain a better, more in-depth understanding of developmental change from childhood through adolescence and into adulthood. Adolescents can help "fill in the gap" between childhood and adulthood to examine how changes in the entire brain influence diverse cognitive functions. For instance, the longitudinal findings reviewed in the previous section provided an interesting picture of the brain from childhood through adulthood by showing that some brain regions do not develop in a linear fashion; in other words, the inclusion of an adolescent group showed that certain brain regions ramp up in size through late childhood but then start to decrease in size around adolescence and into early adulthood. In a separate study, Sowell and colleagues (Sowell et al., 2003) found that the most significant anatomical changes in the brain during the adolescent period occur in brain regions that are critically involved in affective processing; these findings served as an important point of departure for fMRI studies that subsequently examined reward and emotion systems.

The few longitudinal fMRI studies that have been published reported interesting changes in how the brain processes information during adolescence (Braams, van Duijvenvoorde, Peper, and Crone, 2015; Koolschijn, Schel, de Rooij, Rombouts, and Crone, 2011; Pfeifer et al., 2011). A 3-year longitudinal study that included participants aged 8–27 found that task performance in children and adolescents was more tightly linked to brain activation over time than age (Koolschijn et al., 2011). A separate longitudinal study reported that adolescence is a critical period for brain responses to affective facial stimuli (Pfeifer et al., 2011). The study found that from late childhood (10 years) to adolescence (13 years) there was a marked shift in activation of reward regions such that increased activation was associated with decreased likelihood of self-reported peer influence (Pfeifer et al., 2011).

Second, the only way to understand the relationship between puberty and neurodevelopment is to study adolescents. As we will read about in Chapter 2, puberty is a highly significant event in all species that coincides with the onset of adolescence. During pubertal development, the physical, psychological, and hormonal changes that ensue have consequential effects on concurrent and future behavior and well-being. There is a lot known about the effects of pubertal hormones on brain development in animals but there is still much to learn in humans.

Third, because adolescence is a period of identity exploration, increased orientation toward peers, and changing social roles, adolescents serve as a good model group in which to address sophisticated questions about the relationship between socioemotional development and brain development. Studies with adolescent participants are used to examine how the progression from dependence to autonomy is subserved by changes in how the brain processes social information.

Last, adolescence marks the period in development when the onset of psychiatric disorders is most prevalent. It is therefore important to include adolescents into brain imaging studies to address an important question: Why is there an increase in psychiatric disorders during adolescence? (Paus, Keshavan, and Giedd, 2008). Converging evidence suggests that brain changes within regions involved in processing emotional or affectively charged information and in behavioral regulation contribute to this phenomenon. A better understanding of brain development in both typically developing and clinical populations could provide opportunities for treatment or prevention.

1.9 The Importance of Animal Models

The goal of this book is to teach you about adolescent brain development. However, you will notice that some of the research that is reviewed is based on animal models of development. Human and nonhuman animals clearly differ in many respects. But many of the guiding principles and much of the knowledge about the human developing brain were informed by research in other species. In fact, numerous hypotheses and theories about brain development were initially motivated by animal models.

There are several reasons that animal models are helpful. First, animal models allow for investigations that are either ethically or practically impossible in human samples. Because animals typically have shorter lifespans, researchers can ask questions about development using longitudinal approaches that can be conducted within a few months, as opposed to the many years the same type of experiment would take in humans. Second, we share much of the same genetic makeup as non-human primates (monkeys, chimps, and apes) and rodents, all of which are species often used to study basic cognition. This is important because it gives scientists the opportunity to test whether particular sets of genes are implicated in cognitive processes of interest. Third, questions about the role of experience in shaping brain development that are of great interest to developmental cognitive neuroscientists can more easily be addressed with animals. In animals, it is possible to manipulate, or alter, the experience or environment of the individual in ways that are impossible in humans. We can ask such questions as: What is the role of poor (or enriched) caregiving on brain development and behavior? Whereas we must rely on naturalistic cases that limit the sample size and specificity in humans, we can control these factors in animals.

Animal models are not perfect, of course. A developing rodent, for example, is the product of a very different dynamic system from a developing human. In addition, appropriate age comparisons are challenging to discern. Does the "juvenile" period of a rat directly match up with the adolescent period in humans? One way to avoid this issue is to consider the developmental niche or needs of the organism at the particular development window of interest. In both species, sexual maturation instigates a cascade of activities that include heightened risk-taking, novelty exploration, and increased peer affiliation, all in the service of making the individual more confident and independent from caregivers. Nonetheless, animal models are highly valuable to the field of human brain development so you will learn about them throughout this book.

1.10 Chapter Summary

- World leaders and health advocates have given increasing attention to the period of adolescence.
- Adolescence is a period of transition between childhood and adulthood and includes individuals roughly 10 to 25 years of age.
- Historically, hormones and puberty were thought to account for adolescent behavior but the advent of neuroimaging is challenging that view.
- Characteristic adolescent behavior, including emotional reactivity and risk-taking, is similar across cultures and species.

- Theoretical frameworks on adolescence range in their focus from biologically based to societally based perspectives.
- The function of adolescence is for individuals to become independent from adult caregivers.
- The brain matures as based on normative biological changes and interactions with the environment.

1.11 Review Questions

1 What are three prevailing theories of adolescent brain development?
2 How has societal perception of adolescence changed throughout history?
3 What is the role of the developing brain in facilitating adolescent independence?
4 What purpose does a larger cortex in humans relative to nonhuman animals serve?

Further Reading

Casey, B.J. (2015). Beyond simple models of self-control to circuit-based accounts of adolescent behavior. *Annual Review of Psychology*, 66, 295–319.

Johnson, M.H. (2011). Interactive specialization: a domain-general framework for human functional brain development? *Developmental Cognitive Neuroscience*, 1, 7–21.

Paus, T. (2013). How environment and genes shape the adolescent brain. *Hormones and Behavior*, 64, 195–202.

Spear, L.P. (2013). Adolescent neurodevelopment. *Journal of Adolescent Health*, 52, S7–S13.

CHAPTER TWO

Puberty

Learning Objectives

- Learn about the hormonal changes during puberty.
- Describe factors that influence pubertal onset.
- Describe physical changes at puberty.
- Characterize sex differences in pubertal change.
- Describe the influence of puberty on brain development.
- Review psychological impacts of puberty.

2.1 Introduction

The survival of our species rests on one important event that occurs in early adolescence: puberty. Puberty is the result of a series of hormonal events during which young adolescents undergo the physical and neuro-endocrine changes that are required to reach sexual maturity. Most people remember the dramatic physical changes that overcame them in early adolescence: the significant growth spurt, the increased facial hair in boys, perhaps the unwanted acne? All of these changes originate in the brain, where the pubertal hormones are released. A book on the adolescent brain would be incomplete without a chapter on puberty because it plays such a central role in jumpstarting the adolescent period of life. The adolescent-specific changes in cognition and emotion processing that we will read about in later chapters are also directly and indirectly related to puberty, through increases in pubertal hormones as well as the physical transformation that characterizes puberty. In this chapter, we will introduce the most significant physical and hormonal changes that are launched and sustained throughout the metamorphosis that is puberty.

Three characteristics describe puberty: (1) it is controlled and sustained by hormones, (2) there are changes in body height, weight, and shape, and (3) it is associated with changes in behavior and mood. What is perhaps most fascinating about puberty is that, although the physical manifestations occur at a discrete point in development, puberty is actually a long process that is influenced by many factors, including some that occur

---

Box 2.1 Is puberty synonymous with adolescence?

The beginning of puberty and adolescence occur at roughly the same age, in late childhood. However, adolescence is not synonymous with puberty. Puberty is a long process that is characterized by the biological, physical, and hormonal changes that initiate reproductive capability and sexual maturation. The term adolescence also captures the behavioral changes, swings in mood states, and awareness of self that occur during this time, in addition to biological maturation. Hall coined the phrase "storm and stress" (Hall, 1904) in reference to the conflict with parents, mood disruptions, and risky behavior commonly associated with adolescence. Scholars broadly define adolescence as a "transitional" period in life between childhood and adulthood (Dahl, 2004; Steinberg, 2008) that generally begins at the onset of puberty and ends when individuals attain independence from caregivers.

---

much earlier in life. Even characteristics that are observed in infancy are linked to puberty in adolescence. In fact, puberty is simply one aspect of reproductive life rather than the only event. It is also strongly influenced by sociocultural and environmental factors.

Take a brief moment to think about what you know about puberty. Most people associate puberty with a girl's first menstrual period or facial hair in boys; although those are certainly key characteristics of puberty, it is much more complex and interesting than that. Did you know that a girl's first period occurs pretty late in her pubertal development? Or that puberty is beginning earlier and earlier across generations? Throughout this chapter we'll review the basic characteristics of puberty, including the physical growth spurt and which hormones are key players in the beginning of puberty, learn about the variable timing of puberty within our species, and discuss the implications of puberty on psychosocial behaviors. See Box 2.1 for a discussion of how puberty differs from adolescence.

2.2 Pubertal Hormones

Hormones are the body's chemical messengers that are secreted by the endocrine system into the bloodstream to stimulate specific cells into action. Although there are many different types of hormones, in this book we will focus on those related to sexual reproduction: androgens, the primary type of male sex hormones, and estrogens, the primary type of female sex hormones. **Testosterone**, which is secreted from testes in males, is an androgen that plays a central role in male pubertal development. As boys start to undergo puberty, they release increasing levels of testosterone, a process that promotes the physical changes observed in boys during this time, including the development of external genitals, an increase in height, and voice changes. **Estradiol**, which is secreted from ovaries in females, is the equivalent hormone in girls that is responsible for much of female pubertal development, including breast development, pubic hair growth, and the onset of the first menstrual period. Although these hormones are more prevalent in one sex or the other (i.e. males tend to have higher levels of testosterone than females), both males and females produce both types of these hormones. In fact, there is considerable variability in the level of these hormones in each person. While there are men who have high levels of testosterone, there are also men with relatively lower levels of testosterone; women also vary in their level of testosterone.

2.3 Neuroendocrine System

Pubertal hormones are released in the brain. It is through activation of the **hypothalamic-pituitary-gonadal (HPG)** axis that the brain starts to communicate to the gonads (sex glands) that it is time to begin the process of puberty. There is one brain region in particular, the **hypothalamus**, which plays a central role in this process. The hypothalamus is more generally responsible for monitoring basic human needs, such as eating, drinking, and sex. At the onset of puberty, it plays a special role of governing the **pituitary gland**, through **gonadotropin-releasing hormone (GnRH) neurons**. The close proximity of these regions to one another, as you can see in Figure 2.1, makes it easy for them to communicate. It is the pituitary gland that produces the hormones, called **gonadotropins**, necessary to stimulate the release of sex hormones from gonads. The level of sex hormones that need to be released from the gonads is regulated by two hormones secreted from the pituitary gland: **follicle-stimulating hormone** (FSH) and **luteinizing hormone** (LH). FSH stimulates sperm production in males and follicle development in females. LH regulates testosterone production in males and estrogen secretion and ovum development in females.

The amount of FSH and LH released is important because too much or too little can have significant effects on the development of primary sex characteristics (e.g. development of sex organs) and/or on the appearance of secondary sex characteristics (e.g. facial hair and breast development). How does the system know how much of these hormones to release?

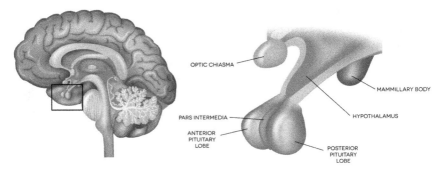

Figure 2.1 The hypothalamus regulates hormone release from the pituitary gland. See color plate 1.

Think of the system like a thermostat. If a room becomes too cold, the thermostat signals the furnace to turn on. Eventually, the room becomes warm and this eventually triggers the thermostat to turn off the furnace. Over time, the room temperature may begin to fall again until the thermostat once again signals the furnace to turn on. This repetitive cycle is called a *negative feedback loop* because an increase in temperature turns the furnace off while a decrease in temperature turns the furnace on. The endocrine system works in a similar "need-based" way: it receives instructions from GnRH neurons to increase FSH and LH release when the level of these hormones drops below a particular set point – secretion stops when the level of the set point is reached to prevent too much of the hormone from acting on the gonads. This flexibility allows hormone levels to be tailored for each specific person, as all individuals are different in how much of a particular hormone they need. Each person's need is based on their genetic makeup and is influenced by environmental factors or other internal bodily conditions.

You may be thinking that all of these vocabulary words and sequential processes are hard to remember. This process is indeed complex! But rather than focusing on the vocabulary words, take a moment to appreciate how well regulated and mapped out the neuroendocrine system is. Puberty is not random: it follows a prescribed sequence of events, involving the same neural regions and hormones in every individual. It is also always initiated in early adolescence, not in toddlerhood or in the late teenage years. This means that over evolutionary time all species have determined the optimal developmental time for members of that species to approximate sexual maturation.

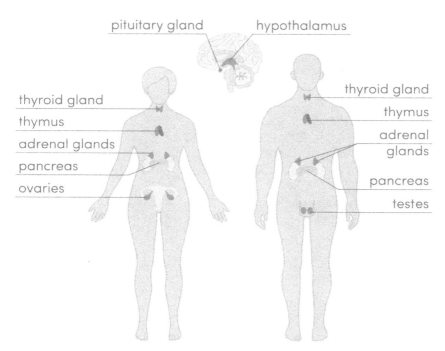

Figure 2.2 The endocrine system includes the hypothalamus and the pituitary gland in the brain, which release hormones that circulate through other glands and organs in the body, including the thyroid gland, thymus, adrenal gland, pancreas, ovaries (in females) and testes (in males).

2.3.1 Adrenarche and Gonadarche

Two distinct phases of puberty occur as a result of interactions between the pituitary gland and other glands throughout the body. The pituitary gland interacts with the thyroid gland, located in the neck area, and the adrenal glands, which sit on top of the kidneys, to stimulate additional pubertal changes. Together, they comprise the endocrine system, which is shown in Figure 2.2. **Adrenarche** is an early sexual maturation stage of puberty that typically begins early, around 6 to 8 years of age. Figure 2.3 (from Dorn et al., 2006) is a good depiction of the timeline during which each of these stages occurs. During adrenarche, the adrenal glands secrete adrenal androgens, such as dehydroepiandrosterone (DHEA) and dehydroepiandrosterone sulfate (DHEAS). Secretion of these hormones leads to *androgen effects*, including the emergence of pubic hair and body odor because of changes in sweat composition. It

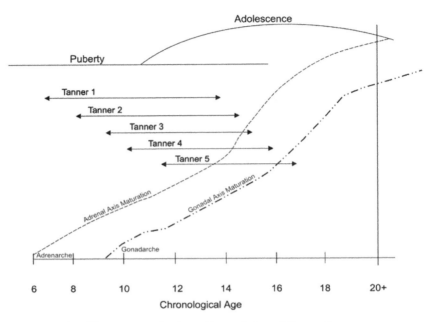

Figure 2.3 The different stages of puberty (Tanner 1 through Tanner 5) occur across a broad age span and interact with the major milestones, including adrenarche and gonarche, at various ages in different individuals (Dorn et al., 2006).

also appears to play a role in changes in the oiliness of the skin that leads to acne.

Gonadarche begins later than adrenarche, typically around 8 to 10 years of age (Figure 2.3), but there is considerable variability among individuals as to when it begins. It is the period most commonly thought of as puberty because it involves the maturation of observable sexual characteristics. Gonadarche includes **menarche**, the first menstrual period, which occurs in mid to late gonadarche in girls, and **spermarche**, a boy's first ejaculation of semen, that occurs in early to mid gonadarche.

2.4 What Triggers Puberty?

In contrast to common misconceptions that puberty is one single event, it is actually a long process that involves a series of related, but distinct, neural and hormonal changes. Some of these changes, such as the first menstrual period or the deepening of a boy's voice, are obvious, but others, such as increases in height or appearance of body hair, occur so gradually that only after they are well underway do they become noticeable. While it is the case that the HPG axis is most active during pubertal onset, it wears many hats and is actually also active much earlier in life, long before adolescence. In fact, it plays an **organizational role** in organizing the brain prenatally, in the developing fetus. In the organization phase, the HPG helps create sexual differentiation of certain brain structures. Sex hormones guide male and female brains along slightly different paths. Three areas of the brain in particular – the hypothalamus, amygdala, and hippocampus – exhibit sex differences in structure and size. These differences are not very obvious until adolescence and in adulthood but the divergent paths begin to occur prenatally. These regions are involved in reproduction, both in terms of hormone release (hypothalamus) and in orientation toward social stimuli in adolescence and adulthood (amygdala).

By the time adolescence comes around, the HPG axis takes on an **activational role**, in which it activates hormonal changes in ways that subsequently influence the changes in behavior and cognition that are characteristic of adolescence. Interestingly, the HPG axis is quite dormant during childhood, a departure from the organizational and activational roles it plays in childhood and adolescence, respectively. In Figure 2.4 you will see the pattern of hormonal fluctuations across development;

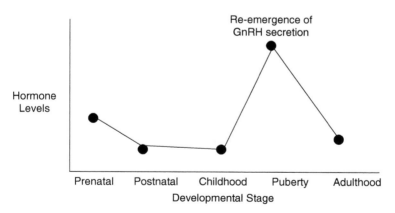

Figure 2.4 Gonadotropin-releasing hormone (GnRH) fluctuates throughout development. It is released prenatally, is relatively inactive in childhood, and then surges at puberty before decreasing throughout adolescence and adulthood.

a rise in hormones in prenatal development wanes during early postnatal development and childhood. In adolescence there is a sharp increase before decreasing again in adulthood. This means that the HPG axis and its hormones take a long break when individuals are children and therefore do not exert much influence on body structure, brain development, or behavior during childhood. So what "reawakens" the HPG axis during adolescence?

Surprisingly, scientists do not have an answer to this question! Decades of research in animals and humans have not identified any one hormone, event, age, or environmental experience that triggers puberty. Instead, all of these factors come together to signal that the organism is healthy enough and physically mature enough for sexual reproduction. These factors have been called "permissive signals" because they permit (or stop inhibiting) pubertal onset (Sisk and Foster, 2004). These signals include changing levels of melatonin, body fat, and leptin, all of which are related to weight and energy balance. It is believed that individuals do not go through puberty until they are energetically and metabolically capable of doing so. Frisch and Revelle suggested that there may be a critical weight or amount of body fat required for the establishment of normal menstrual cycles (Frisch and Revelle, 1970). Why might that be? Consider for a moment some of the potential consequences of being sexually mature: pregnancy, caring for offspring, and defending one's territory or mate. All of these activities are energetically expensive so perhaps delaying puberty until the organism is energetically balanced is nature's built-in trick to ensure that individuals who are not yet physically ready are not placed in the position to attend to the potential outcomes associated with puberty.

Decades of research have led to the conclusion that metabolic conditions and the amount of energy reserves of the organism play an essential role in the regulation of pubertal timing (Fernandez-Fernandez et al., 2006; Martos-Moreno, Chowen, and Argente, 2010). This makes good biological sense, especially in the female. The reproductive capacity, which refers to the potential metabolic drainage of pregnancy and breastfeeding, is only acquired when threshold energy stores and optimal metabolic conditions are achieved (Sanchez-Garrido and Tena-Sempere, 2013). The influence of metabolic signals on puberty and fertility is also found in the male (Castellano et al., 2009), in which energy demands for proper reproduction are not so evident but are probably required as well (e.g. for territoriality and partner selection) (Elias, 2012).

Figure 2.5 A group of young adolescents. Despite being in the same grade (7th grade) and roughly the same age, there are obvious differences in pubertal maturation, with some exhibiting greater physical growth and more advanced pubertal stage than others. See color plate 2.

2.5 Timing Is Everything

One wrinkle in determining when puberty starts is that the onset of puberty is quite varied across individuals. Even though everyone starts puberty around the time of adolescence, everyone's timing is slightly different. This point is illustrated in Figure 2.5, which shows a group of 7th graders who are all roughly the same age but who exhibit vast variation in pubertal maturation and physical development. Because of the many factors that influence puberty in each individual, there is no one single age at which everyone undergoes puberty. It is similar to the variability in motor development milestones; most infants begin walking by 18 months but some begin much earlier than that and others at a later time. Neither is better or worse, just different. The range of pubertal onset is similarly variable, between 9 and 16 years of age in most individuals (Nottelmann et al., 1987). The pubertal transition lasts between 1.5 and 6 years in girls and 2 to 5 years in boys. This duration is quite a long time, especially when contrasted against the comparable intervals in other species who range from a few weeks (mice) to a few months (nonhuman primates). The prolonged period of pubertal transition in humans can probably be attributed to the much more complex environments in which human adolescents are reared. In humans, variations in diet and physical activity, stress, ethnicity, and family all impact the timing and duration of puberty.

2.5.1 Genetic Factors

Genetic factors play a strong role in pubertal timing, with a heritability rate of approximately 49–82% (Anderson, Dallal, and Must, 2003; Morris, Jones, Schoemaker, Ashworth, and Swerdlow, 2011). A girl experiences her first period at roughly the same age as her mom and her sisters did. Identical twins, who share all the same genes, undergo puberty at roughly the same time. However, identifying the exact genes that help regulate puberty is still a puzzle that scientists are working to solve. Research does suggest that genes coding for the protein Kisspeptin, encoded by the *Kiss1* gene, are involved in the control of puberty (Tolson and Chappell, 2012) by regulating GnRH function. Experimental evidence from animals demonstrates that during puberty the *Kiss1* system in the hypothalamus undergoes an extensive and complex activational program that seems essential for proper pubertal timing (Sanchez-Garrido and Tena-Sempere, 2013). This evidence includes an increase in the expression of the *Kiss1* gene during pubertal maturation (Navarro et al., 2004), a sharp rise in the number of kisspeptin neurons during early puberty, and the fact that overexpression of kisspeptin leads to precocious puberty (Teles, Silveira, Tusset, and Latronico, 2011). Together, the expression of the kisspeptin system seems to get the brain (and body) ready for puberty.

2.5.2 Psychosocial Factors

Across generations, people are undergoing puberty at younger and younger ages. Although the average age of menarche has not fallen much in the past 70 years, the lower age limit for pubertal onset appears to be getting earlier and earlier with each successive generation, with a general decline of 1–4 months per decade in industrialized European countries and the United States over the last 150 years (Demerath et al., 2004). Since the 1990s there has been a trend toward earlier age of breast budding in the United States (Chumlea et al., 2003; Herman-Giddens et al., 1997), and a lesser decrease in the age at menarche (Anderson et al., 2003; Morris et al., 2011). This secular trend of younger and younger age of menarche has also been observed in other countries, including China, India, England, and Japan.

Scientists have speculated that this trend is due to the significant change in our diet from a leaner diet to one that is richer in calories and fat: trends in pubertal timing are paralleled by increasing rates of obesity and higher body mass index (BMI), a measure of body fat based on height and weight. At least one study has reported that BMI is associated with age of pubertal onset, such that obese or overweight boys and girls are reaching puberty earlier (De Leonibus et al., 2014). Another study found that diet quality was indeed associated with earlier puberty (Cheng et al., 2010). Recent analysis from a large dataset indicated that children of normal BMI values rarely showed breast or pubic hair development before 8 years (3.2% and 0.6%), but overweight and obese girls had earlier breast budding, pubic hair, and menarche, independent of race or ethnicity (Rosenfield, Lipton, and Drum, 2009).

Theories about the role of weight and pubertal timing are controversial today but were quite pioneering when they were first proposed. The discovery of leptin in 1994 (Zhang et al., 1994) offered a candidate hormone that links body fat to the endocrine changes associated with puberty.

Leptin is a hormone that helps inhibit hunger. An early longitudinal study of eight boys showed a small peak in leptin level prior to the onset of puberty (Mantzoros, Flier, and Rogol, 1997). The small sample size made it hard for some scientists to find the results credible, but subsequent larger studies corroborate the initial study by reporting a slow and steady rise in leptin levels prior to puberty (Ahmed et al., 1999). Sex differences in leptin have also been reported: in girls, leptin continues to rise after the onset of puberty, whereas in boys, leptin declines sharply (Ahmed et al., 1999). Another piece of evidence linking leptin to puberty is that children who lack leptin for one clinical reason or another do not begin puberty until leptin is artificially introduced into the body (Farooqi, 2002). These and other studies suggest that leptin is necessary for pubertal development and that it may play a role in the tempo of its progression, but is not sufficient to trigger puberty (Roa et al., 2010; Sanchez-Garrido and Tena-Sempere, 2013). It is now considered to play a more permissive, rather than active, role in pubertal timing.

2.5.3 Ethnic Differences

A seminal, cross-sectional study in the late 1990s suggested that the onset of puberty in American girls was occurring earlier than previous studies had documented (Herman-Giddens et al., 1997). It also revealed ethnic differences in pubertal development. Between 1966 and 1970, mean ages of menarche in the United States were 12.8 years for Caucasian girls and 12.5 years for African American girls (Harlan, Harlan, and Grillo, 1980). Herman-Giddens and colleagues (1997) observed a mean age of 12.88 years for Caucasians and 12.16 for African Americans. Similarly, Wu, Mendola, and Buck (2002) reported means of 12.7 for Caucasians, 12.1 for African Americans, and 12.2 for Mexican Americans, from another national survey suggesting that girls from ethnic minority groups are experiencing earlier and earlier menarche, with each subsequent generation at a greater rate of change than non-minority girls.

A separate study showed that whereas children of normal weight rarely have breast development before 8 years (3.2%), significantly more African American and Latina girls with normal weight achieved breast development by age 8 years compared to Caucasian girls (12.1% and 19.2% versus 1.3%, respectively) (Rosenfield et al., 2009). Leptin levels are greater in African American girls, even with adjustment for fat mass and pubertal maturation (Wong et al., 1998), which may provide one factor relating to the ethnic difference in onset of puberty. In general, available research suggests that African American girls start to menstruate the earliest, followed by Latina girls and then Caucasian girls (Chumlea et al., 2003). Furthermore, the racial difference was most evident in girls who entered puberty earliest (Wu et al., 2002), and the racial difference appears to have widened over the past half-century (Freedman et al., 2002).

There is less available research on pubertal onset in boys. One large national survey study reported that African American boys showed pubic hair growth approximately 9 months earlier than Caucasian boys and more than 1 year earlier than Latino boys, in agreement with previous data (Herman-Giddens, Wang, and Koch, 2001). In a more recent national study, there was a higher percentage of African American boys at any given age with both genital and pubic hair development compared to Caucasian and Latino boys, but Caucasian and Latino boys showed no difference from each other (Herman-Giddens et al., 2012).

These ethnic differences are intriguing. Several theories have been proposed to explain them: genetic differences, dietary and activity differences, generational changes, and variability in rearing environment and resources are but a few hypotheses. All of these factors likely contribute to ethnic differences in pubertal tempo and timing but it is important to consider the methodological considerations: initial assessments of secondary sex characteristics on which all subsequent assessments were based were conducted in a rather homogenous group of youth; therefore, generational "trends" that suggest earlier and earlier puberty may actually be a reflection of increased diversity in the group of youth who are now sampled. In addition, *how* puberty is assessed is an ongoing conversation among developmental psychologists and pediatricians that undoubtedly has implications for pubertal staging (Box 2.2).

2.5.4 Early and Late Maturation

Early Maturation

Variations in the environment have been linked to variability in pubertal timing. Some of these findings have surprised researchers because the exact mechanisms by which environments "speed up" or delay pubertal onset are unknown. For instance, family composition can exert important effects on timing. Girls who grow up in homes where the father is absent (Ellis, 2004) or who are physically or sexually abused in childhood (Mendle, Leve, Van Ryzin, Natsuaki, and Ge, 2011) tend to reach puberty earlier in life. One explanation for these findings is that girls in these environments experience greater stress than girls who are not in these circumstances. Stress leads to the release of a hormone called **cortisol** and to the activation of the hypothalamic-pituitary-adrenal (HPA) axis, which influences all hormonal secretions. Another argument is based on *Life History* theory, which posits that the timing of reproductive readiness (i.e. puberty) is tied to the environment in order to optimize the chance for reproductive success (Belsky, Steinberg, and Draper, 1991). The rationale is as follows: individuals reared in harmful or unpredictable environments (e.g. uncertain resources, high mortality rates, father absence) may have attempted to increase their reproductive success by accelerating sexual maturation and beginning sexual activity and reproduction at a relatively earlier age. A shortened reproductive timetable in this context may have increased the probability of having at least one offspring that would survive and reproduce (Ellis, 2013). In contrast, individuals growing up in a relatively stable and supportive environment would increase their reproductive success by maturing on time or delaying reproductive maturation, within a biologically acceptable range, in order to reap the benefits of an extended period of development (Ellis, 2004). In such environments, deferring reproduction would allow individuals to acquire the sociocompetitive skills and resources necessary for successful mating and subsequent high-quality parental investment in offspring (Ellis, 2013).

Box 2.2 Measuring Puberty

You may be asking yourself why there are so few studies on brain development and its relation to puberty. It certainly is not for lack of interest! Many researchers are curious to know how the surge of pubertal hormones and psychosocial aspects of sexual maturation influence (or are influenced by) changes in brain development. The main hurdle in learning more about this relationship is a methodological one. Assessing pubertal stage is actually quite challenging and an imprecise science at best. There are excellent readings that describe these challenges in detail (see Dorn et al., 2006) so they will only briefly be described here. First, precise assessment of pubertal development requires a qualified clinician to conduct a physical exam. This practice has issues concerning privacy, convenience, and cost. Clinician time and compensation, required equipment and a private room for the physical exam, and extra burden on participants make a physical exam prohibitively inconvenient for most investigators. An alternative "short cut" that some investigators use to quantify pubertal maturation as based on Tanner staging is the Petersen Development Scale (PDS; Petersen, Crockett, Richards, and Boxer, 1988). The PDS is a short questionnaire that asks participants to provide ratings of their hair growth, skin changes, and growth spurt with sex-specific items (e.g. menarche and breast development for girls, and genital growth and facial hair for boys). Unfortunately, adolescents in this age range are notoriously imprecise in assessing these variables. In fact, correlations with clinician-assessed Tanner staging (i.e. physical exams conducted by a clinician) are low: one study reported correlations between 0.61 and 0.67 in early adolescent girls for the self-reported PDS (Brooks-Gunn, Warren, Rosso, and Gargiulo, 1987).

Hormonal assays are often used as another metric of pubertal development. As already mentioned in this chapter, some researchers assess levels of testosterone or estradiol, among other sex hormones, and use them to determine whether having more (or less) of a particular hormone is associated with changes in behavior or brain development of interest. This has yielded promising results but it is still unclear how these hormone levels relate to Tanner staging: is there a normative range of hormone levels for youth in a particular Tanner stage? Might hormone levels differ by ethnicity, socioeconomic status, or rearing environment? If so, interpretation of results from studies using hormone assays might be challenging. Additionally, hormonal assays also present logistical challenges, including high costs, subject burden, and the fluctuating levels based on monthly and circadian cycles (Blakemore, Burnett, and Dahl, 2010).

Fortunately, the increasing interest in uncovering the association between brain development and pubertal maturation has encouraged scientists to think creatively about how to measure this relationship. As we learn more about the physical and hormonal changes associated with puberty in humans, we will be better able to assess these variables meaningfully.

Late Maturation

Most (approximately 95%) girls and boys have commenced puberty by 13 years and 14 years respectively. However, there are examples of youth passing the normal age range for puberty without showing any signs of body changes. This is called delayed puberty. It is characterized by a failure to develop secondary sexual characteristics by a certain age, usually set as two standard deviations from the population mean. In girls, delayed puberty is defined as lack of any breast development by age 12–13 years, lack of pubic hair by age 14 years, lack of menarche by age 16 years, or greater than 5 years between initial breast budding and menarche. In boys, puberty is considered delayed if testicular enlargement does not occur by 14 years of age, there is lack of pubic hair by age 15 years, or more than 5 years are required to complete genital enlargement.

Puberty can be delayed for several reasons. Usually, youth who undergo delayed puberty are simply following a family pattern of delayed puberty that can be traced back to genetic underpinnings in the timing of puberty, a phenomenon known as **constitutional delay of puberty** (CDP) (or more colloquially as being a "late bloomer").

In other circumstances, delayed puberty occurs because of diet and physical activity. Girls who are very physically active (on sports teams, dance teams, or other physically rigorous activity) may experience delayed puberty because of their high level of energy expenditure. Girls' bodies require a certain amount of fat before they can go through puberty or get their first menstrual period. It is for this reason that girls who suffer from food restrictive eating disorders, such as anorexia nervosa, also typically sexually mature later relative to their peers. In addition to the relatively lower body fat, anorexia is associated with a hypogonadotropic state that can delay or arrest the onset of puberty (Warren and Vu, 2003) because of aberrant hormone levels. Individuals with anorexia and bulimia (an eating disorder characterized by binge eating that is followed by vomiting or fasting) display elevated levels of the androgen hormones DHEA and DHEAS (Monteleone et al., 2001) and decreased levels of luteinizing hormone, FSH and estradiol (Devlin et al., 1989), which are all necessary for normative development of primary and secondary sex characteristics. These variations in hormone levels contribute to atypical pubertal timing.

Delayed puberty may also be caused by a medical condition. These include chronic illnesses, such as kidney disease, severe asthma, cystic fibrosis, rheumatoid arthritis, celiac disease, or hypothyroidism. Deficiencies in the production of gonadotrophins (FSH and LH) from the pituitary gland or in the production of sex steroids (estrogens and testosterone) can also lead to delayed puberty as is the case in girls with Turner syndrome, a genetic condition in which a female does not have the usual pair of two X chromosomes. In these circumstances, endocrinologists typically prescribe treatment with sex steroids (gradually increasing doses of estrogen for girls and testosterone for boys).

2.6 Pubertal Implications on Behavior

The timing of puberty has important implications for adolescent behavior. Parents, educators, and policymakers are all well aware of the changes in mood and behavior that accompany sexual maturation. Although all individuals seem to undergo at least some of these behavioral changes during puberty, they are more dramatic in some people. Early puberty has been associated with a host of poor psychosocial outcomes and health-compromising behaviors (Blumenthal et al., 2011). Particularly in girls, early physical development coupled with relatively slower psychosocial maturity can lead to troublesome outcomes. Girls who mature early are more likely to smoke, drink, exhibit disordered eating and depressive symptoms, have lower self-esteem, be sexually promiscuous, experience conflict with parents, and have older friends (Waylen and Wolke, 2004) than girls who undergo puberty later. They are also more likely to have a live-in boyfriend and to marry younger and are less likely to graduate from high school.

Are hormones responsible for these negative effects? It would seem a logical argument that the surge in sex hormones would somehow influence these behaviors but research suggests the story is much more complicated. Studies suggest that, instead of hormones as the direct culprit, it is the physical appearance in early-maturing girls that is more directly related to the outcomes. Early-maturing girls are very aware of their appearance and social relationship with others because the physical changes elicit reactions, expectations, and treatment from others that should be reserved for older girls. They take on behaviors of older individuals at a time when they are not yet ready to be cognitively aware of the consequences of their actions. This discordance is probably what leads to lower feelings of self-worth, poor self-esteem, and conflicts with peers.

2.6.1 Pubertal Timing Effects on Psychopathology

Early pubertal maturation has been linked to a broad range of psychopathological symptoms during adolescence for girls and boys. For boys, earlier maturation has most consistently been associated with higher frequency of internalizing and externalizing symptoms during early and mid adolescence. Internalizing symptoms include depression, worry, fear, self-injury, and social withdrawal, whereas externalizing symptoms may include aggression, angry outbursts, law-breaking, or hyperactivity. The effects of early pubertal maturation in girls seem to be much greater: early timing is associated with higher rates of depressive disorders, substance disorders, eating disorders, and disruptive behavior disorders (Graber, 2013). Sexual behavior in those who mature earlier is also accelerated; these girls tend to experience first sexual intercourse, first pregnancy, and first childbirth at earlier ages (Ellis, 2004); although there are only a few longitudinal studies, there is some evidence that issues facing early maturers in adolescence persist in young adulthood and beyond (Graber, Seeley, Brooks-Gunn, and Lewinsohn, 2004).

Late-maturing boys and girls differ from their early-maturing counterparts. In girls, those who mature later than their peers have more successful psychosocial, academic and other outcomes (Graber, Nichols, and Brooks-Gunn, 2010). Boys, however, tend to exhibit greater depressive symptoms and externalizing problems (*Dusky v. U.S.*, 362 U.S. 402, 1960; Negriff, Susman, and Trickett, 2011), as well as substance use and disruptive behaviors (Graber et al., 2004).

There are two well-known hypotheses regarding the association between pubertal timing and negative behavioral outcomes. The **early timing or developmental readiness** hypothesis predicts that someone who reaches puberty earlier than peers will not be prepared for the sudden emotional and increased drive in adolescence. The **off-time or maturational deviance hypothesis** proposes that adolescents who develop either earlier or later relative to their peers experience psychological distress and manifest behavioral problems.

The **maturational compression hypothesis** was proposed to explain the relationship between tempo of puberty and psychosocial and behavioral problems (Mendle, Harden, Brooks-Gunn, and Graber, 2010). This hypothesis predicts that early maturers who advance through pubertal stages quickly develop psychological problems because they do not have the developmental time to become accustomed to the biological and social changes they experience.

Another possibility is that the surge in emotional reactivity associated with puberty outpaces the cognitive abilities of the adolescent. As we will learn in later chapters, brain regions implicated in behavioral regulation and self-control lag behind development of regions underlying emotion processing. As such, early maturers may struggle to regulate the strong emotions typically associated with pubertal onset because of normative delays in brain regions that play a strong role in emotion regulation.

2.7 "You've Gotten so Tall!"

"You've grown so much!" is an exclamation you probably heard often when you were an adolescent. It may have seemed that it was because adults do not have much else to say to teenagers but it was actually because they were right: you *had* grown so much. Reproductive success requires that individuals need to be not only hormonally ready, but physically prepared as well; for this reason, there are substantial physical and biological changes that coincide with the increasing levels of sexual hormones as individuals reach sexual maturation. In fact, there is no other time in life when one gains as much height and weight as during the adolescent years (besides during toddlerhood of course). This rapid growth is formally referred to as the adolescent growth spurt. During this time, girls increase in height about 3.5 inches per year and boys about 4 inches per year on average – that's roughly the equivalent of gaining the length of a candy bar every year for a few years! During peak height velocity, boys and girls gain 15–25% of the height they will have for the rest of their adult lives; people gain very little height after about age 18. The linear growth spurt lasts approximately 2 years, ceasing by 17 years of age in most girls. In boys, the growth spurt lasts longer and does not end until about 18–21 years of age. But by about age 14, boys tend to be taller than girls.

Weight increases significantly during adolescence as well. Before puberty, boys and girls do not differ much in body fat or muscle development but sex differences emerge during puberty as girls tend to have greater increases in body fat than boys. At peak weight gain (Stang and Story, 2005), girls gain 18.5 pounds on average per year with a mean average weight gain of about 38 pounds overall by the time puberty is over. In boys, average weight gain is about 20 pounds per year, with an average weight gain of 52 pounds overall. However, it is important to recognize that there are vast individual differences in weight gain in both boys and girls; the range in overall weight gain across puberty is between 15 and 60 pounds. This physical difference has implications for many outcomes, including athletic ability and strength, diet, and body satisfaction. Although normal and critical for development, some adolescents, particularly females, have negative perceptions of this dramatic weight gain.

Weight dissatisfaction is, unfortunately, quite prevalent among adolescent girls and can lead to disordered eating, body image distortions, and negative self-views.

How does the body know when to stop growing? Heredity plays a strong role in a person's height and weight. Individuals from different races and ethnic groups tend to differ in their body fat distribution or body composition. How tall a person will be is also partially determined by genetic makeup: if his parents are tall, there is a good chance that he will also be tall. A pretty accurate rule of thumb is that a person's terminal height is the midpoint between the biological mother's and the biological father's height.

However, individuals share more than just genes with family members. They also share eating habits, levels of activity and exercise, and home environment, all of which can contribute to body weight and height as well. Families who tend to eat high-caloric foods or snacks (e.g. junk food) or who do not engage in much exercise are more likely to exhibit high weight gain; this is particularly true of the teenagers in the family, who are developmentally primed to experience weight gain. In terms of height, youth who are encouraged to "sit up straight" are more likely to appear taller and practice good posture later in life.

2.8 Bone Age

Bone age is a measurement of biological age rather than actual or chronological age. It changes throughout development, until the end of puberty, and is generally a good marker of the end of pubertal-related growth. To determine bone age, a simple X-ray is taken of the left hand and wrist, and this is compared with a set of photographic standards to assess how mature the child's bones are. Beginning in fetal development, the bones take shape in ways that support motor skills. As you can see in Figure 2.6,

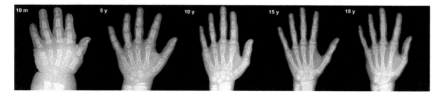

Figure 2.6 This image illustrates changes in bone structure and size across development. Bone age is a measurement of biological age rather than actual or chronological age. It changes throughout development, until the end of puberty.

only the **metaphyses** (wide portions) of the long bones in the legs, arms, fingers, and toes are present in early postnatal life (~2 years old). At either end of a child's long bones, there are gaps, called growth plates, which allow the bone to grow. Across childhood, these gaps gradually get smaller, and by the time puberty is complete they disappear, the growth plates "fuse" and the bones cannot get any longer. Growth occurs when the **epiphysis** at the end of the growing bones is elongated. This process coincides with the increasing levels of sex steroids and tapers off as puberty comes to an end. Once all of the growth plates are fused, the potential for further growth, or height gain, is minimal. The closing of the gap between bones, at the epiphysis, is often used as a marker that signifies the end of puberty (Figure 2.6). No further lengthening occurs after this point, as the bones are the size and shape of adult bones and adult height.

2.9 Puberty and Brain Structure

Although puberty and brain development have been independently studied for decades, relatively little is known about the relationship between the two in humans. Luckily, animal research has provided valuable insight and suggests that the hormonal events at the onset of puberty exert significant effects on brain maturation (Sisk and Foster, 2004). Sex hormones exert three primary effects on behavior by acting on particular brain regions. First, via the hypothalamus, hormones facilitate reproductive behaviors. Second, reorganization of sensory and association regions of the brain, including visual cortex, amygdala, and hippocampus, results in altered sensory recognition of meaningful conspecifics (e.g. a potential mate or competitor). Finally, changes in reward circuitry encourage strong motivation to seek out reproductive opportunities (Sato, Schulz, Sisk, and Wood, 2008). We will discuss changes in reward-related circuitry in greater detail in Chapter 6.

The emergence of neuroimaging technologies, including magnetic resonance imaging (MRI) and functional magnetic resonance imaging (fMRI), revolutionized the study of human brain development in healthy children and adolescents. These non-invasive tools allow researchers to obtain clear and detailed pictures of the developing brain without causing any harm or pain. Whereas MRI is used to examine the anatomy of the brain, fMRI is used to study the brain "in motion" (Galván, 2014). Researchers use fMRI to study how the brain reacts, when processing information. With appropriate instruction, patience, and youth-friendly tasks, children and adolescents can perform quite well and provide useful insights into the developing human brain. Details of these methodological tools will be described in the next chapter.

2.9.1 Gray Matter

MRI studies are used to characterize the size and shape of brain structures. MRI studies in humans suggest that pubertal hormones influence brain structure and function (Herting et al., 2014; Peper and Dahl, 2013). Many of these studies categorize youth into pubertal stages based on a standardized system called *Tanner staging* (described in greater detail in Box 2.3). A large longitudinal study of 275 individuals aged 7–20 years revealed that pubertal development was significantly linked to the size of regions involved in emotion and reward processing, including the amygdala, hippocampus, and striatum (Goddings et al., 2014), as illustrated in Figure 2.7. MRI studies have also identified the gradual emergence of differences between boys and girls across the pubertal transition. In general, there are increases in amygdala size in males only and increases in hippocampal size in females only across puberty (Lenroot et al., 2007), regions dense in sex hormones. This means that, as these regions become more populated with sex hormones, there are greater differences in size, with adolescents who are further along in their pubertal development (e.g. have more sex hormones) exhibiting greater structural size of these regions than those who have relatively fewer sex hormones. Bigger does not necessarily mean better or more mature, as this too varies by gender: in boys, greater sexual maturation is associated with bigger size of medial temporal lobe structures while it is associated with smaller medial temporal lobe structures in girls. These differences highlight the *activational effects* that hormones have during adolescence, by further expanding the sexual dimorphism that occurs during the prenatal *organizational* period.

Assessments of circulating levels of hormones have revealed sex differences in cortical thickness based on differences in testosterone or estradiol levels. Cortical thickness is simply a brain measure used to describe the combined thickness of the layers of the cerebral cortex. These studies suggest that testosterone has the opposite effect on boys and girls, such that higher testosterone levels are associated with thicker cortex in boys but thinner cortex in girls (Bramen et al., 2012). As reviewed in Chapter 1, whether it is "better" or "more mature" to have thinner or thicker cortex depends on the gender of the individual, the association to behavior, and individual differences.

Box 2.3 Tanner Staging

The staging system Tanner developed to describe normal progression of puberty in males and females over 50 years ago is utilized for clinical descriptions in terms of Sexual Maturation Rating (SMR) or Tanner stages (Marshall and Tanner, 1969, 1970).

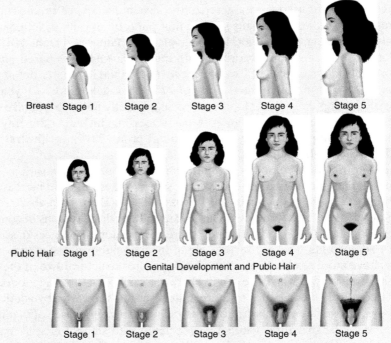

Breast   Stage 1   Stage 2   Stage 3   Stage 4   Stage 5

Pubic Hair   Stage 1   Stage 2   Stage 3   Stage 4   Stage 5

Genital Development and Pubic Hair

Stage 1   Stage 2   Stage 3   Stage 4   Stage 5

Female Development

Stage 1.
   Breast: No breast development; only the nipple is elevated slightly.
   Pubic Hair: No pubic hair.
Stage 2.
   Breast: The "breast bud" stage. The areola widens, darkens slightly, and elevates from the rest of breast as a small mound.
   Pubic Hair: Sparse growth of slightly pigmented, longer hair but still straight or only slightly curled, appearing mainly along the labia.
Stage 3.
   Breast: The breast and areola further enlarge and exhibit a rounded contour. There is no separation of contour between the nipple and areola and the rest of the breast. The breast tissue creates a small cone.

Pubic Hair: The hair is considerably darker, coarser, and more curled. The hair spreads sparsely over the mons.

Stage 4.

Breast: The breast is further enlarged to form a secondary mound. The areola becomes more pigmented and enlarged, and the nipple also becomes pigmented. This is the most variable of all the stages.

Pubic Hair: Hair adult in type but covering smaller area than adult: no spread to medial surface of thighs.

Stage 5.

Breast: Development is the mature, adult breast but there is significant variability in size. There is projection of only the nipple with recession of the areola back to the contour of the breast. The hair is adult-like in appearance and distributed in the classic female triangle. Some individuals may have hair spread to the medial thighs.

Menarche.

Menarche, or the first menstrual period, is not part of the Tanner staging system. Girls need a certain amount of estrogen to menstruate, but it can happen at Tanner stage 2, 3, 4, or even 5. As noted in the text, the exact specifications for the onset of menarche remain a mystery.

Male Development

Stage 1.

The testes, scrotal sac, and penis have a size and proportion similar to those seen in childhood. There is no pubic hair.

Stage 2.

There is an enlargement of the scrotum and testes and a change in the texture of the scrotal skin, which may be reddened. Sparse growth of lightly colored, mostly straight hair begins to emerge at the base of the penis.

Stage 3.

Further growth of the penis has occurred, initially in length, although with some increase in circumference. There is also increased growth of the scrotum and testes. The hair is darker, coarser, and more curled and has spread to thinly cover a larger area.

Stage 4.

The penis is significantly enlarged in length and circumference and the glans (head) is bigger. The scrotum and testes continue to enlarge, and there is a distinct darkening of the scrotal skin. The texture of the pubic hair is similar to that seen in adults but covers a smaller area. There is no spread to the inside of the thighs.

Stage 5.
    The genitalia are adult in size and shape. The hair is distributed in an inverse
    triangle and has spread to the inside of the thighs.

Source: The American College of Obstetricians and Gynecologists

Examination of DHEA has suggested that it too plays a critical role in cortical thickness. A recent longitudinal study reported that DHEA levels were associated with increases in cortical thickness of prefrontal cortex regions, which are implicated in behavioral regulation, between the ages of 4 and 13 years, a period marked by the androgenic changes of adrenarche (Nguyen et al., 2013). This study also found sex differences: testosterone levels were associated with cortical thickness changes in regions of the left hemisphere in males and of the right hemisphere in females. These data suggest that DHEA and testosterone interact and modulate the complex process of cortical maturation during the pubertal transition, consistent with evidence at the molecular level of mechanisms underlying androgen-related brain development.

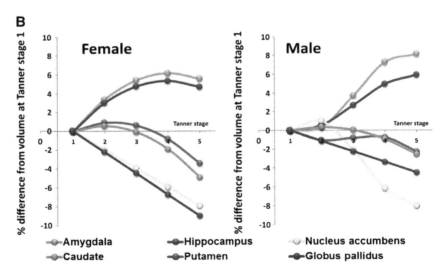

Figure 2.7 The greatest brain volume changes from early pubertal stage (Tanner 1) to latest pubertal stage (Tanner 5) occur in the amygdala and hippocampus in both girls (*left*) and boys (*right*) (Goddings et al., 2014). See color plate 3.

2.9.2 White Matter

White matter consists of myelin-insulated axons that are bundled into tracts that facilitate communication between brain regions. Methods used to measure white matter are reviewed in greater detail in Chapter 3. In brief, there are automated software tools that segment the different parts of the brain into **white matter** and **gray matter**; researchers use these tools to quantify the amount of white matter that an individual has. This approach has yielded interesting relations between white matter development and puberty.

Results from a large study of 9-year-old twin-pairs show that there is a strong relationship between higher levels of luteinizing hormone and the proportion of overall white matter volume (Peper et al., 2008). A follow-up study, however, showed that levels of sex steroids (testosterone and estradiol) are not associated with white matter volume in either boys or girls (Peper et al., 2009), suggesting that pubertal hormones may each play a unique role in brain structure. However, the metric used for puberty seems to influence the findings: A study using Tanner rating scales (instead of hormone levels) did indeed find that white matter density in frontal, parietal, and temporal lobes increases with pubertal maturation in boys only (Perrin et al., 2009). There are only a few studies that have examined associations between puberty and white matter development. Nonetheless, findings from these studies suggest that there may be unique pubertal influences on white matter development in adolescence (Ladouceur, Peper, Crone, and Dahl, 2012).

2.10 Puberty and Brain Function

Along with the many intriguing physical, biological, and neuroanatomical changes that sweep adolescents during puberty, there is a marked change in how the brain *functions*. Pubertal hormones are so powerful that key brain regions critical for inducing increased attention toward reproductive behaviors and social interactions become very engaged and active during adolescence. Hormonal changes during puberty are thought to serve as the impetus for behavioral changes that will orient the adolescent toward increased social behavior. Research suggests that there is a strong relationship between brain development and developmental changes in social behavior (Nelson, Lieibenluft, McClure, and Pine, 2005). The increase of gonadal steroids at puberty induces changes within the limbic system that alter the emotional attributions applied to social stimuli, while the gradual maturation of the prefrontal cortex enables increasingly complex and controlled responses to social information. For instance, regions implicated in emotion processing undergo significant change during adolescence, as well as regions implicated in reward processing and motivation.

These hormones launch sexually dimorphic trajectories in brain development and play a role in reorganizing cortical-striatal circuitry, particularly the circuitry that supports social behaviors relevant to mate selection and the act of mating (Sisk and Zehr, 2005). Changes in specific neural networks help orient the pubertal adolescent toward greater desire of sexual partners. As reviewed in a model put forth by Scherf and colleagues, three core systems are reorganized during puberty that drive orientation toward social-emotional information processing (Scherf, Behrmann, and Dahl, 2012), which is critical for directing individuals toward stimuli that will encourage reproductive behaviors and social experience more broadly.

The first neural network is involved in processing basic attention and visual orientation; it includes the inferior occipital cortex ("occipital face area" (OFA): Gauthier and Nelson, 2001), the posterior fusiform gyrus ("fusiform face area" (FFA): Kanwisher, McDermott, and Chun, 1997), the superior temporal sulcus (STS: Hoffman and Haxby, 2000), and auxiliary visuoperceptual regions of visual cortex (Scherf et al., 2012). Research in this network has shown significant changes in these regions across the pubertal transition. For instance, when presented with images of faces, adolescents (11–14 year olds) activate the fusiform face area that is similar to FFA activation in adults and which is notably absent in children (5–8 year olds) (Scherf, Behrmann, Humphreys, and Luna, 2007). This result has been replicated and extended in other recent studies (Golarai et al., 2007; Golarai, Liberman, Yoon, and Grill-Spector, 2010; Scherf, Luna, Avidan, and Behrmann, 2011), indicating that the core face processing regions continue to exhibit ongoing development in adolescence. This development has significant implications for social engagement: as individuals become more skilled in "reading" faces, emotional expressions, and affect, they become more experienced in social interactions.

The second neural network is critically involved in "mentalizing," the ability to understand the mental state of oneself and of others. This network includes the medial prefrontal cortex (mPFC), temporoparietal junction (TPJ), anterior temporal cortex, and cingulate gyrus. These regions underlie the ability for individuals to "mentalize" or understand the mental state, thoughts, and feelings of other people. This ability is critical for normative and successful social interaction and significantly increases during adolescence (Burnett, Sebastian, Cohen Kadosh, and Blakemore, 2011). Neuroimaging studies show that, during self-reflection, adolescents demonstrate greater activation than adults in this neural network; interestingly, the increased activation in adolescents is associated with more accurate self-appraisals than adults (Pfeifer et al., 2009). Research on this topic also suggests that adolescents exhibit greater activation in the mPFC, a classic mentalizing region, than adults when judging emotional response others may have to social emotions such as embarrassment and guilt (Burnett, Bird, Moll, Frith, and Blakemore, 2009).

The third network is important for emotion processing and includes the amygdala, insula, and striatum. These regions are the core limbic circuitry that supports emotion discrimination, affect, and threat (Feinstein, Adolphs, Damasio, and Tranel, 2011) and undergo significant maturation from childhood through adolescence. For example, explicit memory for emotional expression improves from late childhood through adolescence (Pine et al., 2004), particularly for fear, anger, and disgust (Thomas et al., 2001). Similarly, the ability to recognize face identity follows a delayed developmental trajectory even beyond adolescence (Carey and Diamond, 1977). Using emotional faces as stimuli, researchers have described a U-shaped pattern of functional development in the amygdala with increasing activation through adolescence (Baird et al., 1999) and an age-related decline in activation from adolescence to adulthood (Guyer et al., 2008). There is also evidence of a qualitative shift in amygdala function from late childhood to adulthood such that children show greater activation to neutral faces while adults show greater activation to fearful faces (Thomas et al., 2001).

The changes that occur in the striatum around puberty are related to changes in reward processing. Reward circuitry is rich in the neurotransmitter dopamine, which has been linked to reward processing (Schultz, Dayan, and Montague, 1997). Evidence from animal models suggests that the dopamine system undergoes significant remodeling during puberty (Bell and Sisk, 2013).

Despite the strong evidence from animal studies, there are surprisingly few empirical studies in human adolescents. The few published studies on this topic have suggested that greater levels of testosterone are associated with increased activation in reward circuitry when participants are performing a risk-taking or rewarding computer task. Forbes and Dahl report that plasma testosterone levels are positively related to activation in a reward-related brain region during reward anticipation in boys (Forbes and Dahl, 2010), a finding also reported by Op de Macks and colleageus in both boys and girls (Op de Macks et al., 2011). A more recent study reported that pubertal increases in testosterone predicted increased activation in threat-sensing (e.g. the amygdala) regions as well as the reward-related regions when participants felt strong emotions (Spielberg, Olino, Forbes, and Dahl, 2014). However, a longitudinal study found no associations between reward-related brain activation and pubertal status (van Duijvenvoorde et al., 2014). Using a social processing task, Goddings and colleagues found that increasing levels of pubertal hormones were associated with greater activation in brain regions involved in social information processing (Goddings, Burnett Hayes, Bird, Viner, and Blakemore, 2012); the same group found that communication between these regions was enhanced in girls with higher levels of estradiol and more advanced pubertal status (Klapwijk, Peters, Vermeiren, and Lelieveld, 2013). Although these studies do suggest an association between puberty, hormonal changes, and brain function sensitivity, the discrepant and few results underscore the need for more empirical studies on this topic.

Collectively, these data suggest that the hormonal changes that occur during puberty are the impetus for behavioral increases in motivation related to social information processing. However, much more research in this area is necessary.

2.11 Chapter Summary

- Puberty is a long process that occurs over several years in late childhood and early adolescence.
- Physical changes include significant increases in height, weight, and bone development.
- Multiple factors serve as "permissive signals" that trigger the beginning of puberty.
- Pubertal onset has gotten successively earlier across generations.

2.12 Review Questions

1 Which brain regions are involved in pubertal onset?
2 What are the primary physical changes that occur at the onset of puberty?
3 What are the benefits of puberty?

4 Are there potential negative consequences of variability in pubertal timing?
5 What are the main factors that contribute to the onset of puberty?

Further Reading

Blakemore, S.J., Burnett, S., and Dahl, R.E. (2010). The role of puberty in the developing adolescent brain. *Human Brain Mapping*, 31, 926–933.
Sisk, C.L., and Foster, D.L. (2004). The neural basis of puberty and adolescence. *Nature Neuroscience*, 7, 1040–1047.

CHAPTER THREE

Cognitive Neuroscience Methods to Study the Adolescent Brain

Learning Objectives

- How do scientists study the brain in humans?
- What are the different tools used to study the brain?
- What are the strengths and limitations of brain imaging technology?

3.1 Introduction

In the 1990s, one study revolutionized the understanding of the developing brain. B.J. Casey and colleagues successfully did what no one had attempted to do previously: peek into the brains of healthy (and awake!) children to determine how their brains worked. Dr. Casey did this by asking a group of children to undergo a brain scan while they performed a computerized task. This study was really exciting and novel because previous brain imaging studies in healthy children and adolescents had only examined the anatomy, not the function, of the brain. It sparked a tidal wave of studies that have accumulated into a rich knowledge base of how the brain functions across childhood and into adolescence.

Throughout this book we will read about these studies. All of them use at least one brain imaging tool designed to measure brain activity so it is important for you to have a working understanding of the technology. In this chapter, we will not dig too deeply into the physics and technical aspects of the techniques but we will learn about the most commonly used tools, how they work, what the research participant experiences and what type of data they produce. Unfortunately this requires using some cognitive neuroscience "jargon" but it cannot be avoided when speaking about technical terms. Brain scans are the most common way to study the developing brain so we will start our tour there before reading about other tools used to measure brain waves. Finally, we will circle back to learn how scientists sometimes combine different methods to yield the most informative research. These tools have taught us a great deal about the human brain but, as no technology is perfect, they are not without their limitations. We will review the strengths and limitations of each method and then discuss how scientists use the data to make conclusions about the developing brain.

3.2 Brain Scans

What is a brain scan? A **brain scan** is a picture of the brain that is taken using a machine that operates like a giant camera. There are several different types of brain scans, including those that come under the broad umbrella of brain imaging (sometimes referred to as neuroimaging). Brain imaging falls into two general groups: (1) **structural imaging**, which allows visualization of the anatomy and structure of the brain, and (2) **functional imaging**, which shows how the brain processes information. It is this type of imaging that produces images that show where the brain "lights up" in response to particular stimuli.

There is another type of brain imaging technology, called Positron Emission Tomography (PET), commonly used to study brain function in adults. A PET scan uses a radioactive tracer to show activity in the tissue or organ of interest. The tracer, which contains a tiny amount of a radioactive substance, is injected, swallowed, or inhaled into the research participant (or patient if the PET scan is being conducted for a clinical or diagnostic purpose). The tracer gathers in areas of the brain that have higher levels of chemical activity. The PET scanner detects pairs of γ-rays emitted by the positron-emitting radiotracers. On PET scan images, these areas show up as bright spots. PET imaging has been very useful in identifying neural activation involved in complex processing. However, because it requires the injection of radioactive tracers, this technique remains prohibitively invasive for use in children and adolescent brain research. Therefore, there will be no further mention of PET in this book.

3.2.1 Structural Magnetic Resonance Imaging (sMRI)

Magnetic resonance imaging (MRI) is a noninvasive technique for visualizing many different body tissues. An MRI is not an **X-ray**, which is a type of electromagnetic radiation. To produce an X-ray image, an X-ray machine sends individual X-ray particles throughout the body and the images are recorded on a computer or film. Unlike X-rays, MRI does not use any radiation so there is no radiation exposure. Instead, it uses radio waves, a large magnet, and a computer to create images. This makes it preferable for use with developmental populations because it means nothing pokes, prods, or hurts the research participant while they are receiving a brain scan. There are also no known long-term side effects of

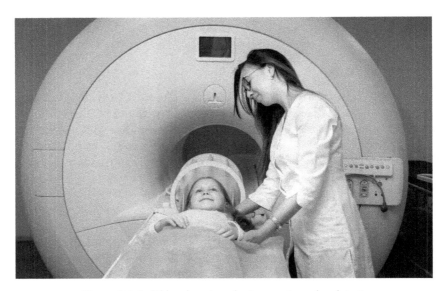

Figure 3.1 A child undergoing a brain scan. See color plate 4.

brain imaging so it is safe too. The first MRI exam was conducted on a human in 1977 and since then the procedure has become quite routine, with over 25,000 MRI machines worldwide (www.magnetic-resonance .org/ch/21-01.html).

As you can see in Figure 3.1, the MRI is a large machine (sometimes referred to as a scanner) with a circular tunnel built through it, like the hole of a donut. A research participant lies on his back on a narrow table that can be moved back and forth into the tunnel by an MRI technician, a person who is specifically trained to operate the scanner. The device you see in the picture over the participant's head is the head coil, which is what takes the brain images. There are some loud noises from the machine as the pictures are being acquired. To minimize the noise, participants are outfitted with earplugs and a headset. Because the participant needs to remain very still to avoid blurry images, participants are also "cushioned" into the tunnel with comfortable pillows. Participants will often also wear goggles to view a computer screen that is programmed from the control room (some imaging facilities instead have a small screen attached to the scanner). During structural MRI (sMRI) scanning, participants often watch a movie through the goggles to help keep them entertained. See Box 3.1 to learn how researchers help participants become comfortable in the scanner.

Box 3.1 Getting Acclimated to the MRI Scanner

Movement Training, Pillows

Unsurprisingly, children and some adolescents tend to wiggle more while getting a brain scan than adults. This wiggling causes more artifact in the data and hence more challenges in analyzing and interpreting the results. Many researchers therefore acclimate youth to the MRI scanner using a mock (pretend) scanner. During the mock scanning session, they are trained to lie still and about how to communicate with the technician (without moving their head) during the scan. This introduction to the MRI scanner helps alleviate any concerns they have also because they have an opportunity to ask questions and see that the scanner is safe.

Mock scan training does a good job at helping youth stay still but it does not always eliminate head movement. Researchers therefore also account for head motion in their analyses. First, we measure the amount of movement (in millimeters) in six head orientations and degree of rotation to account for the multiple ways individuals can move their heads – these include head tilting down, to the back, sidewise left, sidewise right, and head tilts at an angle. Typically, any participant who moves more than a given threshold is removed from the analyses. If a participant only has a handful of head movements that exceed threshold then researchers sometimes only remove those particular timepoints of data but this too can be tricky because it interferes with the timing and may lead to incorrect assumptions about the data. Second, researchers conduct correlation analyses to ensure that brain activation patterns are not correlated with movement. Finally, most researchers include the movement as a covariate of no interest in the initial single-subject general linear model to regress out the effects of movement on brain activation.

How are the brain pictures created? The MRI scanner is a giant magnet, similar to magnets on your refrigerator but there is an important difference. The refrigerator magnets are made of alloys and are technically referred to as permanent magnets whereas the MRI magnet is a **superconducting magnet**. In permanent magnets the magnetic field is generated by the internal structure of the material itself but in a superconducting magnet, the magnetic field is created by conducting electricity. In an MRI experiment, this magnetic field runs horizontally through the research participant from head to toe.

MRI magnets are also much more powerful than refrigerator magnets. Scientists measure magnetic strength in units called **tesla** and **gauss** – 1 tesla is equal to 10,000 gauss. To give you a sense of the relative

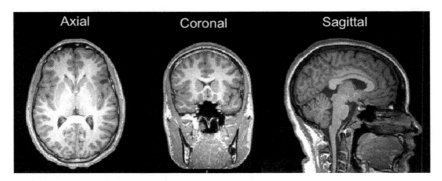

Figure 3.2 MRI images are typically presented in three planes. The transverse (axial) plane slices the brain from top to bottom, the coronal plane slices the brain lengthwise from front to back, and the sagittal plane slices the brain lengthwise from side to side.

difference, consider this: the fridge magnet is about 10 gauss whereas the MRI magnet is typically 3 tesla – 60,000 times the force of the Earth's magnetic field! Such a powerful magnet has the force to pull any metal toward it, which is why potential research volunteers are carefully screened to ensure there is no metal in their body.

Each MRI picture shows a different "slice," or cross-section, of the area being viewed, similar to a sliced loaf of bread. Because these slices are usually spaced about a quarter-inch apart, researchers can get a detailed image of a particular brain area. Often there is interest in a particular brain region, known to be important for processing certain types of stimuli or implicated in particular psychiatric disorders, or which undergoes unique maturational changes across development. As we will learn in Chapter 5, for example, the prefrontal cortex undergoes a long period of development that spans over two decades, so developmental scientists are keen to understand how the protracted development influences cognition.

MRI allows us to view each "slice of bread" from multiple dimensions. The three main dimensions, or planes, are the transverse (or axial, x–y), coronal (x–z) and sagittal (y–x) plans. As illustrated in Figure 3.2, the **transverse** plane slices the brain from top to bottom, the **coronal** plane slices the brain lengthwise from front to back, and the **sagittal** plane slices the brain lengthwise from side to side.

sMRI: Strengths and Limitations

The MRI does not change anything about the research participant's body or its chemistry. It is for this reason that it is often hailed for its

MRI Image   fMRI Image

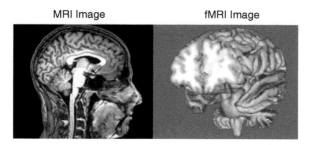

Figure 3.3 The MRI scan (*left*) provides a high level of anatomical detail. The fMRI scan (*right*) illustrates brain activation.

"noninvasive" nature. Participants can receive as many scans as necessary without causing any harm. It is therefore also ideal for longitudinal studies, in which a participant receives a brain scan multiple times, often over several months or years. Longitudinal studies are quite informative in developmental research to determine how the brain changes over time, as individuals get older.

Another strength is that MRIs provide very detailed images of the brain. The 3-D images allow researchers to study the brain from all angles, and to determine whether there are changes in the size or shape of particular brain structures. This level of anatomical detail, called **spatial resolution**, is not available with some other tools that we will review later in this chapter, such as EEG, that are used to study the developing brain. Importantly, MRI captures images of the entire brain, even those regions that are located deep within the brain, which contrasts with tools that only measure electrical brain activity from the surface of the brain. Notice the high level of detail in the MRI image in the left panel of Figure 3.3. You can see the tree-like branching of the cerebellum at the base of the brain and the thick myelin tissue of the corpus callosum in the middle that connects the front and back of the brain.

The limitations of sMRI are mainly related to the restrictions necessary for producing high-quality images. First, research participants need to remain very still. (Most researchers do not include data in their analyses in which the participant moved more than about 3 millimeters!) Although remaining still is pretty easy for an adult, children and adolescents sometimes struggle to remain so for the hour or so in which they are in the scanner. Second, as mentioned previously, participants who have metal in their body cannot receive a brain scan so braces or permanent retainers render a good portion of teenagers ineligible for brain imaging studies. Third, individuals who are claustrophobic may feel uncomfortable in the enclosed MRI space so they too are ineligible to participate in brain studies.

3.2.2 Diffusion Tensor Imaging (DTI)

You may have noticed in Figures 3.2 and 3.3 that some brain regions span multiple areas in the brain, as is the case with the corpus callosum or the gyri of the brain (the hose-like tissue that dominates the brain image). This tissue is called white matter, which consists of bundles of axons covered in myelin, a fatty lipid that speeds up neuronal transmission (Pierpaoli, Jezzard, Basser, Barnett, and Di Chiro, 1996). What we see in the image is actually dense packing of the myelin that wraps around axons, which are the main freeways for neural communication. Researchers have long been interested in studying how white matter is structured and now they can, with a technique called **diffusion tensor imaging** (DTI).

DTI allows for the assessment of brain pathways through the measurement of something called water molecule dispersion (Le Bihan, 1995). This provides insight into the orientation of myelinated fiber bundles that constitute white matter. Diffusion measurements of white matter are meant to approximate organization of white matter tracts (i.e. diameter or packing density of axons).

Diffusion data are acquired during MRI using a rapid echo-planar imaging (EPI) sequence, which captures the rate and direction of water diffusion within brain tissue. The obtained diffusion-weighted images are then used to generate a matrix to reconstruct the white matter tracts of the brain (Figure 3.4). These values form the basis for the calculation of the two most common variables used to infer tissue structure: mean diffusivity (MD) and fractional anisotropy (FA). MD simply refers to the overall magnitude of water diffusion and is hypothesized to reflect white matter volume (Basser and Pierpaoli, 2011). FA is a more specific value, commonly used to infer tissue microstructure (i.e. axon size and density). FA values range from 0 for isotropic (unrestricted) diffusion to 1 for anisotropic (restricted diffusion). Thus, high FA values indicate greater anisotropy and more highly organized and myelinated bundles (Lebel et al., 2012).

DTI: Strengths and Limitations

White matter continues to develop and change from childhood into adolescence (Sowell et al., 2003), supporting neural communication between

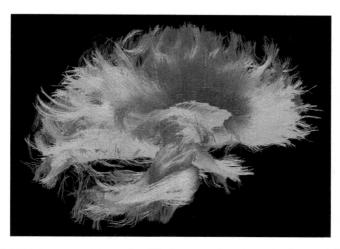

Figure 3.4 This image was taken using diffusion tensor imaging technology and illustrates white matter fibers. The fibers are color-coded by direction: red = left–right, green = anterior–posterior, blue = ascending–descending. See color plate 5.

functionally connected regions that have been coupled through learning and experience. Examining the maturation of these structural connections throughout childhood and into early adulthood, during which white matter growth peaks, provides a deeper understanding of the anatomical links between brain regions and the developmentally appropriate behaviors these connections support.

While DTI offers a powerful tool to examine white matter development, it suffers from inherent artifacts and limitations. Specifically, DTI relies on two assumptions that are not necessarily true for white matter tissue in the brain. The first is that the displacement probability of water molecules follows a Gaussian distribution (Basser, Mattiello, and LeBihan, 1994). Experimental evidence points to non-Gaussian diffusion in white matter (Treit, Chen, Rasmussen, and Beaulieu, 2014), as diffusion within fiber tracts is restricted (Jensen, Helpern, Ramani, Lu, and Kaczynski, 2005). The second assumption of DTI is that a single matrix to fit each voxel of acquired diffusion data is sufficient to characterize the microstructure of white matter tracts. In reality, a single pixel includes tens of thousands of axons and glial cells, and a single diffusion tensor is an average of tens of thousands of axons and glial cells. Thus, areas of tissue partial volume (where white matter resides in the same pixel as gray matter, for instance) or of white matter partial volume (a pixel with crossing tract fibers) cannot be accurately assessed by DTI models (Jansons and Alexander, 2003).

3.2.3 Functional Magnetic Resonance Imaging (fMRI)

Functional MRI is similar to MRI but it allows scientists to see the brain "in motion." This means that researchers can determine how the brain processes information. Because of fMRI, scientists know where the brain processes different types of cognitive operations, ranging from how you solve a math problem to how you store memories to how you process emotional facial expressions. In developmental research, fMRI has been helpful in uncovering how the brain functions differently across different ages. Although the brain does not change very much in its anatomical structure after about age 5, how it *functions* changes throughout the lifespan.

If structural MRIs are photographs, then functional MRIs are like videos. It works by taking advantage of the fact that when a particular part of the brain is used, blood rushes to that brain region. Increases in blood flow and blood oxygenation in the brain (collectively known as **hemodynamics**) are closely linked to neuronal activity. When we think about something, experience an emotion, learn a new fact, or simply look at the world around us, the brain becomes active. More specifically, the neurons of the brain are called into action, ready to help the brain process the information it is presented with. When this happens, local blood flow to those brain regions increases, and oxygen-rich (oxygenated) blood displaces oxygen-poor (deoxygenated) blood. Oxygen is carried by the hemoglobin molecule in red blood cells. Deoxygenated hemoglobin (dHb) is more magnetic (the formal term for this is paramagnetic) than oxygenated hemoglobin (Hb). The difference in magnetic properties between oxygenated and deoxygenated blood is what causes a contrast that can be visualized with fMRI and is considered an index of neuronal activity. The right panel of Figure 3.3 is an example of an fMRI image. The yellow pixels illustrate brain regions that show strong neuronal activity in response to a stimulus the participant is viewing.

BOLD

The brain signal scientists typically use in their analyses is called the Blood-Oxygen-Level-Dependent (BOLD) signal. The BOLD signal

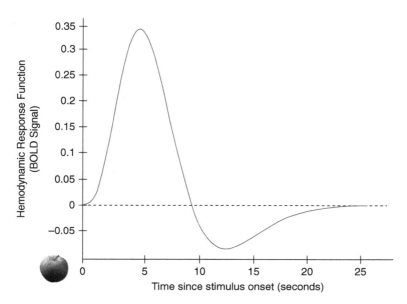

Figure 3.5 The hemodynamic response function of the BOLD signal peaks at approximately 4–6 seconds after stimulus onset (a picture of an apple, for example). Before reaching baseline again, the signal exhibits an "undershoot" (dips below baseline).

refers to the contrast difference between the deoxygenated and oxygenated blood described above. The change in the MR signal from neuronal activity is called the hemodynamic response (HDR). It lags the neuronal events that trigger it by a few seconds, since it takes that long for the vascular system to respond to the brain's need for glucose. From this point it typically rises to a peak at about 5 seconds after the stimulus. If the neurons keep firing, say from a continuous stimulus, the peak spreads to a flat plateau while the neurons stay active. After activity stops, the BOLD signal falls below the original level, the baseline, a phenomenon called the undershoot. Over time the signal recovers to the baseline. Figure 3.5 illustrates the rise and fall of the BOLD signal on the y-axis as a function of time since the stimulus was presented on the x-axis. A hypothetical stimulus, say a picture of an apple, is presented at time 0. There is a slow increase in the neural response in the first few seconds after the research participant sees the apple, peaking approximately 4–6 seconds after it was first presented. The neural response then slowly decreases back to baseline.

fMRI: Strengths and Limitations

Since the early 1990s, fMRI has dominated brain mapping research because it provides powerful and informative images of the brain and because it is non-invasive. Its strengths are similar to those listed for MRI, including the ability to examine the live, healthy, and developing brain, and the detailed images it renders.

In addition to the limitations that involve subject movement and the inability of some individuals to undergo an fMRI scan due to claustrophobia or metal in the body, fMRI has some analytical limitations. There is no consensus as to how exactly to analyze fMRI data. This affords researchers a lot of flexibility, which is good for generating creativity and autonomy, but also can be limiting in how replicable studies are. If everyone is using their own processing approach, then generating the same results is not always possible. Luckily, the cognitive neuroscience community has recently banded together to describe some standard guidelines to help streamline fMRI analyses and reproducibility (Nichols et al., 2015). There are also limitations in interpretation, particularly when comparing two groups of individuals, such as adolescents and adults. We will review these limitations as cautionary warnings at the end of this chapter.

3.2.4 Functional Connectivity

fMRI has been instrumental in learning about the developing brain since the 1990s. We have learned that although particular brain regions are experts in processing particular stimuli (a region called the striatum is adept at processing things that are pleasurable, for instance), brain regions do not typically work in isolation. Instead, individual regions operate as part of a team. You can think of it like a sports team. Although each member of the team specializes in one aspect of the game (a pitcher in a baseball team, for instance), they rely on other members to perform optimally in *their* particular skill to achieve a win. A team that works really well together, and which is comprised of team members who are each highly talented in their own skill, will ultimately be faster, better, and more victorious than a team with weak players and/or poor communication between players. The brain works in a similar way, except that we refer to the collaboration between "team members" (brain regions) as a network rather than a team. The ultimate goal of the network is not, of course, to win a game but to process incoming information as quickly and efficiently as possible. Over time, brain regions that often work together form what is called a "functional network" because they work, or function, together. How do scientists know this if we do not have the ability to actually "see" how brain regions work together? This is relatively easy to observe in task-based fMRI because the researcher can determine which regions are activated together during the task.

Another method researchers use is one called **resting state fMRI (rsfMRI)**. It is a method with which to evaluate the interactions between brain regions when the participant is not performing an explicit computerized task. In the previous section you learned about BOLD, the signal that is measured with fMRI. rsfMRI also uses BOLD to determine which brain regions co-activate by measuring spontaneous fluctuations in blood flow; it is referred to as "spontaneous" because it refers to fluctuations that occur naturally, and not in response to a particular stimulus or cognitive task. The advantage of studying networks this way is that we can determine which brain regions exhibit similar fluctuations in BOLD, which is an indication of which brain regions have worked together over time.

The acquisition of resting state data is simple. It involves scanning participants as they lie in the scanner, fixated on a cross-hair on a screen or with eyes closed. Once the data are collected, there are a few ways to analyze the data. In one approach, researchers choose one brain region to focus on (e.g. the striatum) and conduct a correlation analysis between the BOLD activation in that region and BOLD signals in all other brain regions, resulting in a **functional connectivity map (fcMap)** (Biswal, Yetkin, Haughton, and Hyde, 1995). The fcMap provides information about which regions the selected seed region is functionally linked to, and to what extent (Goldenberg and Galván, 2015). If the researcher does not have a preselected region of particular interest, they can use an approach that allows them to examine whole-brain connectivity patterns. Whole-brain connectivity methods are designed to determine the degree of functional connectivity between regions all over the brain. This is good because the analysis may yield relationships between two (or more) regions that the researcher did not predict would be related.

Resting state fMRI has been used to identify major functional networks in adults and in developing populations, including primary motor, visual, and auditory networks, in addition to higher-order cognitive systems (Fox et al., 2005). It was also used to identify the **default mode network**, which exhibits higher brain activation when the participant is "at rest" compared to when the participants is performing a computerized task or attuned to the outside world (Raichle and Snyder, 2007), suggesting that the activity of this network reflects a default state of neuronal activity.

Note that "at rest" is meant to connote a state in which the participant is not performing a researcher-imposed cognitive task and is instead "daydreaming" or "mind wandering"; "at rest" is not intended to imply that there are moments when our brain is not "on."

Resting State fMRI in Developing Populations

Resting state has helped researchers gain important knowledge about how the brain is constructed and about brain development. One long-standing hypothesis was that the neural system involved in controlling movement (the "motor network") developed before the neural system that processes social and emotional information; resting state has demonstrated that this hypothesis is correct. Several studies have shown that whereas motor system development is similar in children, adolescents, and adults, the neural systems that help support processing of social and emotional information change considerably across age (Kelly et al., 2009). This makes sense if we consider how motor behavior differs from emotional behavior. Aside from acquiring new expertise and practice on a particular motor activity (such as what one gains on a sports team), your motor development did not change much once you learned to walk. In contrast, your social and emotional development continues to change to this day! As we will learn in Chapter 7, the uptick in social skills and increased interest in social interactions around the time of puberty, and again as adolescents transition into adulthood, are supported by changes in *how* the brain processes, stores, and learns from these new experiences. It is for this reason that resting state data on social and emotional brain networks yield differences across age groups.

Several resting state studies have demonstrated that, in the development of large-scale brain systems, functional connectivity shifts from a local to a distributed architecture. This means that stronger bonds are observed in regions close to each other earlier in life, as in infancy (Fransson, Aden, Blennow, and Lagercrantz, 2011); stronger bonds are observed in regions farther apart later in development, as in childhood and adolescence (Fair et al., 2008). One analogy that might be helpful in understanding this is to think of the individual brain regions as representing different friends you may have had throughout college. As a college first-year most of your friends may have been people who lived near you in the dorms. The friendships may not have been very strong, but because you were proximally close you established a bond. As you progressed in your college career, your friendship circle may have shifted to include people who may not necessarily have lived in the same dorm but with whom you shared deeper interests. The bonds you shared in these latter friendships were probably stronger but not as physically proximal. The same is true in network connections in the brain: regions that are further apart become stronger with age.

Strengths and Weaknesses

As with all brain imaging tools, resting state acquisition and analysis techniques undergo continual standardization and refinement. Although the conclusions drawn from resting state data appear to be relatively robust, only time will tell the extent of potentially spurious findings due to motion as researchers continue to search for the most effective preprocessing for raw resting state data. The technique, although still evolving, provides invaluable information on the intrinsic functional architecture of the developing brain.

Resting state's biggest strength is that we can learn a lot about the brain without burdening the research participant too much. Because resting state data are collected while the participant is resting quietly in the scanner, there are no task instructions or demands to burden him. However, this feature is actually what some skeptics say is its major weakness. In the absence of an explicit task, the participant likely does what most of us do when asked to "rest": we daydream, plan our next activity, or ruminate about a current worry. All of these thoughts are impossible to account for so they may influence the results in ways that are unknown to the researcher. Furthermore, the daydreaming brain may look different in children as compared to adolescents and as compared to adults.

A second limitation is how sensitive resting state data acquisition is to participant movement. In the section on MRI we reviewed the importance of stillness for capturing good pictures of the brain. The same is true in resting state and to an even greater extent. Scientists who have used resting state to draw conclusions about the developing brain admit that, even when applying meticulous attention to the exclusion of participants who wiggle too much in the scanner, participant movement can inadvertently lead to misleading conclusions (Power, Barnes, Snyder, Schlaggar, and Petersen, 2012). This is a particular concern in developmental research because kids tend to wiggle more than adults, which may influence their data in a way that is not observed in adults. Given the potentially large implications that the relatively small movements can have, many scientists have worked hard to create algorithms that help them statistically account for the subtle movements (Satterthwaite et al., 2012; van Dijk, Sabuncu, and Buckner, 2012). For a description of how different preprocessing strategies may alter the way motion artifact manifests, the reader is referred to Satterthwaite et al. (2013).

The last thing you should know is that resting state data is influenced by what researchers call "physiological noise" (Biswal et al., 1995). This refers to all the things that are challenging to control and that likely vary from person to person, including heart rate, blood flow rate, and respiration. Researchers have worked hard to develop techniques to remove this noise but it is still a work in progress.

Multivoxel Pattern Analysis (MVPA) Methods

For many years, fMRI data were analyzed in pretty much the same way: analyses on the BOLD signal aimed to identify how experimental variables affected the overall engagement (activation) of a region (or set of regions) of interest (Friston, Worsley, Frackowiak, Mazziotta, and Evans, 1994). These are generally referred to as univariate methods because they characterize the relationship between cognitive variables and individual brain voxels. A voxel is shorthand for **volume pixel**, the smallest perceptible box-shaped part of a three-dimensional image. In brain imaging data, a voxel represents a single data point in the brain. Voxels are commonly used to visualize and analyze medical and scientific data. Univariate methods are no longer the only (or most popular) way to analyze neuroimaging data. In recent years, Multivoxel Pattern Analysis (MVPA) approaches have significantly shifted fMRI analytic convention. Why adopt a new approach when the old one works just fine?

First, MVPA is a technique that allows researchers to test how multiple patterns of BOLD signal across many voxels in the brain relate to experimental variables (Haxby et al., 2001; Norman, Polyn, Detre, and Haxby, 2006). This allows us to detect a broader range of task-related effects than voxel-wise analysis because the analysis does not focus on individual voxels. This approach relies on algorithms that analyze more than one voxel at once to yield multi-voxel patterns of activity.

Second, MVPA affords increased sensitivity because it circumvents the need to spatially average across voxels, a step that is important in individual-voxel-based analyses for reducing noise (i.e. spurious brain activation). Spatial averaging is effective at reducing noise because it increases the likelihood of increasing detection of voxels that show statistically significant responses to the experimental condition of interest.

However, this approach also decreases fMRI signal that is actually pertinent because it misses voxels that have weaker responses that do not reach statistically significance at $p < .05$ but that nonetheless carry some information about the cognitive variable of interest. MVPA does not routinely involve spatial averaging of voxel responses. Instead, the MVPA approach uses pattern-classification techniques to extract the signal that is present in the pattern of response across multiple voxels, even if (considered individually) the voxels might not be significantly responsive to any of the conditions of interest (Norman et al., 2006).

Third, MVPA makes it possible to identify brain response to a cognitive variable when it elicits activation in multiple types of voxels; in other words, MVPA combines information from voxels that focus on different aspects of a construct. Consider the neural processing of something as complex as attractiveness. Not only are there individual differences in what each of us considers attractive, there are also differences in what goes into each of our equations for classifying the attractiveness of a face. You might consider the shape of the face or the color of the eyes while your neighbor takes into account facial symmetry or cheekbone structure. Both of you probably consider all of these factors to some extent but the degree to which one or the other takes precedence will vary among individuals. MVPA makes it possible to detect which voxels combine information to yield a rating of attractiveness.

Fourth, MVPA allows us to examine brain activity on a trial-by-trial basis. In real life, our cognitive states change rapidly, sometimes on a second-to-second basis, and this dynamic is challenging to capture with non-MVPA methods. MVPA makes it possible to track brain activity with greater fine-grained temporal resolution to determine how it tracks with changes in behavioral responses.

The strengths of MVPA may make it promising for fMRI analyses. However, it is important to note that it is best to think of it as complementary, rather than superior, to conventional fMRI analytic methods (reviewed in Davis et al., 2014). In fact, some researchers have suggested that inherent methodological confounds in MVPA may lead to misinterpretation of results (Todd, Nystrom, and Cohen, 2013). Like all emerging tools, the utility, strengths, and weaknesses of MVPA continue to evolve. For now, you can think of MVPA as simply another tool in our neuroimaging toolbox that can provide additional information about how the brain processes information. Most researchers who use MVPA do so in conjunction with traditional univariate methods.

Multivoxel Pattern Analysis (MVPA) Methods: Developmental Applications

Functional connectivity, and MVPA more specifically, holds great promise for classifying and making predictions about individuals with regard to clinical diagnosis, behavior, age, or other variable that varies greatly across people. Indeed, a seminal paper by a research group at Washington University in St. Louis cleverly used it to classify individuals' brain maturation in a sample of participants between the ages of 7 and 30 (Dosenbach et al., 2010). They harnessed the ability to classify individuals based on the multiple functional connections between different brain regions they had acquired using resting state data. They started their analysis by focusing on the 200 functional connections known to be most reliably different between children (7–11 years old) and adults (24–30 years old). They then used an MVPA algorithm to generate a predicted "brain age" as an approximation of each participant's functional connectivity maturation level. The overall rate of change was greatest between the early and later adolescent years, consistent with physical and neurobiological knowledge about teenage development. There were also numerous individual differences within age that were most variable during the early to late adolescent years. Consistent with the "use it or lose it" principle we will discuss in Chapter 4, this analysis also identified which functional connections became stronger and which became weaker with age, presumably based on experience. For instance, connections important for making increasingly sophisticated decisions, such as the fronto-parietal control networks, evinced important strengthening during the adolescent years.

This study also identified interesting structural changes across development. Functional connections that grew in strength across development were significantly longer than functional connections that diminished in strength. In addition, they found that functional connections increasing in strength were significantly more likely to run along the anterior–posterior (AP) axis in the horizontal plane than the functional connections that became weaker. Results indicated the greatest contributor to predicting individual brain maturity was the strengthening of the adult brain's major functional networks, as well as the sharpening of the boundaries between these networks (Dosenbach et al., 2010).

This is considered a breakthrough study because the researchers moved beyond comparing groups of individuals based on their age (e.g. children versus adults) to let the classification algorithm place them on a "maturity" continuum. As discussed in Chapter 1, age truly is just a number. Simply because people were born in the same year does not mean they exhibit the same behavior, process information in the same way, or make the same decisions. This is especially true during the adolescent years when there is vast variability in "maturity" as based on differences in environment, pubertal status, and motivation.

3.3 Electrophysiology

3.3.1 Electroencephalography (EEG)

We have spent a lot of time learning about MRI scanner based imaging techniques. However, equally useful tools do not rely on the scanner to yield information about the brain.

When brain cells (neurons) communicate with one another, they produce tiny electrical signals, called impulses. An electroencephalogram (EEG) is a test used to measure these impulses. During the procedure, electrodes consisting of small metal discs with thin wires are pasted on the scalp and it is through these discs that the electrical impulses are measured (as illustrated on a young research participant in Figure 3.6). The impulses are amplified and appear as a graph on a computer screen.

There are five basic waveforms in the brain: alpha, beta, gamma, theta, and delta rhythms. These different waveforms have been implicated in different cognitive processes that tap into different brain regions. **Alpha waves** occur at a frequency of 8 to 15 cycles per second (Hz) in a regular rhythm. They are only present when a person is awake with closed eyes and usually disappear when the person opens her eyes or starts mentally concentrating. **Beta waves** occur at a frequency of 16 to 30 Hz. They are usually associated with anxiety, depression, or the use of sedatives. **Gamma waves** occur at 31 to100 Hz and are typically associated with peak focus and consciousness. **Theta waves** occur at a frequency of 4 to 7 Hz and are most common in children and young adults. **Delta waves** occur at a frequency of 0.1 to 3.5 Hz and generally occur only in young children during sleep. Figure 3.7 gives you an idea of the different waveforms observed in these rhythms.

3.3.2 Magnetoencephalography (MEG)

Magnetoencephalography (MEG) is another, less often used, technique used to measure neural activity in the brain. MEG scanners use sophisticated technology to detect the magnetic fields naturally generated by

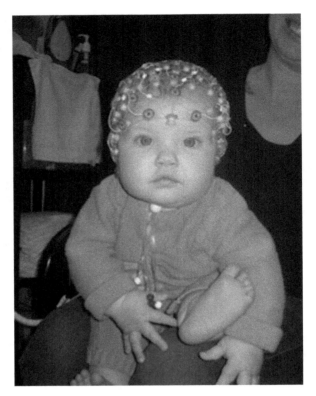

Figure 3.6 A young research participant undergoes an EEG experiment. See color plate 6.

neurons and then amplify them so that they can be measured. Very small electromagnetic fields are created when one neuron communicates with another neuron; this one-to-one communication would be very difficult to detect with any neuroimaging tool, even MEG. However, as you will read in subsequent chapters, every single neuron in your brain is always talking to many other neurons so the effect of multiple "conversations" between neurons (for example, 50,000–100,000!) yields electromagnetic fields that can be detected, and measured with MEG. The magnetic fields are analyzed to find the locations of the neuronal sources within the brain. This is a major advantage over EEG, which does not provide the location in the brain where the neuronal activity is generated.

To collect MEG data, the research participant sits in a magnetically shielded room. A researcher places a "sensor" on the participant's head. The sensor just looks like a helmet but it has special electrodes that help

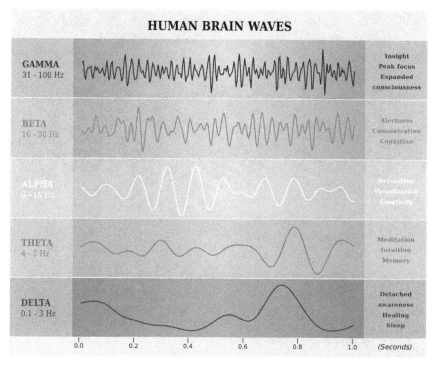

Figure 3.7 An illustration of the five basic waveforms in the human brain.

read the electromagnetic fields that neurons generate as the participant performs a computer game and/or views images on a computer screen. See an illustration of an MEG machine in Figure 3.8.

3.3.3 Strengths and Limitations

EEG has been used for many years and is considered a safe procedure. The test causes no discomfort because the electrodes only record activity and do not produce any sensation. This makes it quite useful for conducting experiments with very young children, including infants. Infants can typically sit on the caregiver's lap while viewing stimuli on a computer screen so they feel safe. Also, EEG is much less sensitive to participant movement than MRI methods so the experiments can last longer. Perhaps the biggest strength is that it has excellent temporal resolution, meaning that there is no lag between stimulus presentation and brain activity. Remember that with fMRI there is a hemodynamic response

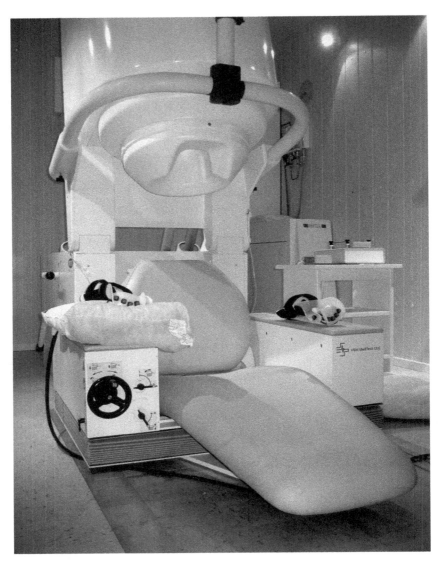

Figure 3.8 A magnetoencephalography machine.

lag that precludes acquiring a BOLD signal at the same moment that the participant views a stimulus or conducts a cognitive operation. With EEG, in contrast, we can map brain activity to stimulus presentation in real time.

The major limitation of EEG is that the spatial resolution is poor. This means that it does not provide detailed images of the brain. Instead, only impulses from the surface of the brain are acquired. This precludes examination of brain regions in the deeper layers.

MEG has advantages over both fMRI and EEG. The technologies complement each other, but only MEG provides timing as well as spatial information about brain activity. fMRI signals reflect brain activity indirectly, by measuring the oxygenation of blood flowing near active neurons. MEG signals are obtained directly from neuronal electrical activity. MEG signals are able to show absolute neuronal activity whereas the fMRI signals show relative neuronal activity, meaning that the fMRI signal analysis can always be compared to reference neuronal activity. This means that MEG can be recorded in sleeping subjects. MEG does not make any operational noise, unlike fMRI. Similar to all the other techniques we have reviewed, MEG is completely non-invasive. It does not require the injection of isotopes or exposure to X-rays or magnetic fields. Children or infants can be studied, and repeated tests are possible.

The main drawback of MEG is that the MEG signals of interest are extremely small, several orders of magnitude smaller than other signals in a typical environment that can obscure the signal. Thus, specialized shielding is required to eliminate the magnetic interference found in a typical urban clinical environment.

3.4 Eye-Tracking

There is an English proverb that says the eyes are the window of the soul. In science, eye movements are one window into the brain. The job of cognitive neuroscientists is to determine how the brain supports information processing, but in order to do that we must first learn *what* individuals are thinking. What someone is thinking is a very challenging question to answer. You may be asking yourself, "if scientists want to know what a person is thinking, why don't they just ask?" This is possible sometimes, but at other times the researcher wants to learn answers to questions that participants themselves do not know the answer to. For instance, participants may not be aware of certain preferences or biases that they have, or the researcher may want to know what a person who is nonverbal, such as an infant, is thinking. In these cases, researchers need to devise a clever way to tap into a person's thoughts without their conscious awareness of it.

One way to do this is to track a person's eye movements using an eye tracker. We humans tend to focus our eye gaze on things we find particularly interesting, novel, or preferable. The human brain automatically directs the eye to information it is processing, so by observing what a person is looking at we can get a glimpse of the information the brain is processing. Leading consumer goods companies use eye-tracking to optimize product packaging and retail shelf design. Market research companies and major advertisers use it to optimize print and TV ads. Web companies use it to optimize online user experiences. And scientists use it for research in psychology and cognitive neuroscience.

Most of us use our eyes to track information every second that we are awake. Right now, you are clearly tracking the pages of this book as you read this paragraph. You might also drive a car, check out your friend's pictures on social media, or search the aisles of a grocery store later today. Basically, any shift of the eyes can be tracked, thereby providing even just a sliver of information of what you are thinking about or attending to. Even though researchers cannot know *exactly* what someone is thinking, there are certain things they can infer; when you look at pictures of your friend online, the researcher will not know how you feel about that friend but will know that you will be looking at facial features and the color of your friend's shirt, thereby giving some information about whether you look longer at pictures of your friend smiling or frowning, for instance.

Eye-tracking is the measurement of eye activity. Where does a person look? What does she ignore? How often does she blink? Does the pupil react differently to different stimuli? Eye-tracking data is collected using either a remote or a head-mounted "eye tracker" that is connected to a computer. An infrared light source (also called a **microprojector**) is directed toward the eye, while a camera (**optical sensor**) tracks the reflection of the light source along with visual ocular features such as the pupil with very high accuracy. Sophisticated mathematical models use these data to determine the eyes' position and rotation, and direction of gaze. The eye tracker can also detect blink frequency and changes in pupil dilation. Pupil dilation is an indicator of excitement so it is a useful metric in studies assessing preference. The procedure is completely non-invasive so it is very easy to implement and there is a camera at the bottom of the computer that tracks the infant's gaze as he watches images on a computer screen. In fact, many infant research volunteers participate without even knowing they are advancing science!

The most common way researchers use eye trackers, particularly to study the developing child and adolescent, is to analyze a research participant's visual path across a computer screen. What is on the computer screen varies from study to study and depends on what the researcher is interested in investigating. Some studies in infants test babies' social cognition: Do they prefer looking at pictures of an attachment figure, such as mom, or pictures of a novel stranger? Do they gaze longer at negative emotional faces, such as a picture of an angry face, or at happy smiling faces? Other studies examine more basic knowledge to determine what babies know (and don't know!). This type of research has generated interesting and sometimes surprising results. For instance, eye-tracking was used to show that, even before the first birthday, infants perceive objects as complete and coherent across space even when part of the object is occluded. In other words, even when part of a toy is hidden from view, the infant knows that that part of the toy didn't just disappear but that it continues to exist even if he can't see it.

3.4.1 Strengths and Limitations

There are four primary strengths of eye-tracking. First, eye trackers have the ability to continuously track eyes and gaze on all users in varying environments. This means that the eye tracker can be implemented in participants who vary on eye color, eyewear, contact lenses, and age. Second, it is highly accurate at measuring the point of gaze, regardless of head movements. This is particularly important with young participants who tend to fidget. Third, participants in eye-tracking studies are not physically confined in any way, in contrast to other tools such as MRI, which require participants to lie still in a tunnel for approximately an hour. Finally, eye-tracking is relatively inexpensive compared to the other available tools. Brain scanners can be prohibitively expensive for some investigators who do not have institutional or grant support. Eye trackers are less expensive at initial purchase and do not require a usage fee per use.

The main limitation with eye-tracking is that it does not directly measure brain activity. Even though eye gaze is a great indicator of what someone is thinking or attending to, it does not directly tap into how the brain is processing information.

3.5 Recruiting Adolescent Research Volunteers

Now that you have learned a bit about the technology used to test how the brain processes information, you might be asking yourself an important question. Who are the research participants? How do researchers convince children and adolescents (and their parents) to serve as research participants? Scientists who study the developing human brain make the experience as fun as possible by designing clever computer tasks, sending kids home with a picture of their brain, and reminding participants that they are making important contributions to science by serving as research volunteers. A small monetary compensation probably helps sweeten the deal as well.

The first step is finding interested and eligible youth to participate. Many researchers partner with schools to recruit volunteers. Others post flyers in youth-friendly places (e.g. the mall) or online ads. But the most effective way is often word of mouth. Once adolescents have a positive experience in a research lab, they are apt to tell their friends and encourage them to participate as well.

The next step is to determine if the potential research participant is eligible for the study. What determines the eligibility criteria? This often depends on the specific research questions: Does the researcher want to learn more about brain processing in a particular age group? Does the study aim to test individuals afflicted with a particular psychiatric condition? There are some criteria that are relevant for all brain imaging studies that are based on the technology itself. For instance, it is not permissible for participants with metal in their body to receive a brain scan because the MRI is actually a large magnet that will pull on metal objects implanted in the body. The metal will also interfere with acquiring good pictures and these will look blurry. So at the very least the data will be unusable and, in worse scenarios, a research participant with metal will feel uncomfortable while receiving a brain scan. For this reason, participants are carefully screened prior to the study to determine if they are metal-free; this means no braces, pacemakers, metal pins or plates, or surgical staples. Because participants are asked to remain still in a relatively enclosed space, those who report being claustrophobic are also excluded from participation. Women who are pregnant may not participate in brain imaging studies because it is unknown if there are risks of the magnetic field to unborn fetuses.

3.6 Computerized Tasks

fMRI studies measure neural responses to stimuli of interest. In most studies, researchers create computerized tasks or games that present stimuli, questions, or events that the participant must passively (simply view the image) or actively (via button press) respond to. Acquiring meaningful data rests entirely on ensuring that participants comprehend, and are engaged in, the fMRI tasks they are asked to perform (Galván,

Van Leijenhorst, and McGlennen, 2012). Researchers therefore spend considerable time and energy creating computerized tasks that are easy to understand and perform (unless of course the goal of the researcher is to frustrate and stress out the participant, in which case they create computerized puzzles that are impossible to solve). For this reason, many tasks that are used with developmental populations include stimuli that are interesting to adolescents, such as faces, and/or that look like video games. One popular task that was originated by Steinberg and colleagues simulated a driving track that looked very similar to video games that teens are familiar with (Chein, Albert, O'Brien, Uckert, and Steinberg, 2011). Their goal was to measure behavioral and neural responses during risky behavior in the presence or absence of friends.

In most fMRI studies, researchers use rewards to encourage motivation and maintain task compliance. With young children (Raschle et al., 2009) or with participants who cannot receive money (e.g. drug-using participants), researchers sometimes give small prizes, such as stickers, pens, or gift certificates, as rewards. Aside from these situations, most researchers compensate participants for their time and effort with money. Sometimes this is a standard amount given to every participant at the end of the study. Other times, participants earn their compensation by performing well on the computer task. In cases where participation needs to be sustained over multiple visits to the laboratory, researchers often encourage the participants' continued involvement by paying them a small amount every time they complete some portion of the study instead of giving one lump sum at the end.

The effectiveness of doling out compensation to increase compliance has been empirically studied (Schlund et al., 2011). Small rewards, such as a pencil or trinket, may not encourage optimal task compliance and engagement because they do not have the ability to function as a reinforcer, which strengthens or makes a behavior more likely to occur (e.g., completing an fMRI task). Thus, while a subject may report that they "like" or "want" a preselected reward, it may simply not encourage or maintain a target behavior. The authors tested different payment types to determine which are most effective. They report three useful tips: (1) ask participants which prizes/incentives they prefer and tell them they are working toward that prize; (2) increase reinforcement rates during the scan such that the participant earns a reward for completing successive portions of the scan; and (3) present a "visual road map" during the imaging session so that participants can keep track of their progress and earnings. Implementation of these approaches yielded significantly greater task compliance (e.g. completion of, and engagement, in fMRI tasks) relative to studies in which participants received a standard reward at the end of the experiment (Schlund et al., 2011).

3.7 Analytical Considerations

We learn a great deal about the developing brain using brain imaging technology. Many researchers use it to compare differences in brain function between adults and children and/or adolescents. Sounds simple, right? Unfortunately, it is not so simple. There are actually a lot of methodological considerations to take into account when analyzing data. In this section we will discuss some of the analytical challenges (and how to address them) that arise in developmental brain imaging work. For further detail, the reader is encouraged to review Church, Petersen, and Schlaggar (2010).

3.7.1 Performance Differences

Inherent in the study of developmental differences is the assumption that youth and adults likely differ in brain function and behavior. This is also a concern when comparing any two groups, such as healthy controls compared to a clinical population. It is safe to assume that a task that is easy for healthy adults will be more challenging for children and, to some extent, adolescents. A difference in task performance creates a potential confound in the brain imaging analyses. As described by Church and colleagues, "Any differences in activation observed between groups might be due to less successful performance (e.g. inattentiveness, misunderstanding of instructions, guessing) in one group and not necessarily by a fundamental difference in the way the brains of members of the two groups process the task" (Church et al., 2010). Discrepant behavioral performance implies that the brain is not performing the same cognitive operation in both groups, so any differences in brain function that are observed in this case may not actually be revealing true developmental differences. An example to elucidate this point might be helpful: Imagine that adolescents and adults were each asked to view a picture while they were undergoing a scan. If they were both presented with a picture of an apple and the adolescent brain responded with activation in brain region A while adults showed activation in brain region B, then we could conclude that their brains processed the picture of the apple differently. However, if adolescents were presented with a picture of an orange but adults were presented with a picture of an apple and they showed

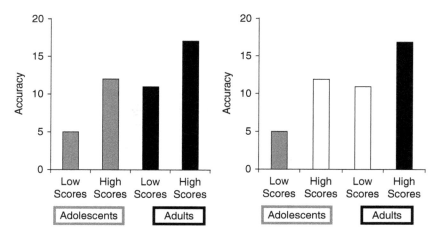

Figure 3.9 Performance matching between groups. Adolescent and adult participants are grouped into those who score high on the cognitive test and those who score low on the cognitive test (*left*). The participants in the adolescent group who receive high scores are compared to participants in the adult group who receive low score (white bars) (*right*).

activation in different brain regions, it would not be fair to conclude that they processed the picture of the apple differently. Why? Because the adolescents were not in fact processing the apple to begin with. The same principle applies to performance differences. If adolescents and adults are processing a task differently (as evident by differences in their performance during the task), then it is unreasonable to expect to see similar activations in the brain. For this reason, it is important to equate behavioral difficulty and comprehension of the task between groups as much as possible.

Calibrating task difficulty to be suitable for both groups being examined is not always possible. In these cases, researchers sometimes rely on a technique called *performance matching*. In this approach, both groups perform the same task. As is inherent in any cognitive task, some people will perform better and some people will perform worse than others on the task, regardless of age. Within both groups there will be variability in performance. Researchers take advantage of this variability to categorize individuals based on behavioral performance rather than strictly on age when conducting the analyses. This grouping leads to four total groups: a high-performing adult group, a low-performing adult group, a high-performing adolescent group, and a low-performing adolescent group. An illustration of these groups is provided in Figure 3.9. The brain analyses are then conducted on the groups that are the most similar to one another behaviorally. As you can see in Figure 3.9, the groups most similar to each other are the low-performing adults and high-performing adolescents (illustrated by white bars). In a performance matching analysis, it is these groups whose brain activation is compared. Brown and colleagues (Brown et al., 2005; Schlaggar et al., 2002) have used this analytical method to identify (1) brain regions that exhibit group differences only when performance differs between groups and (2) regions that continue to show activation differences between groups even when performance is matched. In other words, they identified regions that showed true developmental differences (those that showed activation differences despite behavioral similarity) and regions that showed activation differences that were confounded by behavioral performance. Although there is some concern that this method biases the results by including the most obtuse adults and the brightest adolescents, it provides important insights into the effects of behavior on brain activation between age groups.

Another way around the performance issue is to avoid subgrouping altogether. Instead, researchers regress performance variables as covariates of interest. This method allows us to determine whether variability in task performance is related to variability in brain activation. If it is, then increasing accuracy on the task is associated with increasing (or decreasing) activation in the brain in a linear fashion.

3.7.2 The "Task B" Problem

Jessica Church, Steven Petersen, and Bradley Schlaggar coined the term the "Task B Problem" to describe a potentially disastrous, but surprisingly overlooked, methodological concern. To understand the problem let's first remember that neuroimaging analyses for fMRI data are usually conducted by comparing two conditions; typically these include a psychological condition and a "control" condition that is presumably unrelated to the psychological condition. The psychological condition is referred to as "Task A" and the control condition is referred to as "Task B." For example, scientists who are interested in identifying brain activation in response to faces have conducted studies in which Task A consists of showing participants pictures of faces. In these studies, Task B consists of showing participants pictures of some other non-face stimuli (such as houses). The logic behind this approach is that by subtracting out brain activation in response to Task B from Task A, we can eliminate brain activation common to both types of stimuli to then isolate activation specific to Task A. Suppose there was a region in the brain that responded to all objects, including houses and faces, and another part of the brain

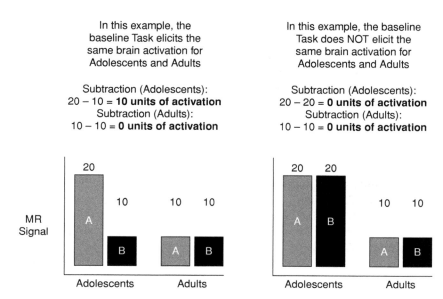

Figure 3.10 A graphical representation of the Task B problem.

that only responded to faces. Subtracting out Task B (brain response to houses) from Task A (brain response to faces) yields activation only to faces.

In and of themselves, subtraction analyses are not problematic. The problem, however, emerges when considering two groups that differ on age or other factor because it rests on the assumption that Task B elicits the same activation in both groups. When comparing adolescents and adults, this assumption can lead to inaccurate interpretations of the data. Indeed, many developmental cognitive neuroscience studies compare age groups after conducting a subtraction analysis within each group and then interpret the results as though they were simply comparing Task A in adolescents to Task A in adults. This is imprecise because the comparison is actually between (Task $A_{adolescent}$ – Task $B_{adolescent}$) and (Task A_{adult} – Task B_{adult}), so it is important to account for the fact that Task B has the potential to differ between groups. If the two groups recruit distinct regions, or patterns of activation, or both in response to Task B, then the subtraction between Task A and Task B within a group will differ across groups. Figure 3.10 (adapted from Church et al., 2010) graphically illustrates this point. We have added arbitrary numbers to help explain the graph. Notice that interpretations from each panel differ simply because there are differences in the magnitude of activation in Task B in the adolescent group. In the panel on the left, Task B is equal in adults and adolescents. In the panel on the right, Task B is significantly greater in the adolescents as compared to the adults. The overall interpretation from the left-hand panel is that adolescents exhibit greater activation than adults because their overall activation to Task A is 10 (Task A_{adol} − Task B_{adol} = 20 − 10 = 10) whereas the overall activation for adults is 0 because they do not respond differently to Task A and Task B (Task A_{adult} − Task B_{adult} = 10 − 10 = 0). The overall interpretation from the right-hand panel is that adults do not differ from adolescents. However, this is incorrect because adolescents are actually more responsive to Task A than adults; this is masked because adolescents do not differ in brain activation to Task A and Task B. In both cases the differences between Task A and B is 0 in the adolescent group, but only in the left-hand panel is it appropriate to conclude that adolescents truly exhibit greater activation to Task A.

What is the methodological solution to the Task B problem? One approach is to directly compare the two groups on Task B (Task B_{adult} − Task $B_{adolescent}$) and proceed with the standard subtraction analysis if there are no differences (essentially demonstrating that the left-hand panel is true). Another approach is to examine the statistical interaction in a 2 (Task) × 2 (Group) analysis of variance (ANOVA) and then determine which group and/or task is driving the effect using a post hoc analysis. Finally, fMRI designs can be used that allow estimation of the hemodynamic response to individual trial types.

3.7.3 Physiological Differences

The brain images produced from fMRI data are based on the BOLD response, as reviewed above, that reflects a net increase in blood oxygenation during psychological processing. Because adolescents (and children) may differ from adults in their neurovascular system, there is some concern that developmental differences observed between adolescents and adults are simply a reflection of this confound instead of a true difference in neural response to psychological processing. Luckily, developmental neuroscientists have conducted meticulous experiments to ensure that this is not the case. If differences in neurovascular responses accounted for the observed BOLD differences between age groups, then one group would always exhibit greater neural activation regardless of the cognitive task. This is not the case, as studies show that sometimes youth show greater activation during psychological processing and sometimes adults show greater activation (Brown et al., 2005). Also, differences in neural activation between groups are observed in different brain regions, based on the task the participants are performing, suggesting that, despite differences across the brain in neurovasculature, we observe group differences. Perhaps the strongest evidence is that activation patterns across time on the task are similar in youth and adults when performing a very simple visual processing task; that is, when cognitive processing is at a minimum because participants are merely asked to view simple shapes on a screen, the BOLD activation does not differ (Kang, Burgund, Lugar, Petersen, and Schlaggar, 2003).

3.7.4 Interpreting Group Differences

In this book we will read about a lot of interesting research that reports differences in how youth and adults process psychological or cognitive information. You may start to notice that sometimes the studies report greater activation in adults compared to the younger group and sometimes they report greater activation in youth compared to adults. Perhaps this is not too surprising, since we'll be learning about studies that test different cognitive processes. However, we will also see examples of these discrepancies between studies that test the same cognitive process. Does this mean one of the studies is wrong? Not necessarily. Keep in mind that each cognitive process, cognitive control for instance, is often comprised of multiple types of processing that may be subtly different. Whereas one study will use the term cognitive control to refer to response inhibition (the act of suppressing a motor response), another will use it to describe impulsivity (the act of carrying out a behavior suddenly and without forethought). Because these studies are actually examining two sides (inhibition versus impulsivity) of the same coin (cognitive control), the activation patterns may differ.

Another consideration is that psychologists and neuroscientists use a variety of computerized tasks to study the same phenomenon. In fact, websites such as www.cognitiveatlas.org list over 600 cognitive tasks used to test over 700 psychological constructs. The field is fortunate to have so many task options but you can probably imagine how each task will have different parameters, including distinct stimuli, task duration, and instructions, that can potentially alter how participants perform them, and subsequently how the brain processes them.

The more complex explanation is one cognitive neuroscientists are still puzzling through. What does greater (versus less) activation indicate from a processing perspective? Does greater activation mean the brain is "better" or does it mean it is impaired or immature somehow? These questions are crucial ones to consider in developmental cognitive neuroscience research. The short answer is that assigning value to greater or lesser activation is nonsensical. Now for the longer answer: Concluding that more activation is somehow beneficial is a residual assumption from the notion that "bigger is better." This idea is simply not true in terms of brain structure or brain activation patterns. In contrast, some investigators conclude that less activation, particularly when it is the adults exhibiting less activation, is a manifestation of more "efficient" processing. This interpretation is problematic too. Russell Poldrack eloquently delineates why an argument for efficiency does not satisfyingly explain group differences in activation (Poldrack, 2015). The reader is encouraged to read his article on this topic as we only discuss the main points here. When used to explain group differences in activation, efficiency is intended to convey that one group expends less metabolic energy to perform the same task or computation. However, there are unexplored reasons rarely discussed in these articles that could also account for group activation differences that "look like" less energy expenditure by one group.

First, the cognitive processes underlying the computation might be different. Assuming that adolescents and adults are using their brains in the same way simply because they are asked to perform the same computer task is inappropriate. You may recognize that this idea is similar to one introduced earlier when discussing performance differences. Although the computer task may be the same, the "meta-task that the subject must perform in order to comply with the experimenter's demands" (Poldrack, 2015) might differ between groups. The meta-task includes the requirements imposed by the fMRI environment, including lying very still and alone in an unfamiliar place for a long time.

Second, *how* the brain solves a problem differs across individuals and certainly across age groups. Adults may rely on additional or different brain regions relative to younger groups to perform a task that diminish local activation of one brain region of interest. This may then appear as less activation overall even though global activation is the same. It is therefore important to consider whether computation is the same across groups.

Finally, and perhaps most aligned with the concept of efficiency, is consideration of differences in "neural energetics." Neural energetics refers to energy usage of neural activity. Neurons use a number of different energetic pathways, including oxidative phosphorylation (Sibson et al., 1998), aerobic glycolysis (Fox, Raichle, Mintun, and Dence, 1988), and metabolism of ketone bodies (Sokoloff, 1973) to varying degrees across development. This is relevant because these pathways significantly vary in their energetic efficiency, which may influence neural activation patterns depending on which pathways are being used at particular ages. For instance, comparison of these pathways revealed that aerobic glycolysis dominates in childhood, perhaps because regional increases in glycolysis are related to synaptic development (Goyal, Hawrylycz, Miller, Snyder, and Raichle, 2014). Age differences in activation may therefore seem to reflect differences in "efficiency" but may in fact be a result of the systems drawing on distinct metabolic resources. A better understanding of developmental changes in neural energetics across development and their relation to functional imaging signals could provide important calibration to help understand the degree to which development effects in imaging studies reflect neuronal versus energetic differences (Poldrack, 2015).

In sum, claiming that one developmental group over another is more efficient is usually an unsatisfying explanation. A better approach is to provide potential reasons to explain the differences in activation. Does one group exhibit better accuracy on the task that is related to brain activation? Is one group devoting greater cognitive computations to ancillary tasks, such as staying still, that are not directly related to the task? Are there developmental differences in underlying neurotransmitter availability in one particular brain region? Consideration of these deeper explanations will ultimately yield greater understanding of developmental differences in brain activation and the meaning behind them.

3.8 Chapter Summary

- A brain scan is a picture of the brain taken with an MRI magnet.
- There are two categories of brain research tools: those that assess brain structure and those that assess brain function. Structural MRI yields anatomical pictures of the brain while functional MRI yields functional pictures of the brain "in motion."
- Functional connectivity examines communication and connections between brain regions.
- Resting state MRI is used to visualize brain structure and function absent a researcher-imposed cognitive test.
- Multi-voxel pattern analysis (MVPA) is a newer tool that allows researchers to determine how multiple patterns of brain activity from an array of voxels contribute to behavior.
- Electrophysiological tools, such as EEG, have better temporal resolution than imaging tools, but do not provide the same level of detail about brain structure.

- Recruiting and engaging adolescent research participants is important for acquiring good data.
- Analytic considerations include age differences in behavioral performance, task motivation, and motion.

3.9 Review Questions

- Which tools use computerized tasks and which do not?
- Identify two brain research tools and list their strengths and weaknesses.
- Why is it important to equate behavioral difficulty and comprehension of the task between age groups?
- What is the Task B problem?

Further Reading

Church, J.A., Petersen, S.E., and Schlaggar, B. (2010). The "Task B problem" and other considerations in developmental functional neuroimaging. *Human Brain Mapping*, 31(6), 852–862.

Galván, A., Van Leijenhorst, L., and McGlennen, K.M. (2012). Considerations for imaging the adolescent brain. *Developmental Cognitive Neuroscience*, 2, 293–302.

Goldenberg, D., and Galván, A, (2015). The use of functional and effective connectivity techniques to understand the developing brain. *Developmental Cognitive Neuroscience*, 12, 155–164.

Poldrack, R.A. (2015). Is "efficiency" a useful concept in cognitive neuroscience? *Developmental Cognitive Neuroscience*, 11, 12–17.

CHAPTER FOUR

Brain Plasticity

Learning Objectives

- Learn about the malleability of the brain.
- Describe how the brain responds to the environment.
- Learn about the neural mechanisms that underlie neuroplasticity.
- Understand why neuroplasticity has implications for development and behavior.

4.1 Introduction

When was the last time you had an "aha" moment? A moment when you had sudden inspiration, insight, or comprehension? Perhaps it was something you learned from a lecture in this class or the last time you made a major life decision you were struggling with. An "aha" moment is the feeling of learning, of changing your perspective, or of solving a long-puzzling problem. A neuroscientist might argue that it's the feeling of neuroplasticity (also known as brain plasticity), which refers to changes in the brain. "Plastic" is derived from the Greek word "plastos" which means "to mold." Being plastic refers to the ability to undergo a change in shape. Every single time you have a new thought or create a new memory, whether in your conscious awareness or not, your brain changes. It may surprise you to know that the brain is remarkably malleable. In response to new experiences, social interactions, and learning opportunities, the brain reshapes and refines itself. This phenomenon is particularly true during periods of development such as childhood and adolescence, when the brain is developing at rapid speed. In this chapter we will learn why plasticity is the mechanism for development, learning, and adaptive change, as much as it is a cause of psychopathology and addiction. These powerful agents of change induce significant and observable structural and functional plasticity in neural systems. Understanding these concepts will set the stage for themes that we will return to throughout the book.

4.2 Neuroplasticity, Defined

In *The principles of psychology* (1890), William James was the first to introduce the term plasticity to the neurosciences in reference to the susceptibility of human behavior to adaptation. Fifteen years after James made this observation, the Spanish neuroscientist Ramón y Cajal noted that behavioral adaptation must have an anatomical basis in the brain and coined the term "neuroplasticity" in *Textura del sistema nervioso* (1899). Since these momentous observations, neuroscientists have worked diligently to examine the reciprocal relationship between behavioral modification and brain changes.

Neuroplasticity refers to changes in the brain, in either neural pathways or synapses or both, that arise in response to the environment, experience, or use. It is a normal ongoing state of the nervous system throughout the lifespan. Although neuroplasticity is now a widely accepted phenomenon with abundant evidence from animal and human research, for many years it was believed that the brain was a physiologically static organ that did not change much after birth. Thank goodness that is not true because our species would be quite limited in its ability to learn and grow. In fact, all learning you have done and will do throughout your life is only possible because your brain can incorporate and use new information.

4.3 Neural Mechanisms of Plasticity

Over half a centruy ago, Donald Hebb established a theoretical framework describing the phenomenon that the brain adapts to its environment based on experience and development (Hebb, 1949). According to theories of neuroplasticity, thinking and learning change both the brain's physical structure and its functional organization. That means that your brain is probably changing at this very moment, as you learn about how learning changes the brain! Basic mechanisms that are involved in plasticity include neurogenesis (the birth of new neurons), programmed cell death, and activity-dependent synaptic plasticity (changes in synaptic strength based on repeated use). Repetitive stimulation of synapses can cause what is referred to as *long-term potentiation* or *long-term depression* of neurotransmission, which we'll review later in this section. Together, these changes are associated with physical changes in dendritic spines and neuronal circuits that eventually influence behavior. These same mechanisms stand out as important contributors to the developing brain's ability to acquire new information, adapt to the rapidly changing environment, and recover from injury (Johnston, 2009).

4.3.1 Neuroplasticity Mechanisms

Two main things occur during neuroplasticity. One is **neurogenesis**, the birth of new neurons, and the other is **synaptogenesis**, which is the generation of new synapses.

Neurogenesis

Neurons are the nerve cells in the brain. The generation of new neurons occurs mostly prior to birth. It is this process that populates the growing brain. In postnatal and adult animals, neurogenesis is restricted mostly to the dentate gyrus of the hippocampus, and to the olfactory bulb via the subventricular zone that lines the lateral ventricles of the brain. Some scientists have suggested that neurogenesis also occurs in the neocortex (Gould, Reeves, Graziano, and Gross, 1999) but this finding is less universally accepted.

What causes neurogenesis? In addition to normal neuronal turnover, neurogenesis is triggered by certain environmental factors. Exercise and enriched environments promote the birth of new neurons. On the other hand, chronic stress can lead to decreased neurogenesis, a topic we will return to at the end of this chapter. Neurogenesis is also a response to the need for new or additional neural resources to support important behaviors relevant to the organism's survival. The best example of this comes from fascinating research in songbirds. In the early 1980s, Fernando Nottebohm, a professor at Rockefeller University, hypothesized that when birds learn new songs they generate new neurons to support the new song information. To test this hypothesis, he studied adult canaries, which use new songs every season to woo female canaries for mating purposes. He labeled their neurons using a dye called bromodeoxyuridine (BrdU), which is commonly used to detect new cells. Dr. Nottebohm found that every time the adult canary learns a new song, it grows new neurons! In fact, the size of the part of a male canary's brain that controls song-making peaks in the spring when the need to mate demands the most of a suitor's musical prowess. This same brain region shrinks in the summer when he is not devoting himself to mating. It then starts to expand again in the fall when it is again time to learn and rehearse new melodies. This finding was remarkable not only because it displaced one of the central dogmas of neurobiology (that when neurons die they are not replaced by new ones), but because it directly tied neurogenesis to the experience of the animal.

Synaptogenesis

Communication between neurons is critical for our brains to work efficiently. Neurons communicate at **synapses**, structures that permit the passage of an electrical or chemical signal from one to the other – a conjunction of sorts. Synapses are critical players in neuronal functioning. Generally there is a "sender" neuron, also known as the **presynaptic neuron**, that passes information to its neighbor, which we can call the "receiving" neuron. At a synapse, the membrane of the sender neuron comes into close contact with the membrane of the receiving neuron. Through some sophisticated molecular changes, the two membranes are temporarily linked together to carry out the transfer of information.

There are two types of synapses, each of which represents the different types of information that can be passed from neuron to neuron. In a **chemical synapse**, electrical activity in the presynaptic neuron helps release a chemical called a neurotransmitter that binds to receptors located on the surface of the postsynaptic cell (see Figure 4.1 for an illustration). In an **electrical synapse**, the presynaptic and postsynaptic cell membranes are connected by special channels called **gap junctions**. Gap junctions are like mini-bridges or tunnels that have the capability to pass electric current, causing voltage changes in the presynaptic cell to induce voltage changes in the postsynaptic cell.

Synaptogenesis refers to the formation of synapses between neurons. Neurons form new synapses to incorporate new information. As described in greater detail below, every time you learn something new or form a new memory, that information is stored in many neurons, so once one neuron receives the information, it needs to pass it along to multiple neurons. If the "sender" neuron does not already have a way to communicate with the "receiver" neuron, synaptogenesis occurs in order to form that pathway of communication. A useful analogy is to think of it like adding a new contact to your address book every time you make a new friend or meet a relevant business associate. Over time, you will have frequent communication with some of these new contacts and little to no contact with others, which may lead you to eliminate them from your address book. The same is true with new synapses. Whenever synaptogenesis occurs, it is unknown whether the two neurons will become frequent communicators or if the new relationship will wane over time – the brain's flexibility allows for either outcome.

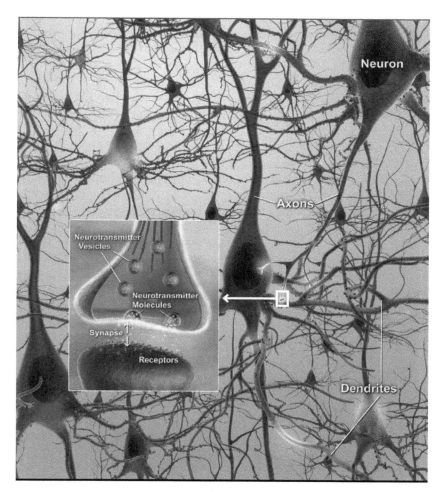

Figure 4.1 A chemical synapse. Neurotransmitters are released from neurotransmitter vesicles in the presynaptic neuron into the space between two neurons (synapse). The neurotransmitter molecules attach to receptors on the postsynaptic neurons. See color plate 7.

Long-Term Potentiation

Long-term potentiation (LTP) is a well-established phenomenon in neuroscience. It refers to the long-lasting increase in signal transmission (communication) between two neurons. LTP is the persistent strengthening of synapses based on recent patterns of activity. This means that increased communication between two neurons occurs because the passage of information is valuable enough to occur repeatedly. In other words, the flow of information (in the form of chemical or electrical signals) changes the strength and eventually the number of synapses over time. Referring back to the address book analogy, the increased bond with a new friend (synapse) strengthens the synapse. This phenomenon underlies plasticity. As new information (or memories) is encoded permanently, it induces LTP.

LTP involves simultaneous presynaptic and postsynaptic activation. Presynaptic activation causes the release of the excitatory neurotransmitter glutamate, which can then bind with and open postsynaptic N-methyl-D-aspartate (NMDA) receptors. The NMDA receptor specifically binds glutamate and is an ion channel protein found in neurons. It is very important for controlling synaptic plasticity and memory formation. Postsynaptic activation causes magnesium ions to move out of the opening of NMDA receptor channels, which they would otherwise block. Calcium ions can then enter the postsynaptic neuron, where they are involved in a series of molecular changes that ultimately increase overall synaptic efficacy. Both presynaptic and postsynaptic activation are thus required for this process (Munakata and Pfaffly, 2004). This complex process is illustrated in Figure 4.2.

Long-Term Depression

Long-term depression is the opposite of LTP. It refers to the *decrease* in synaptic strength following decreasing use or communication between two neurons. It is similar to cleaning up the contacts in your address book when you realize you never ended up connecting much with that new friend or business associate. This process ensures that the brain is not expending valuable metabolic energy on synapses that are not in use. LTD is one of several processes that helps selectively weaken specific synapses in order to make constructive use of synaptic strengthening caused by LTP. If all synapses were allowed to continue increasing in strength exponentially, they would eventually inhibit the encoding of new information. LTD results mainly from a decrease in postsynaptic receptor density, although a decrease in presynaptic neurotransmitter release may also play a role. In the hippocampus, LTD may be important for clearing out old memory traces. It is for this reason that information that was once very important may now just be a faded and distant memory. Moving to a new town often has this effect – you may recall that you used to visit a great coffee shop frequently in your previous town but perhaps now you

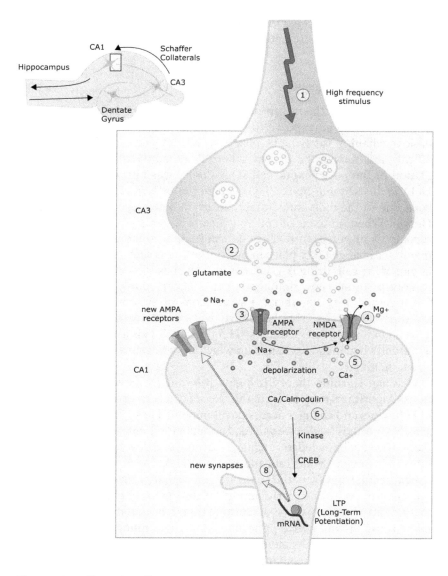

Figure 4.2 An illustration of long-term potentiation (LTP). A high-frequency stimulus (1) triggers release of glutamate (2) from the presynaptic neuron. An influx of sodium (Na$^+$) (3) leads to chemical changes (4–6) that induce LTP (7), which leads to new synapses and AMPA receptors (8) over repeated stimulation. See color plate 8.

cannot recall the exact name of the coffee shop or which street it was on. The irrelevance of these details helps your brain "forget" them through LTD.

Hebbian Learning Theory

Hebbian learning theory proposes a mechanistic explanation for neuronal adaptation in response to learning new information. It describes a basic mechanism for synaptic plasticity, whereby an increase in synaptic efficacy arises from the presynaptic cell's repeated and persistent stimulation of the postsynaptic cell. This theory was introduced by Donald Hebb in his seminal book *The organization of behavior* (1949) and has been one of the most influential theories in neuroscience. According to Hebb, "When an axon of cell A is near enough to excite a cell B and repeatedly or persistently takes part in firing it, some growth process or metabolic change takes place in one or both cells such that A's efficiency, as one of the cells firing B, is increased." The basic assertion derived from this observation is now simplified to an adage in neuroscience, "cells that fire together, wire together." Two neurons or systems of neurons that are repeatedly active simultaneously will become associated over time. This is commonly referred to as "Hebb's Law." This association leads to a mutually beneficial exchange, in which both neurons undergo synaptic strengthening.

Hebbian learning theory is highly relevant for developmental questions. Algorithms derived from this theory can help explain a wide range of behaviors and changes across development. These include critical and sensitive periods (which we will read about below), rule learning, development of object knowledge, language learning and development, and flexibility in behavior (Munakata and Pfaffly, 2004). The ability to extract statistical regularities from the environment is a hallmark of learning across the lifespan and particularly important during early postnatal development. It is through this type of learning that infants and toddlers begin to make sense of, and notice patterns in, the environment (e.g. every time I cry my caregiver picks me up, the infant might think). Infants are also very good at learning regular patterns after brief exposures to auditory or visual stimuli (Kirkham, Slemmer, and Johnson, 2002). Hebbian learning supports such statistical learning by updating information in relevant neural circuits.

4.4 Critical Periods

Have you ever heard the phrase "you learn something new every day"? You do! And your brain takes note. But imagine that your brain stored every single piece of information you ever learned? Or changed its structure on a daily or minute-to-minute basis? That would be highly inefficient and metabolically expensive because it would require restructuring neural architecture every day or every minute. So how does the brain know which pieces of information or experience to hold on to and which to discard? This is a question that continues to bewilder scientists even today but in the past century we have learned a few things that help address it. Although the brain can change throughout the entire life of an organism, there are special moments in life that are more amenable to environmental input. The brain is more sensitive or responsive to the environment during particular periods of development and when a particular experience occurs repeatedly. Later in this chapter we will see how extreme versions of this (being too responsive or experiencing a negative event too many times) can be harmful for the brain.

In many regions of the developing brain, neuronal circuits undergo defined phases of enhanced plasticity, termed **critical periods** (Levelt and Hübener, 2012). The term critical period is sometimes used synonymously with **sensitive period** but they are actually not interchangeable. Critical periods are narrow periods during which particular input to the organism is *expected*. They represent a time when the brain is most easily influenced or vulnerable to environmental effects (or lack of effects). For example, if an infant does not see light during the first few months of life, visual neurons and circuits do not develop normally. Sensitive periods refer to opportunity for certain types of learning but they are not as rigidly tied to specific ages or passage of time. They also span a longer time period compared to critical periods. During a sensitive period, if there is a lack of opportunity for a certain type of learning, it is not gone forever (as it is for critical periods). Simply put, sensitive periods are quite wide periods across the lifespan when it is easier to learn things (e.g. easier to learn languages at a younger age but not impossible to do at later ages) and depends on the personal experience of the individual.

4.4.1 Experience-Expectant Mechanisms

How does the organism know to *expect* particular input or a specific experience? As defined by Greenough and colleagues, experience-expectant mechanisms utilize environmental information that has been common to all members of a species across evolutionary history. The neural system comes to "expect" an experience under normal development to shape sensory and motor neural systems. Experience-expectant processes "appear to have evolved as a neural preparation for incorporating specific information" (Greenough, Black, and Wallace, 1987). Take the visual system in humans as an example. Humans are highly visual creatures who rely on their vision to navigate the world (as opposed to rodents, for instance, who rely more heavily on their olfactory system). If a human infant is not exposed to visual information very soon after birth, the neural circuits that underlie the visual system develop abnormally because the brain has not received the visual input that it expected. This came to light in seminal experiments conducted in the 1960s by Wiesel and Hubel. They used an experimental technique to study visual system plasticity called **monocular deprivation** in which one of an animal's eyes is sutured shut during a period of high cortical plasticity (approximately one month after birth in rodents). They first performed this technique in kittens because they have a visual system that is similar to the human visual system. They focused on the ocular dominance columns (the bands of neurons that are organized to represent visual information for each eye separately) in the lateral geniculate nucleus of the thalamus and found that they were significantly reorganized when one eye was sewn shut for two months (Wiesel and Hubel, 1963). In subsequent work, they demonstrated the anatomical reorganization of this effect: (1) thinner columns in the bands of neurons that represented the deprived eye, suggesting that these neurons had atrophied; and (2) significant enlargement of the columns representing the open eye. These results suggest that the monocular deprivation led to a competitive process in which the columns representing the open eye became more connected to other neurons while those representing the sutured eye became less connected (LeVay, Wiesel, and Hubel, 1980). At the neurophysiological level, the deprived eye becomes functionally disconnected from other visual cortex neurons. Importantly, the results suggest that depriving an animal of expected information (visual information in this case) during the expected period of development leads to neural plasticity in the form of aberrant neural organization. If a normal pattern of experience occurs, a normal pattern of neural organization is observed, but if an abnormal experience occurs (i.e. visual deprivation), then an abnormal pattern of neural organization will occur (Greenough et al., 1987). Wiesel and Hubel were awarded the Nobel Prize in Physiology (1981) for their influential scientific contribution.

Why might we have evolved *expectations* of sensory experience? At first glance it does not seem to make evolutionary sense for an organism to be permanently damaged if it does not receive a particular set of inputs at a particular, critical, period of development. However, evolution is adaptive and these mechanisms are not randomly in place. Research suggests that sensory systems can develop much greater performance capabilities and much faster by taking advantage of experiences that can be expected to be available in the environment of all young animals. Why do we need to be ready for visual input the second we are born? Because our evolutionary history tells us that we are visual creatures who rely on this sensory modality to survive. Imagine if a newborn had to wait a month or longer after birth to be able to see and experience visual input while his visual system figured out how to organize itself? That infant would miss out on significant aspects of development, such as bonding with a caregiver, experiencing edges and contrast to boost the visual development, and learning about colors in the world. Instead, infants can start seeing immediately after they are born because their visual system has been getting ready for the main event (birth!) for several months. Although the visual system is still developing at birth, it is nonetheless ready to participate in the world. Most humans are born after approximately 9 months of gestation; our species takes advantage of this consistently timed length of gestation to organize development of sensory systems at roughly the same time in each individual member of the species. Think of it in this way: the system is simply planning ahead (by preparing the neural circuitry necessary to support visual processing) for what evolutionary history has told us will most likely happen (receipt of visual input upon birth). To give a concrete example, think of the last time it rained in your town for a whole week from Monday through Thursday. By Friday morning, you probably left your house with an umbrella because you assumed it would continue raining that day. You planned ahead (by bringing an umbrella) because rain was a likely event that day; this is an experience-expectant behavior.

How exactly does the brain "prepare" the visual system for visual input? It does so by gradually building up the synapses necessary to support successful visual processing. The diagram in Figure 4.3 is a nice illustration, based on many years of research, of how this works. It represents the density of synapses (on the y-axis and in the dotted line) as a function of development from conception through death in the primary visual cortex of the macaque monkey. This development is demarcated by five distinct phases. In the first and second phases, shortly after conception and in mid gestation, the density of synapses is rather low. But in phase 3 there begins a steady increase in the density of synapses just before and after birth. The rise before birth occurs precisely to prepare the organism for birth, which occurs in the middle of phase 3, and the rise after birth represents the rapid increase in synapses in response to visual input. The explosion of synapse formation that occurs very early in brain development (prenatally) is referred to as exuberant synaptogenesis or synaptic overproduction. How is this well-timed procedure

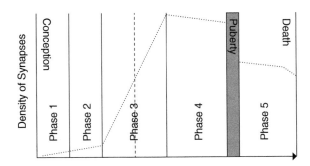

Figure 4.3 Synaptic density changes across development in five distinct phases. It is very low in phases 1 and 2 but increases rapidly just prior to birth in phase 3. The rise in synapses following birth is directly related to the increased visual input to the organism. Synaptic density remains steady in phase 4, which roughly corresponds to childhood. After puberty, there is a steady decline of synapses (synaptic pruning) in phase 5.

possible? Species seem to have evolved such that genes provide only a rough outline of the pattern of neural circuits in the sensory system; and since timing of birth is pretty consistent, the organism knows when to start preparing for birth by increasing the number of synapses. The rough outline is then filled in by experience and the specific environment of the organism. Therefore, experience-dependent mechanisms are pretty unique to each individual and differ in timing across individuals.

Around the time of puberty, a remarkable thing happens to synapses. Notice in Figure 4.3 that not only is there limited synaptogenesis, but there is actually a decrease in the number of synapses in the brain! This process is called pruning. Similar to pruning in the gardening sense of the word, which refers to the practice of selectively removing parts of a plant, branches or roots that are impeding growth, neuronal pruning refers to the elimination of neurons or synapses that are not helping the brain. As with gardening, pruning at the right time encourages healthy growth and flowering. In humans, and in most mammals, the "right" time is puberty, when the organism eliminates relatively unused or irrelevant neurons and synapses.

4.4.2 Experience-Dependent Processes

Having expectations about life is great but life is full of surprises. How can the organism adapt to events that are *unexpected* or *specific to each individual*? We are able to adapt due to *experience-dependent* mechanisms. In this case, neural circuitry changes in response to, not in anticipation of, events that that organism experiences. Let's think back to the rain expectation example above. Your expectation of rain led you to leave the house with an umbrella. But suppose it actually didn't rain as expected? Would you still hold the umbrella over your head? Of course not: you would modify your behavior and leave the umbrella in your bag. In this case your behavior was dependent on your actual experience (no rain) rather than on your expectations (of a fifth day of rain) so it is an *experience-dependent* behavior. The generation of new neurons in response to new songs in the canary bird is a great example of an experience-dependent process.

Experience-dependent plasticity appears to peak in adolescence and young adulthood and shows a gradual but consistent decrease as organisms age. Animal studies have shown that this age-associated decline in synaptic plasticity in specific brain regions correlates with neurocognitive impairments (Oberman and Pascual-Leone, 2013).

Environmental Complexity Paradigm

A large body of work has been conducted to characterize experience-dependent mechanisms. Most of this work has involved manipulating the complexity of the animal's environment by either enriching the environment through stimulating objects or simplifying it by removing all interesting or "enriching" objects. This **environmental complexity paradigm** was pioneered by Donald Hebb and involves the use of two or all of the following three conditions: (1) in the *Environmental Complexity* (EC) condition, animals are housed together in groups of about 12. The large cage in which they are housed contains numerous toys and objects, such as balls, tunnels, and ladders, that are changed daily to provide a continuously stimulating environment; (2) in the *Social Cage* (SC) condition, animals are housed in pairs in standard plastic shoebox cages with sawdust bedding, food, and water; and (3) in the *Individual Condition* (IC), animals are housed alone in similarly unenriched cages. Using this approach, Greenough and colleagues found that the postsynaptic architecture differed, based on the level of complexity and enrichment of the animal's housing. To measure postsynaptic architecture they simply measured the total length of the dendritic field as if all the branch segments that make it up were laid end to end (Greenough, Withers, and Anderson, 1992). They found that dendritic fields in visual cortex were largest in the EC animals, as they had approximately 20% more dendrites than the rats in the IC; SC animals had an intermediate number of dendrites. These results indicated that rats with access to more complex environments developed increased dendritic space for synapses (Greenough and Volkmar, 1973). Importantly, these effects were not limited to the visual cortex: dendritic fields in the temporal cortex (Greenough, Volkmar, and Juraska, 1973) and in the dentate gyrus of the hippocampus (Juraska, Fitch, Henderson, and Rivers, 1985) were also larger in EC rats than in SC or IC rats. It is worth noting that the rats in each of the three conditions did not differ in their dendritic fields or postsynaptic architecture *prior* to being assigned to one of the conditions, suggesting that the environment itself caused the differences in the neural architecture.

Do these synaptic effects have implications for behavior? A large number of studies have demonstrated that animals reared in a complex environment are generally superior on complex tasks compared to individually housed or socially housed animals, particularly on memory tests. These tests include the Hebb-Williams maze (Mohammed, Jonsson, and Archer, 1986), the Morris water maze (Leggio et al., 2005), and the radial arm maze (Galani, Coutureau, and Kelche, 1998), all of which are methods for measuring spatial learning and working memory of rats. For instance, while learning a Hebb-Williams maze, EC animals made fewer errors than IC animals (Hymovitch, 1952). Interestingly, this superior performance in EC animals cannot simply be attributed to greater visual processing, since it was shown that even blinded EC rats performed better on these memory tests than blind IC rats (Rosenzweig, Krech, Bennett, and Diamond, 1962).

4.5 Neuroimaging Evidence of Plasticity in Humans

4.5.1 Research in Adults

Visualizing synaptic plasticity in the human brain is impossible because of the methodological limitations we read about in Chapter 3. However, we do have the ability to view the effects of plasticity using neuroimaging and neurophysiological tools. They can be studied as changes in functional activity and anatomical connectivity using these techniques and as changes in behavior as assessed by measures of learning, memory, and adaptation. Brain imaging studies using structural and functional magnetic resonance imaging (MRI) and diffusion tensor imaging (DTI) have provided evidence of modifications in activation patterns and structural changes that are suggestive of plastic changes (Guye, Bartolomei, and Ranjeva, 2008; Voss and Schiff, 2009). These circuit modifications are believed to be indirect measures of what researchers assume is occurring at the cellular and synaptic levels.

Neuroimaging studies of plasticity tend to use two main experimental approaches. The first approach is a cross-sectional one, in which individuals with varying levels of expertise on a given skill are compared and differences in neural structure or function related to their skill level are identified. One of the first studies demonstrating the effects of experience on the brain showed that London taxi drivers had posterior hippocampi that were larger than controls in proportion to the length of driving experience (Maguire et al., 2000). This study showed that the hippocampus, which is critical for spatial representation, is structurally altered by increased navigational experience. Subsequent studies showed structural changes using a variety of training paradigms, including complex visuo-motor tasks such as juggling (Draganski et al., 2004) and music training (Zatorre, Chen, and Penhune, 2007), which each yielded changes in gray matter in motor cortex and regions in the parietal sulci. Decreased experience is similarly related to the converse condition, as is the case with limb amputation, which is associated with cortical reorganization (Flor et al., 1995).

Musicians are a popular group of subjects to enroll for such studies because there is wide variability in their musical skills and because their skills are cross-domain (often involving motor cortex as well as auditory cortex). One study found that string players have greater cortical representations of the fingers of the left hand than non-musicians and that the extent of this representation is correlated with the age at which the person began to play (Elbert, Pantev, Wienbruch, Rockstroh, and Taub, 1995), suggesting that over time the experience of playing music leads to changes (neuroplasticity) in the musicians. These studies suggest that neural plasticity of relevant cortices depends on use and that it changes to accommodate the needs and experiences of the individual.

Whether training and experience increases or decreases neural activation or the extent of activation is still up for debate. Some studies have shown general decreases in neural activity following training (e.g. Chein and Schneider, 2005). One explanation for this phenomenon is that enhanced engagement of neural systems (leading to greater activation) serves a scaffolding role to help the novice learn to optimally perform the task at hand, but that this extra help becomes less essential as the novice becomes more skilled at the task (Chein and Schneider, 2005). With training, therefore, changes in fMRI signal are generalized as decreases in the extent and/or magnitude of activity. Other studies have shown general increases in neural activation as a result of training or experience (e.g. Karni et al., 1995; Westerberg and Klingberg, 2007). Klingberg and colleagues reported that increased prefrontal and parietal activation was related to working memory capacity in children (Klingberg, Forssberg, and Westerberg, 2002). In adults, several groups have reported increased activation following skill learning (Constantinidis and Klingberg, 2016) and other interventions such as meditation (Davidson et al., 2003), suggesting that these findings reflect the recruitment of additional cortical resources with practice.

The second strategy to study neural plasticity is to examine participants at multiple time points. In this longitudinal approach, participants are examined multiple times over the course of a learning or training period. Training is a way to flood the organism with experience-dependent processes by saturating it with one particular experience. In humans, functional neural activation is assessed in a cognitive task before and after (and sometimes during) training on a task, in comparison with a baseline task that is not practiced. Then it is determined whether brain activity has changed in association with training on the task. In one study, a group of adults practiced two rapid sequences of finger movements daily over several weeks (Karni et al., 1995). Each participant was randomly assigned one sequence to practice for 10–20 minutes each day for several weeks while the other sequence was to be performed only during the fMRI scanning. Initial accuracy on both sequences did not differ, but after 3 weeks of practicing, the speed at which the practiced sequence could be performed increased significantly. Remarkably, these improvements in performance were observable in the brain. Whereas there were no differences in brain activation to the sequences initially, by the end of the 3 weeks the extent of activation evoked by the practiced sequence was larger than the extent of activation evoked by the control sequence. This result indicates that practicing something over and over changes the brain! You already knew that, but now you know the neural mechanisms that underlie that effect. This example is specific to motor movement but the effect is observed in other domains, including visual attention and memory.

One important point to make is that plasticity itself is plastic and not necessarily permanent. Several studies have shown that changes in the brain based on a particular experience can and do revert back to baseline once that experience is removed. For instance, individuals who underwent extensive training on how to juggle evinced structural changes in motor regions of the brain (as observed with MRI) (Draganski et al., 2004). However, once they ceased juggling practice, the structural changes induced by the juggling reverted back to their pre-juggling structure.

Recent advances in the use of transcranial magnetic stimulation (TMS) have demonstrated the utility of this tool in the study of neural plasticity as well. Since its introduction, it has been known that repeated TMS (rTMS) of the motor cortex in healthy adult human participants can lead to relatively lasting effects (usually of the order of 30–60 minutes) on the excitability of the corticospinal output (Siebner and Rothwell, 2003). One study showed that rTMS delivered to the superior temporal cortex causes macroscopic cortical changes in gray matter in the auditory cortex as early as within 5 days of continuous intervention (May et al., 2007).

4.5.2 Research in Children

Although most studies on neural plasticity have been conducted in adults, the knowledge learned from them has yielded important insights that help inform developmental work. Currently there are a few published studies that have examined plasticity based on skill training in children.

Building on previous studies in adult musicians and nonmusicians that have revealed structural and functional differences in brain regions relevant to music production (Schlaug et al., 2009; Zatorre et al., 2007), one study compared structural neural changes in relation to behavioral changes in young children who received 15 months of instrumental musical training relative to a group of children who did not (Hyde et al., 2009). The children who received private keyboard lessons showed greater behavioral improvements on music ability than the non-trained children; neither group showed differences between baseline and testing on non-musical tasks. In addition, the musically trained children showed greater structural changes in the right precentral gyrus, corpus callosum, and the primary auditory region (Hyde et al., 2009), consistent with findings in adults (Zatorre et al., 2007). Their data provide new evidence for training-induced structural brain plasticity in early childhood. Another study also identified structural differences in the corpus callosum in young musicians. Based on total weekly practice time, the researchers divided a sample of 5- to 7-year-old children into three groups: high-practicing, low-practicing, and controls (no practice). There were no differences in corpus callosum size at baseline but differences did emerge after approximately 29 months, with the greatest increased change in the high-practicing group of children (Schlaug et al., 2009).

Collectively, these studies indicate that the developing brain exhibits plasticity that is similar to plasticity in the adult system. Behavioral improvements related to intensive training or experience are associated with neural plasticity specific to the task at hand (e.g. increased activation of the motor cortex following training). What this suggests is that experience-dependent mechanisms do not differ greatly across the lifespan. Neural regions previously associated with experience-expectant mechanisms, such as motor abilities and language, show a high degree of plasticity across development, suggesting that perhaps there is plasticity in processes that are initially precipitated by expectant interactions with the environment.

These studies have also led to more questions that will undoubtedly be addressed in the next generation of research on this topic. First, which neural systems show greater or less training-related plasticity earlier in development? There is significantly greater plasticity in receiving and learning from language input during infancy than at any other point in life. As infants receive increasing exposure to their native language, neural systems responsive to language lose plasticity, which is translated into more difficulty discriminating speech sounds of foreign languages and learning new languages (Doupe and Kuhl, 2008). It is for this reason that many adult-age learners of a new language have accents. Are there other examples of such extreme behavioral and neural loss of plasticity across the lifespan, whereby learning itself imposes constraints on plasticity? Second, how do the timescales of neural plasticity change across development? That is, do observed behavioral and neural changes occur more or less quickly in the developing brain? Again, to borrow from the language literature, young children learn to discriminate foreign languages more quickly and more proficiently than adults (Snow and Hoefnagel-Hohle, 1977). Last, which behaviors cannot be "sped up" by exposure earlier in development because of time-locked experience-expectant mechanisms? Certainly, pubertal constraints impose at least some limits on plasticity associated with behavioral and neurobiological changes.

4.5.3 The Plasticity of Developmental Timing

Now that you have learned a bit about plasticity, you might be asking yourself a question that researchers have puzzled over for many decades: Can cognitive and brain development be "sped up" with training or developmentally delayed with experience? Animal work suggests that the "window" of plasticity can actually be manipulated. Returning to experiments with the visual system in kittens, Cynader and Mitchell demonstrated this effect (1977). Remember that kittens reared normally, which is to say under normal light conditions, show peak sensitivity to monocular deprivation within the first 2 months of life (Wiesel and Hubel, 1963). Cynader and Mitchell found that kittens reared in the dark until

6, 8, or 10 months of age, with absolutely no exposure to light, remained highly sensitive to monocular deprivation effects well beyond the first 2 months of life. This suggests that the brain remained in a plastic (or flexible) state well beyond normal when reared in abnormal conditions. In humans, the most insightful experiments to address these questions have been conducted in infants. In addition to being cute and fun to play with, infants teach researchers about basic cognition and plasticity. In these experiments, researchers introduce tools that facilitate motor skills early in development, before the age at which these behaviors are typically observed.

Despite their seemingly relaxed lives in which they spend the majority of time sleeping or eating, newborn infants are actually in quite a demanding phase of life. As soon as they are born, infants are working hard on learning basic things such as eating on their own, recognizing their caregiver's face, and crying to get their needs met. These relatively demanding requirements leave them little room for learning more complex behaviors that involve motor skill. In general, infants do not systematically reach for objects until ~5 months of age (Butterworth and Hopkins, 1988), likely a reflection of their relatively immature gross motor skills (e.g. arm and hand strength, fine motor control) prior to this time (Halverson, 1933). Researchers have cleverly taken advantage of this delayed motor development to test whether plasticity can be manipulated by "speeding up" motor skills. By providing infants with scaffolding tools that they are not typically exposed to before a certain age, they can be trained to exhibit motor characteristics earlier than normal.

In one study, 3-month-old infants who had not yet demonstrated spontaneous reaching and grasping skills were tested using an "enrichment experience" (Needham, Barrett, and Peterman, 2002). The enrichment experience consisted of 12–14 brief parent-led object play sessions held at the infant's home. During the play sessions, the infant sat on a parent's lap at a table and wore mittens with the soft side of Velcro covering the palms. On the table in front of the infant were small, lightweight objects with edges covered in the corresponding side of the Velcro. With a quick swipe of the hand, the infant could easily "pick up" an object as it stuck to the mitten. After the enrichment phase, infants in the experimental condition as well as infants in a control condition (who did not play with the "sticky mittens") were taken to the lab for an assessment of object exploration skills. Infants who had had the enrichment experience showed advanced reaching behavior toward the new objects compared to control infants, even when not wearing the sticky mittens. These data suggest that experience may be a critical factor in manipulating processes considered to be under developmental constraint. Furthermore, it suggests that plasticity can be "sped up"!

Another research team used a different, but equally brilliant, experiment to test infants. In this paradigm, the goal was to determine if infants could be trained to manipulate objects before they typically do so on their own in normative development (Rovee-Collier and Hayne, 2000). The researchers tied a ribbon to an infant's ankle and tied the other end to an overhead crib mobile. Without explicitly telling the infant to kick her leg in order to move the mobile (they couldn't even if they had wanted to because infants, of course, do not talk!), the researchers noticed that over time infants learned the association between their ankle kicks and the rewarding mobile movement. At first this happened by chance, as the infants randomly moved a leg and noticed that this movement caused the overhead mobile to move. Once they became aware of the association, the infant's rate of leg kicks increased sharply. They had learned that their motor actions were tied to a reward (the moving mobile). It remains an open question as to whether this experience with leg-kicking and mobile-moving would generalize to other abilities. Nonetheless, these experiments suggest that behaviors that seem developmentally constrained can, in fact, be manipulated in developmental time.

4.6 Why Is Plasticity Adaptive?

Why would our species have evolved in such a way as to allow (and even encourage) constant change of the most fragile and important organ in our body? The main reason is that this plasticity is what allows humans to keep learning new things throughout life. Imagine if you could not move to a new neighborhood because your brain was unable to learn the new route home from school? Or if going to college was pointless because your brain could not incorporate the new knowledge you were learning? This would be very sad and frustrating! In fact, our brain is very good at learning new spatial information and at consolidating new information from all types of sources throughout our lives. This ability is very adaptive because it allows us to update our working representation of the world around us with remarkable speed. Plasticity is also adaptive because it provides the potential for the brain to repair itself, to a certain extent, following atypical development, trauma, or psychopathology. All behavioral interventions, in fact, rest on the assumption that the brain is plastic.

4.6.1 Opportunities for Intervention and Remediation

Intervention Studies

Children afflicted with developmental disorders, such as Attention-Deficit Hyperactivity Disorder (ADHD), are characterized as having atypical development. This means that their brains do not exhibit the typical developmental patterns observed in their non-afflicted peers. This atypical neurodevelopment often means that their behavior is also different from that of typically developing peers. In the case of ADHD, youth exhibit hyperactive behavior (i.e. difficulty sitting still) and a limited attention span. You can imagine that this behavior can be quite disruptive in settings where staying still and paying attention are necessary, as in the classroom. Therefore, researchers, parents, and educators are keen on creating treatments and interventions that help individuals with ADHD and other common disorders.

Working memory, the ability to temporarily hold information in mind and use it to perform basic cognitive functions, is impaired in many common neuropsychiatric disorders, including ADHD. Therefore, a number of training interventions have been created that specifically target working memory abilities in an effort to improve them. The assumption is that any behavioral improvements in working memory following a working memory intervention are a manifestation of the plasticity in the underlying neural systems. There are numerous training interventions that target other cognitive processes, such as impulse control, but we will review some promising findings with working memory interventions to keep the example simple.

One way to improve working memory is through computerized training where participants practice their working memory through computer games. These trainings typically entail 20 or more sessions over a 5-week period (Spencer-Smith and Klingberg, 2015). A certified training coach monitors the training by tracking the user's progress online. An analysis of over 12 studies using this intervention found that the training helped decrease inattention and increase working memory in daily life, as reported by teacher and/or parent reports of the target child's behavior in daily life. This type of training was also conducted in a group of adults who received a brain scan before and after they received the training for 5 weeks. During the brain scan, participants completed a visuo-spatial working memory task and a control (non-working memory) task. Compared to the brain scan they received before training, participants exhibited greater activation in the prefrontal cortex and parietal cortex of the brain after the training period, but only during the working memory task. These results indicate that there was an increase in brain activation following working memory training, which was associated with improved task performance (that is, better working memory) (Olesen, Westerberg, and Klingberg, 2004; Nemmi et al., 2016). These changes in cortical activity are good evidence of training-induced plasticity in the neural systems that underlie working memory.

Dyslexia Intervention

Several studies have provided strong support for the claim that children with reading disabilities can benefit significantly from intervention techniques; the impact of such interventions on neural plasticity has been assessed using fMRI (McCandliss and Noble, 2003). In one study, children with dyslexia, a condition in which individuals experience a reading difficulty despite a normal intelligence, were examined (Simos et al., 2002). They received an 80-hour intervention that consisted of intensive remedial instruction. All children were initially diagnosed with dyslexia, marked by severe difficulties in word recognition and phonologic processing. Before intervention, all children with dyslexia showed distinctly aberrant activation profiles featuring little or no activation of the posterior portion of the superior temporal gyrus (STGp), an area normally involved in phonologic processing (Simos et al., 2002). An initial baseline scan showed the typical reduced activation of the left posterior superior temporal gyrus (STG) during a phonologically challenging task. Following the intervention, all children with dyslexia showed significant increases in reading skill, as well as increased activation in the left posterior STG. The authors of the study concluded that the deficit in functional brain organization underlying dyslexia can be reversed after sufficiently intense intervention lasting as little as 2 months, and are consistent with current proposals that reading difficulties in many children represent a variation of typical development that can be altered by intensive intervention. Indeed, other researchers have reported similar findings.

4.6.2 Cross-Modal Plasticity

One remarkable feature of neuroplasticity is in its cross-modality, which means that when one sensory modality (e.g. vision) is compromised, other sensory modalities (e.g. touch or hearing) are enhanced. Sensory compensation observed in blind individuals is one example of this phenomenon. Blind individuals exhibit superior skills in touch and hearing as compared to the average non-blind population (Doucet et al., 2005;

Voss et al., 2010). In one ground-breaking study, blind participants were found to be better at localizing sound sources than sighted participants (Lessard, Pare, Lepore, and Lassonde, 1998). Studies in animals have also shown the profound effects of visual loss on somatosensory functions. For example, blind newborn rats use somatosensory perception from their whiskers to successfully perform maze tasks; this effect is associated with concomitant changes in the size and sensitivity of the receptive fields of the barrel cortex (the part of the brain that represents whisker sensitivity) (Toldi, Rojik, and Feher, 1994). Interestingly, this compensatory effect is much greater if the sensory deprivation occurs earlier rather than later in life (Volgyi, Farkas, and Toldi, 1993). In cats, visual deprivation from birth leads to improved auditory localization and greater auditory spatial tuning of cells in the auditory cortex (Rauschecker, 1995).

The cross-modal plasticity is not limited to the visual system. MEG, ERP, and neuroimaging studies have shown in humans that auditory cortex areas are active during visual and somatosensory processing in deaf individuals (Finney, Fine, and Dobkins, 2001; Bola et al., 2017), suggesting that the sensory deprivation leads to reorganization of primary sensory cortices.

What are the neural mechanisms underlying cross-modal plasticity? We know that the brain reorganizes, but how does it do it? Reorganization might be due to modifications in local connectivity at the synaptic level or in connectivity between long-range connections in the brain (Lee and Whitt, 2015). Regardless of the exact mechanism, observed manifestations of plasticity, whether behavioral or neural, depend on the nature of the altered experience, the developmental timing of the altered experience, and the particular brain systems that are modified (see Bavelier and Neville, 2002 for an extensive review on this topic).

4.6.3 Psychotherapy

Plasticity underlies the basic implicit assumptions about psychotherapy. The English word therapy comes via Latin *therapīa* from Greek θεραπεία, and literally means "curing" or "healing." Indeed, the goal of therapy and psychotherapy is to help an individual work through and eventually eliminate a problem behavior or intrusive and debilitating thoughts. Psychotherapy is therapy for a person's mental or emotional problems and is typically conducted by conversing with a mental health professional such as a psychiatrist, psychologist, clinical social worker, or member of the clergy. An exhaustive discussion of all the many types of therapies and schools of thought about psychotherapy is beyond the scope of this book. However, most forms of psychotherapy involve an interactive process between the afflicted individual who is seeking help and the psychotherapist. Through this process, the goal is to explore and resolve troublesome thoughts, feelings, and/or behaviors to achieve higher levels of day-to-day functioning. Often, this process leads to changes in behavior and cognition. For example, if a patient undergoes psychotherapy to diminish troublesome memories associated with a traumatic event, a common approach is for the therapist to help that person change her cognitive representation of the traumatic event. The shift in thinking will require reorganization of the neuronal representation of the event, thereby drawing on the mechanisms of neuroplasticity. Indeed, studies suggest that the behavioral and cognitive changes induced by therapy are paralleled by neuroplasticity. One study examined the effect of cognitive therapy on a group of patients afflicted with chronic fatigue syndrome (de Lange et al., 2008). Following 16 sessions of therapy, the patients exhibited increased prefrontal cortex volume compared to baseline.

4.6.4 Exercise

Physical activity, such as aerobic exercise, improves neurocognitive function (Hillman, Erickson, and Kramer, 2008). In older adults, exercise leads to improved learning, which is associated with increased neurogenesis and survival in rodents (van Praag, Shubert, Zhao, and Gage, 2005). To determine the neural mechanism underlying improved cognition in humans, recent work examined hippocampal volume and spatial memory performance. In a single-blind, randomized controlled trial, adults were randomly assigned to either the experimental condition in which they received moderate-intensity aerobic exercise 3 days per week for 1 year or to the control condition which involved simple stretching exercises (Erickson et al., 2011). MRI images to measure anatomical volume were collected before the intervention, 6 months after the intervention started, and again at the completion of the program. The hippocampal volumes of individuals in the experimental condition did not differ from those of individuals in the control condition at baseline. However, hippocampal volume increased significantly only in the aerobic exercise group (Erickson et al., 2011). Although MRI does not have the resolution to detect changes at the neuronal level, we know from animal studies that the hippocampus is the major site of neurogenesis, suggesting that the observed exercise-related increases in hippocampal volume may be a manifestation of underlying neurogenesis processes. Furthermore, these hippocampal changes were associated with improved performance on a memory test.

4.7 Adverse Environments and Plasticity

The malleability of the brain helps support learning, facilitates interventions, and plays a key role in development. However, the brain is also sensitive to the negative effects of the environment. A long line of research in both animals and humans shows that individuals reared in adverse or stressful environments exhibit neural reorganization. Stress is the brain's and the body's way of reacting to daily challenges, pressures, and conflicts. It leads to changes in physiological systems and psychological well-being. Although it may be hard to believe, stress is quite useful for the organism. Without the psychological feelings of stress, it would be challenging to generate the motivation necessary to study for a boring class, for instance, or spring into action in life-threatening situations. Like most other systems in the body, the sympathetic nervous system that stimulates the "fight or flight" response under conditions of stress is regulated by a feedback loop. Like the feedback loop we discussed in Chapter 2 regarding puberty, the stress feedback loop works in a similar way: the body (and brain) kicks into the fight or flight response during stress but returns to **homeostasis** once the stressor has passed. In the stress literature, this process of achieving stability through physiological or behavioral change is referred to as **allostasis**. However, sometimes the system can go awry, leading to a feedback loop that does not "turn off" the stress response. This leads to a chronic stress condition in which the body believes it needs to be in a hypervigilant state, which is psychologically, metabolically, and physically expensive for the organism. This stress-induced "wear and tear" on the body is referred to as **allostatic load**. Furthermore, it can lead to maladaptive changes in the brain.

Perhaps the most well-known experiments addressing this issue come from Bruce McEwen's lab at Rockefeller University. Dr. McEwen and his colleagues, most notably his former graduate students Elizabeth Gould (now at Princeton University) and Robert Sapolsky (now at Stanford University), showed that stressors have direct effects on neural organization.

McEwen and colleagues were first drawn to this research because they aimed to uncover how stress hormones, more formally known as **glucocorticoids** (or **cortisol** in humans), affect the brain. They examined both acute and chronic stress in a series of clever experiments that varied the source of the stressor, which included physically restraining the animal (restraint stress) (Watanabe, Gould, and McEwen, 1992), placing subordinate animals in the presence of dominant animals (psychosocial stress) (Magarinos, McEwen, Flugge, and Fuchs, 1996), and treating the animal with glucocorticoid injections (Woolley, Gould, and McEwen, 1990). In all of these experiments and a host of others, both acute and chronic stress yielded altered spine density and decreased dendritic length in the hippocampus and prefrontal cortex regions of the brain (Lupien, McEwen, Gunnar, and Heim, 2009). The decreased branching pattern in the stressed dendrites as compared with the dendrites from the control animal (Magarinos et al., 1996) is evidence for dendritic **atrophy** (which is the neuroscientific term for neuronal degeneration). These regions also show decreased neurogenesis in the dentate gyrus of the hippocampus.

Think back to what we read about earlier in this chapter: neurogenesis is stimulated by physical activity and enriched environments. Now you have learned that hippocampal neurogenesis is inhibited by stress and glucocorticoids. This should give you an indication of how malleable neurogenesis is and that it is largely based on experiential conditions. Interestingly, the same stressors produce the opposite effects in an area of the brain known as the amygdala, which is a region associated with emotion processing and threat detection. The amygdala actually reacts to stress with increased dendritic growth, along with increased anxiety symptoms and aggression (Vyas, Mitra, Shankaranarayana Rao, and Chattarji, 2002). Why might this be? Since the role of the amygdala is to help the organism detect threat and potential harm in the environment, then perhaps it makes ecological sense for this region to grow in neural resources to face the challenges of a stressful and potentially dangerous environment. Evidence in support of this hypothesis comes from research on children who experienced early adversity in the form of poor caregiving in an impoverished orphanage (Tottenham et al., 2010). Children in this study differed on how long they had been institutionalized. When the authors divided the sample into those who had been adopted at an early age (that is, they were only in the institution for a short period of time) versus those who had been adopted at a later age (they were in the institution for a longer period of time and presumably, therefore, experienced more adversity and early life stress), they found that the later-adopted post-institutionalized children had significantly larger amygdala than those who had been adopted early in life (Tottenham et al., 2010). Higher parental ratings of internalizing problems and anxiety were correlated with larger amygdala volume. These findings are consistent with the idea that early life stress induces structural change that is not necessarily in the form of a *decreased* brain structure size in the developing brain.

Although stress causes neurons to shrink or grow, it does not necessarily cause them to die. In the hippocampus, prefrontal cortex, and amygdala, stress-induced decreases and increases in dendritic spine density and neurogenesis are largely reversible in young adult animals (Davidson and McEwen, 2012). This was shown experimentally using the restraint stress paradigm in rats. Animals received daily restraint stress for 3 weeks and then were allowed to recover for another 3 weeks. There was a significant reduction in dendritic length and branch number in the medial prefrontal cortex following the restraint stress period compared to the recovery period, where the dendritic architecture looked similar to that observed prior to the stress period (Radley et al., 2005). Interestingly, the same effect is observed in humans! To demonstrate this, Liston and colleagues took advantage of the fact that medical students experience a significant amount of stress as they prepare for their medical board exams. The researchers obtained an fMRI scan of each participant while they performed a cognitive test after 4 weeks of the stress exposure as they prepared for the exam; their performance was worse compared with a group of control participants (not undergoing stress) matched for age, gender, and occupation. Once the stressor had passed (i.e. after the participants had taken the medical boards), they received another fMRI scan and were again compared to matched control participants, thus yielding an assessment of the reversibility of stress effects on brain function. Data from the second scan showed that after the stressor had passed, the previously stressed participants did not differ in either cognitive performance or functional patterns of the prefrontal cortex from the control group. These results are strong evidence for the reversibility of stress-induced cognition and plasticity of the prefrontal cortex (Liston, McEwen, and Casey, 2009).

4.7.1 Socioeconomic Status and Plasticity

Socioeconomic status (SES), a measure that aggregates one's overall income, education, and status in society, significantly influences an individual's experiences from childhood through adolescence and into adulthood. Relative to individuals who are raised in a mid-to-high SES home, growing up in a family with low SES is associated with a number of poorer outcomes, including worse health and psychological well-being, impaired cognitive and emotional development, and academic obstacles (Johnson, Riis, and Noble, 2016). Numerous factors contribute to this disparity, including income, material resources, education, occupation, neighborhood factors, family stressors and conflict, exposure to violence and toxins, and parental care. A growing body of research has also begun to study how SES affects brain development and has identified the specific neural mechanisms and changes that underlie this disadvantage.

Language Development

Neurocognitive studies have shown that the most deleterious effects of lower SES during childhood are on language processing and executive functioning. An early, influential study found differences in vocabulary size among children of professional, working class, and low SES families that were observable from the beginning of normative speech production (around 1 year old) and that increased with development (Hart and Risley, 2003). By 3 years of age, the children from higher SES homes had produced over 1,000 different words while the children from lower SES homes had produced half that many. Subsequent research found that the utterances produced by the more advantaged children were also more complex (Vasilyeva, Waterfall, and Huttenlocher, 2008) and grammatically advanced (Dollaghan et al., 1999). Does this suggest that the brain "knows" that the individual is reared in a lower-resourced home and therefore somehow alters the language network? No. Remember that the brain simply matures according to the input it receives. With this in mind, researchers examined how much language input children who varied on SES received. Using all-day recordings of parent–infant interactions at home revealed that infants who experienced more child-directed speech became more efficient at language processing and had a more demonstrative vocabulary by age 2 than those whose caregivers provided more limited child-directed speech (Weisleder and Fernald, 2013). This research suggests that the deficits in language production, language comprehension, and syntax in youth from lower versus higher SES homes may perhaps be attributed to gaps in language exposure and opportunities to "practice" engaging in language interactions. As the authors note in the title of their study, "talking to children matters" (Weisleder and Fernald, 2013).

The neural mechanisms of this effect have been studied. A recent study that examined youth ages 5–20 found that differences in income level and parental education were associated with relatively large differences in brain surface area, a measure that is thought to reflect experience-dependent changes. Youth from higher-income homes had greater surface area than those from lower-income homes (Noble et al., 2015). Using fMRI, SES has been found to be positively correlated with the degree to which the inferior frontal gyrus is activated during a language task (Hackman et al., 2010), indicating that perhaps there is decreased specialization of language function in the neural systems of children from low SES homes.

Executive Functions

Executive functions commonly refer to a cluster of cognitive processes that are critically involved in higher cognition. These include working memory, task flexibility, inhibitory control, and planning. Research suggests that executive function ability varies based on SES from childhood through adolescence (Noble, McCandliss, and Farah, 2007). ERP studies reveal that children from lower SES homes do not engage the common executive function neural network, namely the prefrontal cortex, while engaged in executive function tasks, such as distractor suppression or rule learning (Kishiyama, Boyce, Jimenez, Perry, and Knight, 2009).

Social Causation Hypothesis

Scientists who work at the intersection of SES and brain development have identified the social causation hypothesis in an attempt to explain this relationship. This hypothesis posits that the experiences that are typical of different levels of SES affect brain development (Hackman et al., 2010). A few pieces of evidence support this hypothesis. First, cross-fostering studies that compared children who were adopted within or between SES levels report that there is a strong effect of the environment on cognitive factors such as IQ (Capron and Duyme, 1989). Second, the negative effects of poverty are significantly greater if poverty is experienced in earlier rather than later childhood (Duncan, Brooks-Gunn, and Klebanov, 1994). Third, twin studies indicate that the magnitude of genetic effects on IQ depends on SES, such that cognitive ability is almost entirely predicted by environmental factors at lower SES levels (Turkheimer, Haley, Waldron, D'Onofrio, and Gottesman, 2003). Finally, one last piece of (very encouraging) evidence is that some of the negative effects of SES on brain development may be reversible: interventions conducted in preschool children suggest that executive functions can be improved in children (Diamond, Barnett, Thomas, and Munro, 2007; Thorell, Lindqvist, Bergman Nutley, Bohlin, and Klingberg, 2009).

While no single factor can explain how deprived environments impact the brain, there are numerous candidate explanations. Health care access and good-quality education likely play a significant role, especially because they are both better for children in higher levels of SES (Hackman et al., 2010). There is also evidence linking prenatal influences (such as low birthweight and nutrition) (Spencer, Bambang, Logan, and Gill, 1999), parental care (including greater irritability and mood disorders and harsh discipline) (Belsky and Jaffe, 2006), and cognitive stimulation in the home environment (including the availability of books, computers, and cultural excursions) (McLoyd, 1998). The promising news is that each of these factors has been shown to be amenable to interventions that benefit cognition and child well-being. These interventions have been shown to boost academic achievement, increase self-esteem and social competence, and reduce aggression across time (Seitz, Rosenbaum, and Apfel, 1985).

4.8 Chapter Summary

- Neuroplasticity refers to the neuroanatomical basis of behavioral adaptation.
- Neurogenesis and synaptogenesis underlie neuroplasticity.
- Neuroimaging tools are often used to indirectly examine neuroplasticity in humans.
- Neuroplasticity underlies changes in brain and behavior that arise across development.
- Neuroplasticity is adaptive for behavior and interventions.

4.9 Review Questions

1 What is the difference between a critical period versus a sensitive period?
2 Define neurogenesis and synaptogenesis.
3 List two examples each of how the brain responds to positive and negative effects of the environment.
4 What is the difference between experience-expectant and experience-dependent modes of plasticity?
5 Provide examples of how neuroplasticity is reversible.

Further Reading

Bavelier, D., and Neville, H.J. (2002). Cross-modal plasticity: where and how? *Nature Reviews Neuroscience*, 3, 443–52.
Greenough, W.T., Black, J.E., and Wallace, C.E. (1987). Experience and brain development. *Child Development*, 58, 3, 539–559.

Hackman, D.A., Farah, M.J., and Meaney, M.J. (2010) Socioeconomic status and the brain: mechanistic insights from human and animal research. *Nature Reviews Neuroscience*, 11(9), 651–659.

Hebb, D.O. (1949). *The organization of behavior: a neuropsychological theory.* New York: Wiley and Sons.

CHAPTER FIVE

Neurocognitive Development

Learning Objectives

- Consider how higher cognition makes humans distinct among primates.
- Learn about the development of higher cognition across adolescence.
- Learn about the prefrontal cortex.
- Examine the protracted development of the prefrontal cortex.
- Discuss neurobiological models of adolescent behavior within the context of the protracted development of the prefrontal cortex.

5.1 Introduction

From the moment we are born, our brains are thinking, processing information, and learning from the surrounding world. *How* we think changes with development. Not only do we become faster, and better at processing information, we use different neural regions to support our thinking as we get older.

In this chapter we will discuss why and how this important shift happens. The majority of this conversation will focus on the prefrontal cortex. Its development occurs over a prolonged period of development that spans over two decades. The prefrontal cortex receives significant auxiliary support from other brain structures, largely via connections that become stronger and stronger over development. We will learn about its partners in cognition as well.

The protracted development of the prefrontal cortex has significant implications for behavior. With increased development of this region comes increased processing speed and future planning abilities, better motor control and self-regulation, and improved understanding of abstract concepts. The prefrontal cortex is, arguably, the brain region that helps differentiate humans from nonhuman animals because it supports goal-directed behavior. It is no coincidence that the observable shift in adolescent cognition coincides with the significant developmental changes in the prefrontal cortex. During this time, individuals exhibit enhanced higher cognition and greater sophistication in thinking. Why then do adolescents also exhibit some of the *least* sophisticated actions, in the form of poor decisions and increased health-compromising risky behavior? At the end of the chapter we will revisit the theoretical models that were introduced in Chapter 1 to learn how different developmental trajectories of motivational and cognitive systems help explain this paradox.

5.2 Cognition, Defined

Cognition is a broad concept that encompasses many mental abilities. These include attention, inhibitory control (self-regulation), memory, problem solving, language, reasoning, and decision-making. This is by no means an exhaustive list, as any mental ability that supports thinking and the acquisition of knowledge is relevant. The word cognition comes from the Latin verb *cognosco* (*con* "with" and *gnōscō* "know"), itself a cognate of the Greek verb γι(γ)νώσκω (*gi(g)nósko*), meaning "I know, perceive" (noun: γνῶσις *gnósis* "knowledge").

More than any other mental ability, cognition changes considerably over the lifespan. Even language, which also changes rapidly within the first few years of life, does not exhibit as much prolonged development and variability among individuals as cognition. This process has been a longstanding fascination among developmental psychologists. Studies on cognitive development generated several influential theories about the construction of human thought and mental processing, which are briefly reviewed in Box 5.1.

5.3 Prefrontal Cortex – an Evolutionary History

The **prefrontal cortex** is the swatch of brain tissue that spans the top, most anterior, part of the brain, right above your eyes. It has received considerable attention from scientists over the last century as we have come to appreciate the important role it plays in human cognition. Although other animals have an analogue of the brain that is similar to the prefrontal cortex, no other animal has one that is as complex, proportionally large, and prominent as humans. As you can see in Figure 5.1, the human prefrontal cortex takes up much more real estate in the brain relative to other nonhuman primates, at about 25% of all the cerebral cortex in the human brain (Diamond, 2002). In comparison, it only makes up 15% of the entire cortex in chimpanzees, 7% in dogs, and 4% in cats. Compared to almost all other species, the human brain is larger as a

Box 5.1 Stages of Development

The famous developmental psychologist, Jean Piaget, was captivated by the question of how infants and children acquired knowledge. He is credited with making significant contributions to the study of cognitive development. Based on his observations of his three children, he proposed that children and adolescents throughout the world advance through four stages of development that help shape their mental abilities. The table below describes each stage. Piaget placed great importance on the third stage, when children transition into early adolescents. During this concrete operational stage, he reasoned, there is an obvious shift toward more logical thought.

Similar to Piaget, Lev Vygotsky was intrigued by the question of how children acquire knowledge. Unlike Piaget, Vygotsky placed great emphasis on the role of the social world in cognitive development. Specifically, he proposed that reasoning and increased mental abilities emerge through practical activity in a social environment. Thus, culture is a significant contributor to cognition, according to Vygotsky.

Stage	Age	Description
Sensorimotor stage	Infancy (0–2 years)	During the sensorimotor stage infants learn mostly through trial and error. Children initially rely on reflexes, eventually modifying them to adapt to their world. Behaviors become goal-directed, progressing from concrete to abstract goals. Objects and events can be mentally represented by the child (sometimes called object permanence).
Pre-operational stage	Toddler and early childhood (2–7 years)	During the pre-operational stage, children can mentally represent events and objects and engage in symbolic play. Their thoughts and communications are typically egocentric and they assume that what other people see, hear, and feel are exactly as their own.

Stage	Age	Description
Concrete operational stage	Elementary and early adolescence (7–12 years)	During the concrete operational stage, the individual can apply logical thought or rules to physical objects (hence *concrete* operations). Children become less egocentric and come to understand that something stays the same in quantity even though its appearance changes (e.g. transferring water from a tall thin glass to a short wide glass).
Formal operational stage	Adolescence and adulthood (12 years and on)	As adolescents enter this stage, they gain the ability to think in an abstract manner, the ability to combine and classify items in a more sophisticated way, and the capacity for higher-order reasoning. The adolescent can do mathematical calculations, think creatively, use abstract reasoning, and imagine the outcome of particular actions.

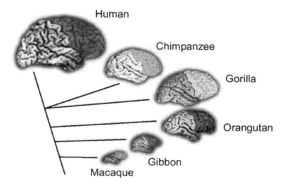

Figure 5.1 The prefrontal cortex is disproportionately larger in humans than in other primates.

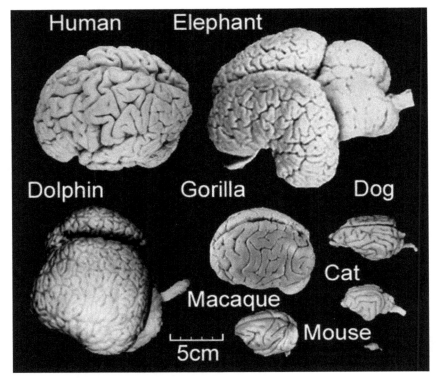

Figure 5.2 The African elephant has a larger overall brain size than the human brain but a proportionately smaller prefrontal cortex.

percentage of body weight, making it disproportionately large in humans (Preuss, 2000). Since the emergence of the first species in our *Homo* genus (*Homo habilis*) approximately 2 million years ago, the human brain has doubled in size. When compared to earlier ancestors who lived about 4 million years ago, the human brain is three times as large. However, this does not mean that humans have the largest brain in the animal kingdom but that we have proportionally the largest prefrontal cortex. As you can see in Figure 5.2, the African elephant has a larger overall brain size (check out the size of the cerebellum!) but a relatively smaller prefrontal cortex.

This steady increase in prefrontal cortex size begs two important questions: (1) what accounts for this increase, and (2) what (if any) advantages does it confer for humans over other species? Bigger brains take much more energy to power. Surely there is a reason that our metabolically conservative brain has devoted so much space to one region. Indeed, there is. In other species, it is dedicated mostly to voluntary motor control, but in primates it has developed considerably beyond motor skills. For many years, scientists believed that humans' unparalleled abilities for planning and abstract reasoning were attributable to their having a more developed prefrontal cortex than other primates. However, it is important to understand that complex brain organization, not overall size, may be the key feature that has advantaged primates over evolutionary time. The end result is enhanced flexibility of behavior, which facilitates sophisticated decision-making, inhibitory control, and working memory.

5.3.1 Why Do We Need a Prefrontal Cortex?

Our nonhuman ancestors and cousins have survived just fine without the complex prefrontal cortex that humans have. Simple, automatic behaviors such as the inclination to instinctively orient to an unexpected sound or movement or to recoil from hot flames do not necessitate the prefrontal cortex. So why do humans need a prefrontal cortex? Simple behaviors are inflexible, stereotyped reactions elicited by particular events in the environment that are not malleable to novel situations (Miller and Cohen, 2001). Given the dynamic nature of human life and the ubiquity of novel situations, our behaviors require greater complexity. This complexity comes at a metabolic cost: the development of the prefrontal cortex is a lengthy process that uses many neuronal resources, requires reorganization continually throughout childhood and adolescence, and, because of its functional variability among individuals, yields vast individual differences in its efficiency. So why would we have evolved to rely on such an (initially) unreliable, energetically expensive, and occasionally vulnerable brain region?

The answer is simple: the prefrontal cortex affords humans the cognitive flexibility that other species do not have by serving an integrative function between sensory, motor, and higher cognitive regions. Animals without the complex prefrontal cortex that humans have are limited to (relatively) simple approach and avoid behaviors. They can approach appetitive stimuli such as food and potential reproductive mates and avoid threats such as predators or poisonous food, but they cannot anticipate what others are thinking, consider abstract concepts, switch easily from one cognitive task to another, or learn languages (sometimes even multiple ones!) like humans can.

The prefrontal cortex also serves an important regulatory role that is sometimes referred to as "top-down" processing. This refers to the governance that prefrontal cortex regions have over other brain regions, typically those in subcortical systems, to facilitate internal representations of current and future goals and the means to achieve them. Studies in lesion patients with damage to the prefrontal cortex were instrumental in establishing this important function of the prefrontal cortex. Patients with frontal impairment struggle on tasks that require holding multiple rules and goals in mind. They are impaired in their ability to select the correct response on the Stroop task (described in Box 5.3) because they are unable to suppress the distracting information contained within the task (Cohen and Servan-Schreiber, 1992). Tasks with frequently changing rules, such as the Wisconsin Card Sorting Task, are also challenging for patients with prefrontal cortex damage. Similar to control subjects (without prefrontal damage), they can acquire the initial rule easily, but in contrast to them, they are unable to flexibly adapt their behavior when the rule changes (Milner, 1963). There are numerous other studies that exemplify the importance of the prefrontal cortex in guiding behavior. This occurs because of the ability of prefrontal cortex neurons to maintain task-relevant information (Fuster and Alexander, 1971; Goldman-Rakic, 1996) that is resistant to interference from distraction (Miller and Desimone, 1994). Together, these studies suggest that the prefrontal cortex is critical for integrating information from various regions and maintaining representations of goals.

Some theorists take this idea a step further to suggest that the role of the prefrontal cortex is not simply to represent internal goals and guide behavior but also to *bias* behavior. Miller and Cohen's influential integrative theory of the prefrontal cortex posits that neural activity of the prefrontal cortex yields bias signals that "guide the flow of neural activity along pathways that establish the proper mappings between inputs (from the environment), internal states, and outputs (behavior) needed to perform a given task" (Miller and Cohen, 2001). In other words, the prefrontal cortex serves as a central hub of traffic control that guides relevant neural activity and behavioral output based on its bird's eye view of the various neural representations of cognitive demands, needs, and desires of the individual.

The prefrontal cortex is not born this way. It takes many years to develop the skills, flexibility, and neural processing speed to enact this important cognitive role. Linda Wilbrecht, a creative neuroscientist, likens the extended shaping of the prefrontal cortex to topiary art, the horticultural practice of clipping the foliage of trees and shrubs into defined (often ornamental) shapes. See an example of the brain as

Figure 5.3 The brain as topiary art. See color plate 9.

topiary art in Figure 5.3. A central question in developmental cognitive neuroscience has been to understand the timing and influence of ontogenetic and environmental factors that help sculpt the prefrontal cortex into its mature form.

5.4 The A-not-B Task

The A-not-B task is a simple object-hiding task that is among the most enduring and well known in development psychology for studying cognitive development in infants and toddlers. It is also used to study prefrontal cortex development in older youth. There are variations on how it is implemented but in the typical A-not-B task an experimenter hides a desired object (usually a toy) within the baby's reach in a well (Well A) under a cloth. The baby searches for the toy by uncovering the cloth in Well A and finds the toy. This activity is repeated several times to establish that the baby expects to find the toy in Well A. Then, the experimenter moves the toy to a second well (Well B). This switch is conducted in plain view so that the baby sees the transfer of the toy from Well A to Well B. The baby is then invited to remove the toy and this is where it gets interesting. Jean Piaget, who first described this task, observed that infants under the age of 10 months make a consistent error in which they search for the toy under Well A, even though they saw the experimenter put the toy in Well B! This is now famously known as the A-not-B error, and decades of research have been devoted to understanding what causes this error and identifying the factors and conditions that eliminate it.

Several explanations, all under the premise that the executive functions are immature in infants, have been offered. Smith and Thelen explained the error using a dynamic systems approach in which they argue that various components converge to produce the A-not-B error (Smith and Thelen, 2003). They reasoned that the strength of the memory trace, salience of the toy, length of the delay between hiding and searching, and posture all combine to determine whether or not the infant will make the error. Experimenters have been able to make the error come and go by eliminating the delay between hiding the toy in Well B and asking the infant to reach for it. If the infant is asked to reach for the toy immediately after it is hidden, when it is most salient, he will not make the error. By 12 months of age, human infants succeed on the task even at delays as long as 10 seconds (Diamond, 2002). The error also disappears when the hiding event into Well B is made extremely exciting or salient. In one experiment, the A-not-B error vanished simply by shifting the posture of the infant (Smith, Thelen, Titzer, and McLin, 1999). An infant who had being been sitting on his mother's lap during the initial hiding of the toy in Well A would then be stood up so that he had a bird's eye view of the wells. This shift in posture led to correct searching in Well B even by 8- and 10-month-old infants. Other experiments that also manipulated physical aspects of reaching, along with the observation that between 10 months of age (when infants still make the error) and 12 months of age (when they no longer make the error) there is a dramatic increase in crawling, which improves the spatial memory of infants (Bertenthal and Campos, 1990), led Smith and Thelen to propose that "the relevant memories are in the language of the body" (Smith and Thelen, 2003).

According to dynamic systems theory, which we learned about in Chapter 1, the reason these manipulations can make the error appear or disappear is because there are multiple causes for the error, each of which taps into a different aspect of cognitive development (including memory representation, physical ability, and inhibitory control) that each develop on unique developmental and individual timescales.

5.4.1 The Role of the Dorsolateral Prefrontal Cortex in A-not-B

To identify the neural mechanisms underlying the A-not-B error, Diamond and Goldman-Rakic compared task performance between human infants and cortically lesioned rhesus monkeys (Diamond and Goldman-Rakic, 1989). They found that monkeys with dorsolateral prefrontal lesions committed the A-not-B error as frequently (and under the same delay conditions) as infants 12 months old and younger. Monkeys with lesions in other brain regions or who were not lesioned at all did not exhibit the classic error. These results suggest that success on the A-not-B task depends on an intact and mature dorsolateral prefrontal cortex. Although adult humans with damage to the dorsolateral prefrontal cortex have never been tested on the A-not-B task, amnesiac patients with frontal damage exhibit the same error, lending further support to the hypothesis that this task relies on the integrity of the dorsolateral prefrontal cortex. More generally, these studies point to the role of the prefrontal cortex in supporting the complex skills that are working memory, inhibitory control, and attention. In particular, the neurotransmitter dopamine plays a role in supporting these skills, as described in Box 5.2.

5.5 Structural Development of the Prefrontal Cortex

One fascinating aspect of the prefrontal cortex is that it is the most dynamic brain region not only in terms of phylogeny but also in terms of ontogeny. Phylogeny refers to evolutionary development (change across species) whereas ontogeny refers to the development of an individual organism, and from immaturity to maturity. The prefrontal cortex changes considerably in size and function from birth through death. It encompasses a collection of interconnected cortical areas that sends and receives projections from virtually all cortical sensory systems, motor systems, and many subcortical structures (Miller and Cohen, 2001) but we are not born with this complex web of interconnections. In fact, it is the brain region that changes the most throughout our lifetime and which undergoes the longest process of development, taking over two decades to reach full maturity in humans. Its malleability is precisely what makes it so helpful in advancing our cognition as we acquire greater knowledge throughout our lives.

During the first year of life, there is marked growth of the length and extent of the dendritic branches in the dorsolateral prefrontal cortex

Box 5.2 PKU: A Model System for Studying the Role of Dopamine in Prefrontal Cortex Function

Phenylketonuria (PKU) is a condition characterized by significantly reduced levels of dopamine in the prefrontal cortex. A mutation of the gene on chromosome 12 (12q22–12q24.1), which codes for the enzyme phenylalanine hydroxylase, leads to excess levels of phenylalanine and reduced (sometimes non-existent) levels of tyrosine, the precursor to dopamine. This imbalance occurs because the function of phenylalanine hydroxylase, which is to metabolize (convert) phenylalanine to tyrosine, is disrupted. When PKU is untreated, levels of Phe in the bloodstream dangerously rise to over 10 times normal and cause pervasive brain damage and severe mental retardation (Koch and Wenz, 1987).

Luckily, there is a treatment for PKU that can obviate mental retardation. The treatment consists of a low-Phe diet, which restricts intake of dairy products (milk, ice cream, butter, and cheese) and all meat and fish. This may seem quite restrictive and indeed it is, but people with PKU learn to avoid these foods from an early age so it becomes second nature to them. Despite the low-Phe diet, individuals with PKU do have higher levels of Phe because they need to eat protein, which contains Phe. The US National Collaborative Study of Treated PKU states that persons with PKU are considered to be under adequate control so long as their Phe levels do not exceed 5 times the normal amount. Remember, however, that this means that people with PKU have abnormally low levels of tyrosine, a chemical that is necessary for the production of dopamine. Although dopamine projections are found throughout the brain, those in the prefrontal cortex are particularly vulnerable to even small changes in the amount of available tyrosine. The dopamine neurons that project to the prefrontal cortex are unusual in that they have higher firing rate and dopamine turnover than dopamine neurons in other parts of the brain (Diamond, 2002). Thus, decreased tyrosine availability in people with PKU leads to low dopamine levels in the prefrontal cortex. This condition unfortunately yields cognitive deficits, particularly in cognitive domains that rely heavily on dopamine and/or the prefrontal cortex. They tend to have lower IQs (Berry, O'Grady, Perlmutter, and Bofinger, 1979) and deficits in cognitive control functions, including working memory, problem solving, and information processing (Brunner, Berch, and Berry, 1987; Smith and Beasley, 1989). You may notice that these deficits are similar to those that rely on the prefrontal cortex. Adele Diamond made this same association and pioneered the idea that PKU is a useful model for studying the role of dopamine in cognitive functions that rely on the prefrontal cortex.

To investigate this hypothesis empirically, Diamond and colleagues studied a sample of roughly 150 children longitudinally and 364 children cross-sectionally (Diamond, Prevor, Callender, and Druin, 1997). All of the children with PKU in the study had started the low-Phe dietary treatment soon after birth (80% began the treatment within 14 days of birth and all had been placed on a low-Phe diet within 1 month of birth) and had continuously maintained the diet thereafter. All had birthweights and IQ within the normal range, no known learning disability or serious medical problem, and were born at full-term. These characteristics were true of the control groups as well. All the children were studied using 19 age-appropriate cognitive tests that did and did not rely on the prefrontal cortex: one for infants (6–12 months of age), one for toddlers (15–30 months of age), and one for young children (3.5–7 years old). The study yielded a massive amount of data, too many findings to review here, so we will only review the key points.

In sum, they found that children with PKU whose plasma Phe levels were 3 to 5 times normal (6–10 mg/dl) performed worse than other PKU children with lower Phe levels, matched controls, their own siblings, and children from the general population on tasks that required the working memory and inhibitory control abilities dependent on dorsolateral prefrontal cortex. The impairment was evident in children of all age ranges, from 6 months to 7 years of age. The higher a child's Phe level, the worse that child's performance. Girls were more adversely affected than boys. The deficit appears to be selective, affecting principally one neural system, since even PKU children with Phe levels three to five times normal performed well on the 13 control tasks (Diamond et al., 1997). For comprehensive explanation of the results, the reader is encouraged to read Diamond's work.

(Koenderink, Ulyings, and Mrzljiak, 1994). These dendritic branches reach a plateau, in terms of total length and in radial distance, at approximately age 1, a plateau that extends at least through 27 years of age (Diamond, 2002). At around age 2, the density of neurons in the dorsolateral prefrontal cortex is 55% above the adult mean, but only about 10% above adult levels by age 7 years (Huttenlocher, 1990), indicative of the prolonged pruning process during this time. From 7 years of age through adolescence and into early adulthood, significant changes occur in both myelination and cell body size in the prefrontal cortex. Recall from Chapter 1 that the white matter of the brain represents the myelin wrapped around axons whereas gray matter refers to portions of the neuron that are unmyelinated, such as the cell body, which have a gray appearance.

Anatomical MRI studies have been quite informative in mapping out developmental changes in gray and white matter from mid childhood through early adulthood. Longitudinal MRI studies, which take a snapshot of the developing brain every few years, have afforded researchers the ability to observe developmental trajectories (i.e. change in size over time). The largest (and longest-running) study to date is an ongoing longitudinal neuroimaging study at the Child Psychiatry Branch of the National Institute of Mental Health (NIMH), currently comprised of individuals aged 5–25 years of age. Participants visit the NIMH at roughly 2-year intervals for MRI scans, neuropsychological testing, and genetic assays. As of August 2014, the database consists of 6,000+ scans from over 2,000 research participants, approximately half from clinical populations with developmental disorders and half from typically developing individuals (Giedd et al., 2015). The general developmental trajectory that has emerged from these data during childhood and adolescence is an increase in white matter volumes and inverted U-shaped trajectories in both cortical and subcortical gray matter volumes, with peak numbers occurring at different times in different brain regions. Total cerebral volume, including the prefrontal cortex, reaches 95% of its maximum size by kindergarten, increases slightly during middle childhood, and then declines through the 20s.

5.5.1 Gray Matter

Gray matter is comprised predominantly of cell bodies and dendrites (Braitenberg, 2001). Gray matter volume peaks the earliest in the primary sensorimotor area and the latest in higher-order association areas, including the dorsolateral prefrontal cortex, inferior parietal cortex, and superior temporal gyrus. This peak occurs as children transition into puberty, which leads to sex differences given the distinct pubertal trajectories of boys and girls. Subcortical regions, including the striatum and thalamus, also exhibit an inverted U-shaped developmental trajectory (Raznahan et al., 2014). Research comparing adults and adolescents indicates that the regions that show the biggest developmental differences are the prefrontal cortex and basal ganglia (Sowell et al., 2003), regions that have significant implications for changes in cognition observed during adolescence.

The fact that gray matter is still changing through adolescence initially surprised scientists. Although it was known that early postnatal neurodevelopment involved an overproduction of synapses that then were eventually pruned if unused (the "use it or lose it" principle), it was surprising to learn that the more significant amount of pruning occurs in adolescence. Recall that the brain over-produces neurons and synapses initially and then, based on experience, starts pruning them back around the age of 3. The process is much like the pruning of a tree. By cutting back weak branches, others thrive.

Although it may seem counterintuitive that having fewer synapses is better, the brain is actually more efficient with less "noise" in the system. By pruning away ineffective synapses, greater metabolic energy can be devoted to the more valuable neurons and synapses. Increased myelination around them also helps to stabilize and strengthen them. The period of pruning, in which the brain actually loses gray matter, is as important for brain development as the period of growth.

5.5.2 White Matter

White matter consists of glia and myelinated axons. Myelin is a fatty protein that acts as a sheath that increases the speed of transmission of all neurons. In contrast to the inverted U-shaped developmental trajectories of gray matter, white matter volumes increase about 1–2% per year throughout childhood and adolescence (Giedd et al., 2015). Also in contrast to GM, WM increases are roughly similar across the major lobes (i.e. the frontal, temporal, and parietal lobes) and the corpus callosum, which connects homologous areas of the left and right brain hemispheres and which, with roughly 200 million myelinated axons, is the most prominent white matter structure. Diffusion tensor imaging studies, commonly used to assay white matter, indicate that white matter organization improves with age in ways that facilitate improvements in an array of cognitive domains, including, but not limited to, language (Nagy, Westerberg, and Klingberg, 2004), reading ability (Myers et al., 2014), self-regulation (Treit, Chen, Rasmussen, and Beaulieu, 2014), and memory (Nagy et al., 2004).

5.5.3 Sex Differences

Although it is a fact that there are some general ontogenetic patterns of brain development, there is also considerable variability among individuals and between males and females. For instance, although total cerebral volume peaks just before puberty in the majority of individuals, girls exhibit an earlier peak (at age 10.5) compared to boys (who exhibit the peak at 14.5 years on average). Peak volumes of subcortical regions, such as the striatum and thalamus, also occur later in males. Furthermore, group-average total brain size is approximately 10% larger in males, and the magnitude of this difference is fairly stable across the lifespan (Giedd et al., 2015). This sex difference in brain size is not to be interpreted as imparting any sort of functional advantage or disadvantage.

5.5.4 Structural Developmental in Clinical Populations

Characterization of structural brain development in typically developing samples has been highly important for understanding deviations from typical development. In the NIMH study described above, half of the sample consists of individuals afflicted with a neurodevelopmental disorder. Analyses that have examined brain development in individuals diagnosed with Attention-Deficit Hyperactivity Disorder or childhood-onset schizophrenia have yielded some particularly interesting results.

Attention-Deficit Hyperactivity Disorder (ADHD)

ADHD is the most common neurodevelopmental disorder in the United States, afflicting between 5 and 10% of school-age children (Kessler et al., 2005). Anatomical imaging studies indicate that youth with ADHD have decreased volume of the frontal lobes (Castellanos et al., 2002), parietal lobes (Sowell et al., 2003), basal ganglia (Castellanos et al., 2002), corpus callosum (Giedd et al., 1994), and cerebellum (Berquin et al., 1998). Studies using fMRI in youth with ADHD also show impaired functioning, particularly in the basal ganglia, a region critically involved in motor control and response inhibition. Compared to typically developing youth (without ADHD), youth with ADHD exhibit less engagement of the ventrolateral prefrontal cortex during inhibitory control tasks, an effect that is associated with poorer task performance (Durston, Mulder, Casey, Ziermans, and van Engeland, 2006).

Although the cross-sectional anatomical and functional studies are informative, they are limited in their ability to provide insight into the neurodevelopmental trajectory of individuals with ADHD. How is their brain development distinct from typically developing youth? And how can it explain the phenomenon that some children "age out" of ADHD by young adulthood? A seminal study by Shaw and colleagues, also at the NIMH, provided a glimpse into these questions (Shaw, Gogtay, and Rapoport, 2010). The study included over 200 children with ADHD, within the age range of 4–20 years, who were assessed at least twice over several years. Using MRI, the researchers examined cortical thickness, considered to be a marker for cortical maturation. The data yielded three atypical neurodevelopmental paths: **delayed shifts**, **disrupted veloc-ity**, and **deviant trajectories**. Although this study focused on youth with ADHD, the conceptual ideas can be applied to any pathological group.

Delayed Shifts

A delayed shift neurodevelopmental trajectory refers to the observation that the pathological group of interest (ADHD in this case) exhibits the same general shape of cortical thickness development as healthy individuals across age, albeit shifted to the right. As illustrated in the top panel (Figure 5.4a), this suggests that, while both pathological and healthy groups show the normative increase in cortical thickness in early childhood that peaks around the time of puberty before exhibiting a pruning-induced decrease, the shifted curve in the pathological group indicates that peak cortical thickness peaks at a later age. Panel (a) in the figure shows the average cortical thickness in the prefrontal cortex. By the age of 10, 95% of the children in the healthy group had achieved peak cortical thickness while only 45% of children in the ADHD group had done so. This pattern means that the age of attaining peak cortical thickness is later in the pathological group and may help explain ADHD deficits in core cognitive control, including response inhibition, working memory, and temporal processing, all of which rely on the prefrontal cortex.

The maturational delay may also help explain why some individuals seem to "grow out of" ADHD. Figure 5.5 may help explain this point. Shaw and colleagues observed that, although all children in the study had a diagnosis of ADHD at baseline (a criterion for being in the study in the first place), by mid adolescence only 37% of them still had an ADHD diagnosis at a follow-up assessment approximately 5 years later (Shaw et al., 2010). The remaining patients had either partial remission (42% of participants) or full remission (21% of participants), which is consistent with a striking feature of ADHD, the tendency for symptomatic improve-ment in roughly 30–40% as children move into adolescence (Mannuzza et al., 1991). This observation suggests that developmental disorders are not stable and that maturational changes may help ameliorate problem-atic phenotypes. Examination of the neurodevelopmental trajectories of these three groups suggests that there was convergence between the trajectories of the remitted ADHD group and the typically developing group such that by late adolescence there was "normalization" of corti-cal thickness in the parietal cortex and in the prefrontal cortex of those whose ADHD symptoms were no longer present. In contrast, the group

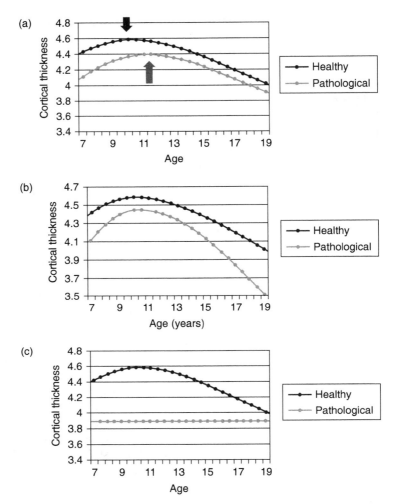

Figure 5.4 Hypothetical developmental trajectories of cortical development proposed by Shaw et al. (2010). The top panel illustrates a hypothetical *delayed* trajectory whereby a pathological group experiences delayed cortical development compared to a healthy (non-pathological) group. The middle panel illustrates an *accelerated velocity* in the pathological compared to the healthy group. The bottom panel illustrates a *deviant* trajectory whereby the pathological group exhibits a developmental trajectory unlike the form of the healthy group.

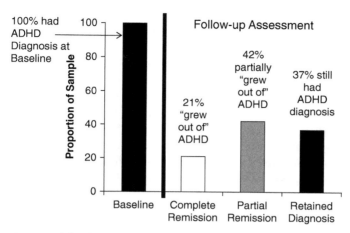

Figure 5.5 In a study by Shaw, Gogtay, and Rapoport (2010), there was a change in ADHD diagnosis among some research participants who had received an ADHD diagnosis at baseline. Over half the sample exhibited either complete or partial remission at a follow-up visit whereas only 37% of the sample retained the original ADHD diagnosis.

of ADHD subjects who retained ADHD symptoms at follow-up continued to show non-progressive cortical deficits (Shaw et al., 2010). This suggests that initial presentation of ADHD in some children (those who eventually remit) may be a reflection of delayed neurodevelopmental maturation such that they eventually "catch up" to their non-ADHD peers. In some cases, this occurs following pharmacological treatment (Shaw et al., 2009). Once their neurodevelopmental trajectory converges with typical development (that is, they no longer differ from children who never had ADHD), there is significant clinical improvement. In contrast, persistence of ADHD (children who do not "grow out of" the disorder) is associated with increasing divergence from typical development. This means that over time these children look less and less like their typically developing peers.

Disrupted Velocity
The middle panel (Figure 5.4b) illustrates the hypothesized possibility that children with a pathology evince an accelerated velocity of the same developmental trajectory healthy children experience. A disrupted velocity refers to neurodevelopmental trajectories that exhibit the same general pattern as in typical development but at an aberrant *speed*. Youth with disrupted velocity exhibit the same childhood phase of cortical thickening followed by the adolescent phase of cortical thinning but this

process occurs earlier than it should. The acceleration of the pruning process (cortical thinning) coincides with the emergence of pathological behavior. The best example of this is in a developmental disorder that is called childhood-onset schizophrenia (COS). Schizophrenia involves a range of problems with thinking (cognition), behavior, or emotions. Schizophrenia may result in some combination of hallucinations, delusions, and disordered thinking and behavior. Signs and symptoms may vary, but they reflect an impaired ability to function. COS is basically the same as schizophrenia in adults, but it is defined by the onset of psychotic symptoms before age 13 years. Although rare, occurring ~1/500th as often as adult-onset schizophrenia, the COS cases ($n = 102$ to date) exhibit neurobiological and behavioral phenotypes that are consistent with severe adult-onset schizophrenia (Gogtay and Rapoport, 2008). This has a profound impact on a youth's behavior and development. With childhood schizophrenia, the early age of onset presents special challenges for diagnosis, treatment, educational needs, and emotional and social development.

A longitudinal study of 100 patients with COS revealed that they exhibit disrupted velocity neurodevelopmental trajectories. As shown in Figure 5.4b, the gray matter loss rate was much faster (in that it occurred at an earlier age) in youth with schizophrenia relative to healthy adolescents (Vidal et al., 2006). This effect was observed in multiple cortical regions, including the superior frontal gyrus, superior parietal lobe, and lateral temporal cortex (Thompson et al., 2004).

Deviant Trajectories

As illustrated in Figure 5.4c, individuals with deviant trajectories exhibit patterns that do not at all resemble typical development. This means that, in contrast to delayed or disrupted velocity trajectories, individuals in this group will never "catch up" to peers. Instead, these individuals experience a completely distinct pattern of brain development, an effect that is reflected in their atypical behavioral development as well. For instance, children and adolescents with Down's syndrome evince brain development that is distinct from other neurodevelopmental disorders in terms of anatomical size and brain function.

5.5.5 Effects of Psychopharmacological Treatment on Neurodevelopment

The stimulant methylphenidate (also known as Ritalin) is the most commonly prescribed drug for the treatment of ADHD. Neuroanatomical studies reveal that long-term stimulant treatment may normalize structural brain changes typically observed in white matter, the anterior cingulate cortex, the thalamus, and the cerebellum in ADHD, meaning that the treatment eventually leads to structural changes that resemble youth without ADHD (Schweren, de Zeeuw, and Durston, 2013). Similar effects have been observed with functional MRI, suggesting that, in addition to acute effects on brain functioning, children with ADHD who use methylphenidate neurobiologically function more similarly to children without ADHD than those with the disorder who do not use the stimulant (Schweren et al., 2013). However, it is important to note that there are vast individual differences in the effects of the drug on behavior and brain profiles. Genetic predispositions, age, symptom severity, and rearing environment all contribute to how effective and neurobiologically impactful drugs are.

5.6 Functional Development of the Prefrontal Cortex

Since the early 2000s there has been much interest in the popular press about the adolescent brain. Most of this coverage has focused on the prefrontal cortex because it is the last brain region to mature anatomically and functionally. Adult-like patterns of brain function in the prefrontal cortex begin to emerge during adolescence.

In the previous section we discussed the anatomical changes that occur in the adolescent brain. These changes are important and have been associated with differences in behavior and well-being. However, structural changes in the brain do not necessarily implicate the same functional changes. Data suggest that anatomical immaturity is related to functional immaturity, but remember that structure and function are distinct.

What is *functional development*? It refers to the development of how the brain works, solves problems, processes information, and responds to new situations. Over two decades of research on the functional development of the prefrontal cortex has taught us that children and adolescents use their prefrontal cortex differently from how they will eventually use it as adults. This phenomenon is particularly true in neurocognitive behaviors that rely on the prefrontal cortex the most, including cognitive control, working memory, decision-making, and goal-oriented behavior. The development of the prefrontal cortex, particularly the ventrolateral prefrontal cortex (VLPFC) and dorsolateral prefrontal cortex (DLPFC), is believed to play an important role in the maturation of higher cognitive abilities. The VLPFC and DLPFC have connections to other prefrontal regions as well as sensory and motor regions, all of which support response inhibition. Moreover, evidence of late structural changes in these regions makes them particularly important for studying neurocognitive development. Tasks that recruit and rely on these regions are therefore ideally suited for investigating the neurobiological changes that underlie neurocognitive maturation.

5.6.1 Cognitive Control

Broadly defined, **cognitive control** refers to the ability to ignore distracting or irrelevant information, thoughts, and actions in favor of relevant ones (Casey, Tottenham, and Fossella, 2002). The ability to suppress attention or action when appropriate develops over the first two decades of life. The change in cognitive control across this time is very apparent. A 1 year old has a much harder time sitting still in a restaurant than a 10 year old, for instance. Around the transition to adolescence, the still-developing cognitive control skills are also apparent, as adolescents must increasingly self-regulate and make decisions in the absence of adult guidance and supervision. Of course there are individual differences in this behavior but this developmental pattern is the norm.

Studies to examine the neurobiological correlates of this phenomenon have tended to use child-friendly versions of standard cognitive control tasks, including the Flanker task, Stroop task, Antisaccade task, and Go/No-Go task (Casey, Giedd, and Thomas, 2000; Luna et al., 2001; Tamm, Menon, and Reiss, 2002). Box 5.3 provides greater detail on these tasks.

A seminal study by Casey and colleagues used the Go/No-Go task to measure cognitive control (Casey et al., 1997). This study revolutionized the field of developmental cognitive neuroscience for two reasons. First, it demonstrated the feasibility of assaying brain function in healthy, awake youth. Second, it provided evidence that there are developmental differences in how the prefrontal cortex functions. Since then, other studies using either the Go/No-Go task or other cognitive control tasks have shown that younger participants rely on a larger, more diffuse swath of the prefrontal cortex than adults when engaged in a cognitive control challenge (Casey, Galván, and Hare, 2005). It is now widely accepted that delayed functional development of the prefrontal cortex contributes to limitations in self-control and behavioral regulation in young participants (Casey and Caudle, 2013). There is also evidence that the pattern of functional activation in the prefrontal cortex that correlates with task performance becomes more focal or fine-tuned with increased activation,

Box 5.3 Cognitive Control Tasks

Many different computer tasks are used to assess cognitive control. The most commonly used to study the development of cognitive control are described here.

Flanker task. The task is used to assess the ability to suppress responses that are inappropriate in a particular context. The target stimulus is flanked (surrounded) by non-target stimuli which correspond either to the same directional response as the target (congruent flankers), to the opposite response (incongruent flankers), or to neither (neutral flankers) (Eriksen and Eriksen, 1974). In the images below, the target stimulus is the middle arrow

Trial type	Stimuli
Congruent Flanker trial	> > >
Incongruent Flanker trial	< > <
Neutral trial	x > x

Go/No-Go task. A task in which stimuli are presented in a continuous stream and participants perform a binary decision on each stimulus. One of the outcomes requires participants to make a motor response (go), whereas the other requires participants to withhold a response (no-go). Accuracy and reaction time are measured for each event. Go events typically occur with higher frequency than no-go events. Participants are instructed to press for all stimuli except for one particular type of stimulus. In adults, the stimuli are commonly letters of the alphabet and they are instructed to press for all letters except for X. Child-friendly versions of this often include cartoon

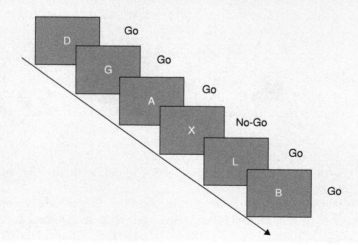

characters. For instance, a Pokemon version instructs participants to press for all characters except Meowth. Go/No-go tasks that examine responses to emotion typically use a range of emotions (either pictures or words). Participants are instructed to press for all emotions and to withhold a response to a particular emotion (e.g. "Press to all emotions except happy faces").

Stroop task. In this task, participants view color names presented in various ink colors and are instructed to name the color of the ink. In incongruent stimuli, color names and ink colors are non-matching. When the name of a color (e.g., "blue," "green," or "red") is printed in a color not denoted by the name (e.g., the word "red" printed in blue ink instead of red ink), naming the color of the word takes longer and is more prone to errors than when the color of the ink matches the name of the color.

BLUE   GREEN   YELLOW

PINK   RED   ORANGE

GRAY   BLACK   PURPLE

TAN   WHITE   BROWN

Antisaccade task. In this task, the participant is asked to fixate on a centrally located target. A stimulus, such as a light, is presented to one side of the target. The participant is instructed to make a saccade (directional eye movement) to the opposite direction from the light.

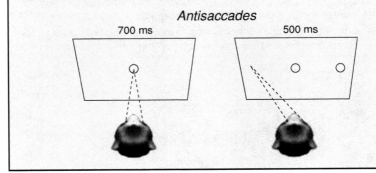

Antisaccades

whereas brain regions that are not correlated with how well a participant performs on the task decrease in activity with age (Durston, Davidson, et al., 2006).

To test whether different aspects of cognitive control are supported by the same neural regions, Bunge and colleagues conducted an fMRI study using the Flanker task and the Go/No-Go task (Bunge, Dudukovic,

Box 5.4 Prefrontal Cortex Neuron Number in Atypical Development

The development of the prefrontal cortex is prolonged in humans. It is also one of the brain regions that shows the greatest variability across age, individuals, and pathological states. For instance, clinical phenotypes associated with autism are often preceded by atypical growth in the prefrontal cortex. Overgrowth and neural dysfunction are evident in children as young as 9–18 months of age (Courchesne, Carper, and Akshoomoff, 2003) and yield a neurobiological trajectory that is distinctly different by the time individuals with autism reach adolescence. Postmortem tissue of youth with and without autism from national brain banks and the National Institutes of Health was used to quantify the number of neurons in the prefrontal cortex. The children and adolescents ranged in age from 2 to 16 years old. Most of the children died of acute global ischemic hypoxia (drowning, hanging, electrocution) but one each died of an automobile crash, rhabdomyosarcoma, and cardiac arrest. Brain weight in the autistic group deviated by 17.6% from the normative mean weight for age, while brain weight in controls was 0.2% greater than the normative mean for age, which yielded a significant difference in brain weight between the autistic and control group. Additionally, prefrontal cortex neuron counts were significantly different between the groups: there were 67% more neurons in the dorsolateral prefrontal cortex in the autistic cases compared with the control cases. The average neuron count was 1.94 billion neurons in the youth with autism compared to 1.16 billion in the youth without autism. These significant differences remained even after controlling for age of the individual. Interestingly these postmortem data coincide with anatomical differences observed using MRI volumetric data in living toddlers with autism (Carper and Courchesne, 2005). As we learned about in Chapter 4, an overwhelming majority of cortical neurons are generated in prenatal life (and the evidence is in fact mixed as to whether there is cortical neurogenesis after birth). Therefore, the authors note that the pathological increase in neuron numbers they observed in children with autism suggests prenatal causes, including overabundant proliferation, reduced pruning, or both (Gohlke, Griffith, and Faustman, 2007). Cortical neuron proliferation typically results in a net overabundance of neurons by as much as 100% between 10 and 20 weeks' gestation. During the third trimester of gestation and shortly after birth, normative cell removal mechanisms (apoptosis) remove neurons. Aberrations in this process could lead to excess neurons in the brain (Kanold, 2009).

Thomason, Vaidya, and Gabrieli, 2002). The Flanker task was used to measure interference suppression and the Go/No-Go task to measure response inhibition. Behaviorally, children performed just as well as adults in the congruent and neutral trials of the Flanker task (the easier trials) but were less accurate than them in the incongruent trials and the no-go trials (the more difficult trials). This suggests that, although children were as adept at adults at some aspects of cognitive control, they struggled to a greater extent when they were tasked with suppressing interfering information and inhibiting a response. They were also slower to respond than adults in all conditions, probably a reflection of their immaturely myelinated axons. Evidence of the interference effect comes from the finding that the incongruent flankers tacked on 45 milliseconds to the children's response as compared to their reaction time for the neutral (easier) trials. In comparison, the incongruent flankers added only 22 milliseconds to the adult response time. Forty-five milliseconds may not seem like a lot of time, but, given that our brains process visual information in ~15 milliseconds, it is actually quite a delay.

What helps adults overcome the potentially interfering effects of a distracting stimulus? They exhibit greater activation in areas of ventrolateral prefrontal cortex on the right hemisphere, and in particular Brodmann area 44 (pars opercularis of the inferior frontal gyrus) and Brodmann area 47 (orbital cortex) than children during the incongruent trials. In contrast, children rely on the areas in the left ventrolateral prefrontal cortex, including Brodmann area 45 (pars triangularis of the inferior frontal cortex) and Brodmann area 13 (posterior insular cortex). In fact, the magnitude of activation children exhibited in the left ventrolateral prefrontal cortex was the same as that exhibited by adults in the right ventrolateral prefrontal cortex. This explains why children *can* perform the task but just not as well (or as quickly) as adults: because they rely on a brain region that is simply not as helpful as the ones adults use. It is similar to how we can imagine using a Swiss army knife to open a cardboard box, but that a box-cutter is better suited for the task. Similarly, just because one particular brain region *can* (and does) help perform a task does not mean it is the best candidate for the job. One major function of neurocognitive development is to help the developing brain determine, typically through trial and error, which brain regions and systems are optimal for particular cognitive challenges. The data from the Bunge study support this view, and suggest that there is a shift in cognitive strategy and supporting neural regions as the prefrontal cortex becomes more mature.

In general, studies from different labs indicate that the inferior frontal gyrus (IFG) and premotor regions increase in activation with age (Bunge et al., 2002; Rubia et al., 2000) on tasks such as the Go/No-go (Rubia et al., 2006; Tamm et al., 2002), Flanker (Bunge et al., 2002), Stop (Rubia, Smith, Taylor, and Brammer, 2007), Stroop (Marsh et al., 2006), and Antisaccade tasks (Luna, Padmanabhan, and O'Hearn, 2010).

However, more activation is not necessarily superior or always indicative of greater maturation. Some of these same studies, as well as others, report age-related decreases in the activation of other prefrontal regions, including IFG and medial frontal gyri. For instance, a Go/No-Go study on 8 to 20 year olds showed increases in activation in the medial frontal gyrus as well as decreases in the IFG (Tamm et al., 2002). These authors hypothesized that age-related increases in medial frontal activation reflect improved inhibitory processes with age, related to limitations in the processing of information in this region in younger individuals, while age-related decreases in IFG activation reflect the decreased effort required to exert inhibitory control with age (Luna et al., 2010). Luna and colleagues have also reported that adolescents exhibit increased DLPFC activation relative to either younger or older groups, perhaps reflecting that although adolescents show adult-like inhibition, this achievement requires greater effort (Luna et al., 2001).

Motivated Cognitive Control

In the next chapter, we will learn about the strong influence that motivational systems have on behavior in adolescence. In a clever study, researchers aimed to determine whether this reward and motivation bias might be useful during cognitive control challenges in adolescents (Geier and Luna, 2009). They added a reward component to the traditional Antisaccade task (Box 5.3); in this version participants were given the opportunity to earn money on some of the trials. Adults performed very well (at around 90% accuracy) on both rewarded and unrewarded trials and there were no significant differences in performance between the two trial types. However, this was not the case in the adolescent group, whose performance was significantly improved on the trials in which they knew that their performance would be rewarded with money. This behavioral change in adolescents was associated with greater activation in the ventral striatum on rewarded trials versus unrewarded trials. In fact, the adult brain activation was relatively unchanged on rewarded versus unrewarded trials, as if the adult brain was not using that information to perform the task. In contrast, the adolescent brain was squarely focused on that information to perform the task! This suggests that incentives can improve cognitive control performance in adolescents.

Emotional Interference

Susceptibility to interference is one reason that children and adolescents exhibit worse cognitive control than adults. Research suggests that when the interference is of an emotional nature, the developmental differences in cognition are even stronger. This is particularly important to understand across adolescence, given the heightened emotional affective reactivity. Emotions must frequently be regulated so that appropriate behavior can be displayed, such as when frustration must be controlled or temptation avoided. To study the effects of emotion on cognitive control, researchers often add an emotional component to cognitive control tasks. The Go/No-Go task presents letters against a plain white screen. In an emotional version of the Go/No-Go task, the letters are presented against a backdrop of emotional scenes or images. These images might include a crying boy or a ferocious snake displaying its fangs. Positive and non-emotional images, of cute puppies or household items for instance, are also included as controls. Using this task, Cohen-Gilbert and Thomas (2013) found that pre-adolescents and adolescents do not differ from adults in how well they perform on the task when the letters are presented on positive or neutral images. However, their cognitive control significantly suffers when the letters are presented on a negative image. The authors interpret these findings to mean that younger adolescents, when required to exert inhibitory control, are more readily disrupted by emotional information than are older adolescents and adults (Cohen-Gilbert and Thomas, 2013). Furthermore, emotional inputs appear to derail regulatory efforts more easily in this age range, even when the emotion information is not directly relevant to the regulatory task.

A neuroimaging study that also examined the effects of affect on cognitive control found similar behavioral effects. Using an emotional Go/No-Go task that used emotional faces instead of letters, Somerville and colleagues reported that performance falters when participants must exert cognitive control in the presence of an emotional cue versus a neutral cue (Somerville, Hare, and Casey, 2011). This behavioral deficit was paralleled by enhanced activation of the ventral striatum, an effect that was not observed in children or adults. In fact, in the unemotional conditions, the teens performed just as well as adults. These data remind us that although cognitive control and the neural systems that support it continue to undergo maturation during the adolescent years, adolescents are indeed quite capable of effective cognitive control in unemotional contexts. However, under emotional contexts, cognitive control requires a bit more (maybe sometimes a lot more) behavioral and neural resources in adolescents than it does in adults.

Individual Differences in Cognitive Control

Asserting that all children and adolescents struggle with cognitive control or that they lack self-control due to an immature prefrontal cortex is an oversimplification. Clearly, some youth exhibit this phenotype to a lesser or greater extent, highlighting the importance of considering the role of individual differences in behavior and brain development.

One innovative study examined this question by assessing participants at two time points: 40 years apart! This is highly unusual and innovative in a psychological study. In the original study, a cohort of 4-year-old preschoolers were assessed on their *delay of gratification*, the ability to resist the temptation of an immediate reward in favor of a large reward. Delay of gratification is considered one form of cognitive control. Walter Mischel and colleagues used the now famous "marshmallow test" to examine whether children would choose a small reward (one marshmallow) immediately or a larger reward (two marshmallows) after a short delay of a few minutes. Figure 5.6 depicts a child performing this experiment, which has been replicated in laboratories all around the world. Children's behavior fell into two categories in the original study: (1) limited self-control in children who ate the treat almost immediately (low delayers) or (2) greater self-control in children who waited for some instructed amount of time in order to gain two treats (high delayers). These two types of behaviors provide an example of individual differences in self-control.

In a follow-up longitudinal study on the same sample of individuals (now in their 40s), Mischel collaborated with B.J. Casey to examine the stability of individual differences in self-control. They found that individuals who had more difficulty delaying gratification at age 4 continued to show reduced self-control 40 years later (Casey et al., 2011). At the follow-up visit, participants performed a Go/No-Go task while undergoing fMRI. Individuals who had been classified as low delayers (poor self-control) as children had greater difficulty controlling their behavior than those who had been classified as high delayers. They also exhibited less activation in the VLPFC, suggesting that the poor response inhibition was due to suboptimal engagement of the prefrontal cortex. What is particularly interesting is that this effect was not restricted to the laboratory:

Figure 5.6 A young participant resisting temptation during the delay of gratification task. See color plate 10.

individuals who are classified as high delayers evince advantages in other aspects of life. On average, they have higher SAT scores of roughly 210 points, earn higher incomes as adults, and have generally better psychological well-being. In contrast, those who are classified as low delayers experience more relationship problems, higher rates of obesity, criminal behavior and drug addiction, and poorer academic and work performance. These findings highlight individual differences in self-control that are independent of age and which can persist throughout the lifespan.

5.7 Functional Connectivity

One of the most valuable innovations in cognitive neuroscience was the creation of statistical tools that allow us to measure functional connectivity in the brain. In Chapter 3 we learned in greater detail about functional

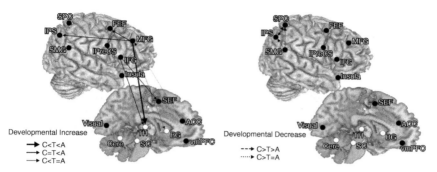

Figure 5.7 Developmental patterns of functional connectivity underlying cognitive control. This figure illustrates nodes that exhibit developmental increases in connectivity (*left*) and developmental decreases in connectivity (*right*) among children (C), adolescent (T), and adult (A) participants. SPC = bilateral superior parietal cortex; IPS = bilateral intraparietal sulcus; SMG = bilateral supramarginal gyrus; FEF = frontal eye field; MFG = medial frontal gyrus; IPreCS = bilateral inferior of precentral sulcus; IFG = inferior frontal gyrus; Cere = cerebellum; TH = bilateral dorsal medial thalamus; SC = superior colliculus; SEF = supplementary eye field; ACC = anterior cingulate cortex; vmPFC = ventromedial prefrontal cortex; BG = basal ganglia.

connectivity. It is the study of how different brain regions and neural networks communicate with one another when performing a particular task (or even when simply at rest).

Cognitive control of behavior is supported by a wide network of brain regions, including prefrontal and parietal cortices, that interact with subcortical areas, including the striatum, thalamus, cerebellum, and brain stem, forming a circuitry that supports top-down control of behavior (Sweeney et al., 1996). Beatriz Luna and her colleagues used one method of functional connectivity to show that connections that are governed by the prefrontal cortex become established from childhood to adolescence and strengthened into adulthood (Hwang, Velanova, and Luna, 2010). Figure 5.7 illustrates these findings. Notice the black circles on the brain rendering; these represent the different brain regions (nodes) that are found to be most involved in cognitive control. Although this chapter has focused mainly on the prefrontal cortex there are many other regions all over the cortex that play an important role as well. The arrows on the image indicate the direction of control. For instance, these data indicate that an important region in the prefrontal cortex, the IFG, controls subcortical regions. The thickness of the arrows indicates whether these connections become stronger or weaker across development. Enhanced communication in the adults and adolescents is associated with age-related improvements in cognitive processing (Stevens, Kiehl, Pearlson, and Calhoun, 2007). Since the same basic connections are evident since childhood, these data suggest that the basic architecture and cross-talk between brain regions is set up fairly early in life and that there is great architectural stability across the lifespan. However, what changes is the strength of these connections. In addition to normative maturation, experience largely feeds this strengthening.

5.8 Working Memory

Working memory refers to the temporary storage and processing of new and previously learned information. Since it is the ability to keep information online for a short period of time for cognitive processing, working memory is a critical component of neurocognition. Without it, it would be very challenging to reason, to learn, and to maintain attention. It would also be very hard to stay focused in a conversation, remember how to drive a car, or study for an exam. Although fundamental working memory skills and their neural substrates are established early in life, the refinement and maturation of working memory persists through adolescence Luna et al., 2015.

Working memory can be assessed in a variety of ways, including through verbal, numerical, and spatial working memory tasks. Improvement in all domains occurs throughout childhood but perhaps the most useful are tasks that rely on spatial working memory, because they are devoid of sophisticated verbal comprehension and strategies (which tend to be better in older children and adults). The oculomotor delayed response task (ODR) is a classic spatial working memory task in which participants make an eye movement (also referred to as a saccade) to the location on a computer screen where they remember having previously seen a target, after a varying delay period during which they maintain their gaze on a central fixation stimulus (Luna et al., 2010). You can imagine that the longer the delay period is, the harder it is to remember where the target stimulus appeared. Adults are quite good at this task but research has shown that children lag in this ability until the late teenage years, when accuracy begins to match that of adults (Luna et al., 2004). This developmental pattern was evident across different difficulty levels of the task (manipulated by changing the delay periods).

What accounts for the protracted development of working memory? In addition to the ongoing development of the neural substrates required to sustain working memory, there are maturational limitations in related cognitive constructs. For instance, younger children have greater difficulty ignoring distracting information, primarily due to immaturities in inhibition, which weakens the ability to exhibit mature working memory. This interference is particularly evident in tasks that present competing information during the delay period (Bjorklund and Harnishfeger, 1990). Adults are also more likely to use strategies such as verbal rehearsal or employing associations between to-be-remembered items during working memory maintenance than are adolescents (Van Leijenhorst, Crone, and van der Molen, 2007). These strategies help the individual tap into other neural systems that support the task at hand. When children and adolescents are explicitly instructed to use auxiliary strategies, as adults automatically do, they do show improvements in working memory. However, their improvement is limited and typically does not approximate adult levels of accuracy. This suggests that working memory is a holistic process that relies on distributed cognitive strategies and neural substrates. Luna and colleagues (2010) propose that what continues to improve through adolescence is the "ability to be precise, to control distraction, and to monitor performance, resulting in more exact and adaptable working memory. That is, working memory is on-line early in development but processes related to precision of the maintained representation continue to improve with age."

Similar to other aspects of cognitive control, working memory is supported by a broad network of neural regions, each of which matures across development. Increasing working memory capacity in children and adolescents is positively correlated with brain activity, most consistently localized to the intraparietal cortex, superior frontal sulcus, and dorsolateral prefrontal cortex (Klingberg, Forssberg, and Westerberg, 2002; Kwon, Reiss, and Menon, 2002). The VLPFC, striatum, middle temporal gyrus, and cerebellum are also active during working memory (see Fuster, 2001 for a comprehensive review).

fMRI studies using simple working memory tasks, such as the n-back task, which requires online maintenance of the arrangement of previous cues, have consistently shown that prefrontal and parietal systems in particular are engaged as early as 8 years of age but that the magnitude of activation changes across development. In contrast, studies using more complex working memory tasks that require manipulation (Crone, Wendelken, Donohue, Van Leijenhorst, and Bunge, 2006) and monitoring of information (Oleson, Macoveanu, Tegner, and Klingberg, 2007) show that children and adults differ in the regions they use to complete the task. Adolescents exhibit an interesting pattern of activation and behavior that is distinct from both children and adults: although they outperform children (and do just as well as adults), they require a broader magnitude of activation in the DLPFC, suggesting that they may require greater effort to do so. Based on many working memory studies, scientists have suggested that, whereas the prefrontal cortex may support general executive aspects of working memory including suppression of distractors and manipulation of relevant information, the parietal cortex may support the mnemonic aspects of working memory (Luna et al., 2010). Evidence suggests that these regions do not work in isolation but rather that the improvements in working memory capacity are associated with the integration of these regions. Longitudinal research shows that an important basis for the development of working memory is the white matter connectivity of fronto-parietal and fronto-striatal tracts (Darki and Klingberg, 2014).

5.9 Implications

Throughout this chapter we have learned about the complex, dynamic, and protracted development of the prefrontal cortex. It should be clear that these characteristics are what make the prefrontal cortex "shapeable" by the environment. It is both reliant on and receptive to input from the world in which it lives. This narrative should remind you of what we learned in Chapter 4 about neuroplasticity. Is the prefrontal cortex plastic? As with every other scientific question, the answer is yes and no and it depends. Yes, it is receptive to the environment, particularly during the "topiary" phase of earlier development. No, this level of plasticity does not persist throughout life and it is certainly unclear as to whether it occurs at the neuronal level. And it depends on the timing of the input and the neural targets of the input. What we do know is that the cognitive elements that undergo the most dynamic and protracted development are the ones most amenable to change.

The strongest evidence that cognition and neurocognitive development are malleable comes from intervention studies that specifically target cognitive control functions. Most of these interventions have focused on inhibitory control, working memory, and cognitive flexibility, which collectively are sometimes called "executive functions" and which all rely on the prefrontal cortex. The majority of these studies have been conducted in children and adolescents who struggle with their executive functions and who therefore exhibit academic, relationship, and mental health impairments. Boosting these cognitive skills earlier rather than later in life is critical because executive function problems in early childhood predict them later in life (Friedman et al., 2007).

There is no shortage of cognitive interventions in the literature so a review of them all is a book unto itself. The reader is directed to Diamond (2012) for a comprehensive review of these interventions. We will instead focus on the common themes the field has deduced from the interventions that have proven to be the most reliable, efficacious, and generalizable to the real world. First, youth who have the biggest room for improvement are those who improve most (Diamond, 2012). Second, practice makes perfect. The majority of these training programs occur over several weeks to leverage the fact that the brain learns best through repeated exposure. Third, not all cognitive domains are created equally. There are many variations on working memory training, for instance, and whether a child is trained on spatial versus temporal working memory will have effects on the overall gains in working memory. Fourth, one size does not fit all. What may be very effective for one population of participants (perhaps who vary on age, ethnicity, or income status) may be terrible for another population. It is certainly the case that the success of inhibitory control training depends on the age of participants. Although 9 year olds exhibit improvements in cognitive flexibility and inhibitory control using a computerized training program, no evidence thus far has found similar gains in 4 to 6 year olds. Finally, physical activity can be helpful in improving cognitive control. Although there is less research on the benefits of physical activity (such as exercise programs and yoga/mindfulness programs) as compared to computerized programs, encouraging evidence suggests that it is worth pursuing. One study found that adolescent girls (10 to 13 years old) who were randomly assigned to yoga training showed greater improvements in planning and cognitive flexibility than counterparts who did not receive yoga (Manjunath and Telles, 2001). Other studies have shown that activities that include both physical activity and character development help youth improve basic neurocognition such as working memory and inhibition and academic performance (Esteban-Cornejo et al., 2015).

How long-lasting the effects of cognitive training are over time is still uncharted territory. However, there is good evidence to suggest that there are (at least some) improvements following these programs. In addition to determining *how* effective they are, it remains to be seen whether it is a good idea to implement them in children who are not struggling with neurocognition. We know that the relative deficits in neurocognition in children versus adults are due to an immaturity in the prefrontal cortex. Perhaps this is biology's way of saying that being in a state of immaturity is adaptive for our species.

5.10 Chapter Summary

- Higher cognition differentiates humans from nonhuman animals.
- The prefrontal cortex is the primary hub for higher cognition.
- The prefrontal cortex exhibits protracted development through the mid-20s and is the last brain region to develop.
- The prefrontal cortex works with other cortical regions and subcortical regions to support cognitive control, working memory, and response inhibition.
- Developmental disorders show deficits in prefrontal cortex structure and function.
- Cognitive control deficits in children and adolescents correspond with delayed development of the prefrontal cortex.
- Working memory also exhibits delayed development that is based on the delayed development of the prefrontal cortex and interactions with other brain regions.

5.11 Review Questions

1 What are the three primary domains that encompass neurocognition?
2 What is the role of the prefrontal cortex in neurocognition?
3 How do the neural mechanisms supporting cognitive control change across development?
4 How do neural mechanisms underlying cognitive control and motivation interact during adolescence?

Further Reading

Casey, B.J., and Caudle, K. (2013). The teenage brain: self control. *Current Directions in Psychological Science*, 22, 82–87.

Diamond, A. (2012). Activities and programs that improve children's executive functions. *Current Directions in Psychological Science*, 21(5), 335–341.

Luna, B., Marek, S., Larsen, B., Tervo-Clemmens, B., and Chahal, R. (2015). An integrative model of the maturation of cognitive control. *Annual Review of Neuroscience*, 38, 151–170.

Miller, E.K., and Cohen, J.D. (2001). An integrative theory of prefrontal cortex function. *Annual Review of Neuroscience*, 24, 167–202.

CHAPTER SIX

Motivational Systems

Learning Objectives

- Learn about neural systems that support reward processing.
- Discuss the role of dopamine in reward processing.
- Learn about the development of the dopamine system.
- Discuss how the adolescent brain supports heightened sensitivity to reward.
- Discuss the relationship between reward circuitry and risk-taking.

6.1 Introduction

Take a moment to think of your fondest memory. If you are like most people, you are probably thinking of a time in your adolescence or maybe in your early adulthood. Is it a coincidence that teenagers are usually the ones having the most fun? But as we will review in this chapter, there are neurobiological explanations for the adolescent tendency to have fun, to seek out rewards, and to engage in greater risk-taking behavior than children or adults. It turns out it is not simply because of their close friendships but also has to do with the changes occurring in mesolimbic brain regions. The mesolimbic system is commonly referred to as the motivational system in the brain because it plays a large role in motivating and mobilizing organisms. In the first half of this chapter we will focus on what is known about the neural systems that process rewards and risky behavior in adolescents. In the second half we will review the role that the mesolimbic system has in learning.

6.2 What Is a Reward?

A reward is any stimulus that an organism finds pleasurable. For some of us, that stimulus might be a piece of chocolate (Figure 6.1) or a good grade on an exam. Although there are vast individual differences in what each person finds rewarding, the neural regions that govern reward share a few characteristics. First, they are rich in the neurotransmitter dopamine

Figure 6.1 A chocolate reward.

and are in frequent communication with one another, comprising what is known as the "reward system." Second, the neural systems that process reward are conserved across age, organisms, and species. This means that the brain of a monkey processes reward in much the same way that a human brain does, by using the neurotransmitter dopamine. Third, the brain is consistent in how it processes different *types* of reward, including primary rewards, such as sugar, and secondary rewards, such as money.

There is a marked *change* in how organisms respond to, seek out, and work for rewards across development. The greatest changes occur at two key points in development: as individuals transition in and transition out of puberty, making adolescents more sensitive and responsive to reward than other age groups. Relative to children or adults, adolescents exhibit increased behavioral motivation to obtain rewards and greater arousal in response to rewards (Galván, 2013b). There is also a peak in reward- and sensation-seeking behaviors (Steinberg et al., 2009), sensitivity to monetary incentives (Smith, Xiao, and Bechara, 2012) and social rewards (Albert, Chein, and Steinberg, 2013), and even greater reactivity to sweet substances in mid adolescence (Galván and McGlennen, 2013; Post and Kemper, 1993) compared to older and younger individuals.

6.3 The Reward System

The **reward system**, one of the most studied brain systems, was discovered by accident. James Olds, a postdoctoral scholar at McGill University, was working with Peter Milner when he came upon the curious observation that rats seemed to enjoy being stimulated in a particular region of the brain. He and Milner had been stimulating certain areas of the rat brain, mainly the limbic system, to test the hypothesis that electrical stimulation was uncomfortable. In the experiment, he implanted electrodes into the rats' brains and passed an electric current when they entered a certain corner of a cage. He predicted that they would scurry away from that corner if they found the electrical stimulation uncomfortable. What he saw surprised him. Instead of running away he noticed that the rats came back around quickly to that corner after the first stimulation and even faster after the second! Olds and Milner quickly realized that the rats found stimulation of the brain region pleasurable. To confirm this hypothesis, they rigged up the testing apparatus so that rats could press a lever to stimulate their brain themselves. Consistent with their hypothesis, the rats pressed the lever as much as 700 times per hour! Soon after, they declared this brain region, the mesolimbic dopamine system, the "pleasure center" (Olds and Milner, 1954). It is now more commonly referred to as the reward system. Stimulation of this system is so powerfully rewarding that rats will self-stimulate repeatedly, preferring to do so over eating or drinking, so much so that they eventually die from exhaustion (Routtenberg, 1978).

They did not know it at the time but Olds and Milner's discovery unleashed a tidal wave of research on the reward system. In the decades since, there have been thousands of studies aimed at better characterizing the reward system in rodents, nonhuman primates, and humans.

6.3.1 The Development of the Dopamine System

At the heart of the reward system is the neurotransmitter **dopamine**. Although other neurotransmitters also fire when an organism experiences a reward, it is dopamine that does so most consistently and vigorously. It is not possible to measure actual levels of dopamine in the human brain, but luckily many mammalian species, including rodents and nonhuman primates, show similar patterns of reward-related behavior as humans. This conservation of dopamine-mediated reward processing across evolution (Spear, 2011) allows us to learn about the dopamine system from animals.

Studies comparing rats of different ages show that juvenile rats exhibit greater reward- and novelty-seeking (Douglas, Varlinskaya, and Spear, 2003), **risk-taking**, social interactions (Douglas, Varlinskaya, and Spear, 2004), and consummatory behavior (Friemel, Spanagel, and Schneider,

2010) than younger or older rats. For instance, adolescent rats are more sensitive than adult rats to the hedonic properties of sucrose (Wilmouth and Spear, 2009). They also demonstrate enhanced behavioral responses to novelty and social peers (Varlinskaya and Spear, 2008) compared to adult rats. The increased proclivity toward drugs in human adolescents versus adults is also observed in rats (Brenhouse and Andersen, 2008) and nonhuman primates (Nelson et al., 2009). In fact, adolescent mice are more likely to consume alcohol in the presence of other mice than when they are alone (Logue, Chein, Gould, Holliday, and Steinberg, 2014). Sounds eerily similar to the behavior of human adolescents, doesn't it? These observations dispel the idea that human adolescents are driven to reward-seeking and risk-taking behaviors simply because they model their friends' behaviors. Instead, the conservation of juvenile/adolescent-specific behavior across species suggests that there may be some neuro-biological reasons to explain heightened reward-seeking and risk-taking during adolescence.

Rodent models have shown that the mesolimbic dopamine system undergoes significant changes during adolescence. In a key brain region called the striatum, dopamine levels increase during adolescence and dopamine receptor expression increases from pre-adolescence to adolescence (Andersen, Dumont, and Teicher, 1997). Several reports have also noted that there is dopamine receptor overproduction followed by pruning during adolescence (Teicher, Andersen, and Hostetter, 1995). Striatal dopamine receptor binding peaks in adolescence at levels that are about 30–45% greater than those seen in adulthood (Teicher et al., 1995). Bolanos and colleagues demonstrated that striatal slices from adolescent rat brain were more sensitive to the dopamine uptake inhibitors cocaine and nomifensine than adults (Bolanos, Glatt, and Jackson, 1998), indicating that the adolescent brain is more neurochemically responsive to drugs of abuse.

Compared to adults, the adolescent rat brain releases more dopamine if stimulated by environmental or pharmacological challenges (Laviola, Pasucci, and Pieretti, 2001), despite reduced dopamine release in basal conditions (Andersen and Gazzara, 1993), and exhibit longer-sustained dopamine release following a social interaction (Robinson, Zitzman, Smith, and Spear, 2011).

A similar pattern of dopaminergic reorganization during adolescence is observed in the prefrontal cortex, albeit with a more protracted elimination period (Andersen, Thompson, Rutstein, Hostetter, and Teicher, 2000). Neurons in the prefrontal cortex also express higher levels of dopamine receptors during adolescence than older or younger rodents

(Brenhouse, Sonntag, and Andersen, 2008). Similarly, firing rates of dopamine neurons (McCutcheon and Marinelli, 2009) and the number of dopamine neurons that are activated in anticipation of reward (Sturman and Moghaddam, 2012) peak during the juvenile period. Together, these data suggest that, during adolescence, changes in dopamine neurochemistry may alter reward sensitivity in response to drugs, social interactions, and consummatory behaviors.

6.3.2 Reward Neurocircuitry

Neurocircuitry involved in reward processing is comprised of regions rich in dopamine and/or which receive innervation from dopaminergic neurons. Dopamine is a neurotransmitter, a chemical released by neurons as a signal to other neurons, that is critically involved in detecting, responding to, and learning from rewarding events (Schultz, Dayan, and Montague, 1997). Dopamine neurons fire when the organism experiences rewards (Roitman, Wheeler, Wightman, and Carelli, 2008), consumes drugs or food (Volkow, Wang, Fowler, and Tomasi, 2012), engages in social interactions (Robinson, Heien, and Wightman, 2002), and in response to unexpected events or stimuli (Takahashi et al., 2009).

At the center of this network is the cortico-ventral basal ganglia circuit (Haber, 2011) which consists of a distributed neural network that includes the ventral striatum, the anterior cingulate cortex, the orbitofrontal cortex, the ventral pallidum, and the midbrain dopamine neurons. The complex organization is illustrated in Figure 6.2. Additionally, auxiliary structures, including the dorsolateral prefrontal cortex, amygdala, hippocampus, thalamus, habenula, and regions in the brainstem help regulate reward neurocircuitry (Haber and Knutson, 2010). This network works in concert to integrate reward-related information from the environment in order to produce a relevant motor output (Everitt and Robbins, 2005).

The ventral striatum is the striatal region that has been most strongly implicated in reward in humans. It includes the nucleus accumbens and the broad continuity between the caudate nucleus and the putamen (Heimer et al., 1999). Most of the neuronal signaling that reaches the ventral striatum comes from the orbitofrontal cortex, insular cortex, cingulate cortex, and amygdala (Haber, 2011). Together, this complex network facilitates the coordinated effort that is required for an organism to predict, evaluate, and respond to a reward. Within the basal ganglia there is an elegant division of labor that produces a system in which specific regions are responsible for different aspects of reward

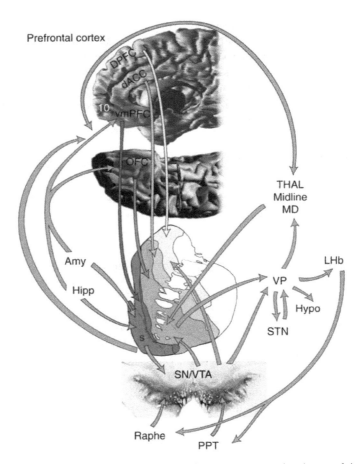

Figure 6.2 A schematic illustrating the primary brain structures and pathways of the reward circuit. 10 refers to Brodmann area 10; red arrow = input from the vmPFC; dark orange arrow = input from the OFC; light orange arrow = input from the dACC; yellow arrow = input from the dPFC; brown arrows = other main connections of the reward circuit. Amy = amygdala; dACC = dorsal anterior cingulate cortex; dPFC = dorsal prefrontal cortex; Hipp = hippocampus; LHb = lateral habenula; MD = mediodorsal; Hypo = hypothalamus; OFC = orbital frontal cortex; PPT = pedunculopontine nucleus; S = shell; SNc = substantia nigra, pars compacta; STN = subthalamic nucleus; Thal = thalamus; VP = ventral pallidum; VTA = ventral tegmental area; vmPFC = ventral medial prefrontal cortex. (Haber and Knutson, 2010.) See color plate 11.

processing, including evaluation of reward value, anticipation of reward, predictability, and risk. The anterior cingulate cortex and orbitofrontal regions mostly mediate error prediction, value, and the choice between short- and long-term gains (Haber, 2011). Cells in the ventral striatum and ventral pallidum respond to anticipation of reward and reward detection. Reward prediction and error detection signals are generated, in part, from the dopamine cells in the midbrain section of the brain. Additionally, reward-responsive activation is found throughout the striatum and substantia nigra, pars compacta. Together, the frontal regions that mediate reward, motivation, and affect regulation project primarily to the rostral striatum, including the nucleus accumbens, the medial caudate nucleus, and the medial and ventral rostral putamen. Another important region in the reward system is the lateral habenular nucleus, which mediates inhibition of dopamine activity by providing a negative reward-related signal to the substantia nigra when an expected reward does not occur (Matsumoto and Hikosaka, 2009). However, the habenula has received relatively less attention than the striatum in the adult human literature (Salas, Baldwin, de Biasi, and Montague, 2010) and no published studies in youth have reported the role of this region in the context of reward processing.

6.3.3 MRI Studies of the Adolescent Reward System

The brain regions implicated in reward processing undergo significant maturation in anatomical size during adolescence. Although the size of the overall brain remains relatively stable after approximately age 6, various regions of the brain undergo subtle but significant anatomical and functional changes throughout development. Sowell and colleagues reported significant differences between adolescents and adults in frontal cortex and striatum (Sowell, Thompson, Holmes, Jernigan, and Toga, 1999). In a longitudinal sample of almost 400 children, adolescents, and young adults, Giedd and colleagues at the National Institute of Mental Health examined gray matter volume and found differences between boys and girls in how several brain regions, including the frontal lobe and caudate nucleus, develop over time (Lenroot et al., 2007). Specifically, the peak in cerebral and caudate volumes occurs at about age 10.5 in girls and 14.5 in boys whereas the total gray matter peaks at age 8.5 in girls and 10.5 in boys (Lenroot et al., 2007). These data are a good reminder that not all brain regions mature at the same time and that there are significant sex differences. A more recent longitudinal study in a sample of 9 to 23 year olds paints a similar picture by reporting that nucleus accumbens volume peaks in adolescence and then decreases into the early 20s (Urošević, Collins, Muetzel, Lim, and Luciana, 2012). Moreover, this nonlinear developmental pattern in the nucleus accumbens was associated with increased reward sensitivity from early to late adolescence, which subsequently declined in the early 20s (Urošević et al., 2012). As discussed in the next section, these structural changes appear to be functionally meaningful and may contribute to reward-related behaviors in adolescence.

6.3.4 fMRI Studies of the Adolescent Reward System

To examine the reward system "in motion" many scientists use fMRI to scan participants' brains while they perform a computerized reward task. These tasks typically involve presenting research subjects with the opportunity for earning various types of rewards, including monetary, social, or appetitive rewards such as a drop of juice or sugar.

The first fMRI studies of reward in adolescents set out to address relatively simple questions about reward processing. Does the brain process reward similarly across development? Is the adolescent brain more or less reactive to reward than younger or older individuals? It was hypothesized by some that adolescent reward-seeking and risk-taking is the result of a relative deficit in the activity of motivational circuitry whereby rewards of higher intensity or frequency are necessary to achieve the same reward sensitivity as adults (Blum et al., 2000). They reasoned that adolescents generally attain less positive feelings from rewarding stimuli, which drives them to pursue new appetitive reinforcers through increases in reward-seeking behavior that increases activity in dopamine-related circuitry. An opposing theory posited that adolescents engage in greater reward-seeking behavior than individuals of other age groups because of *greater* activation of mesolimbic circuitry (Chambers, Taylor, and Potenza, 2003).

The first study to address this question used the monetary incentive delay (MID) task, a task commonly used in adults to study reward processing, and found that adolescents showed less activation of the reward system than adults (Bjork et al., 2004). Since then, many studies have found the exact opposite results. Bjork and colleagues thus conducted a replication study using an improved version of the MID task, increased statistical power, and an upgraded MRJ head coil for better brain image quality (Bjork, Smith, Chen, and Hommer, 2010). Despite these methodological modifications, the authors observed a similar result, whereby adolescents exhibited less reactivity to rewards than adults. The authors speculate that differences in task engagement, vigilance required, and amount of reward may explain divergent findings from studies that use the MID task versus those that use more youth-friendly tasks (Bjork et al., 2010).

Using reward tasks that vary on stimuli and the type of incentive, the majority of studies on reward processing have found support for enhanced reward sensitivity in striatal regions in adolescents compared to children and adults. In one fMRI study, children, adolescents, and adults performed a reward task in which three cues were each associated with three reward values (small, medium, and large) (Galván et al., 2006). The task was based on a reward learning task previously used in nonhuman primates to show that dopamine firing patterns temporally shift to track the most meaningful reward information (Fiorillo, Tobler, and Schultz, 2003). In the monkey studies, dopamine firing was initially greatest when the thirsty monkey, who had been deprived of food or water for hours prior to the experiment, received the reward (a drop of juice). This observation was consistent with the older studies from Olds and Milner suggesting that dopamine is responsive to the experience of a reward. However, Fiorillo and colleagues noticed that as the animal learned that a particular cue (i.e. shape that was presented on a computer screen) predicted the size of the upcoming drop of juice, the dopamine neurons become increasingly more responsive to the reward-predicting cue. By the end of the experiment the dopamine neurons were minimally responsive to the actual reward delivery when the animal received the drop of juice and instead fired most vigorously to the cue (Fiorillo et al., 2003). This shift in firing pattern suggested that dopamine neurons were doing much more than simply responding to reward but that they were helping the animal *learn* how to anticipate reward.

The adolescent fMRI reward study showed similar findings: early in the experiment, children, adolescents, and adults all exhibited robust activation in the reward system when the participant saw their earnings on a computer screen. By the end of the experiment, adolescents showed the overall greatest activation to the reward, while adults showed the least. Notice that the bar graph in Figure 6.3 shows greater activation in the adolescent group compared to children and adults. However, within the adult group, the greatest activation was in response to the cue (e.g. a shape) that predicted the reward and not to the actual reward outcome, which paralleled the monkey data. Particularly interesting is that these neural patterns of activation mapped onto the behavioral differences between groups. In the beginning of the experiment, none of

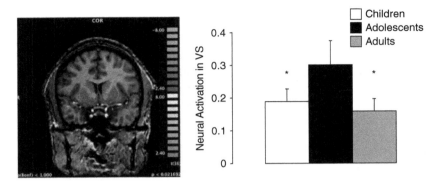

Figure 6.3 Monetary reward elicited activation in the ventral striatum during fMRI in child, adolescent, and adult research participants (*left*). Neural activation in the ventral striatum (VS) was greatest in the adolescent group compared to the children and adults (*right*). ∗ = significant at p < .05 (Galván et al., 2006). See color plate 12.

the age groups showed differences in reaction time to the three reward types. However, by the end of the experiment, adults had learned to discriminate between them, as evidenced by faster reaction time to the large reward and slowest reaction time to the small reward. Adolescents became significantly slower to the small reward and children continued to show no differences in reaction between the three reward types. The authors concluded that differences in how the reward system responds to rewards of different values is associated with behavior and that adolescents show heightened neural sensitivity to reward compared to children and adults (Galván et al., 2006). Results from other laboratories using a variety of tasks, including a probabilistic monetary reward task (Ernst et al., 2005), a reward-based antisaccade task (Geier, Terwilliger, Teslovich, Velanova, and Luna, 2010), a decision-making reward task (Jarcho et al., 2012), a social rewards task (Chein, Albert, O'Brien, Uckert, and Steinberg, 2011), and a prediction error task (Cohen et al., 2010), also found that, compared to adults, adolescents showed heightened ventral striatal activation when experiencing rewards. Longitudinal assessments, in which over 200 participants between the ages of ~10 and 25 were scanned twice, confirmed that the striatum shows peak activation during the adolescent period (Braams, van Duijvenvoorde, Peper, and Crone, 2015).

Earnings on all these tasks were based on participant performance. It is therefore possible that if participant performance differed across age groups, group differences in brain activation simply reflect behavioral differences and not differential neural sensitivity to reward. This notion is similar to the "Task B problem" discussed in Chapter 2. However, fMRI studies that used "passive tasks" (i.e. those that require participants not to perform a behavior but instead to passively experience the reward) led to similar conclusions as the performance-based reward studies. In a study by Linda van Leijenhorst and colleagues, participants passively viewed shapes that predicted subsequent reward with varying degrees of probability. Results showed that adolescents exhibited greater striatal activation than children or adults in response to reward receipt (van Leijenhorst et al., 2010), suggesting that even when reward is not contingent on behavior or differences in motivation, adolescents show a hyperactive striatal response to reward. Another study eliminated the use of money as reward altogether by instead mimicking the monkey studies and using sugar water as the reward. In this study, hungry and thirsty participants passively consume sugar water while undergoing fMRI (Galván and McGlennen, 2013). Compared to adults, adolescent participants not only reported that the sugar water was more pleasurable than the adults did, but also showed enhanced engagement of the striatum. This study provides evidence for the notion that the reward system is responsive to both primary (e.g. sugar water) and secondary (e.g. monetary) rewards and that both types of rewards elicit greater striatal activation in teens versus adults. Collectively, findings from both performance-based and passive tasks lend support for the hypothesis that disproportionately increased activation of the reward systems characterizes adolescent neurodevelopment (Chambers et al., 2003).

6.3.5 Neurophysiological Maturation of the Reward System

The striatum is rich in tissue-iron concentration (Haacke et al., 2005) which supports dopamine receptor density (Erikson, Jones, and Beard, 2000), as well as the function and regulation of dopamine neurons (Beard, 2003). Larsen and Luna (2015) leveraged this knowledge to gain further insight into dopaminergic function during adolescence. They measured tissue-iron concentration using MRI. Tissue-iron is paramagnetic and thus strongly influences the signal of MRI images known as $T2^*$-weighted images. They also took a clever approach in their analysis by using multivariate pattern analyses (MVPA, which we learned about in Chapter 3) rather than traditional fMRI processing analyses. They reasoned that MVPA would allow them to characterize all the subregions within the striatum, including the caudate, putamen, and ventral striatum, which are heterogeneous in terms of function, connectivity, and underlying neurobiology. With MVPA, they assessed age-related differences in the striatum on a voxel-wise basis, a much more fine-grained approach than with traditional MRI analyses. The analysis revealed strong predictability of age based on the T2*-weighted images. Interestingly, different subregions of the striatum evinced different developmental trajectories, with the dorsal region (caudate) showing increasing T2* intensity with age and the ventral region (nucleus accumbens) showing decreasing T2* intensity with age. These patterns may provide some insight into why regulatory systems (including the caudate) have increasing influence on behavior with age relative to limbic systems (including the nucleus accumbens), which have progressively less overall input on behavior with age. A separate analysis showed that age was predicted most significantly in the nucleus accumbens, indicating that T2* (as an index of iron concentrations) has a particularly strong relationship with adolescent development in the region of the brain that is strongly associated with dopaminergic functioning. Overall, this study provides strong evidence that the reward system undergoes significant neurophysiological development during adolescence. This research also made an important methodological contribution to the literature by showing that the multivariate approach was much better at detecting age-related changes in the subdivisions of the striatum than traditional univariate approaches (Larsen and Luna, 2015).

6.3.6 Reward Influences on Cognitive Control

Within the dual-process framework discussed in Chapter 1, the studies we have reviewed thus far lend support for the notion that affective systems in subcortical brain regions have significant influence over behavior and that there seems to be a developmental tug of war where the inclination to seek out risk and reward competes with an immaturity to inhibit those inclinations. Indeed, increased activation in prefrontal regions does seem to assuage the effects of an overactive affective system. Until recently, most studies did not explicitly examine these systems in conjunction. However, a few recent noteworthy studies examined the integration of cognitive control and reward-related processes by implementing tasks that test how well participants are able to control their behavior, even when they are tempted to do otherwise by potential rewards. Using an antisaccade task as a measure of inhibitory control, a series of studies have shown that adolescent participants show better behavioral control when they are rewarded for doing so (Geier et al., 2010; Padmanabhan, Geier,

Ordaz, Teslovich, and Luna, 2011). In a clever manipulation, Luna and colleagues presented participants with a simple cognitive task that they have used previously to measure inhibitory control (Luna et al., 2001). In this task, participants are asked to focus their gaze on the center of a computer screen. Every few seconds, a light is presented on one side of the screen and their job is to shift their eye gaze in the *opposite* direction of the light (see Box 5.3 in Chapter 5 for an illustration). Seems easy but is actually quite challenging and requires considerable effort. In a new version of the task, participants knew that on some trials they would receive a monetary reward for good behavioral control (shifting their gaze in the opposite direction from the light); these trials were called rewarded trials. Relative to trials in which good behavior was not rewarded, adolescents significantly improved their ability to control their behavior when they knew there was a reward attached to it. During anticipation of reward on the rewarded trials, adolescent participants showed increased activation in the ventral striatum and medial frontal gyrus compared to adults, despite equitable task performance between groups (Geier et al., 2010). This increased activation is speculated to contribute to significant improvements in accuracy in adolescents. In a follow-up study that included children as well as adolescents and adults, the authors report that children and adolescents, but not adults, made fewer errors during rewarded versus neutral trials on the same task (Padmanabhan et al., 2011). Across a range of regions, including the putamen, ventral striatum, and parietal cortex, adolescents exhibited increased activation compared to children and adults in the rewarded trials. Collectively, these results indicate that adolescents have the ability to perform as well as adults when they are motivated to do so, suggesting that rewards (or other motivational tools) may act to enhance or improve behavioral regulation in youth.

6.3.7 Neural Response to Immediate versus Delayed Rewards

In the previous section we reviewed research showing that the adolescent brain is hyperresponsive to rewards. All of these studies involved rewards that were immediately delivered to the participant, in the form of either money or sugar. But in the real world, rewards are often temporally delayed in time. For instance, teens are often unable to obtain rewards immediately after identifying a desire for them – they usually must save up an allowance or wait for a special holiday or birthday to receive the reward. Does the adolescent brain process immediate versus delayed rewards differently? And if so, does it provide some insight into why adolescents are generally less patient than adults at waiting for rewards that are delayed in time?

Delay discounting tasks, which examine the temporal dynamics of reward-seeking behavior. They quantify the ability to choose a delayed, larger reward over an immediate, smaller reward. Recent neuroimaging work has shown that age-related reductions in choosing immediate versus delayed rewards are associated with changes in neural activation. From childhood to adulthood, this behavioral shift is associated with decreased activation in ventrolateral prefrontal cortex, ventral striatum, insula, and medial temporal lobe, and increased activation in ventromedial and dorsolateral prefrontal cortex and bilateral temporal regions (Christakou, Brammer, and Rubia, 2011). This age-related engagement of distinct neural systems suggests that more mature preferences (i.e. choosing rewards that are temporally delayed but more valuable) may be the product of two interrelated changes: decreased engagement of limbic regions and increased engagement of regulatory prefrontal regions.

6.3.8 Functional Connectivity Studies of Reward Processing

In recent years there has been an uptick in the use of functional connectivity methods. This type of analysis can provide new insight into functional organization of the brain by empirically testing conceptual theories about reward-driven behavior in adolescents. For instance, connectivity can help disentangle whether adolescents exhibit greater reward-seeking behavior than adults because signals from the ventral striatum exert robust influence over cognitive control regions or because there is limited regulatory influence from the prefrontal cortex onto reward neurocircuitry. The answer is likely a combination of both scenarios.

Using functional connectivity analyses, Cho and colleagues (2013) examined reward processing using the monetary incentive delay task in a group of adolescents and adults. They found a core incentive processing network that involved the nucleus accumbens, thalamus, and insula in both groups, with robust thalamic influence on insula and nucleus accumbens, as well as insula influence on the nucleus accumbens. Adolescents additionally demonstrated significant connectivity from the nucleus accumbens to thalamus (Cho et al., 2013). Interestingly, there were no statistically significant differences in connectivity modulation between adolescents and adults, which the authors speculate may be due to high individual variability among the sample. Nonetheless, this study suggests that the thalamus and insula provide the nucleus accumbens with extero-ceptive signals about cues and interoceptive signals about drive, given their respective roles in identifying and responding to appetitive stimuli in the environment.

Results from a delay discounting study suggest that enhanced age-related coupling between ventromedial prefrontal cortex and ventral striatum accounts for reduced discounting across development (Chris-takou et al., 2011). The authors speculate that this implicates the frontal regulatory regions as redirecting the decision-making process that guides the pursuit of an immediately available reward away from ventral stri-atal hyperresponsiveness to proximal rewards in younger individuals, toward context-sensitive value-driven evaluation of the available alter-natives in older individuals (Christakou et al., 2011). These initial studies have already begun to fill in the empirical gaps of current conceptual frameworks by supporting the notion that progressive strengthening of functional connections between frontal and subcortical regions con-tributes to age-related increases in affect and reward-related regulation. Similar to the burst in knowledge about the developing brain that arose when fMRI was first used to study children and adolescents (Casey et al., 1997), functional connectivity studies will yield important new insights and generate novel ways to conceptualize the development of neural networks.

6.4 Neural Correlates of Risk-Taking in Adolescents

The murmurs of rebellion and defiance that emerge in early puberty reach a sharp crescendo during the adolescent years when risk-taking behaviors climax. Adolescents have higher rates of just about any risky behavior you can think of, including experimentation with alcohol, cigarettes, and illicit drugs, higher rates of risky sexual activity, petty and violent crime, and reckless driving. Parents, educators, and policymakers have long wondered why this occurs. Before the advent of neuroimaging, this phenomenon was primarily attributed to shifts in pubertal hormones. However, the neuroimaging studies of the adolescent reward system reviewed above undeniably suggested that hormones are not the whole story. Scientists reasoned that the increase in risk-taking behaviors in adolescents is also due to heightened reward sensitivity in the adolescent brain. Research has corroborated this hypothesis.

Laboratory measures of risk-taking (listed in Box 6.1), including tasks that give participants the option of accepting monetary gambles (risky choice) or cashing out (safe choice), have shown that risky behavior

Box 6.1 Common Laboratory Risk-Taking Tasks

Balloon Analogue Risk Task (BART). On each trial, participants pump a simulated balloon without knowing when it will explode. Each pump increases the potential reward to be gained but also the probability of explosion, which wipes out all potential gains for that trial. In most studies, balloon explosion probabilities are drawn from a uniform distribution, and participants must learn explosion probabilities through trial and error.

Cambridge Gambling Task. Participants see ten boxes at the top of a screen, each of which is red or blue in some ratio. Under one of these boxes is a token, and participants must guess whether the token is under red or blue. On a gambling trial, participants can select some proportion of their allotted points to bet on their judgment. A youth-friendly version of this task is called the **Cake Gambling Task**.

Cups Task. On each trial, participants choose between a risky and a safe option. Each trial involves either gains or losses. The options are presented as a choice of cups. The risky option involves two to five cups, one containing a gain (loss) of $4, $6, or $10, and the others containing $0. If the latter option is selected, the payoff from one cup is selected at random. The safe cup offers a sure gain (loss) of $2.

Hungry Donkey Task. The Hungry Donkey Task is a version of Bechera's Iowa Gambling Task for children; it is a test in the areas of cognition and emotion that was originally developed to assist in detecting decision-making impairment in patients with prefrontal cortex damage. The experiment is often computerized, is carried out in real time, and resembles real-world contingencies. A donkey chooses from four doors, each with a cost or reward in apples. The objective is to give the donkey the most apples possible.

Mixed Gambles Task. Subjects are presented with gambles in which they have a 50% chance of gaining some amount of money and a 50% chance of losing some other amount of money. The subject decides whether or not they would accept the gamble. The amount of the potential gain and loss are varied across trials. Gambles are not resolved during performance of the task; after the end of the task, some gambles are chosen at random and played for real money if they were accepted.

Probabilistic Gambling Task. Two cards are drawn without replacement from a deck containing cards numbered from one to ten (one of each). After the first card is presented, participants bet whether the next card will be higher or lower than the first card. Thus there is maximal risk when the first card is five or six, zero risk when it is ten or one.

Risky Gains Task. Subjects are presented with a sequence of three numbers in ascending order (20, 40, and 80). Each number is displayed onscreen for one second and, if the subject presses a button while that number is displayed, she receives that number of points along with immediate positive visual and auditory feedback. When a 40 or 80 appears, however, there is a chance that it will appear in an alternate color, along with immediate negative feedback signaling a loss of 40 or 80 points, respectively. When this occurs, the trial ends immediately (i.e. the subject may not make a response).

increases from childhood to adolescence and decreases from adolescence to adulthood (Braams et al., 2015). Figure 6.4 illustrates this developmental pattern, with peak risk-taking behavior, as indexed by behavior on the BART task, in adolescence. This pattern is similar to previous studies that examined risk-taking in the laboratory (Burnett, Bault, Coricelli, and Blakemore, 2010; Figner, Mackinlay, Wilkening, and Weber, 2009), and self-reported sensation-seeking (Steinberg et al., 2008), and real-life risk-taking behavior (Eaton et al., 2012).

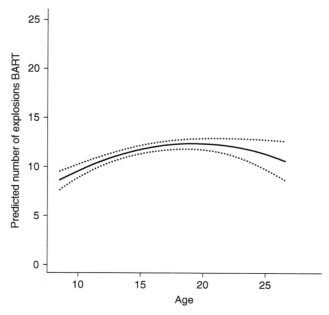

Figure 6.4 A large study in youth reports a curvilinear trend in laboratory-based risk-taking behavior across development that peaks in adolescence. BART = Balloon Analogue Risk Task (Braams et al., 2015).

Brain scans show a similar developmental trend. In response to laboratory risk-taking tasks, the ventral striatum exhibits greater activation in adolescents compared to children and adults (Braams et al., 2015). Even after equating subjective value attributed to the risky behavior, adolescents show greater activation of the ventral striatum than adults (Barkley-Levenson and Galván, 2014).

Asking participants to choose between high-risk/high-reward versus low-risk/low-reward choices yields interesting developmental differences. In adults, this type of decision-making engages a wide network of cortical areas, including the ventral striatum, cingulate cortex, and ventrolateral prefrontal cortex (Krain et al., 2006, 2008). In a sample of participants that varied in age (ages 8–10, 12–14, 15–17, and 19–25), van Leijenhorst and colleagues (2010) found that on trials in which expected value of high- and low-risk options was equal, 8 to 10 year olds chose mostly the high-risk/high-reward options, whereas adults chose mostly the low-risk/low-reward options; adolescents showed an intermediate pattern (van Duijvenvoorde and Crone, 2013). These results seem to indicate a developmental decrease in taste for risk (i.e. increasing risk aversiveness).

Another study examined differences in neural response to *risk* versus *ambiguity* using a gambling task. Although they are very similar constructs, *risk* refers to choices made in which the probabilities of outcomes are known, whereas *ambiguity* refers to choices made in which the probabilities of the potential outcomes are unknown. Compared to adults, adolescents showed similar patterns of risk aversion (both groups avoided risk) but were more tolerant of ambiguity. Adolescents showed a greater tendency to accept gambles than adults, even when the probabilities were unknown (Tymula et al., 2012). The authors suggest that the higher level of risk-taking observed among adolescents in the real world may reflect a higher tolerance for the unknown. Biologically, such a tolerance may make sense, because it would allow young organisms to take better advantage of learning opportunities (Tymula et al., 2012).

Do the brain data suggest that hormones have *nothing* to do with the surge in risk-taking in adolescents? Certainly not. Instead, they help construct an integrative model of risk-taking that includes changes in neurobiology as well as changes in hormones as major contributors to this normative behavior. The study mentioned previously by Braams and colleagues with almost 300 participants examined both reward sensitivity in the brain and hormones. The study reports that increases in puberty were related to higher ventral striatal response to rewards. Specifically, testosterone was associated with activation of the reward system whereby individuals with higher testosterone levels across developmental time also showed higher neural sensitivity to rewards. These findings are similar to earlier studies, including a longitudinal study in a small age range (11–13 years) of participants (Spielberg, Olino, Forbes, and Dahl, 2014), a cross-sectional study that found positive correlations between testosterone levels and ventral striatal activation when playing a gambling task (Op de Macks et al., 2011), and a study showing a relationship between laboratory-based risk-taking behavior and testosterone levels (Peper, Koolschijn, and Crone, 2013).

Do these data suggest that the ventral striatum is solely responsible for heightened risk-taking in adolescents? Hardly. As we learned in Chapter 3, no one brain region works in isolation. Although particular brain regions, such as the striatum, may be more heavily involved in processing a particular mental operation, such as reward, it is undoubtedly influenced by other regions. During processing of risk, the prefrontal cortex also plays a significant role. In a longitudinal study in which adolescents were scanned once at age 15 and then again at approximately 17, there was a decrease from the first to second scan in activation of the ventrolateral prefrontal cortex when making risky decisions on a laboratory task (Qu, Galván, Fuligni, Lieberman, and Telzer, 2015). This decline in activation was also associated with greater declines in self-reported risk-taking on real-life behaviors, including smoking, alcohol use, drug use, and stealing. Importantly, adolescents who reported greater declines in real-life risky behavior from the first to the second scanning session also showed greater negative coupling between the ventral striatum and medial prefrontal cortex (Qu et al., 2015), a shift from the association between positive coupling of these regions and greater risk-taking behavior at the first scan. These findings suggest that individuals with better regulation of the ventral striatum by the medial prefrontal cortex exhibit decreases in risky behavior.

6.4.1 Individual Differences in Reward and Risk-Sensitivity

It is important to note that not all adolescents exhibit heightened reward or risk-sensitivity. In fact, the likelihood of reward-seeking behavior is largely influenced by individual differences, including sensitivity to rewards, gender, and personality traits. Reward-seeking and risk-taking behaviors are more frequent in individuals with elevated novelty and sensation-seeking (Rao et al., 2011) and in those who report greater risk-taking among their peers.

Neuroimaging data in adults show that individual differences in activation of reward circuitry predict reward-related risks (Kuhnen and Knutson, 2005). Individuals who exhibit greater ventral striatal activation in response to rewards are subsequently more likely to make risky choices to obtain monetary reward (Kuhnen and Knutson, 2005), to consume unhealthy snacks (Lawrence, Hinton, Parkinson, and Lawrence, 2012), to gain weight, and to report greater sexual desires (Demos, Heatherton, and Kelley, 2012). Recent research using positron emission tomography, a technique used to examine dopamine function in adult humans, found that individual differences in dopamine reactivity in the ventral striatum and ventromedial prefrontal cortex were correlated with a willingness to expend greater effort for larger rewards (Treadway et al., 2012), further implicating individual differences in dopamine activity in reward sensitivity.

Individual differences in activation of reward circuitry have also been observed in developmental populations. By examining individual neural responses to reward and correlating them with self-reported risk-taking behavior in a sample of children, adolescents, and adults, Galván and colleagues found a positive association between ventral striatal activation in response to monetary reward and the likelihood of engaging in risky behavior; that is, individuals more likely to report higher frequency of risky behavior in real life showed greater ventral striatal activation (Galván, Hare, Voss, Glover, and Casey, 2007). These findings were corroborated in a separate study, which reported a positive association between individual differences in reactivity of the ventral striatum in response to reward and externalizing behaviors such as drug use (Bjork, Smith, Chen, and Hommer, 2011).

Using a novel way to estimate dopamine in the brain, Barkley-Levenson and Galván found further evidence for the importance of individual differences (Barkley-Levenson and Galván, 2016). Eyeblink rate has been found to positively correlate with dopamine receptors in the striatum in monkeys and with performance of a dopamine-related task (Groman et al., 2014). Humans with depleted dopamine neurons conversely show decreased eyeblink rate whereas those with elevated dopamine show increased eyeblinke rate (Karson, 1983). In a sample of adolescents and young adults, Barkley-Levenson and Galván (2016) found that individuals with greater spontaneous eyeblink rate were more likely to display higher reward sensitivity than those with lower spontaneous eyeblink rate. Intriguingly, this association was only observed in the adolescent group, suggesting that dopamine may play a greater role in reward-seeking behavior in teens than in adults.

6.5 A Model to Explain Risky Decision-Making in Adolescents

In Chapter 1 we learned about the prevailing theories of adolescent neurodevelopment. They are particularly useful in making sense of adolescent decision-making. In many domains, adolescence is a period of robust cognitive and physical ability. Compared to children (and some adults), adolescents show vast maturational superiority in terms of physical capabilities, concrete reasoning, mathematical ability, and overall intelligence. In most laboratory measures, adolescents have the same reasoning capabilities as adults (Reyna and Farley, 2006; Steinberg and Morris, 2001). They are also physically stronger, more agile, and better coordinated. Their brains are primed to learn and they evince adaptive flexibility in their behavior. And yet, rates of mortality increase during this developmental window. Adolescent risky behavior often leads to health-compromising behaviors and harmful outcomes. Of the approximately 13,000 adolescent deaths recorded in the United States each year by the National Center for Health Statistics, the leading causes are all preventable: motor vehicle crashes, unintentional injuries, homicide, and suicide. Decisions made during adolescence set the stage for future health-compromising behaviors in adulthood. For instance, 80% of adult smokers become addicted to nicotine by age 18 and an estimated 25 million people will die prematurely as adults from smoking-related illness, including 5 million people under 18 years of age (CDC, 2011). Research has suggested that, if people do not start smoking as children or teenagers, it is unlikely that they will ever do so (Sussman, 2002).

Herein lies what Ronald Dahl famously described as an "adolescent paradox" (Dahl, 2004): despite rapid increases in mental and physical abilities during adolescence, a substantial number of adolescents are notoriously poor decision-makers. Why? The research we have reviewed in this chapter and in the chapter on neurocognition suggests that the answer lies in the distinct developmental trajectories of the motivational and regulatory systems.

Both of these neural systems show substantial development during adolescence. Perhaps it is no coincidence that both are also critically involved in decision-making and risky behavior. However, to make this link it is important to understand why and how developmental change in these regions during adolescence leads to characteristic adolescent risky behavior. The models described in Chapter 1 attempt to reconcile the adolescent paradox. Adolescents are quite capable of rational decisions and understanding risks of behaviors in which they engage (Reyna and

Farley, 2006). However, in emotionally salient situations, the peak in risk-taking during adolescence might, at least in part, be due to asymmetrical functional development of the dopaminergic motivational system (including the ventral striatum), which is hyperresponsive to reward in adolescence, and the prefrontal systems implicated in impulse and inhibitory control, which develop more gradually over childhood and adolescence. Figure 6.5 is a cartoon representation of this model (Somerville and Casey, 2010). The left panel depicts a linear pattern of development in the prefrontal cortex (represented by the blue line) and a nonlinear pattern of development of the striatum (represented by the red line), which shows a sharp increase in sensitivity as children transition into adolescence that decreases as individuals transition into adulthood. The panel on the right depicts how the discrepancy between the engagement of motivational and regulatory circuitry may be further exacerbated by emotional and/or social contexts. The bottom panel represents how functional connectivity between these systems changes across development (Somerville and Casey, 2010). In young children the regional signaling of both systems on behavior is relatively light (as indicated by the translucent colors) and the bidirectional input from the striatum to the prefrontal cortex (and vice versa) is relatively immature (as indicated by the dotted lines between them). In adolescents, the striatum exhibits greater regional signaling (as indicated by the deeper red color) than the prefrontal cortex on behavior. The functional connectivity in adolescents is greater from the striatum to the prefrontal cortex (solid line) than from the prefrontal cortex to the striatum (dotted line). In adults, the prefrontal cortex exhibits greater regional signaling (as indicated by the deeper blue color) than the striatum on behavior. The functional connectivity in adults is equally strong from the striatum to the prefrontal cortex and from the prefrontal cortex to the striatum.

6.5.1 Peer Influence on Risk-Taking

Risk-taking does not occur in a vacuum. It is therefore too simplistic to attribute heightened risk-taking in adolescents to the asymmetrical functional development of motivational and regulatory systems. Risk-taking is a very social behavior, particularly during adolescence. For every risky behavior you can think of, you can bet that most adolescents do it with their friends. Teenagers spend an astounding amount of time with their friends (or planning to be with, or yearning to be with, their friends). It is thus no surprise that most risky behavior occurs in the presence of friends. But could it be the case that being with friends

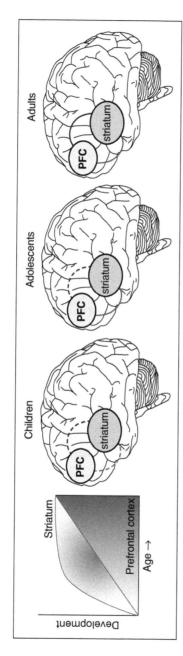

Figure 6.5 A schematic model of striatal and prefrontal interactions across development (*left*). Hypothesized connections between the striatum and the prefrontal cortex change across development (*right*). Deeper color indicates stronger regional signaling such that the striatum exhibits the strongest regional signaling during adolescence. Lines represent the strength of functional connectivity between regions, with a solid line indicating mature connection and a dotted line indicating less mature connection (Somerville and Casey, 2010).

amplifies excitability of the mesolimbic system to an even greater degree than it already is? An interesting question, but how to study it, given the challenges of capturing brain activity while teens are with their friends? One would have to devise an experiment whereby participants were in the company of their friends while receiving a brain scan!

Luckily, a research team at Temple University, led by Laurence Steinberg and Jason Chein, created a clever fMRI experiment in which participants played a risk-taking video game in the presence of their peers while undergoing fMRI (Chein et al., 2011). Three groups of research participants, adolescents (ages 14–18), college students (ages 19–22) and adults (ages 24–29), were recruited to the study and each one played the "Stoplight Game." The Stoplight Game is a first-person task wherein participants must advance a car through a series of street intersections to reach a finish line as quickly as possible to receive a monetary reward. The risky component mimics real-life driving circumstances in which each intersection contains a stoplight that turns yellow as the car approaches and participants must decide whether to make a risky choice by running the yellow light or make the non-risky choice of stepping on the brakes (and thus incurring extra time to get to the finish line). Each participant played the game either alone or in the presence of two same-aged, same-sex friends.

College students and adults exhibited the same behavior (that is, made the same number of risky and non-risky choices, whether or not there was a peer watching them. Not so the adolescents. They made significantly more risky choices when a peer was watching than when they were alone. This finding is especially interesting because their risky behavior did not differ from the other age groups in the alone condition. Interestingly, risky decisions in the presence of peers elicited greater activation in the mesolimbic circuitry (specifically in the ventral striatum) in the adolescent group only. This study provides compelling evidence that, in the company of friends, adolescents' reward sensitivity is amplified when confronted with a risky choice. Keep in mind that these adolescent patterns were observed within the confines of a relatively sterile laboratory environment, so you can imagine what friends do to the teenage brain in real life, in tempting risky behaviors!

6.6 The Adaptive Aspects of Adolescent Risk-Taking

So the adolescent brain likes rewards and risks. When educators, parents, and policymakers hear this, alarm bells go off. Are teenagers victims of their own neurodevelopment? Will they make life-threatening and health-compromising decisions? Some adolescents do indeed engage in behaviors that are a threat to healthy development. However, many adolescents pass through this developmental window relatively unscathed and scientists have long wondered what the adaptive aspects are of a brain that is hyperexcitable, responsive to the social environment, and primed for learning.

The answer is quite simple actually. The brain is built this way to facilitate the important task of transitioning from a state of dependence on caregivers to one of relative independence. Imagine if there *wasn't* a period in life when individuals actively sought out autonomy from their parents. There would be minimal exploration of the environment, not much thirst for learning new things, and little curiosity to meet new people. Our species wouldn't survive. Growth of the human species is dependent on the motivation of individuals to innovate, create, and procreate! At no other time in life is there greater intrinsic motivation to explore the world than during adolescence (Crone and Dahl, 2012). Youth are often at the forefront of new ideas, impassioned defenders of ideals, fervid leaders, and the ones having the most fun in the quest for autonomy. These characteristics are what make adolescents, well, adolescents – despite better cognitive, intellectual, and reasoning abilities than children, adolescents are not simply "mini-adults," and despite immature emotion regulation, inexperience, and dependence on caregivers, adolescents are not overgrown children (Galván, 2014). Instead, they are in a distinct developmental stage that facilitates all of the creativity, rebellion, and progressive thinking that characterizes this period. Puberty jumpstarts this process by giving individuals the biological means to procreate. This is followed by a few years of activities and behaviors that facilitate, and in some cases expedite, moving away from caregivers in order to truly establish independence, including increasing conflict with parents, more time spent with peers, increased risk-taking behavior, and greater desire for romantic partners. By the time late adolescence rolls around, adolescents are motivated to move away. In previous decades this usually occurred because individuals married in late adolescence, but in more modern times many simply move out of their parents' house to live with friends or romantic partners or to attend college. In recent decades, there has been an increase in the number of people (particularly women) who are attending college or university.

Beyond simply being normative, there is research to suggest that a healthy dose of risk-taking in human adolescents is beneficial. Shedler and Block found that popular adolescents who engaged in moderate amounts of risk-taking were found to be more socially competent both in childhood and in adolescence than were those who abstained or who were more frequent risk takers (Allen et al., 2005).

Humans are not the only ones to undergo this characteristic shift in independence-seeking. Nonhuman animals also leave the natal troop to seek out new sexual mates, food resources, and sleeping burrows or trees (Spear, 2000). In fact, risk-taking around the time of sexual maturation is not unique to humans; like their human counterparts, rats undergoing the developmental transition of adolescence show a significant increase in the amount of time spent in social interactions with peers (Varlinskaya and Spear, 2008) and at play. They also are more likely to engage in risk-taking behavior, and they seek out new situations and explore unknown areas more avidly than they do either at a younger age or in adulthood.

American psychologist Jerome Bruner proposed that the function of being "immature" is that the organism can engage in experimental play without serious consequences, and can spend considerable time observing the actions of skilled others in conjunction with oversight by and activity with its caregiver (Bruner, 1972). He went on to suggest that this type of play helps the species practice and perfect imitative acts, such that "re-interpretive imitation" leads to human innovation through extensive exploration of the limits on one's ability to interact with the world. There is evidence that contemporary youth are experiencing a period of extended immaturity, and therefore of "play" and schooling. This may be the result of the increasing complexity of our world and its technologies, which demand an increasing intricacy of skill as well as a more exhaustive set of prerequisite abilities. The outcome has yet to be seen, but some have argued that this extended period of immaturity may serve the adaptive purpose of extending the period of plasticity (Steinberg, 2014).

6.7 The Role of Motivational Systems in Learning

The striatum is heavily implicated in reward and risk processing. However, it wears multiple hats. Another primary responsibility of the striatum, along with the hippocampus, is in helping organisms learn about the environment. This usually occurs through reinforcement learning and prediction error.

Reinforcement learning theory is couched in the notion that we learn by interacting with our environment. Specifically, reinforcement learning is learning how to maximize rewards based on our behavior. The learner learns, through trial and error, which actions yield the most reward. Learning from the environment occurs via computation of what is called a *prediction error signal*, which is derived directly from the **Rescorla-Wagner Model** of classical conditioning. The prediction error signal is coded by dopamine cells (Schultz et al., 1997).

A prediction error occurs when outcomes do not match expectations. This mismatch provides new information for the organism, which then learns new information. A positive prediction error refers to when the outcome is better than expected and a negative prediction error occurs when the outcome is worse than expected. For example, if an adolescent expects her weekly allowance of $50 and instead receives $60, she experiences a positive prediction error of plus $10. If she instead receives $25, then she experiences a negative prediction error of minus $25. One study used a learning task to violate participants' expectations. Sometimes the outcomes on the task were better than expected and sometimes they were worse. When they were better then expected, the adolescent group (ages 14–19 years) showed an elevated positive prediction error signal in the striatum compared with children (ages 8–12) and adults (ages 25–30) (Cohen et al., 2010). With training, all participants became faster and more accurate at responding to predictable stimuli, but only the adolescent group (ages 14–19) responded more quickly to stimuli associated with a higher reward value compared with small rewards. In addition, compared with children and adults, the adolescent group exhibited higher ventral striatum responses to higher, unpredicted reward. This suggests that responsiveness to dopaminergic prediction error is higher in adolescents, which might contribute to elevated reward-seeking in this age group.

Another possibility is that greater sensitivity to prediction errors in adolescents helps facilitate learning. Indeed, a study that tested adolescents' and adults' ability to learn simple associations between cues and outcomes found that adolescents outperformed adults (Davidow, Foerde, Galván, and Shohamy, 2016). This is a remarkable finding, because in many studies adults outperform adolescents. They also showed better memory for positive reinforcement events than for negative reinforcement events, whereas adults' memory did not differentiate between positive and negative events. Adolescents also showed greater prediction error-related activation in the hippocampus than adults, and significant functional connectivity between the hippocampus and striatum that was associated with memory for positive reinforcement events (Davidow et al., 2016).

A related study found that, following positive prediction errors, there was stronger connectivity between the striatum and the medial frontal cortex in adolescents and young adults (ages 13–22) than in children (ages 8–11) (van den Bos, Cohen, Kahnt, and Crone, 2012). Similar studies have also found that adolescents, compared to adults, are more responsive to unpredictable outcomes in terms of modifying behavior in response to new information (van Duijvenvoorde, Jansen, Bredman, and Huizenga, 2012). These studies suggest that prediction error signals help adolescents learn about the environment and, importantly, to flexibly adjust their behavior in response to the dynamic nature of real life. This flexibility is possible because of the malleability of activation in striatal and frontal networks during adolescence (Crone and Dahl, 2012).

6.8 Chapter Summary

- Adolescents evince heightened activation of reward circuitry compared to children and adults.
- Risk-taking is a product of both neural and hormone changes during adolescence.
- Individual differences in reward sensitivity influence risk-taking.
- Heightened reward sensitivity and risk-taking serve both adaptive and maladaptive purposes in adolescence.

6.9 Review Questions

1 What are the primary regions involved in reward processing?
2 Describe the development of the dopamine system.
3 Describe the model to explain adolescent risk-taking behavior.
4 How is adolescent risk-taking adaptive?

Further Reading

Chein, J., Albert, D., O'Brien, L., Uckert, K., and Steinberg, L. (2011). Peers increase adolescent risk taking by enhancing activity in the brain's reward circuitry. *Developmental Science*, 14, F1–F10.
Galván A (2013). Sensitivity to reward in adolescence. *Current Directions in Psychological Science*, 22, 100–105.
Somerville, L.H., and Casey, B.J. (2010). Developmental neurobiology of cognitive control and motivational systems. *Current Opinion in Neurobiology*, 20, 236–241.
Spear, L. (2011). Rewards, aversions and affect in adolescence: emerging convergences across laboratory animal and human data. *Developmental Cognitive Neuroscience*, 1, 392–400.

CHAPTER SEVEN

The Social Brain

Learning Objectives

- To learn about social cognition.
- To review the neural correlates of affect processing.
- To review the neural correlates of face processing.
- To learn about aberrant social development.

7.1 Introduction

Forming and maintaining social bonds is a strong human need (Baumeister and Leary, 1995). In infancy, social attachments are focused on the ones between mother and child (Ainsworth, 1989). As children grow so too does the number of people they are attached to. As children become adolescents there are often new attachments, to friends and significant others. In early to mid adulthood, new attachments are often established to spouses, life-long partners, and/or one's own children. In this chapter we will learn about the neural systems that support all aspects of social cognition, including social attachment, face processing, understanding others, recognizing different emotions, self-development, and peer relationships. These topics are particularly relevant to adolescence because of increased social awareness and interest that emerges during this developmental window.

The social landscape changes significantly during adolescence. Around this time, people exhibit increasing interest in others and build up their social cognition skills (Figure 7.1). Social cognition refers to the ability to use signals by members of the same species to navigate the world (Frith, 2008). Social cognitive processes include basic perceptual skills, such as face processing, biological motion detection, and joint attention (Blakemore and Mills, 2014). More complex social cognitive processing includes understanding others' mental states, emotion processing, and interpersonal interactions. All social cognitive skills involve significant changes in a network of regions called "the social brain"

Figure 7.1 Social relationships are very important in adolescence.

(Blakemore, 2008). It includes the dorsal medial prefrontal cortex (dmPFC), temporoparietal junction (TPJ), amygdala, posterior superior temporal sulcus (pSTS), and anterior temporal cortex (ATC). A representation of these regions and their location in the brain is provided in Figure 7.2. This chapter will be divided into two major sections. The first will focus on basic social cognitive processes and the neural correlates that support them and the second on the more complex social cognitive process, which evince significant developmental change during adolescence.

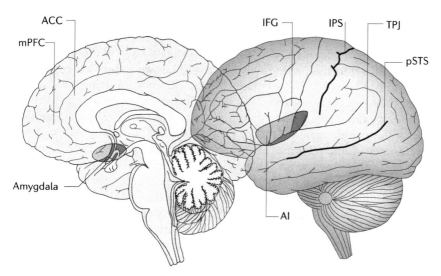

Figure 7.2 An illustration of the primary regions that comprise the social brain, including the medial prefrontal cortex (mPFC) and the temporoparietal junction (TPJ), which are involved in thinking about mental states, and the posterior superior temporal sulcus (pSTS), which is activated by observing faces and biological motion. Other regions of the social brain on the lateral surface are the inferior frontal gyrus (IFG) and the interparietal sulcus (IPS). Regions on the medial surface that are involved in social cognition include the amygdala, the anterior cingulate cortex (ACC), and the anterior insula (AI). (Blakemore, 2008.) See color plate 13.

7.2 Basic Social Cognitive Skills

7.2.1 Face Processing

All humans are "face experts." We encounter faces every single day of our lives, are flooded with facial information from the moment we are born. It is therefore no surprise that we become really good at knowing the general configuration of a face: two eyes near the top, a nose in the middle, and a mouth that opens and closes at the bottom. We are so good at recognizing this particular configuration of objects that we can even note and *remember* subtle differences in this configuration. Within our species, we tend to think there is a lot of variation, including eye shape and color, nose length and width, and mouth size and shape, but in truth we may be more similar than we think. Despite this, we can easily distinguish one person from another. If you happen to have two roommates, you probably never mistake Mary for Anna, for instance. This is because humans have a highly sophisticated way of identifying and storing face information in the brain, a skill known as **face processing**.

Within the first 30 minutes of life, babies will track a moving face farther than they will other patterns of equal contrast, complexity, and spatial frequency (Johnson, Dziurawiec, Ellis, and Morton, 1991), suggesting a particular preference for faces at birth. It is not known why we have this preference. Some scientists reason that it is because there is an "innate" face detecting mechanism (Johnson, 2005) or maybe these early face preferences reflect the basic properties of the immature visual system that are most engaged by the physical properties of the face (Golarai, Grill-Spector, and Reiss, 2006), such as constant moving of the eyes or frequent opening and closing of the mouth when we coo at babies. Regardless of the reason, this early preference for faces is quite important for establishing the early building blocks of face processing and social communication. In Chapter 1 we discussed that experience and input are critically important for building the brain. Face processing and orientation is an excellent example of why. It is also a good illustration of the activity-dependent response we discussed in Chapter 4, because it emerges out of experience. It is a skill that continues throughout childhood and into adolescence (Carey, Diamond, and Woods, 1980). It is not until adulthood that individuals begin to process the face in its entirety, rather than focusing on its constituent parts. This is called **configural processing** and is much more efficient than processing each aspect of the face separately. Configural processing allows us to quickly process and identify faces (Tanaka and Farah, 1993). In fact, faces can be discriminated from other objects in less than 200 milliseconds (Allison et al., 1994), perhaps even as early as 125 milliseconds (Schendan, Ganis, and Kutas, 1998) or 100 milliseconds (Liu, Harris, and Kanwisher, 2002) in adulthood. To give you a point of comparison, it takes 400 milliseconds to complete an eye blink, which is an eternity relative to how quickly you can identify faces.

Developmental studies report that children under 10 years old are less sensitive to the configural properties of faces than those over the age of 10 (Baenninger, 1994). That is, young children are more likely to focus and process each aspect of the face separately, first studying the eyes and then the mouth and finally the nose. We know this because researchers asked children to identify different faces, some of which contained salient features. Children under age 10 made more errors in face recognition when the faces had strong physical features (such as prominent eyebrows or nose) (Diamond and Carey, 1977) suggesting that they were focused on the features rather than the whole face.

As children shift their face processing strategy from a features-based to a whole-face one, they become faster and more accurate at face recognition. This improvement occurs throughout childhood, but surprisingly there is a temporary disruption in face recognition improvement that occurs around puberty. Regardless of age, girls in the midst of puberty encode faces less efficiently than girls who are pre- or post-pubertal (Diamond, Carey, and Back, 1983). No one knows why, but prominent researchers in this field have suggested that the puberty-related timing may provide an important clue. Perhaps, they reason, puberty spurs a reorganization of the neural systems that support face processing and this dip in face processing skills is necessary for the final switch from featural to configural processing. Another possibility is that the increased interest in faces (one's own and others') leads to longer looking time at the face, which may yield slower reaction times on laboratory face processing tasks. Scherf and colleagues argue that the surge of pubertal hormones at puberty influences the behavioral and neural basis of face processing and social information processing more generally (Scherf, Behrmann, and Dahl, 2012). They posit that hormones influence increased *motivation* to pay attention to faces, to bond with same-aged peers, and to initiate romantic relationships. Together, these developmental tasks help tune the neural systems that are eventually the primary social information processing systems. Hormones may also play a more direct role in refining these neural systems by helping to shape the connection between brain regions, and to fundamentally change the dynamical interactions between them (Scherf et al., 2012).

Neural Correlates of Face Processing

Face processing is supported by a distributed neural network (Haxby, Hoffman, and Gobbini, 2000), but is most prominently represented by the fusiform gyrus, a region within the ventral occipitotemporal cortex portion of the ventral visual processing stream. Across a variety of laboratories and using different computer tasks, fMRI studies have shown that when presented with a face, there is robust activation in the fusiform gyrus (Haxby et al., 1991; Kanwisher, McDermott, and Chun, 1997).

One might imagine that such consistent results across multiple sources would mean that the brain is preprogrammed (before birth) to represent faces in this particular brain region, but instead it has led to one of the longest-running debates among neuroscientists. There is currently no consensus about how the fusiform gyrus came to be so robustly and selectively responsive to faces. One camp argues that this is evidence for what is known as the *modular* view of the brain, in which the brain is organized into regions that each specifically respond to one particular type of stimulus. This argument lends support for the prebirth preprogramming. The other camp maintains that the sensitivity to faces in the fusiform gyrus is not evidence that the fusiform gyrus "evolved" to respond to faces. Instead, they argue that the fusiform gyrus happens to respond to objects for which it has acquired expertise. This suggests that the fusiform gyrus responds to objects in general, but because of how often we see faces it became highly attuned to this category of objects.

Fusiform Gyrus Development

The fusiform gyrus response to faces changes considerably across childhood and adolescence. To characterize the fusiform response to faces, scientists typically present research participants with face images and other (non-face) images, such as houses or other easily recognizable objects, and compare the fusiform response to each category of objects. This approach is useful for determining how selective the fusiform response is to faces. In this context, selectivity refers to the preference that a particular region exhibits for a particular object. If the region in question exhibits similar activation intensity to multiple types of objects it means that it is not very discerning to any one object. However, if it is mostly responsive to one object, that means it has been selected either phylogenetically (across evolutionary time) or ontogenetically (across developmental time) to specifically respond to that object type.

Research has consistently found that adolescents exhibit a fusiform gyrus response that is very similar to adults, wherein the fusiform gyrus response to faces is greater for faces than for houses (Aylward et al., 2005). As a result of this finding, this region is sometimes referred to as the **fusiform face area** (FFA) (Kanwisher et al., 1997). Interestingly, children do not show this selectivity, as response in the fusiform gyrus does not differ between faces and houses in children (Aylward et al., 2005). Another study found evidence for large age-related changes in the fusiform gyrus response to faces in a sample of participants that ranged in age from 7 to 37 years old (Cohen Kadosh, Johnson, Dick, Cohen Kadosh, and Blakemore, 2013). This interesting developmental shift suggests that, in contrast to the modular view of face processing that would predict people of all ages would show face selectivity in the fusiform gyrus, this region develops over time based on the interaction of increased experience with faces and brain maturation. This argues against the "preprogrammed" argument.

There is also evidence to suggest that the fusiform gyrus response to faces is more diffuse in children, covering a larger swath of brain tissue, becoming more focal with increasing age. These results are consistent with the notion that the representations of object categories encompass more overlapping regions at younger ages and become increasingly selective and localized to one region (Passarotti et al., 2003). Specifically, linear age-related increases were observed in the activation of the FFA, which was associated with a behavioral improvement in recognition memory for facial identity (Golarai et al., 2007). A more focal, intense response in the fusiform gyrus to faces with increasing age is consistent with experiential tuning and refinement of the representation across adolescence, consistent with the notion that representations of faces become more focal with development and experience (Burnett, Sebastian, Cohen Kadosh, and Blakemore, 2011). Using postmortem tissue, Grill-Spector and colleagues report that development of face-selective regions is dominated by microstructural proliferation in the cortex (Gomez et al., 2017). However, there is a limit to refinement in this region, as studies suggest that not much change occurs past adolescence (Golarai, Liberman, Yoon, and Grill-Spector, 2010; Scherf, Behrmann, Humphreys, and Luna, 2007).

In sum, the neuroimaging evidence suggests that large changes occur in the neural representations of faces in the fusiform gyrus across childhood, adolescence, and adulthood. Another important change is that connections between the fusiform gyrus and other brain region changes show large differences from childhood into adolescence. For example, age-related changes in top-down modulation of fusiform gyrus connections have been observed from childhood through adulthood (Cohen Kadosh, Henson, Cohen Kadosh, Johnson, and Dick, 2010). The face processing literature has not only provided important information about how high-level visual perception develops across adolescence, but also more broadly provides a useful framework for considering how environmental factors and biological readiness interact to shape the social brain during adolescence.

Posterior Superior Temporal Sulcus

If the fusiform gyrus is the Director of face processing, the posterior superior temporal sulcus (pSTS) is an important Associate Director. It is involved in eye gaze processing, which helps link processing of the physical aspects of the face (such as the nose, eyes, and mouth) with the emotional meaning or intentions of the face. The pSTS is selective in what it attends to, as it responds to moving and stationary eyes and mouth, but not to moving checkerboards or contracting circles (Puce, Allison, Bentin, Gore, and McCarthy, 1998). It also shows greater activation when participants are focused specifically on eye gaze rather than face identity (Hoffman and Haxby, 2000) and it responds to other signals important for social communication, including mutual gaze, emotional expression, and limb movements (Allison, Puce, and McCarthy, 2000). More generally, it has been associated with monitoring intentions, regardless of who or what is doing the motions or intentions. One study found that the pSTS was even activated by simple geometric shapes, which had no resemblance to faces or body parts, when the shapes' pattern of motion conveyed "intention" (Schultz, Imamizu, Kawato, and Frith, 2004). When these familiar objects are not moving, participants do not typically assign "intention" to them but adding motion changes how we (and our pSTS) interpret the same shapes!

The majority of studies of the pSTS have been conducted in adults but there are a few developmental findings. One fMRI study found similar responses in the pSTS of adults and children (ages 7–10) during processing of averted gaze (Mosconi, Mack, McCarthy, and Pelphrey, 2005). Around the time of puberty there is a simultaneous decrease in anatomical size and cortical thickness in the pSTS (Mills, Lalonde, Clasen, Giedd, and Blakemore, 2014) and increased connectivity between the pSTS and other regions in the social processing network, including the DMPFC and TPJ during social processing, that is associated with increased pubertal hormone levels (Klapwijk et al., 2013). These findings suggest increased refinement in the pSTS as adolescents gain social information processing skills.

Face Processing in Other Species

Humans are not the only species on this earth who have faces. Nor are they the only species that exhibits strong social bonding. Research in monkeys has demonstrated that they also have strong face processing skills. Remarkably these skills are specific to other monkey faces. There is no evolutionarily good reason for monkeys to be human face experts (just as there is no good reason for us to be monkey face experts) but it does make a lot of sense for them to be able to recognize other monkeys. Adult monkeys also simply have more experience seeing monkey faces than human faces (just as we have more experience seeing human faces than monkey faces). A seminal experiment illustrated this point elegantly.

Pascalis and colleagues were interested in determining whether there is a "sensitive period" for recognizing faces of other species (Pascalis, de Haan, and Nelson, 2002). This idea is similar to the notion that as people get older, they slowly lose the ease of learning a new language. The same is true with face processing. Some proposed that the ability to perceive faces diminishes with development, due in part to the cortical specialization that occurs with increased experience viewing faces. The underlying assumption with this hypothesis is that, because the brain can hold only so much information at one time, the ability to take in new information (or to hold on to less relevant information) diminishes as we acquire expertise. As Pascalis and colleagues hypothesized that younger infants, who have less experience with faces than older infants and than adults, would exhibit better face processing skills than older infants or adults when viewing faces of other species.

They tested this prediction in human infants who presumably were not yet "adult face experts" and who did not have much experience with faces of the other species (Pascalis et al., 2002). They used a visual paired-comparison procedure (VPC) to assess face recognition in both infants and adults. In a VPC, participants are presented with two stimuli, one of which they have seen many times before and one that is novel. An example of the stimuli used in this study during the VPC is shown in Figure 7.3. You probably easily recognize that the faces in the top panel are two different human faces but perhaps it took you a little longer to realize that the two monkey faces in the bottom panel were of two different monkeys. During the experiment, participants' looking time to each of the faces was assessed. If they spent longer time looking at the face they had not previously seen, the experimenters concluded that they could tell the difference between the two faces and saw each one as distinct. However, if there was no difference in looking time to the faces, the experimenters concluded that the participants did not know the two faces were from different individuals.

Infant participants in the study were 30 healthy, full-term 6-month-old infants and 30 healthy, full-term 9-month-old infants. A comparison group of 11 healthy adults was also included. All three age groups looked longer at the human face that they had not seen before as compared to the face they had been familiarized to earlier in the experiment. This confirmed that all three age groups knew the human faces were different from one another. However, the three age groups exhibited behavior that differed from each other when they were presented with the two monkey faces. Only the 6-month-olds showed evidence of face discrimination of the monkey faces! They looked longer at the "new" monkey face than at

Figure 7.3 Examples of monkey and human face study used by Pascalis and colleagues (2002). See color plate 14.

the monkey face they saw first. This means that the 6-month-olds were better at telling the monkeys apart than the 9-month-olds and the adults, both of whom did not exhibit differences in looking time to the monkey they had seen earlier and to the monkey that was new to them. This finding provides strong evidence for the hypothesis that face processing skills narrow with age: people get better at identifying and differentiating faces of humans but get worse at differentiating faces of other species!

7.2.2 Affect Processing

Our world is colored by emotions. The neural processing of emotions or feelings, whether our own or those of others, is called **affect**

processing. The development of affect processing and the neural regions that support it starts very early in life and continues through adolescence. Some evidence even suggests that infants as young as 3 months of age can discriminate between happy or sad facial expressions (Barrera and Maurer, 1981). Between the ages of 2 and 5, recognition of emotional expressions improves by as much as 40% (Golarai et al., 2006) but even 5 year olds struggle with uncommon emotions. There is an interesting gradient of accuracy in identifying emotions in young children. They are best at identifying happiness. They are least accurate at identifying surprise, fear, and neutral expressions (Bullock and Russell, 1985). Their accuracy in identifying sadness and anger lies somewhere in the middle. This pattern is consistently reported from different researchers. One common explanation for this phenomenon is that children are best able to detect happiness and sadness because they have more experience seeing these faces than surprise, fear, and neutral expressions. Indeed, one piece of evidence for this rationale comes from research in children who are reared in abusive homes – they show higher accuracy for identifying angry and sad faces, presumably because they have more experience seeing them than their non-abused counterparts (Pollak et al., 2010). In this section we will focus on the neural correlates that support affect processing and learn how their development is influenced by experience.

Amygdala

When was the last time you were scared? Perhaps it was when you watched a scary movie or when you were walking down a dark alley alone or when you were riding a roller coaster. Regardless of the situation, your amygdala was highly engaged, sending alert signals about potential threat and harm. The amygdala is a subcortical structure in the deep layers of the brain that is composed of nine nuclei. All vertebrate animals have an amygdala and it plays a critical role in monitoring the environment. Our survival heavily depends on it because it helps organisms process emotions in the self and read the emotions of others, detect surrounding threat, and motivate the *fight or flight* response. First described in 1929 (Bradford Cannon, 1929), the fight or flight response refers to the physiological reaction that occurs in response to a perceived threat. The release of hormones in response to threat results in a rush of arousing neurotransmitters, including dopamine, norepinephrine, and epinephrine (the latter two also known as noradrenaline and adrenaline, respectively), that help mobilize the organism. It is perhaps no coincidence that the word "motion" is embedded in "emotion" because emotions, whether positive or negative, help motivate and mobilize us.

Some believe that the amygdala is the most important region in the brain. Although emotion processing is supported by numerous brain regions (Adolphs, 2002), the amygdala takes the lead in recognizing emotion. It is also implicated in positive and negative affect, sensing threat, mood, and a wide range of neurodevelopmental disorders that emerge in adolescence, including depression, anxiety, substance use, and eating disorders. One of the most well-characterized behaviors associated with amygdala function is Pavlovian fear conditioning, a basic form of learning in which an emotional or arousing event is associated with a neutral stimulus or event. This happens so quickly that we often do not even recognize when it is happening but are acutely aware once we have acquired a fear without our awareness of it! Most people consider the movie *The Shining* to be very scary. It was highly effective at pairing an otherwise neutral stimulus, such as an empty hallway, with scary music after having conditioned the viewer to the eerie tone of the movie. The amygdala quickly taught us to feel chills at the sight of the empty hallway! The amygdala is also involved in directing attention to emotionally relevant stimuli for the purposes of learning and maintaining arousal (Kim et al., 2011). Rare instances where the amygdala is damaged lead to impairments in these skills. See Box 7.1 for a case study of an otherwise healthy patient who has lost both of her amygdalae.

fMRI Studies of the Amygdala

Neuroimaging studies in adults find that the amygdala exhibits significant activation in response to facial expressions of emotion. This has been a consistent finding across a wide range of studies, even when subjects were not instructed to judge emotion (Breiter et al., 1996) or when the presentation of faces was subliminal (Whalen et al., 1998). The amygdala response is greater to fear than to happy faces (Morris et al., 1996), as shown in Figure 7.4 (Tottenham et al., 2011). Converging evidence suggests that the amygdala takes the greatest cue about emotions from the eyes (Golarai et al., 2006), as studies that manipulate eye gaze (Kawashima et al., 1999), occlude the eyes, or mask everything but the eyes (Whalen et al., 2004) find decreased amygdala activation. However, the context under which the face is being observed is also important. As described in Box 7.2, neutral faces, not fearful faces, activate the amygdala in children the most; this is due to the negative connotation of neutral faces to children.

Box 7.1 Patient SM

Patient SM is famous among emotion scientists. She is a middle-aged woman who does not have amygdalae because of a rare congenital genetic disorder called Urbach-Wiethe disease. Scientists have been studying her for over two decades to determine what happens to someone's fear conditioning, face processing, and social abilities when they do not have the very region that helps recognize threat, emotions, and people. A comprehensive review of all the experiments they have done with her would take an entire book so only a few will be listed here, but you are encouraged to read a thorough report on the topic by the scientists who have conducted the research (Feinstein, Adolphs, Damasio, and Tranel, 2011).

To provoke fear in SM, the scientists exposed her to many things that make most of us jump, including live snakes and spiders, and a tour of a haunted house, and showed her emotionally evocative films. On not one occasion did she show signs of fear. At a pet store, she held a snake and displayed exploratory behaviors not commonly observed: she rubbed its leathery scales, touched its flicking tongue, and said "This is so cool!" (Feinstein et al., 2011). At a haunted house ranked one of the "most haunted" in the world, SM volunteered to lead a group through the house, reacted to monsters that jumped out at her by laughing and trying to talk to them, and showed absolutely no fear but much excitement. This latter point is important because it suggests that her lack of fear is not simply a result of an under-aroused arousal system. In response to short clips from films most of us consider really scary, including *The Blair Witch Project*, *Arachnophobia*, *The Shining*, *Halloween*, and *Silence of the Lambs*, SM said she found the films to be entertaining but not scary.

SM was also interviewed about her colorful life experiences. These include numerous events that would be considered fear-inducing and traumatic in most people, such as being held up at knife-point and gun-point, being physically assaulted by someone twice her size, and being nearly killed in an act of domestic violence. Despite the intensity of the experiences, SM does not recall feeling fear despite feeling anger and being upset. Police reports corroborate this recollection.

Patient SM's inability to generate fear across the range of scary situations supports the conclusion that the amygdala is a critical brain region for triggering a state of fear when an individual encounters threatening stimuli in the external environment (Feinstein et al., 2011).

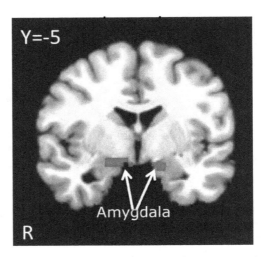

Figure 7.4 The amygdala exhibits enhanced activation during presentation of fearful stimuli (Tottenham et al., 2011).

Similar to research in adults, the amygdala is robustly engaged across development, albeit to a greater extent in adolescents. Several studies have shown greater amygdala response to facial expressions in adolescents relative to adults across a wide range of emotions (Gee et al., 2013; Guyer et al., 2008; Hare et al., 2008; Swartz, Carrasco, Wiggins, Thomason, and Monk, 2014). Interestingly, this age-related difference has even been observed for facial expressions that are presented subliminally and therefore not consciously perceived (Killgore and Yurgelun-Todd, 2007), suggesting that during adolescence the amygdala is highly sensitive to emotional cues even when presented below awareness thresholds.

The amygdala is so important in shaping adolescent behavioral and neural response to the dynamic social world that it has been called an "agent of change in adolescent neural networks" (Scherf, Smyth, and Delgado, 2013). An agent of change refers to the neural region that is the driving force in helping to reorganize neural systems so that they can together support the emergence of completely novel behaviors during adolescence. These behaviors, which include mastery of developmental tasks that are specific to this period of development, including developing romantic partners, increased loyalty to friends, and becoming autonomous from parents, are complex and thus need a "neural leader" to take charge. Similar to a sports coach, it is posited that the

Box. 7.2 The Curious Case of the Neutral Face

Children (and some adolescents) find neutral facial expressions threatening. In fact, they commonly misidentify neutral faces as sad or angry in the laboratory (Walden and Field, 1982). In real life, when a child sees a neutral face directed at them, it typically does mean that the person making that face is displeased with his or her behavior. This is a contrast to adults' experience, wherein seeing a neutral face is the norm, as when we drive a car, ride the subway, or simply sit in class. Think about this next time you are in a lecture. Your professor is flooded with a sea of neutral faces but this is not threatening to her because it is what she sees on a daily basis. But a child receiving that same neutral input would perceive it as having a negative connotation. It is because of our increasing experience with neutral faces across development that we begin to shift our interpretation of neutral faces from one that implies a potential threat to one that is, well, neutral.

The amygdala plays a large role in equating threat with neutral faces in children. If the amygdala's job is to alert us to arousing and scary events then why is it wasting its energy on responding to neutral? The amygdala response to neutral is a nice example of how tightly linked experience and development are with neural activation. Remember that children find neutral faces to connote negative intentions. Indeed, they are least able to concentrate on a laboratory task when presented with neutral faces and actually show the worst performance in face identification to neutral faces, as compared to angry, fearful, happy, and calm faces (Tottenham, Hare, and Casey, 2009). In younger children, this poor accuracy is paralleled by heightened activation in the amygdala to neutral faces (as compared to any other emotion). Is it because neutral faces are scarier than angry faces, for instance? Not necessarily. Instead, it is probably because neutral faces have different meaning in children than for adults, including a stranger connotation, punishment, and because they signal ambiguity. All of these are potential threats to the organism, so the amygdala is called in to monitor the situation until it is known whether there is threat in the environment or not. In adults, the amygdala response is greater to fear than to neutral faces whereas the opposite is true in young adolescents (Thomas et al., 2001). Across age, the amygdala response to neutral faces wanes (Tottenham et al., 2009), presumably due to increasing daily experience with neutral expressions that do not lead to threatening or harmful outcomes.

amygdala helps strengthen the key players (other "social brain" regions) and reorganize their positions in response to dynamic needs of each developmental stage. It is reasonable to focus on the amygdala as the agent of change in this reorganizational process because it is extensively interconnected with the vast majority of cortical and subcortical regions that support social and emotion processing. It has been described as having a "hub-like" architecture because many neural connections pass through it en route to a final destination, similar to an airport hub. It is also really good at receiving signals from the pubertal hormones that emerge at the beginning of adolescence and using them to guide behavior. It is unique in that it is one of only a small number of regions that have receptors for sex hormones (Osterlund, Keller, and Hurd, 1999). Functional neuroimaging studies have shown that sex hormones modulate amygdala activation (Bos, van Honk, Ramsey, Stein, and Hermans, 2013) and functional connectivity between the amygdala and other regions (e.g., ventrolateral prefrontal cortex) in response to social stimuli (Volman, Toni, Verhagen, and Roelofs, 2011).

Amygdala–mPFC Functional Connectivity

The emergence of functional connectivity techniques discussed in Chapter 3 has allowed the field to more deeply explain why amygdala reactivity to emotion decreases across age. The phenomenon seems to rest on the changes in connectivity between the amygdala and regions of the medial prefrontal cortex (mPFC). Interactions between the amygdala and mPFC are fundamental to emotion processing and regulation (Delgado, Nearing, Ledoux, and Phelps, 2008; Wager, Davidson, Hughes, Lindquist, and Ochsner, 2008) and extinction (Hartley, Fischl, and Phelps, 2011), which refers to the reduction or loss of an emotional response to a particular stimulus, in adults. Moreover, individual differences in the strength of amygdala–mPFC functional connectivity are associated with greater amygdala habituation to affective stimuli (Hare et al., 2008), more effective emotion regulation (Banks, Eddy, Angstadt, Nathan, and Phan, 2007), and lower temperamental anxiety (Pezawas et al., 2005), suggesting that the prefrontal regions may help regulate (or decrease) the amygdala's reactivity to emotion.

In adults, these regions exhibit inverse functional coupling, meaning that when one is highly reactive the other is minimally reactive (Hariri, Mattay, Tessitore, Fera, and Weinberger, 2003; Kim et al., 2004). In other words, the mPFC helps dampen the amygdala response to emotional information, and this regulation increases from adolescence to adulthood because of the ongoing maturation of the prefrontal cortex.

The large developmental changes in amygdala and prefrontal connectivity have been reported in numerous studies (Gee et al., 2013; Perlman and Pelphrey, 2011; Swartz et al., 2014). Improvements in emotion regulation across adolescence parallel this development and appear to be mediated by an interesting switch in connectivity: the positive amygdala–prefrontal connectivity in early childhood switches to a negative connectivity during the transition to adolescence that coincides with a steady decline in amygdala activity (Gee et al., 2013). The authors interpret this switch to indicate a shift to greater regulation over the amygdala by the prefrontal cortex with increasing regulatory maturation.

How Emotions Impact Cognition

Emotions serve a useful purpose. They help us direct attention to relevant and salient stimuli in the environment, so much so that sometimes this interferes with our cognitive abilities. This phenomenon seems to be exaggerated in adolescents. For example, in one fMRI study, children, adolescents, and adults were tested on a Go/No-Go task with emotional (happy faces) and non-emotional cues (calm faces) (Somerville, Hare, and Casey, 2011). Participants were asked to press a button every time they were presented with an image of a face but to inhibit their behavioral response to particular facial expressions (on some trials they were instructed to inhibit their response when a happy face was presented and on other trials they were instructed to inhibit their response when a calm face was presented). The ability to inhibit responses to calm faces improved with age whereas the ability to inhibit responses to happy faces was significantly worse in adolescents compared to children and adults. Why would adolescents make more errors when presented with a happy face, even worse than younger children? The explanation became clear when the researchers analyzed the neuroimaging data. The lapse in behavioral control in the adolescent group was associated with enhanced activation of the reward and emotion system and greater connectivity between the reward and cognitive control systems in adolescents versus children and adults (Somerville et al., 2011). This finding shows that greater sensitivity to the emotional stimuli disrupted an otherwise capable cognitive control system. This suggests that emotional information distinctively biases input from the prefrontal cortex and subsequent behavior in adolescents.

7.3 Complex Social Cognitive Skills

We derive a lot of useful information from faces and emotions. However, we have also evolved social cognitive skills that enhance the complexity of our interactions. It is through these skills that we can understand others, sometimes without even exchanging one word. In the remaining section of this chapter we will learn about complex social cognitive skills and the neural systems that support them.

7.3.1 Theory of Mind/Mentalizing

Theory of mind (often abbreviated as ToM or referred to as **mentalizing**) is a sophisticated and rather complex social cognitive skill. It refers to the ability to assign mental states, including beliefs, intents, desires, pretending, knowledge, and sarcasm, to oneself and others. It also refers to the understanding that others have beliefs, desires, intentions, and perspectives that are different from one's own. For instance, if someone accidentally drops their ice cream cone and they say, "Well, that's just terrific!" you know that they do not really believe it is terrific. Your mentalizing skills give you this insight. It is at the very core of understanding what people mean when they say what they mean and also when they say something they do not mean. This is an area of great interest in the social cognition literature, not only because it is highly relevant for effective social communication but because individuals with certain neurodevelopmental disorders suffer from impaired mentalizing abilities.

Mentalizing Theories

How does mentalizing develop? Young children display some rudimentary mentalizing skills but many do not understand or use sarcasm until much later, around adolescence. There are four leading theories about how mentalizing develops (Mahy, Moses, and Pfeifer, 2014).

Modularity theories ascribe to the notion that mentalizing is supported by an innate neural system that cannot be influenced by the environment (e.g. Leslie, Friedman, and German, 2004). In general, innate theories are based on the idea that certain mental faculties are present from birth because they are intrinsic to the individual. This means that they should be observable in very young children. Indeed, there is some evidence for mentalizing in very young infants. Between 6 and 12 months infants develop something called **joint attention** (Grossmann and Johnson, 2007), which means they look in the direction of someone else's gaze, an indication that they are jointly attending to something. Between 12 and

18 months of age, babies will look in the direction that someone is pointing, rather than at the person's finger, and will themselves point to draw someone's attention to something (Wellman, Lopez-Duran, LaBounty, and Hamilton, 2008), suggesting that they understand that the pointing behavior is a window into the person's thought process.

Simulation theories propose that individuals first call up their own representations of psychological states in order to understand mental states of other people (Gordon, 1992). This suggests that we first consider how we would feel/react/act in a particular situation and then project those mental states onto the other person. Evidence for this notion is found in the protracted developmental trajectory of mentalizing. Infants who are initially limited to tasks such as joint attention become increasingly skilled at more sophisticated mentalizing tasks that require more complex understanding of others (Carpendale and Lewis, 2004).

Executive function theories are strongly rooted in the notion that one's inhibitory control and working memory abilities contribute to mentalizing capacity (Carlson and Moses, 2001). These theories basically state that challenges in inhibiting one's own perspective to generate a different one and/or holding both perspectives in working memory will make it difficult to reason or consider the mental states of others. Given that children and adolescents have more limited inhibitory control and working memory skills than adults in general, it follows that they would be worse at mentalizing about others. Indeed, younger individuals have a harder time taking the perspective of someone else. Many laboratory tests have demonstrated the relationship between age-related improvements in executive functions and mentalizing (e.g. Carlson, Moses, and Claxton, 2004).

The final theory is amusingly called *theory theory* (Gopnik and Wellman, 2012). This theory is diametrically opposed to the modular theories. In contrast to the notion that mentalizing is innate and supported by neural mechanisms that are programmed from birth, the *theory* theory proposes that children acquire the knowledge and skills necessary for effective mentalizing through observation. Specifically, this line of thinking supports the idea that the child plays an active role in forming the concepts necessary to link mental states with actions (Pears and Moses, 2003). According to Mahy and colleagues (2014) and much of the developmental psychology literature, the *theory* theory is considered the one that most fully explains extant developmental data. In particular, it satisfactorily accounts for the observed progressions in mentalizing from early childhood through adulthood. It also explains why children make great strides in mentalizing in response to experience (Lohmann and Tomasello, 2003).

Neural Correlates of Mentalizing

Neural support for each of these theories is mixed. To support *modularity theories*, a particular set of regions would need to be consistently engaged during mentalizing tasks, present very early in development and throughout the entire lifespan and only responsive to mentalizing tasks and no other cognitive operation. This is a tall order and so, unsurprisingly, there is little neural evidence to fulfill a strict modularity theory. Although there are particular regions that are typically implicated in mentalizing fMRI tasks in adults, including the medial prefrontal cortex, ACC, TPJ, and posterior parietal cortices (PPC) (Amodio and Frith, 2006), these regions are also regularly engaged for other cognitive operations that do not involve mentalizing. Activation in the TPJ during mentalizing is observed in adulthood but is not observed in younger children and adolescents, who do not consistently exhibit TPJ recruitment during mentalizing tasks (Gweon, Dodell-Feder, Bedny, and Saxe, 2013).

Criteria to support *simulation theories* needs to include some overlap between neural regions that are active when thinking about the self and when thinking about others. Furthermore, the strength of activation should be related to the extent of mentalizing ability (Mahy et al., 2014). Activation of the mPFC, ACC, and PPC supports this perspective, as they are engaged in both self-perception and perspective-taking in typically developing adolescents and adults (Pfeifer et al., 2009). One way researchers have tested this is to examine brain activation when thinking about a similar or dissimilar other person. This research has revealed that the mPFC in adults is more responsive during mentalizing of similar versus dissimilar others (Mitchell, Macrae, and Banaji, 2006). However, there is a change in how the mPFC is engaged across development (Pfeifer, Lieberman, and Dapretto, 2007), suggesting that adults may have a specialized process for simulating and reasoning about dissimilar others (Mahy et al., 2014) whereas children do not yet have this specialized engagement of the mPFC for this purpose.

Simulation theories are also supported by neural evidence for a system known as the *mirror neuron systems* (MNS). The MNS is comprised of regions in the inferior frontal gyrus (IFG) and inferior parietal lobule (IPL) that are active during the perception and execution of actions. The MNS co-activates to the actions, intentions, and emotions of both the self and others in children, adolescents, and adults (Pfeifer, Iacoboni, Mazziotta, and Dapretto, 2008).

There is some neural evidence to support **executive function theories**. First, inhibitory control and mentalizing share neural correlates, most prominently the bilateral inferior frontal gyrus (van der Meer, Groenewold, Nolen, Pijnenborg, and Aleman, 2011), frontal regions, and TPJ (Rothmayr et al., 2010), possibly an indication of a common inhibitory control mechanism. Second, EEG studies in children suggest that EEG waveforms are positively associated with individual differences in mentalizing, after controlling for age and performance variability on the tasks (Sabbagh, Bowman, Evraire, and Ito, 2009). What remains unknown is the extent to which executive functions contribute to, or are necessary for, the acquisition of mentalizing skills.

The neural evidence for *theory* theory is fairly sparse. However, emerging tools that examine how experience shapes brain function, such as functional connectivity or resting state approaches, can help identify neural mechanisms. Nonetheless, the finding that TPJ is consistently and highly engaged during mentalizing tasks supports *theory* theories. The increasing developmental selectivity of the TPJ to mentalizing tasks may reflect advancing skill that comes with age.

Regardless of the particular theory, there is no question that regions implicated in mentalizing evince considerable structural change across adolescence before stabilizing in the early twenties (Mills et al., 2014). In a large sample of almost 300 participants who ranged from 7 to 30 years of age, Mills and colleagues used MRI to identify the structural developmental trajectories of the mentalizing brain network. Gray matter volume and cortical thickness in dmPFC, TPJ, and pSTS decreased from childhood into the early twenties, whereas the ATC increased in gray matter volume until adolescence and in cortical thickness until early adulthood (Blakemore and Mills, 2014). Surface area for each region followed a cubic trajectory, reaching a peak in early adolescence before decreasing into the early twenties (Mills et al., 2014). This protracted development demonstrates that areas of the brain involved in deciphering the mental states of others are still maturing from late childhood into early adulthood. You might be asking yourself what these reductions in gray matter mean. Remember from Chapter 4 that cortical regions continue to eliminate neurons throughout adolescence that are irrelevant or unnecessary, a process known as synaptic pruning (Huttenlocher and Dabholkar, 1997).

7.3.2 Social Evaluation

Among the most consistent and marked shifts in adolescence is an increased orientation toward peers (Steinberg and Morris, 2001). Adolescents go through a period of social reorienting whereby they place greater importance on the opinions of peers than on those of family members (Larson, Richards, Moneta, Holmbeck, and Duckett, 1996). They also spend more face-to-face and digital time with them, with a higher frequency of internet, text messaging, and social media usage in teenagers compared to adults (Perrin, 2015). This shift helps the adolescent become aware of peer norms and to learn about complex social structures more generally. However, peer orientation can lead to maladaptive consequences, such as increased sensitivity to social evaluation (Urberg, 1992), and negative peer influence such as heightened engagement in risky behaviors (Gardner and Steinberg, 2005). Indeed, adolescents are hyperaware of others' evaluations and feel they are under constant scrutiny (Elkind and Bowen, 1979). This phenomenon has been called *social sensitivity*, a reference to the intensification of attention, salience, and emotion "relegated to processing information concerning social evaluations and social standing" (Somerville, 2013).

Several studies have demonstrated the neurobiological correlates of social evaluation. In one study, researchers examined the neural response during adolescents' subjective appraisal of how peers evaluated them (Guyer, McClure-Tone, Shiffrin, Pine, and Nelson, 2009). It is challenging to set up a laboratory version of peer evaluation but the researchers cleverly did so using a "chatroom" scenario. Adolescent participants ranging in age from 8 to 17 were led to believe they were participating in a nationwide investigation of teenagers' online communication through internet chatrooms. Participants were also photographed and told they would be evaluated by other teens in the study. During the brain scan, they viewed pictures of the alleged other participants who presumably had evaluated the research participant. Using a handheld device inside the scanner, the participants rated the degree to which they believed the peer on the screen would be interested in interacting with them. The study revealed interesting gender interactions. Whereas adolescent girls evinced greater activation in the nucleus accumbens, hypothalamus, and hippocampus as they got older, there was no such relationship in males. Given the role of the nucleus accumbens in processing rewarding information, the authors interpret this finding as suggesting that this activation pattern may be "in response to positive social interactions" that mature during adolescence. In the insula, a region implicated in affective processing and in integrating visceral sensation with cognitive appraisals in response to social and emotional stimuli (Craig, 2009), a different pattern was observed. Whereas females did not show increased insula activation with increasing age, males showed decreased activation with increasing age. This may suggest a key difference between males and females in terms of social processing:

males may be showing a reduction in affective engagement while females become increasingly aware of and sensitive to social evaluation (Guyer et al., 2009).

One particularly interesting study reported that adolescents demonstrated heightened self-consciousness and exaggerated engagement of social processing circuitry just by knowing that someone was looking at them! Somerville and colleagues told participants that while they were in the brain scanner a peer would watch them via live video feed (Somerville et al., 2013). Adolescents reported more embarrassment, greater autonomic response (sweatier palms), and more activation of the medial prefrontal cortex than the other age groups.

Unfortunately, some adolescents have good reason to be sensitive to peer evaluation because they experience chronic peer rejection. Studies that have examined the neural response to social exclusion have consistently found activation of the anterior cingulate cortex (ACC), medial PFC, and VLPFC (Masten, Eisenberger, Pfeifer, and Dapretto, 2010; Will, van Lier, Crone, and Guroglu, 2016). Chronically rejected youth showed heightened activation of the ACC during social exclusion, which is consistent with previous work in adults with low self-esteem (Onoda et al., 2010) and in adults who reported low social support and comfort (Eisenberger, Taylor, Gable, Hilmert, and Lieberman, 2007). There are several lines of research that might be helpful in interpreting this result. The ACC has previously been implicated in conflict monitoring (Botvinick, Cohen, and Carter, 2004), violation of expectations (Somerville, Heatherton, and Kelley, 2006), physical pain (Shackman et al., 2011), unfairness (Sanfey, Rilling, Aronson, Nystrom, and Cohen, 2003), and social exclusion in adults (Eisenberger, Lieberman, and Williams, 2003). Furthermore, it has been argued that it is a hub for the integration of emotional and motivational valence of stimuli (Somerville et al., 2006). Thus, it makes sense that it plays a strong role in representing exclusion, a psychological construct that embodies these various emotions and cognitive responses. You may be surprised to learn that being excluded does not consistently elicit robust activation of the amygdala, a center for processing threat, emotion, and feelings. This just goes to show how important it is to consider the various cognitive inputs that influence behaviors and responses that seem purely emotional in nature. It is also a good reminder that, although we may heuristically categorize brain regions and their primary function, the complexity of the human brain (and its development) lies precisely in the fact that many neural regions are called upon to perform various tasks and no one region is responsible for any one cognitive operation.

7.3.3 Prosocial Behavior

A **prosocial behavior** is any action intended to help others. This may include helping, sharing, donating, co-operating, including, and volunteering. Although there are vast individual differences in the extent to which people exhibit prosocial behavior, it becomes more sophisticated with age.

In a series of studies, scientists at Harvard have found that even very young children exhibit helping and cooperative behavior (Warneken and Tomasello, 2009). How can altruism and cooperation be studied in subjects (infants and toddlers) who are preverbal? The basic paradigm Warneken and colleagues used was to set up many situations in which an adult stranger was engaged in a goal-directed activity (e.g. putting books into a cabinet) while a toddler was playing with his or her mother. Then something happened that interfered with the experimenter's goal (e.g. the cabinet door swung shut while the experimenter's arms were loaded with books). (Figure 7.5 shows some examples of young children exhibiting helping behavior in laboratory experiments. To see videos of this helping behavior, visit http://email.eva.mpg .de/~warneken/video). The dependent measure was whether children helped. They find that children as young as 14 months of age naturally and spontaneously help others (Warneken and Tomasello, 2006). Subsequent work then explored the hypothesis that children may have been socialized to be helpful. Warneken found that children are not responsive to potential rewards for helping. They help whether or not their parents are present, and whether or not the experimenter asks for help, and they show the signature of intrinsic motivation: reinforcing them for helping actually decreases the probability of their doing so immediately thereafter (Warneken and Tomasello, 2008). Children also exhibit sharing behavior (Moore, 2009) and pass along relevant information if it would be helpful to another person (Liszkowski, Carpenter, Striano, and Tomasello, 2006).

An important aspect of prosocial behavior is fairness and this too is also observed in very young children. Using economic games that economists and evolutionary psychologists use to study fairness in adults, Warneken and colleagues found that young children will reject an offer in which they get 1 reward (a candy) and another child gets 4 pieces of candy, such that neither child gets the reward. This suggests a value of fairness over the value of a piece of candy. These experiments strongly suggest that human infants are naturally empathetic, helpful, generous, and informative (Warneken and Tomasello, 2009). However, more sophisticated prosocial behavior, such as reciprocity, seems to emerge later in childhood (Warneken and Tomasello, 2013).

Out-of-reach

Physical Obstacle

A person accidentally drops an object on the floor and unsuccessfully reaches for it.

A person wants to put a pile of books into a cabinet, but she cannot open the closed doors because her hands are full.

Wrong Result

Wrong Means

A book slips from a stack as a person attempts to place it on top of the stack.

An object drops through a hole into a box and the person unsuccessfully tries to grasp it through the small hole, ignorant of a flap on the side of the box.

Figure 7.5 Examples of children exhibiting helping behavior in laboratory experiments (Warneken and Tomasello, 2009). See color plate 15.

The later emergence is probably influenced by both experience (and encouragement from parents and adults!) and the continued development of regions implicated in prosocial behavior. Developmental neuro-imaging studies have suggested that the transition from an egocentric form of empathy in young children to a more reciprocal concern for others in adolescence (Nakao and Itakura, 2009) is driven by the development of the social brain, particularly by the regions implicated in mentalizing (Decety and Svetlova, 2012). Empathy is usually defined as the ability to feel and read the affective mental states of others, which helps predict their intentions. Being empathetic is also helpful in building and establishing friendships, so it is perhaps no surprise that there are changes in empathy during adolescence. Researchers examined neural responses in adolescents when they were viewing pictures of negative and positive social situations and how these responses related to self-reported levels of empathy (Overgaauw, Guroglu, Rieffe, and Crone, 2014). Examples of the negative situations include inflicting harm on another person, such as punching them. Examples of positive situations include helping a person who has fallen down. The negative situations elicited activation in the STS, which has been shown to be responsive to the intentions of others, whereas the positive situations elicited activation in mPFC and TPJ, both of which have been associated with understanding and empathizing with others (Overgaauw et al., 2014).

To examine the neural correlates of more sophisticated prosocial acts, such as reciprocity, scientists often employ economic allocation games. These games are commonly used by economists to test how people weigh the pros and cons of helping another person, sometimes at their own expense. For example, when considering how to split a piece of pie between yourself and another person, an important consideration in your decision is how much you are willing to sacrifice your own gain for the benefit of the other person. Extant research in adults shows that most individuals value equity and make choices that will be equally beneficial to both people (Fehr and Fischbacher, 2003). Children exhibit a strong preference for equity around ages 8–10, so much so that they are even willing to waste resources to achieve fairness (Blake and McAuliffe, 2011). To examine sharing and giving across adolescence, participants from four age groups (9 year olds, 12 year olds, 15 year olds, and 18 year olds) were asked to play a series of economic allocation games (Guroglu, van den Bos, and Crone, 2014). They were invited to play with four different partners: friend, antagonist, neutral classmate, and anonymous peer. The 9 and 12 year olds showed similar levels of prosocial behavior to all partners, whereas older adolescents showed increasing differentiation in prosocial behavior depending on the relation with peers, with most prosocial behavior toward friends (Guroglu et al., 2014). These findings suggest that adolescents are increasingly better at incorporating social context and closeness with others into sharing decisions. Uncovering the exact neural mechanisms that underlie these shifts in giving and sharing behavior is an intense area of research, but early studies suggest that giving behavior involves the mesolimbic reward system in adolescents (Telzer, Fuligni, Lieberman, and Galván, 2014).

7.4 Adolescent Self-Development

What is the self? From a psychological perspective, the self encompasses the sense that one has of oneself in terms of self-awareness, agency, self-esteem, and the self within the social context (Leary and Tangney, 2003). It is also the recognition that we all have multiple identities and that our sense of self may differ slightly in different domains. For instance, you may have a strong identity as an athlete but still be working through your career identity. Importantly, recognizing the self is important for understanding others. It is what helps us take the perspective of another person (mentalizing).

Adolescence is a critical time for **self-development**, a time when individuals seek to explore their identity, determine "who they really are," and identify the causes and ideas important to them. It is certainly the case that recognizing oneself, both physically and psychologically, emerges much earlier in life, as when a toddler begins to recognize himself in the mirror and refers to himself as "I" (Lewis and Carmody, 2008), but adolescence is when more sophisticated recognition of the self emerges. Why might this be? First, this is perhaps because of the strong influence that peers and others have on perceptions of self during adolescence. During this time, adolescents frequently question "what do others think of me?" and "do I fit in with everyone else?" This questioning helps the individual, correctly or not, to assign value to different aspects herself. If one is praised by teachers for high academic marks but rejected by social peers, then one may identify more strongly as a "smart kid" and less so as a "popular kid." Second, focusing on the self, and on what the self does and does not relate to, helps the adolescent differentiate herself from caregivers. After all, individuating oneself from parents is at the very core of adolescence. Third, the significant changes in pubertal hormones and physical changes associated with puberty bring about new focus on one's body and, subsequently, how others view one's body. Fourth, the increasing ability to conceptualize abstract concepts, aided by maturation of the prefrontal cortex, supports the increasingly sophisticated understanding of the self as a multifaceted being who is the product of a confluence of identities and values.

Cognitive neuroscience research has identified the neural regions that support this identity exploration. Self-development is supported and influenced by both cognitive and socioemotional neural systems (Pfeifer and Peake, 2012). Shifts often observed during adolescence are directly attributed to the changes in brain structure, activation, and connectivity of the social brain.

In response to the simple question "what do others think of me?" adults exhibit enhanced activation of brain regions involved in perspective-taking, such as the TPJ and the pSTS, and those involved in affective states, including the insula and the amygdala. To identify neural correlates underlying the feeling of "fitting in with others," several studies have conducted social exclusion experiments, in which the target participant feels he is being excluded from a peer group while undergoing fMRI. In adults, social exclusion typically elicits activity in dorsal ACC and anterior insula, which correlates with how socially excluded the participant feels (Burklund, Eisenberger, and Lieberman, 2007).

Research in developmental populations shows similar findings. In one study, children (9 to 11 years old) and young adults (23 to 32 years old) were asked to evaluate themselves in terms of their social and academic abilities as well as the abilities of a familiar, fictional other person (the popular character Harry Potter) (Pfeifer et al., 2007). Both adults and children engaged the mPFC to a greater extent when thinking about their own abilities as compared to Harry Potter's abilities. However, children showed more activation than adults during self-appraisals. A study with adolescents found the same developmental effect, of greater activation compared to adults when thinking about themselves (Pfeifer et al., 2009). The authors offer an intriguing interpretation of these findings. They suggest that perhaps children and adolescents are more actively constructing self-appraisals instead of efficiently relying on automatic representations of self. In other words, the self-appraisals are influenced by a greater number of perspectives (Harter, 1999) and thus require greater neural integration of multiple sources of self-evaluation. If this is the case, these findings suggest that vulnerability of self-perceptions to social influences may be amplified across late childhood and early adolescence (Pfeifer and Peake, 2012).

7.5 Atypical Social Development

7.5.1 Social Anxiety Disorder

Adolescence is the time of peak onset for many anxiety disorders, particularly **social anxiety disorder** (Kessler et al., 2005). Social anxiety is characterized by an intense fear or distress in social situations that causes

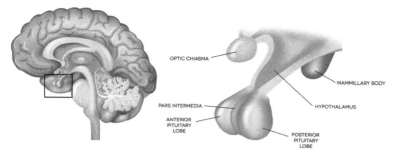

1 The hypothalamus regulates hormone release from the pituitary gland.

2 A group of young adolescents. Despite being in the same grade (7th grade) and roughly the same age, there are obvious differences in pubertal maturation, with some exhibiting greater physical growth and more advanced pubertal stage than others.

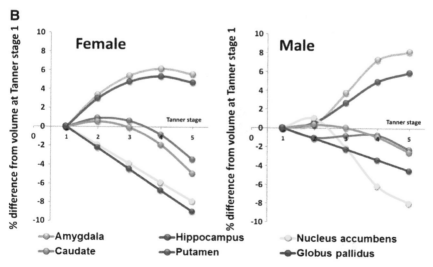

3 The greatest brain volume changes from early pubertal stage (Tanner 1) to latest pubertal stage (Tanner 5) occur in the amygdala and hippocampus in both girls (*left*) and boys (*right*) (Goddings et al., 2014).

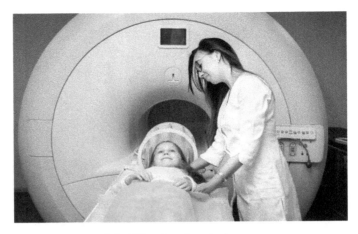

4 A child undergoing a brain scan.

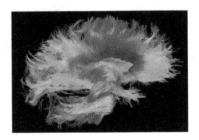

5 This image was taken using diffusion tensor imaging technology and illustrates white matter fibers. The fibers are color-coded by direction: red = left–right, green = anterior–posterior, blue = ascending–descending.

6 A young research participant undergoes an EEG experiment.

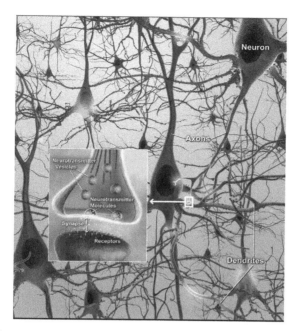

7 A chemical synapse. Neurotransmitters are released from neurotransmitter vesicles in the presynaptic neuron into the space between two neurons (synapse). The neurotransmitter molecules attach to receptors on the postsynaptic neurons.

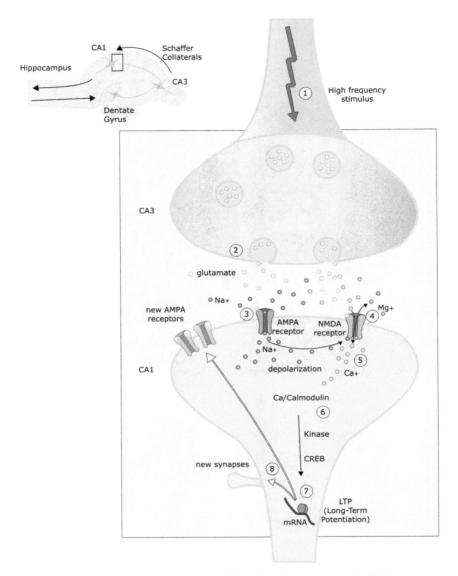

8 An illustration of long-term potentiation (LTP). A high-frequency stimulus (1) triggers release of glutamate (2) from the presynaptic neuron. An influx of sodium (Na$^+$) (3) leads to chemical changes (4–6) that induce LTP (7), which leads to new synapses and AMPA receptors (8) over repeated stimulation.

9 The brain as topiary art.

10 A young participant resisting temptation during the delay of gratification task.

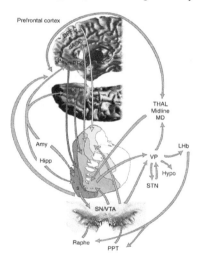

11 A schematic illustrating the primary brain structures and pathways of the reward circuit. 10 refers to Brodmann area 10; red arrow = input from the vmPFC; dark orange arrow = input from the OFC; light orange arrow = input from the dACC; yellow arrow = input from the dPFC; brown arrows = other main connections of the reward circuit. Amy = amygdala; dACC = dorsal anterior cingulate cortex; dPFC = dorsal prefrontal cortex; Hipp = hippocampus; LHb = lateral habenula; MD = mediodorsal; Hypo = hypothalamus; OFC = orbital frontal cortex; PPT = pedunculopontine nucleus; S = shell; SNc = substantia nigra, pars compacta; STN = subthalamic nucleus; Thal = thalamus; VP = ventral pallidum; VTA = ventral tegmental area; vmPFC = ventral medial prefrontal cortex (Haber and Knutson, 2010).

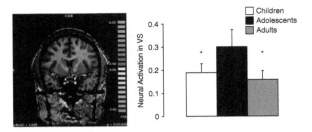

12 Monetary reward elicited activation in the ventral striatum during fMRI in child, adolescent, and adult research participants (*left*). Neural activation in the ventral striatum (VS) was greatest in the adolescent group compared to the children and adults (*right*). ✳ = significant at p < .05 (Galván et al., 2006).

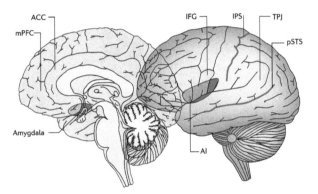

13 An illustration of the primary regions that comprise the social brain, including the medial prefrontal cortex (mPFC) and the temporoparietal junction (TPJ), which are involved in thinking about mental states, and the posterior superior temporal sulcus (pSTS), which is activated by observing faces and biological motion. Other regions of the social brain on the lateral surface are the inferior frontal gyrus (IFG) and the interparietal sulcus (IPS). Regions on the medial surface that are involved in social cognition include the amygdala, the anterior cingulate cortex (ACC), and the anterior insula (AI) (Blakemore, 2008).

14 Examples of monkey and human face study used by Pascalis and colleagues (2002).

Out-of-reach

Physical Obstacle

A person accidentally drops an object on the floor and unsuccessfully reaches for it.

A person wants to put a pile of books into a cabinet, but she cannot open the closed doors because her hands are full.

Wrong Result

Wrong Means

A book slips from a stack as a person attempts to place it on top of the stack.

An object drops through a hole into a box and the person unsuccessfully tries to grasp it through the small hole, ignorant of a flap on the side of the box.

15 Examples of children exhibiting helping behavior in laboratory experiments (Warneken and Tomasello, 2009).

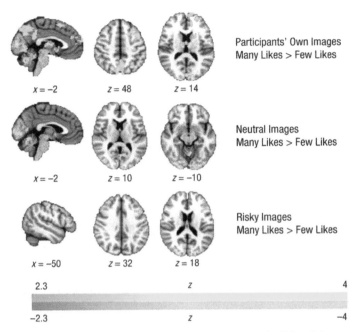

Participants' Own Images
Many Likes > Few Likes

$x = -2$ $z = 48$ $z = 14$

Neutral Images
Many Likes > Few Likes

$x = -2$ $z = 10$ $z = -10$

Risky Images
Many Likes > Few Likes

$x = -50$ $z = 32$ $z = 18$

2.3   z   4

-2.3   z   -4

16 In a study aimed at examining neural responses to social media "likes," there was greater neural activation in response to participants' own photos that generated more versus fewer "likes" (*top* and *bottom*). When participants viewed neutral images (compared with risky images) ostensibly submitted by peers (*middle*), significantly greater activity was observed in the bilateral occipital cortex, the medial prefrontal cortex, and the inferior frontal gyrus (Sherman et al., 2016).

17 High school students engaged in a football tackle.

impairments in daily functioning. Research using simulated social interactions consistently finds differential activation in several brain regions
in anxious (versus non-anxious) youth, including amygdala, striatum,
and medial prefrontal cortex (Spielberg et al., 2015). Unsurprisingly,
youth who suffer from social anxiety are highly sensitive to peer evaluation. Neuroimaging research comparing socially anxious youth with
non-anxious peers has revealed that activation in the amygdala, striatum, ACC, and medial prefrontal cortex is consistently different between
the two groups during peer evaluation (Guyer et al., 2009) and feedback (Guyer, Choate, Pine, and Nelson, 2012) phases of a computer
task. Specifically, anxious participants evidenced greater amygdala activation and greater communication between the rostral anterior cingulate
(rACC) and the amygdala than non-anxious participants during anticipation of feedback from peers they had previously rejected (Spielberg,
Olino, Forbes, and Dahl, 2014). Interestingly, anxious participants exhibited less nucleus accumbens activation during anticipation of feedback
from selected peers. Overall, these data suggest that anxious youth have
greater neural reactivity in threat-sensitive regions in anticipation of feedback from rejected peers and thus may ascribe greater salience to these
potential interactions and increase the likelihood of avoidance behavior
(Spielberg et al., 2015; Spielberg et al., 2014).

7.5.2 Autism

Autism is developmental disorder that falls under the umbrella of Autism
Spectrum Disorders (ASD) (DSM-5 Diagnostic Manual). Milder forms
of ASD include Asperger's Syndrome. These disorders are characterized by difficulties in social interactions, and in verbal and non-verbal
communication, and by stereotyped patterns of behavior. They are also
sometimes associated with intellectual disabilities, motor coordination
impairments, and physical health issues including sleep and gastrointes-
tinal disturbances.

Although the exact causes are unknown, a cluster of genetic, neural,
and perhaps environmental factors seem to play a role in its etiology.
Autism is typically diagnosed by expert clinicians who assess a child's
verbal ability, social communication skills, and repetitive behaviors. This
diagnosis typically occurs between ages 2–3 years, when signs tend to
emerge. Recent statistics from the US Centers for Disease Control and
Prevention (CDC) report that approximately 1 in 68 American children is
on the autism spectrum – an increase that is 10 times greater than 40 years
ago. Research also suggests that autism is 4 to 5 times more commons in

boys than girls, with an estimated 1 out of 42 boys and 1 out of 189 girls in the US. Worldwide, the World Health Organization estimates that 1 in 160 children have an ASD. However, this figure varies substantially across studies and countries, likely due to differences in methodologies used to diagnose, stigma associated with the diagnosis, and access to healthcare.

Early signs of autism typically include deficits in the very social skills we have been discussing in this chapter, including face processing, social communication, and emotion recognition. Physical features include delayed onset of language production and averted eye gaze. Specifically, early indications include lack of mutual eye gaze, a lack of interest in the human face and voice, and preference for inanimate objects (Baron-Cohen et al., 2000).

Mentalizing

The ability to take the perspective of another is at the very core of having meaningful and valuable interactions with others. Emerging research suggests that individuals who struggle to connect with others in typical ways, such as those afflicted with autism and other neurodevelopmental disorders, may have atypical developmental of neural circuitry that underlies mentalizing and self-appraisal. Children and adolescents with autism frequently demonstrate deficits in prospection, self-reference, and other indices of self-development (Lind and Bowler, 2008).

In one fMRI study, regions that are typically activated during self-appraisals, including the ventral and anterior rostral mPFC, showed significantly less activation in adults with autism compared to neurotypical controls (Lombardo et al., 2010). In addition, unlike individuals without autism, they did not exhibit differences in brain activation when thinking about the self versus when thinking about another person. In fact, one brain region, the middle cingulate cortex, exhibited more activation to the other person than to the self in the individuals with autism (Lombardo et al., 2010).

It has been suggested that one core deficit in autism is the inability (or reduced ability) to imitate others (Rogers and Pennington, 1991), which may originate from dysfunctions of the MNS discussed above. Several lines of evidence in adults suggest this hypothesis may be correct. A morphometric study found that patients with autism evince structural abnormalities in MNS regions as compared to typically developing individuals (Hadjikhani, Joseph, Snyder, and Tager-Flusberg, 2006). Patients with autism also displayed reduced mu rhythm suppression during an EEG study when observing others make an action (Oberman et al., 2005) and reduced MNS activation during the imitation of finger movements (Williams et al., 2006).

Although less work has been conducted in children and adolescents to specifically test the MNS deficit hypothesis, one study reports compelling evidence (Dapretto et al., 2006). Children with autism and typically developing control children observed and imitated facial expressions displaying basic emotions (such as happiness, sadness, neutral, and anger). Not only did the children with autism show less MNS activation than healthy controls but the extent of activation in the MNS correlated with the severity of their autism symptoms. Using a widely used clinical scale, the authors found that those with more severe symptoms engaged the MNS system to a lesser extent. This work is promising because it suggests that giving youth with autism training in how to imitate others could be used as an effective treatment approach. Indeed, behavioral data already seem to support this hypothesis. In one study, two groups of children with autism interacted with an adult, and the adult imitated the actions of the children in only one group. Children in the group whose actions were imitated had a higher tendency to initiate social interactions in a later session compared with the group of children that had only a contingent interaction with the adult, with no imitation (Escalona, Field, Nadel, and Lundy, 2002).

Face Processing

Face processing impairments in autism are the focus of intense investigation. The struggle that children and adolescents with autism exhibit during face processing may be attributed to deficits in the skills necessary for face processing, including attention to eye gaze, face identification skills, and emotion recognition.

Eye Gaze

We infer a lot of social information from other people's eyes. Unfortunately, individuals with autism struggle with this ability. Youth with autism are slower at detecting eye gaze than youth without autism (Senju, Yaguchi, Tojo, and Hasegawa, 2003) and adults with autism do not follow the stereotypical pattern of "tracing" a face as controls do. Using eye-tracking, researchers found that whereas adults without autism generally move their eyes in a triangle-like pattern when studying a face, starting at the eyes, then scanning the nose and mouth before returning to the eyes, those with ASD showed an erratic pattern that was less

Autistic Group   Control Group

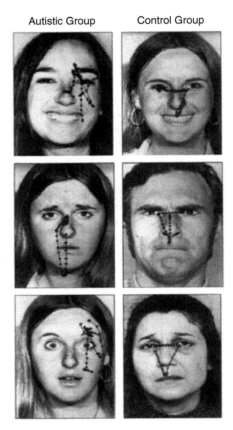

Figure 7.6 Eye-tracking pattern of individuals with autism on the left and individuals without autism on the right.

predictable (Pelphrey, Shultz, Hudac, and Vander Wyk, 2011), sometimes even focusing on peripheral features such as the ear lobe, chin, or hairline. You can see this pattern in Figure 7.6, which shows the eye-tracking patterns of the group with autism on the left and the group without autism on the right. Some researchers interpret this lack of interest in eye gaze as an indication that viewing faces, particularly the eyes, is too arousing and that individuals with autism thus avoid them (Pelphrey et al., 2002).

The lack of mutual eye contact is a phenotype that is observable at a very young age. Home movies of children who were later diagnosed with an ASD reveal atypical social behavior, including poor eye contact, slow or absent mutual gaze, and lack of social engagement (Adrien et al., 1991). Given the importance of experience in shaping the development of particular neural regions, such as the pSTS, lack of mutual eye gaze may lead to long-term deficits or delayed neurodevelopment that subsequently impacts face processing and social cognitive skills more generally. This has actually been reported in otherwise healthy infants (without autism) who are temporarily deprived of visual input due to congenital cataract for an extended period of time. These infants show face recognition deficits 8–29 years later (Le Grand, Mondloch, Maurer, and Brent, 2003), underscoring the important role of early visual face input.

There are some studies that report no difference in eye gaze focus between those with and without autism (van der Geest, Kemner, Verbaten, and van Engeland, 2002). This apparent contradiction of results is likely due to variability in the severity of autism symptoms, experimental methods, and age of research participants. However, a meta-analysis of 14 eye-tracking studies in youth with autism reported that they have significant impairments in gaze fixation to the eyes (Papagiannopoulou, Chitty, Hermens, Hickie, and Lagopoulos, 2014).

Earlier in this chapter we discussed the role of the pSTS in processing eye gaze and intention in others. This region exhibits atypical structural (Boddaert et al., 2004) and functional development in youth with autism. When asked to interpret other people's intention conveyed by gaze shifts, fMRI research suggests that youth with autism do not recruit the pSTS to the same extent as youth without autism (Pelphrey, Morris, and McCarthy, 2005).

Face Recognition
Children and adolescents with autism struggle to remember faces (Boucher and Lewis, 1992). Some research suggests that this is because individuals with ASD focus more on the mouth rather than on the eyes when processing a face (Langdell, 1978) because they do not process the face as a whole, instead studying each part of the face individually (Tantam, Monaghan, Nicholson, and Stirling, 1989). Research using ERP has shown atypical amplitude and delay of the N170 (Golarai et al., 2006), a component of the event-related potential that reflects the neural processing of faces.

A wealth of data suggests that the face processing deficit is due to abnormalities in engagement of the fusiform face area in ASD (e.g. Nomi and Uddin, 2015). One explanation is that the lack of "expertise" for faces in the fusiform is due to a lifelong lack of motivation to viewing faces and social information (Grelotti, Gauthier, and Schultz, 2001) that leads to diminished eye gaze and relevant experience (Golarai et al., 2006). Another possibility is that, instead of being mostly confined to the fusiform gyrus, face processing in ASD occurs across a wider swath of the brain by engaging more regions.

Emotion Recognition

Individuals with ASD struggle with emotion recognition (Golarai et al., 2006). Rather than focusing on emotional expressions as individuals without ASD do, those with ASD focus on other features of a face, including eye color or accessories (earrings or hats for example) (Weeks and Hobson, 1987), suggesting that emotion expressions are less salient for them. Less focus on the eyes when viewing emotional expressions, and subsequent decreased activation of the amygdala, may also account for some of the deficits. In adults with ASD, activation of the fusiform gyrus and amygdala is positively correlated with the time spent fixating on the eyes (Dalton et al., 2005). In a group of children with ASD, fMRI research revealed diminished activation of the amygdala during an emotional face matching task compared to controls (Wang, Dapretto, Hariri, Sigman, and Bookheimer, 2004). However, it remains unclear whether decreased amygdala activation in those with ASD is the cause or the effect of abnormal eye fixation behavior.

While the majority of studies have found decreased amygdala engagement in ASD during emotion processing, there are some that report divergent findings. One study found no difference in amygdala activation to faces between participants with ASD and healthy controls (Pierce, Haist, Sedaghat, and Courchesne, 2004). Another study reported that participants with ASD actually had greater amygdala activation relative to controls (Dalton et al., 2005). Monk and colleagues wondered whether these discrepant results might be due to auxiliary factors that would mask true differences (or similarities) between the groups. They reasoned that differences in activation between ASD and control groups were partially dependent on the cognitive demands specific to the face identification tasks used during fMRI (Monk et al., 2010). Specifically, how much attention one pays to a stimulus influences the neural response to that stimulus, and if individuals with autism exhibit less attention to social stimuli, then perhaps the results are confounded by this auxiliary difference between groups. To address this possibility, Monk and his research team asked a group of participants with ASD and a group without to view emotional (happy, sad, and angry) and neutral face pairs during an attention cuing paradigm that measures attention bias. Using this task, they found that those in the ASD had stronger amygdala activation than those in the control group (Monk et al., 2010), suggesting that, when attention is equitable between ASD and control groups, there is greater amygdala activation in ASD. This finding underscores the importance of being mindful of the experimental conditions under which certain findings emerge.

7.6 Chapter Summary

- Social development involves face processing, affect processing, and prosocial behaviors.
- Maturation of social development occurs throughout childhood and adolescence.
- Social development is supported by the development of the "social brain."
- Mentalizing refers to the attribution of mental states to others.
- Individuals with social anxiety and autism spectrum disorders evince atypical development of the social brain.

7.7 Review Questions

1 Which brain regions comprise the social brain?
2 Why is face processing so important for social development?
3 What is the amygdala's role in emotion?
4 How do peers influence affect processing and decisions?
5 Which deficits are observed in individuals with autism spectrum disorders?

Further Reading

Blakemore, S.J., and Mills, K.L. (2014). Is adolescence a sensitive period for sociocultural processing? *Annual Review of Psychology*, 65, 187–207.
Golarai, G., Grill-Spector, K., and Reiss, A.L. (2006). Autism and the development of face processing. *Clinical Neuroscience Research*, 6, 145–160.
Mahy, C.E., Moses, L.J., and Pfeifer, J.H. (2014). How and where: theory-of-mind in the brain. *Developmental Cognitive Neuroscience*, 9, 68–81.
Tottenham, N. (2014). The importance of early experiences for neuro-affective development. *Current Topics in Behavioral Neuroscience*, 16, 109–129.

CHAPTER EIGHT

The Implications of Adolescent Neuroscience on Policy

Learning Objectives

- Introduce the concepts of maturity and competence.
- Review how adolescent brain research informs public policy.
- Describe the primary policy areas (teenage driving, sex education, and juvenile justice) that have been changed by advances in adolescent research.
- Learn about new areas of policy that will be informed by adolescent brain research.

8.1 Introduction

Adolescent brain research piques the interest of a wide array of individuals. Parents, educators, policy wonks, and legal scholars alike want to know what makes the adolescent brain tick. The advent of brain imaging helped spark this cross-disciplinary conversation and has continued to help bridge communication between researchers and policymakers. In this chapter, policy refers to a course or principle of action adopted by a government, party, business, or individual.

When imaging was first applied to the adolescent brain, some feigned relief that adolescents indeed have a brain. Luckily, this poor attempt at humor is falling out of favor. Scientists and youth advocates are using empirical research to redirect the perception that the developing brain is fragile, troubled, and irrational. It's about time.

Although still relatively new compared to the plethora of research on earlier and later stages of development, adolescent brain research has thus far been impactful in at least three ways. First, it has neurobiologically differentiated adolescents from children and adults. Second, it has helped explain adolescent behavior. Third, it demonstrates that the brain is adaptively plastic well beyond the early postnatal years. These advancements have been essential to the mission of generating developmentally appropriate expectations, policies, and sanctions for adolescents. More broadly, the research has generated a fresh perspective on this powerful period of life. This chapter opens with a discussion on the relevant developmental elements, namely maturity and competence, that are called into question in policy discourse. We then review how the daily lives of adolescents have been impacted by research on the adolescent brain, including in the domains of juvenile justice, teenage driving, school start time and sleep, and health decisions. We will close by describing areas that are currently shifting as a result of this research, including sports-related head concussions and teenage media use.

8.2 Maturity

In this chapter we will review the role of adolescent neuroscience research on a diverse array of policy areas. These seemingly disparate content areas share a common thread: the struggle to define maturity. When is an adolescent mature?

The reason this question is so challenging to answer is because the definition of maturity is not clear-cut and varies on the context and particular topic of interest. Defining it, however, is of utmost importance in policy because it is inherent in the age boundaries our society draws between adolescence and adulthood for purposes of public policy.

We use the word *maturity* synonymously with *adulthood*, which is intended to connote responsibility, wisdom, and sophistication. But age, in terms of how many years one has been alive, is an imprecise measure of these attributes. Although adults *tend* to bear more responsibility and so forth than adolescents, we can all certainly think of adults who are "immature" for their age and adolescents who are "mature" for their age. So what are we truly trying to characterize with the word "maturity"? I would argue that maturity in the policy-relevant sense is actually more akin to **competence**, the capability or skills to understand the circumstances of interest.

Not all of the policy domains that we review in this chapter specifically refer to competence but all aim to establish the age at which an individual is *competent* to make decisions. However, the inherent variability among individuals, their circumstances, and the conditions under which the event of interest occurs makes applying a "one size fits all" calculation impossible. Policymakers and lawmakers recognize this dilemma and thus rely on age as a proxy for competency, fully aware that simply because individuals share the same age does not mean they share the same level of competency.

8.2.1 The Elements of Maturity

Take a moment to think about the characteristics that define maturity. Although we may each have slightly different definitions of the elements necessary for maturity, there are probably some common ones we would agree on. These might include intellectual curiosity, psychosocial skills, emotion regulation, perspective-taking, behavioral control, good decision-making skills, the ability to delay immediate gratification, being secure in one's identity (i.e. not being too shaken by flattery or criticism), making choices based on values (not feelings), and being teachable (keen to learn new things and the recognition that no one is always right).

Now, think back to the chapters describing the different developmental trajectories of particular brain regions. In particular, the difference between the emotional/affect systems and the cognitive control system are relevant here. The latter is necessary for some of the characteristics listed above, including emotion regulation, good decision-making skills, and the ability to delay immediate gratification. The developmental difference between these systems may thus delay the acquisition of these skills until the development of these systems converges.

Another import element of maturity has less to do with the self and is instead based on the self's relation to others, namely parents. The status of maturity implies a shift away from dependence on caregivers or other guardians to reliance on oneself, a concept we reviewed in Chapter 6. Now, the tricky thing is in defining what is appropriate dependence and independence and at what age or developmental stage this occurs. This definition is often tied to culturally relevant barometers of independence that vary as based on current social norms of that society. Because of these factors, the boundary between maturity and immaturity is somewhat speculative and subjective. The juvenile justice system has perhaps made the most headway in identifying the cognitive proxies for competence so we will review it in greater detail below.

8.3 Juvenile Justice

8.3.1 Who Is a Juvenile?

Our society has a complicated understanding of who is considered an adolescent. Most countries define the end of adolescence as when an individual is mature enough to be trusted with certain responsibilities, including driving a vehicle, having legal sexual relations, serving in the armed forces or on a jury, purchasing, selling, and drinking alcohol, voting, finishing certain levels of education, marriage, and renting a car. But even the age at which these rights and privileges are granted varies within a single nation or culture. Even more perplexing is that the established legal age limits seem arbitrary relative to the legal age for comparable or more significant activities. For instance, youth can hold employment in many US states at the age of 14 but are not legally allowed to drive, vote, and buy alcohol until the ages of 16, 18, and 21 years, respectively. They can fight in wars and serve in the armed forces at age 18 but cannot rent a car until age 25.

In the eyes of the law, which refers to adolescents as juveniles, the binary age boundaries include "minors," presumed to be vulnerable, dependent on adults, and inept at making decisions, and adults, who are viewed as autonomous, responsible, and entitled to exercise legal rights and privileges (Scott, 2000). The "age of majority"[1] (a formal way of referring to legal adult status) for most purposes is 18 years of age. But age is just a number, as they say, which is why there is such variability in when youth are legally allowed to do the activities mentioned above. Policies setting these age boundaries are based on many considerations that depend on the issue in question – administrative convenience, parental rights, child welfare, economic impact, and the public interest – as well as assumptions, often rooted primarily in conventional wisdom, about whether young people at a given age are sufficiently mature, as a group, to be treated as adults for the particular statutory purpose (Bonnie and Scott, 2013).

8.3.2 Juvenile Justice Law: A Historical Overview

During most of the twentieth century, young offender cases were handled in a justice system that was separate from the adult justice system, with a primary goal of rehabilitating young offenders. This practice was based on the assumption that juveniles who committed crimes were simply manifesting immaturity, impulsivity, and poor decision-making. However, a wave of violent crimes committed by juveniles in the 1980s and 1990s in the United States scared citizens, and a movement toward greater punitive juvenile law reforms swept the country. Supporters of tougher policies rejected altogether the idea that juveniles were different from adults in any way that was relevant to criminal responsibility or punishment (Scott and Steinberg, 2008). Legislatures enacted harsh laws that

[1] The word majority here refers to having greater years and being of full age; it is opposed to minority, the state of being a minor.

greatly increased confinement and expanded the category of youth subject to criminal court jurisdiction in the juvenile system (Bonnie and Scott, 2013).

8.3.3 Current Juvenile Justice Law

As crimes rates among juveniles continue to drop and growing concerns that imposing harsh adult sentences on adolescents violates basic principles of fairness (Bonnie and Scott, 2013), lawmakers have been increasingly receptive to swing the pendulum back in the other (less punitive) direction. Insights from developmental psychology and cognitive neuroscience research have also helped bolster the rationale for developmentally appropriate sanctions. These include keeping adolescents in juvenile court (instead of sending them to adult court) and striving for less incarceration time. Why might these sanctions be particularly important during adolescence? Research we reviewed in Chapter 4 provides some clues: the adolescent brain is highly plastic. This plasticity makes juveniles vulnerable to environmental input; if they are tried in adult court, they are more likely to receive adult sentencing and be housed with adult offenders (or worse, to be housed in solitary confinement), thereby increasing the likelihood of learning antisocial and criminal habits. Trying them in juvenile court helps preclude these outcomes. On the flip side, plasticity makes adolescents more amenable to remediation and intervention. Therefore, limiting incarceration time and instead directing young offenders to programs that help redirect their criminal behavior is worthwhile. Nonetheless, in most states, people aged 14 (or even younger) can be tried as adults when charged with serious crimes.

8.3.4 Competence

The broad definition of competence is "the ability to do something successfully or efficiently." This could refer to one's competence at computer skills, for instance. In the legal realm, competence refers to a criminal defendant's ability to stand trial, typically as measured by their mental ability to understand the proceedings and to assist their attorneys in advocating for their case (*Dusky v. U.S.*, 362 U.S. 402, 1960).

The rise in harsher penalties for juvenile offenders begged the question of whether youths charged with crimes are competent to participate effectively in their trials. The basic standards for determining competency involve multiple abilities related to comprehension and communication and make up what some scholars (Bonnie, 1993) refer to as "adjudicative

---

Box 8.1 Abilities Related to Legal Competency

- To understand the current legal situation
- To understand the charges
- To understand relevant facts
- To understand the legal issues and procedures
- To understand potential legal defenses
- To understand the possible dispositions, pleas, and penalties
- To appraise the likely outcome
- To appraise the roles of the defense counsel, prosecutor, judge, jury, witnesses, and defendant
- To identify witnesses
- To relate to counsel in a trusting and communicative fashion
- To comprehend instructions and advice
- To make decisions after receiving advice
- To maintain a collaborative relationship with counsel and help plan legal strategy
- To follow testimony for contradictions or errors
- To testify relevantly and be cross-examined if necessary
- To challenge prosecution witnesses
- To tolerate stress at the trial and while awaiting trial
- To refrain from irrational and unmanageable behavior during trial
- To disclose pertinent facts surrounding the alleged offense
- To protect oneself and utilize legal safeguards available

---

competence" or "competence to proceed." This is an umbrella term that encompasses *Understanding*, a basic comprehension of the purpose and nature of the trial process, *Reasoning*, the capacity to provide relevant information to counsel and to process information, and *Appreciation*, the ability to apply information to one's own situation in a manner that is neither distorted nor irrational (Grisso et al., 2003). These competencies are by no means exhaustive. Box 8.1 lists a more comprehensive set of abilities related to the notion of competency. Although questions of competency have been quite prevalent in cases involving the mentally ill or handicapped, there has generally been little recognition that youths in criminal court may also be incompetent because of developmental immaturity (Bonnie and Grisso, 2000).

A seminal study aimed to provide empirical evidence about youths' competence to stand trial (CST) (Grisso et al., 2003). The *MacArthur Competence Assessment Tool–Criminal Adjudication* (MacCAT–CA)

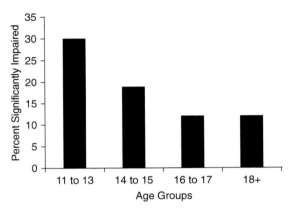

Figure 8.1 In a study aimed at testing adolescents' competence to stand trial, younger adolescents exhibited greater reasoning impairments compared to older adolescents and adults.

was used to test the three types of competencies described above. The *MacArthur Judgment Evaluation* (MacJEN) was used to assess immaturity of judgment. Responses on the MacJEN were scored on three primary variables: *risk appraisal* (including the recognition of risk, the likelihood of negative consequences of risk, and risk impact), *future orientation* (the assessment of the short- or long-range nature of risk consequences), and *resistance to peer influence*. A sample of over 900 11 to 17 year olds and an adult comparison group of over 450 18–24 year olds were included. Half of each group was comprised of a community sample with no current juvenile or criminal court involvement and the other half included individuals currently detained in a juvenile detention center or adult jail.

Results indicate that younger adolescents (11 to 15 year olds) were significantly worse than older adolescents and young adults on the MacCAT–CA, in the *Understanding, Reasoning*, and *Appreciation* subscales. The proportion of individuals who were significantly impaired on the *Understanding* and *Reasoning* subscales differed significantly by age group. Whereas approximately 10% of adults showed impairment on these domains, over 30% of young adolescents did, as illustrated in Figure 8.1. The most significant predictor in the ability to understand, reason, and appreciate was, unsurprisingly, IQ across all ages. Prior experience with the justice system and mental health problems was unrelated to competence on these subscales. An age by IQ analysis revealed

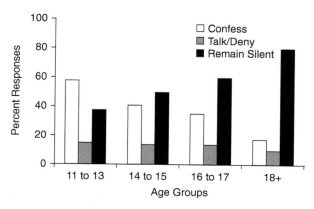

Figure 8.2 In a study aimed at testing adolescents' legal decision-making, younger adolescents reported a greater likelihood to endorse confession compared to older adolescents and young adults, whereas older adolescents and young adults reported a greater likelihood of remaining silent.

that younger individuals of lower IQ were particularly impaired in their capacities on the assessments.

The MacJEN assessment was specifically designed to test participants' legal decision-making in real-life scenarios, including policy interrogation, attorney consultation, and plea agreement. When asked to choose the best response to police interrogation, an alarming 50% of young adolescents chose confession as the best choice, compared to 20% of young adults. Almost 80% of adults chose to remain silent whereas only ~20% of young adolescents did. In Figure 8.2 you'll notice the increasing trend to remain silent with age. Approximately 75% of young adolescents chose to accept the plea agreement compared to 50% of young adults. Here again the trend to "take the deal" decreases with age. There were no age differences in the vignette regarding the full disclosure of criminal involvement with personal attorney or public defender. Notice that the youngest adolescents were more likely to endorse the choice in each vignette that was most compliant with authority: confessing to police, fully disclosing to the attorney, and accepting the prosecutor's plea agreement. Statistical analyses confirmed this age-related observation, which also revealed no significant differences in authority compliance as based on gender, ethnicity, or criminal history.

This important study provided the first empirical evidence (on a large sample size) proving that juveniles aged 15 and younger are incompetent in the domains necessary for a fair and just trial, as compared to young adults and older adolescents. The MacJEN assessment also illuminated an important factor to consider in questions about competence: that psychosocial immaturity may play a significant role, beyond understanding and reasoning, which are explicitly relevant to the competence question. Young adolescents are more likely to implicate themselves in criminal proceedings because of an inherent bias to comply with authority figures. They are also less likely to recognize the long-term risks of their legal decisions. *This age-related propensity puts them at a judicial disadvantage.* In *Dusky v. U.S.* (1960) the Supreme Court ruled that competence to stand trial should be a consideration in judicial proceedings in individuals afflicted with mental illness. The data we just reviewed suggest that competence should also be assessed in individuals who may be incompetent because of immaturity.

8.3.5 The Role of Adolescent Brain Research in Juvenile Justice

Adolescent neuroscience has called into question whether adolescents are as culpable as adults, and relatedly, whether they should receive the same punitive sanctions for similar offenses. Research showing that the adolescent reward and emotion systems outpace development of the regulatory systems in ways that interfere with optimal decision-making has argued against holding adolescents as culpable as adults. That's to say not that young offenders should not be held *accountable* but that the developmental research suggests the court system should consider the developmental stage of the offender when imposing discipline and justice. In fact, the Supreme Court opined that the use of harsh adult sentences on juvenile offenders is "cruel and unusual punishment," unconstitutional under the Eighth Amendment. Three rulings in particular eliminated this practice. In *Roper v. Simmons* (543 U.S. 551, 2005), which abolished the death penalty for juveniles under the age of 18, the Court highlighted behavioral differences between adolescents and adults with little mention of adolescent brain development. However, subsequent cases, including *Graham v. Florida* (560 U.S. 48, 2010), which banned life without parole sentences for juveniles who are convicted of crimes other than homicide, and the joint cases of *Miller v. Alabama* and *Jackson v. Hobbs* (567 U.S. ____, 2012), in which the Court held that it is unconstitutional for states to mandate life without parole for juveniles regardless of the crime, were directly informed by neuroscience research.

Three general characteristics of adolescent behavior, all substantiated by neuroscientific evidence, have influenced the Court. First, in several rulings the Court commented on the role of developing regulatory systems in limiting behavioral regulation. The following quote, from *Miller v. Alabama*, illustrates this point: "It is increasingly clear that adolescent brains are not yet fully mature in regions and systems related to higher-order executive functions such as impulse control, planning ahead, and risk avoidance." Second, in *Roper v. Simmons*, the Court stated that juveniles are "more vulnerable or susceptible to negative influences and outside pressures, including peer pressure" than adults. The experiment we read about in Chapter 6, in which the presence of peers increased risky behavior in adolescent but not adult participants, is just one bit of evidence for this notion. Third, the Court made the astute observation, based on neuroscience research, that the adolescent brain is plastic and thereby more malleable than the less flexible adult brain, by stating: "the character of a juvenile is not as well formed as that of an adult. The personality traits of juveniles are more transitory, less fixed (*Roper v. Simmons*)." The recognition that juveniles show "heightened capacity for change" (*Miller v. Alabama* and *Jackson v. Hobbs*) is particularly important because it has implications for the sanctions imparted on youths convicted of criminal activity (Galván, 2014). Box 8.2 provides greater detail of each of these influential Supreme Court cases.

8.3.6 A Cautionary Note about Adolescent Brain Research in Juvenile Justice Policy

Neurobiological evidence for behavioral phenomena has helped advance policy questions in the juvenile justice system. However, there are limits to its utility, namely because it lacks the predictive power it was initially presumed to have. Huh? Let's back up a bit. When legal scholars first began to take notice of neuroimaging they were excited about the possibility of using neuroscientific evidence in criminal trials to demonstrate that the brain functioning of a particular juvenile facing criminal charges was or was not sufficiently mature to hold the youth responsible for his or her offense (Bonnie and Scott, 2013). However, this has not proven to be very effective, because the very nature of neuroimaging data, in which inferences are drawn from analyses of a *group* of individuals, precludes making predictions about how any *one* individual's past, current, or future behavior relates to their criminal activity. Relatedly, it is unclear how neuroscientists and scholars who rely on neuroscience evidence will

Box 8.2 A Detailed Look at Juvenile Justice Supreme Court Cases

Roper v. Simmons, **543 U.S. 551 (2005)**

The Decision. A landmark decision in which the Supreme Court of the United States abolished the death penalty for juveniles by declaring capital punishment (death penalty) unconstitutional for crimes committed while under the age of 18. The 5–4 decision overruled the Court's prior ruling upholding such sentences on offenders above or at the age of 16, in *Stanford v. Kentucky*, 492 U.S. 361 (1989).

The Criminal Events

In 1993, 17-year-old Christopher Simmons, along with a younger friend, broke into 46-year-old Shirley Crook's home, tied her up, drove her to a state park, and threw her off a bridge in Cape Girardeau County, Missouri. Shortly after, Simmons confessed to the murder and there was testimony from another friend stating that he had discussed the plot in advance and later bragged about the crime. The jury found him guilty and recommended the death sentence.

Opinion of the Supreme Court

Simmons appealed, and after several motions the case found its way to the US Supreme Court. In light of a 2002 US Supreme Court ruling, *Atkins v. Virginia*, 536 U.S. 304, which overturned the death penalty for the mentally retarded, Simmons filed a new petition and the Supreme Court of Missouri reduced Simmons sentence to life imprisonment without parole. Based on the State of Missouri's appeal of the decision, the US Supreme Court argued the case on October 13, 2004.

Invoking the *Atkins v. Virginia* (2002) decision, where the Court opined that evolving standards of decency had made the execution of the mentally retarded cruel and unusual punishment (and thus unconstitutional), the Court held that it was also cruel and unusual punishment to execute a person who was under the age of 18 at the time of the crime.

Justice Kennedy cited research demonstrating juveniles' lack of maturity and self-control and increased impulsivity compared to adults. The Court also cited the relative rarity of executing juvenile offenders around the world, with the United States being the sole country that allowed the execution of juvenile offenders. Since 1990 until 2004 (when the case was argued), only seven other countries, Iran, Pakistan, Saudi Arabia, Yemen, Nigeria, the Democratic Republic of the Congo, and China, had executed juveniles but these countries had since either abolished the death penalty or made movements toward public rejection of it.

Implications of the Ruling

Roper v. Simmons (2005) had two major implications for the United States. First, it impacted 72 juvenile offenders who were on death row by canceling their death sentences. The greatest impact was in Texas, where 29 juvenile offenders were awaiting execution. No other state had more than 5 juvenile offenders on death row. Second, its strong use of scientific research revolutionized the Court's use of empirical evidence to support its rulings, a practice that would become prevalent in subsequent juvenile justice rulings.

Graham v. Florida, 560 U.S. 48 (2010)

The Decision. The Supreme Court of the United States held that juvenile offenders cannot be sentenced to life imprisonment without parole for non-homicide offenses.

The Criminal Events

In 2003, 16-year-old Terrance Jamar Graham, along with two friends, attempted to rob a barbecue restaurant in Jacksonville, Florida and was arrested and charged as an adult for armed burglary with assault and battery. Six months later, he was arrested again for home invasion robbery and charged with life in prison without parole.

Opinion of the Supreme Court

Similar to the *Roper v. Simmons* opinion, the Court held that it is unconstitutional, under the ban of cruel and unusual punishment, to sentence juvenile offenders to life in prison without the possibility of parole for nonhomicide crimes.

Implications of the Ruling

In the case of *State v. Jason Means*, the *Graham v. Florida* ruling was declared retroactive. In 1993 when Means was 17 years old he was convicted of kidnapping and second degree murder and sentenced to life without parole. Following the *Graham v. Florida* ruling the court resentenced Means to life imprisonment with the possibility of parole.

Miller v. Alabama, 567 U.S. 551 (2012)

The Decision. The Supreme Court of the United States held that it is unconstitutional to impose mandatory life sentences without the possibility of parole on juvenile offenders for all crimes, including murder. This ruling extended the ruling of the *Graham v. Florida* (2010) case which held that life without parole sentences were unconstitutional for crimes excluding murder.

The Criminal Events

The Supreme Court decision was based on two cases, *Miller v. Alabama* and *Jackson v. Hobbs*. In 2003, 14-year-old Evan Miller, along with a friend, beat and robbed his neighbor. In an attempt to conceal the crime, they set fire to the neighbor's trailer. The neighbor ultimately died of smoke inhalation and injuries from the beating. A jury trial found Miller guilty of capital murder and sentenced him to life imprisonment without the possibility of parole.

In 1999, 14-year-old Kuntrell Jackson, along with two older boys, attempted to rob a video store. Upon arriving at the store one of the older boys pointed a shotgun at the clerk and demanded money. The clerk refused and the boy shot her in the face. Jackson was inside the store during the killing. In 2003, Jackson was charged as an adult and sentenced to life imprisonment without the possibility of parole.

Opinion of the Supreme Court

The Court held that imposing mandatory life without parole sentences on children "contravenes Graham's (and also Roper's) foundational principle: that imposition of a State's most severe penalties on juvenile offenders cannot proceed as though they were not children." Therefore, regardless of the crime committed, age of offense matters.

Writing for the majority, Justice Kagan said that sentencing should include consideration of a child's chronological age and its hallmark features, such as immaturity, impetuosity, and failure to appreciate risks and consequences. It also should take into account the family and home environment – from which the youth cannot usually extricate himself, even if it is brutal or dysfunctional, as well as the youth's role in the crime and potential to become rehabilitated.

reconcile these group-averaged findings with the vast individual variation in behavior and neurodevelopment. In other words, although scientists recognize that behavior and brain development are highly variable across individuals, most research on the adolescent brain and all research that has been referenced in legal and policy contexts is based on group data (Galván, 2014). One looming question that makes translation from laboratories to courtrooms challenging, therefore, is whether generic guidelines about maturation can be established based on neuroscience research, or is individual variation so great as to preclude the establishment of a biological benchmark for adult-like maturity and judgment? As parents, neuroscientists, and legal scholars continue to grapple with this question it is important to recognize that simply because there are neurobiological correlates for a particular behavioral phenomenon does not necessarily mean that we have any greater understanding of that behavior.

8.4 Driving

The influence of brain research on the Supreme Court is highly significant but it will, thankfully, only impact a relatively small proportion of youth in the United States. A more wide-reaching influence of this research is on teenage driving regulations.

Getting a driver's license is a rite of passage in the United States. To many teenagers it signifies the opportunity to explore, meander along an open road, and see friends on a whim. Similar to the confidence, thrill, and taste of autonomy that preschoolers feel when learning how to ride a bicycle, learning to drive is often the beginning of an exciting journey toward independence. Unfortunately, it is the number one cause of adolescent mortality and morbidity in the United States and most developed countries (CDC, 2012). Figure 8.3 illustrates the disproportionately high rates of car accidents, 73% of all unintentional injuries, which themselves comprise just about half of all deaths, among teenagers aged 12–19 years. Adolescents and young adults under age 20 have the highest rates of crashes per mile driven, at 3 times more likely than drivers 21 years and older. Car accident fatalities are even higher among adolescents who are male, who are driving with a passenger, or who are newly licensed (CDC, 2012).

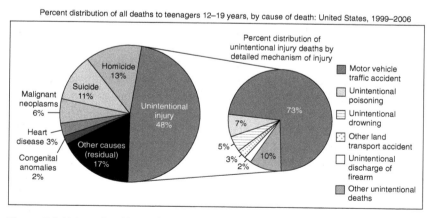

Percent distribution of all deaths to teenagers 12–19 years, by cause of death: United States, 1999–2006

Figure 8.3 Unintentional injury (mainly car accidents) comprises almost half of fatalities among adolescents in the United States.

What explains these statistics? One line of thinking is that young drivers *lack the ability* to attend to driving tasks, including cognitive and motor skills, working memory, visual-spatial attention, and speed of processing (Romer, Lee, McDonald, and Winston, 2014), due to immaturity in brain development (Keating, 2007). For instance, novice drivers lack the skills to effectively and efficiently recognize and respond to hazards; they are often untrained in proper scanning and may focus on noncrucial elements in the driving scene (Dickinson, Chekaluk, and Irwin, 2013). Another possibility is that their driving *inexperience* accounts for the high crash and fatality rates. In the driving literature, the failure to attend to and recognize hazards results from the lack of cognitive and motor schemas that are gained from experience in driving, an ability known as *hazard or situation awareness* (Dickinson et al., 2013). These explanations are not mutually exclusive and it is likely that they both contribute to poor teen driving. In fact, adolescents exhibit deficits stemming from both immaturity and inexperience in the three *situation awareness* schemas (perception, comprehension, and prediction of relevant driving cues) that are necessary for quickly reacting to potential driving hazards. However, the reason policymakers are keen to disentangle them is because they have implications for determining the age at which adolescents should be granted the privilege to obtain a driver's license. The *immaturity* explanation would suggest delaying full licensure for adolescents until they have the requisite maturity to drive safely; while the *inexperience* explanation would suggest more modest policies that consider both brain maturation and experience as important influences on adolescent driving ability (Romer et al., 2014).

The success of the three-stage graduated driver licensing (GDL) at reducing by nearly half the recent number of adolescent car accident fatalities (McCartt, Teoh, Fields, Braitman, and Hellinga, 2010) provides support for the importance of delaying full licensure until they have garnered greater experience behind the wheel. Knowledge about the protracted development of the adolescent brain, and in particular research on limited cognitive control, played a key role in generating GDL policies for young drivers. It has three stages of licensure: (1) a learner's permit; (2) a probationary license; and (3) a full license at 18 years old. These stages reflect our current understanding of adolescent brain and behavior development: the first recognizes that adolescents are inexperienced with behavioral regulation compared to adults and therefore benefit from adult supervision. Requirements for adult-supervised practice driving during the learning period also increase the chances that novice adolescent drivers will gain experience before driving independently (Romer et al., 2014). The second stage reflects the empirical and anecdotal knowledge that adolescents are more susceptible to distraction, particularly social distraction, than adults. Finally, the very nature of being a graduated policy is reflective of the understanding that the adolescent brain changes in response to experience, normative development, and skill, and that changing neural systems are directly related to increasing sophistication in behavior and decision-making (Galván, 2014).

You may notice that the GDL laws are more focused on the compromised cognitive skills in adolescents relative to adults and less so on the known increases in thrill-seeking, the latter of which could conceivably lead to reckless driving. Empirical research suggests that, although risky behavior may lead to reckless driving in adolescents, deficits in cognitive skills are indeed more predictive of car accidents. A study examined sources of teen driving problems in a survey of 16 to 19 year olds in two states. They concluded that "the great majority of non-fatal accidents resulted from errors in attention, visual search, speed relative to conditions, hazard recognition, and emergency maneuvers, rather than to high speeds and patently risky behavior" (McKnight and McKnight, 2003). A second recent analysis of teen crashes based on the US National Motor Vehicle Crash Causation Survey (NMVCCS) found that nearly half of serious crashes (46%) were attributable to failures of surveillance as well as distractions, the greatest one being cell phone use and texting (Westlake and Boyle, 2012), and mind wandering, when drivers monitor the road but focus their thoughts elsewhere (Curry, Hafetz, Kallan, Winston, and Durbin, 2011). The authors noted that too often public health efforts "focus on preventing teen 'problem' behaviors instead of focusing on the skills they need to develop as skilled drivers" (Curry et al., 2011).

8.4.1 Effects of Teenage Passengers

Adolescents like to hang out with adolescents. It is therefore unsurprising that the effects of peer passengers on adolescent driving have been the subject of considerable research, pointing to both distraction and risk-taking (Romer et al., 2014). A study of US drivers found an increasing fatal crash risk among drivers ages 16 and 17 years with each additional peer passenger, a result that was not seen in adult drivers (Chen, Baker, Braver, and Li, 2000). Other research shows that the effects of peers on driving are likely dependent on the situation, the driver, and the passengers. Male drivers ages 16–20 with male passengers, especially those between 13 and 24, were more likely to experience fatal crashes per miles driven than when driving alone (Ouimet et al., 2010). The effect of female passengers was weaker but still present and appeared to be restricted to younger passengers, ages 13–20. A study using NMVCCS data found that males and females differed in the distractions they attended to. Whereas males were more likely to drive aggressively and pay attention to distracting events outside the car, female drivers were more likely to be distracted with events inside the car, such as attending to conversations with passengers (Curry, Mirman, Kallan, Winston, and Durbin, 2012). These studies suggest that the effects of peer passengers differ by gender.

The experimental study we reviewed in Chapter 6 regarding the effects of peers on a simulated driving computer task corroborates these findings, particularly because adults in that study showed no difference in risky behavior whether or not there was a peer present (Chein, Albert, O'Brien, Uckert, and Steinberg, 2011).

8.4.2 Effects of Alcohol and Other Drugs

In Chapter 6 we learned that excitability of the mesolimbic dopamine system is implicated in the rewarding properties of alcohol and other substances. This phenomenon is particularly true of adolescents, who are also excited about the novelty of these drugs. Unfortunately, this may contribute to the higher relative risk of driver fatality while intoxicated for drivers ages 16–20 years than for older drivers (Voas, Torres, Romano, and Lacey, 2012).

Is this because more teenagers than adults drive under the influence of alcohol? Not necessarily. Instead, alcohol may exacerbate the relatively compromised motor and attentional skills of novice drivers as compared to adults (Harrison and Fillmore, 2011). Alcohol, as well as marijuana, increases the risk of driver error and inattention (Hartman and Huestis, 2013). Furthermore, the adolescents who are more likely to use multiple drugs, such as alcohol, nicotine, and marijuana, are more likely to drive under the influence of alcohol (Delcher, Johnson, and Maldonado-Molina, 2013) and to experience crashes (Dunlop and Romer, 2010).

The good news is that reports of adolescents age 16–17 driving under the influence of alcohol have declined significantly from 1999 to 2009 in the US (Cavasos-Rehg, Krauss, and Spitznagel, 2012). Furthermore, the proportion of alcohol-related car fatalities in drivers under age 20 (20%) is lower than in drivers in their 20s (39%) (Pickrell, 2006). These decreases in risky driving point to the power of educating young drivers about the risk and potential consequences of reckless driving, of enacting developmentally appropriate driving laws, and of normalizing "designated driver" practices and the use of car services.

8.4.3 Effects of Drowsy Driving

Approximately one-third of teenage drivers in the United States report driving while drowsy (National Sleep Foundation, 2011). In addition to the negative effects on healthy brain development and consequences for learning, lack of sleep can be fatal for drivers. It is unequivocally linked to deficits in attention and alerting, and the probability of crash rates in adolescents and young adults increases as a function of fewer hours of sleep (Martiniuk et al., 2013). Two matched school districts in Virginia that differed in high school start times not only exhibited differences in academic performance but revealed that the district with later start times also had lower student crash rates (Vorona et al., 2011). Other school districts that have delayed the school start time have also benefited by having reduced rates of student crashes (Danner and Phillips, 2008). Evidence suggests that these reductions are due to improvements in sustained attention administered at the end of the school week as compared to students who start school earlier (Lufi, Tzischinsky, and Hadar, 2011). The results show that encouraging students to sleep longer allows them to improve attention to important tasks, such as driving (Romer et al., 2014).

This brief literature review on adolescent driving points to a confluence of factors, including limited experience, maturing brain systems, and individual differences in propensity for distractibility and risk-taking, that may place young drivers at higher risk than older and more experienced drivers. Although the graduated driver licensing in place has already shown promise in reducing this risk by increasing protected driving experience before allowing adolescents to venture out on their own, identifying and implementing training strategies that will effectively prepare adolescents for competent solo driving are needed (Williams, 2006). As Romer and colleagues (2014) suggest, another important advance in this knowledge will be to disentangle the influence of age versus experience on teenage driving risk (McCartt, Mayhew, Braitman, Ferguson, and Simpson, 2009). With increased driving experience, there are declines in car crash rates but they are still higher for novice adolescent drivers (16 to 19 years old) than for novice adult drivers (20 years and older) (Gregersen and Bjurulf, 1996). This suggests that inexperience is exacerbated by the immaturities in cognitive and brain development inherent in adolescent drivers. However, without empirical evidence it is challenging to determine the age at which most adolescents have the maturity to drive safely, suggesting that an improved assessment of competence, as related to driving skills, would be beneficial for young drivers.

8.4.4 A Decline in Teenage Driving

Although intoxication, drowsy driving, and peer distraction are all important considerations regarding teen driving, there has actually been a decline in the number of teenagers on the road. According to a study published by the Transportation Research Institute at the University of Michigan, there has been a continuous drop in the percentage of people with a driver's license in the past few decades. In 1983, approximately 92% of young adults had a driver's license as compared to 76% in 2014. The decline is even greater among teenagers – in 2014, just 24.5% of 16 year olds had a driver's license, which is a 47% decrease from 1983. Among 19 year olds, 69% had a driver's license in 2014, as compared to 87.3% in 1983. What accounts for these significant, and somewhat surprising, declines? The allure of the driver's license has never really been about the car, but more about the freedom the car provides. Young people can now enjoy that freedom without the potentially frustrating, expensive, and less environmentally friendly experience of car driving. The increased availability of car services such as Uber™, which are easily accessible with a simple phone application, and public transportation eliminate the need for a driver's license for many teens, especially those living in large cities. In fact, some preliminary data suggest that as teens approach the car-driving age of 16, some are forgoing the trouble of obtaining a driver's license and instead getting an Uber account. This trend has already started to lessen the number of car accidents and fatalities among teenage drivers and will undoubtedly continue to do so in upcoming years.

8.5 Adolescent Sleep

More than 90% of adolescents in the United States are chronically sleep deprived, according to the Youth Risk Surveillance System Survey with data collected from over 12,000 high school students (Basch, Basch, Ruggles, and Rajan, 2014). These statistics are leading to what is increasingly regarded as a sleep deprivation epidemic (Carskadon, 2011). More than 25% of adolescents report a bedtime later than 11:30 pm on weeknights, despite early rise times for school (Asarnow, McGlinchey, and Harvey, 2014). Adolescents often try to compensate for this sleep debt by extending sleep times on weekend nights (Crowley and Carskadon, 2010), leading to a phenomenon known as "social jet lag" in which individuals attempt to equilibrate the weekday sleep deficit by sleeping more on the weekends. This practice is ineffective and may even be harmful during adolescence by increasing psychiatric symptoms, fatigue, and academic costs (Gillen-O'Neel, Huynh, and Fuligni, 2013). This phenomenon is concerning because sleep during adolescence helps promote physical, brain, and cognitive development (Gregory and Sadeh, 2012).

8.5.1 Why Adolescents Receive Insufficient Sleep

Parent, educators, and adolescents themselves blame media and technology for increasingly poor sleep that emerges around puberty. Indeed, adolescents report staying up late to juggle social demands, homework, extra-curricular activities, after-school jobs and responsibilities, and technology (Cain and Gradisar, 2010; Knutson and Lauderdale, 2009). However, there are also biological reasons for this shift. At around the time pubertal hormones start to kick in, many adolescents begin to experience what is referred to as sleep–wake "phase delay," which is a preference for later bedtimes and wake times. This phase delay is typically a shift of up to 2 hours compared to children in middle childhood; whereas the average bedtime is 9:24 pm for 6th graders in the US, it is 11:02 pm for 12th graders (Carskadon, 2011). Interestingly, this phenomenon is observed all around the world, in people of all cultures. For instance, the average bedtime of 6th graders and 12th graders in Korea is 10:42 pm and 12:54 am, respectively. Although the Korean teenagers go to bed later overall than American teenagers, the phase delay is consistently about 2 hours in both countries, and in over 20 countries on 6 continents, in cultures ranging from pre-industrial to modern societies (Hagenauer and Lee, 2013). The delay is attributed to two biological factors: (1) across adolescence, nocturnal melatonin release in the body occurs later and later in the night (Crowley, Acebo, and Carskadon, 2007). This makes falling asleep at an earlier bedtime difficult for many teenagers; (2) teenagers experience a change in their "sleep pressure," in which the pressure or desire to fall asleep increases more slowly in the evening than in children. This yields a higher tolerance for being awake. Both factors make it easier for most adolescents to stay awake later without feeling sleepy. Despite higher tolerance for being awake, adolescents continue to *need* as much sleep as children (and no one would argue that a newborn or toddler doesn't need a lot of sleep!). So how are teenagers supposed to get as much sleep as when they were younger if their bodies are encouraging staying up later? The answer is simple. Nature intended for adolescents to go to bed later but also to *wake up later* but modern society threw a wrench in these plans by imposing early school start times. As a result, many adolescents stay up late on school nights, get insufficient sleep, and then struggle to stay awake in class the following day.

A large study by the National Sleep Foundation (2011) suggests that, unlike other aspects of health and well-being, including safe sex practices, drug avoidance, and good nutrition, healthy sleep is not something parents stress to their adolescents. New parents obsess over their newborn's sleep, but over time this obsession wanes. According to the study, 87% of high school students in the United States were receiving less than the recommended 8.5–9.5 hours of sleep on school nights but only 29% of parents surveyed were aware of this deficit. This disconnect points to a troubling lack of parental awareness regarding the extent of insufficient sleep in their adolescents.

8.5.2 The Consequences of Poor Sleep

The effects of poor sleep are pervasive. Reviewing every one of the deleterious outcomes would fill up an entire book so here we will just list the major ones. Please review Box 8.3 for a more comprehensive list of outcomes, as based on empirical research. Unsurprisingly, academic performance suffers. Many studies show an association between decreased sleep duration and lower academic achievement at the middle school, high school, and college levels, as well as higher rates of absenteeism and tardiness, and decreased readiness to learn (Curcio, Ferrara, and De Gennaro, 2006; Fredriksen, Rhodes, Reddy, and Way, 2004), effects that are exacerbated in youth from low socioeconomic conditions (Buckhalt, 2011). The normative prevalence rates of internalizing disorders, including anxiety and depression, that emerge around the time of puberty are amplified by insufficient sleep (Alfano, Reynolds, Scott, Dahl, and Mellman, 2013). From a health perspective, the (poor) sleep habits that are established in adolescence have implications for future onset of cardiovascular diseases, metabolic dysfunction, and type 2 diabetes (Owens; Adolescent Sleep Working Group; Committee on Adolescence, 2014) along with concurrent and future rates of obesity. Several cross-sectional and prospective studies have shown that children and adolescents who get less sleep evince greater body mass index (Cappuccio et al., 2008).

8.5.3 The Role of School Start Time

Insufficient sleep in adolescence is the product of many factors that cannot be changed, including biology and environmental demands.

Box 8.3 Areas Impacted by Poor Sleep in Adolescence

Category	Risk outcomes
Physical health and safety	Increased obesity
	Metabolic dysfunction (hypercholesterolemia, type 2 diabetes mellitus)
	Increased cardiovascular morbidity (hypertension, increased risk of stroke)
	Increased rates of motor vehicle crashes ("drowsy driving")
	Higher rates of caffeine consumption; increased risk of toxicity/overdose
	Nonmedical use of stimulant medications
	Lower levels of physical activity
Mental health and behavior	Increased risk for anxiety, depression, suicidal ideation
	Poor impulse control and self-regulation
	Increased risk-taking behaviors
	Emotional dysregulation
	Decreased positive affect
	Impaired interpretation of social/emotional cues in self and others
	Decreased motivation
	Increased vulnerability to stress
Academic performance	Cognitive deficits, especially with more complex tasks
	Impairments in executive function (working memory, organization)
	Impairments in time management
	Impairments in attention and memory
	Deficits in abstract thinking, verbal creativity
	Decreased performance

Taken directly from *Pediatrics*, 134 (2014), 642–649.

However, scientists, policymakers, and parents have identified one that is the biggest culprit and which is actually the most malleable: early school start time. Statistics from the United States Department of Education note that of the more than 18,000 public high schools in this country, almost half of them start school before 8 am. Isn't getting more school time beneficial for students? Not necessarily. Numerous studies have compared schools with varying start times in terms of adolescent sleep duration, sleepiness, concentration abilities, behavior problems, and absenteeism, and found that students who attend schools that start later fare better in each of these domains (Carrell, Maghakian, and West, 2011), even after accounting for other factors that may contribute to these outcomes, such as socioeconomic status, mental health, and stress.

8.5.4 School Start Time: The Recommendations

After years of research, pediatricians and policymakers are finally listening to proven scientific facts about the detrimental effects of poor sleep on adolescents. What role do pediatricians have in this conversation? An important one, as they are the credible voices who can enact mobility in this movement by underscoring the potentially long-lasting effects of sleep deprivation on adolescent health. In August 2014, the American Academy of Pediatrics put forth a powerful policy statement recommending delayed start times of middle and high schools to combat teen sleep deprivation (Adolescent Sleep Working Group, Committee on Adolescence, and Council on School Health, 2014). Specifically, they recommended a start time of 8:30 am or later, a significant shift from the increasingly earlier start times (some as early at 7:15 am!) that have become popular in recent decades. They noted that "doing so will align school schedules to the biological sleep rhythms of adolescents, whose sleep–wake cycles begin to shift up to two hours later at the start of puberty." They also referenced research implicating early school start times, before 8:30 am, as a key *modifiable* contributor to insufficient sleep. Their recommendations, a complete list of which is found in Box 8.4, are based on research showing that delaying school start times is "an effective countermeasure to chronic sleep loss and has a wide range of potential benefits to students with regard to physical and mental health, safety, and academic achievement." Notice that the general theme of each of these recommendations is to *educate* adolescents, parents, educators, athletic coaches, and lawmakers about the continued importance of sleep and of discussing sleep patterns and issues regularly.

Box 8.4 Sleep Recommendations by the American Academy of Pediatrics

1 Pediatricians should educate adolescents and parents regarding the optimal sleep amount teenagers need to match physiologic sleep needs (8.5–9.5 hours). Although napping, extending sleep on weekends, and caffeine consumption can temporarily counteract sleepiness, these measures do not restore optimal alertness and are not a substitute for regular sufficient sleep.

2 Health care professionals, especially those working in school-based clinics or acting in an advisory capacity to schools, should be aware of adolescent sleep needs. They should educate parents, teenagers, educators, athletic coaches, and other stakeholders about the biological and environmental factors, including early school start times, that contribute to widespread chronic sleep deprivation in America's youth.

3 Educational interventions for parents and adolescents as well as the general public should be developed and disseminated by the American Academy of Pediatrics and other child and sleep health advocacy groups. Content should include the potential risks of chronic sleep loss in adolescents, including depressed mood, deficits in learning, attention and memory problems, poor impulse control, academic performance deficits, an increased risk of fall-asleep motor vehicle crashes, and an elevated risk of obesity, hypertension, and long-term cardiovascular morbidity. Information should also be included about the potential utility of systemic countermeasures, including delaying school start times, in mitigating these effects. Finally, educational efforts should also emphasize the importance of behavior change on the individual level and the personal responsibility that families and students themselves have in modifying their sleep habits.

4 Pediatricians and other pediatric health care providers (e.g. school physicians, school nurses) should provide scientific information, evidence-based rationales, guidance, and support to educate school administrators, parent-teacher associations, and school boards about the benefits of instituting a delay in start times as a potentially highly cost-effective countermeasure to adolescent sleep deprivation and sleepiness. In most districts, middle and high schools should aim for a starting time of no earlier than 8:30 AM. However, individual school districts also need to take average commuting times and other exigencies into account in setting a start time that allows for adequate sleep opportunity for students. Additional information regarding opportunities, challenges, and potential solutions involved in changing school start times

may be found at: http://www.sleepfoundation.org/article/sleep-topics/
school-start-time-and-sleep; http://schoolstarttime.org.

5 Pediatricians should routinely provide education and support to adolescents and families regarding the significance of sleep and healthy sleep
habits as an important component of anticipatory guidance and well-child
care. In particular, pediatricians should endorse parental involvement in setting bedtimes and in supervising sleep practices, such as social networking
and electronic media use in the bedroom; for example, pediatricians could
recommend to parents that they establish a "home media use plan" and
enforce a "media curfew." Adolescents should be regularly queried regarding sleep patterns and duration and counseled about the risks of excessive
caffeine consumption, misuse of stimulant medications as a countermeasure to sleepiness, and the dangers of drowsy driving.

Taken directly from *Pediatrics*, 134 (2014), 642–649.

8.5.5 School Start Time: The Reality

A year later, in August 2015, the Centers for Disease Control and Prevention reported that fewer than 20% of middle and high schools in the
US began the school day at the recommended 8:30 am start time or later.
The report, based on data from the 2011–12 school year of nearly 40,000
public middle and high schools, found that the average start time was
8:03 am. Furthermore, it reported that 42 states admitted that 75–100%
of public schools had start times before 8:30 am. The biggest offenders
were schools in Hawaii, Mississippi, and Wyoming, all of which started
earlier than 8:30 am, while 75% of schools in Alaska and North Dakota
started at 8:30 am or later. Louisiana had the earliest average school start
time at 7:40 am, while Alaska had the latest, at 8:33 am.

8.5.6 School Start Time: Reasons for the Resistance

Some skeptics of shifting school start times have argued that a shift
would simply encourage adolescents to stay up later. This is a reasonable
argument but preliminary research has somewhat assuaged this concern.
A study that followed over 18,000 high school students in Minneapolis
before and after the school district imposed a delayed start time of 8:40
am (almost an hour and a half later than the original 7:15 am start time)
found that bedtimes were unchanged (Wahlstrohm, 2002). This yielded

nearly 1 extra hour of sleep on school nights for those students. A separate study found that a 1-hour delay in school start time resulted in 12 to 30 minutes more nightly sleep, and the percentage of students who reported getting more than 8 hours of sleep increased from 37% to 50% (Danner and Phillips, 2008). One study did find that earlier start times changed bedtimes, but not in the way skeptics predicted. That study reported that after a 1-hour school start delay, students reported bedtimes that were, on average, 18 minutes *earlier* than before the school start shift and average sleep duration increased by 45 minutes (Owens et al., 2014). Finally, a longitudinal study of over 9,000 high school students reported that the percentage of students sleeping more than 8 hours per night was significantly higher in schools that had a later start time (e.g. 33% of students at schools that started at 7:30 am versus 66% of students at schools that started at 8:55 am) (Wahlstrohm et al., 2014). These studies and others like them have also noted additional gains as a result of these school start time shifts, including in academic performance (Owens et al., 2014), mental health (Owens and Jones, 2011), and safe driving (Danner and Phillips, 2008).

Delayed school start time seems like a great idea all around. However, logistical considerations are perhaps the number one reason it has not been systematically implemented across the country. The most common perceived logistical barriers, as reported in a survey of over 300 public high school personnel, included reduced time for athletics and sports games, reduced opportunity for after-school employment, challenges in providing child care for younger siblings, adjustments in parent and family schedules, potential safety issues, and transportation issues. Anecdotal evidence suggests that these concerns are unfounded, but a comprehensive empirical study is warranted to determine just how impactful delayed school start time would be on these factors (Owens et al., 2014). In sum, the evidence is clear: adolescent sleep is critical for success at the individual and societal level, and delaying the school start time in the US is one reasonable way to ensure that youth get the sleep they need.

8.6 Media and the Adolescent Brain

There is growing concern and interest in the effects of media and technology on the developing brain. The sharp increase in media use (and misuse), particularly in young adolescents, has caused spirited debates among parents, educators, and policymakers, and in the media. Whereas some contend that being technologically savvy can only be beneficial in the long run, others worry that excessive media use is corrupting, or at the very least changing, brain development. Choudhury and McKinney (2013) argue that the latter is based on two broader concerns about social behaviors: (1) existing moral panics about adolescent behavior, an issue that has plagued every generation, and (2) growing concern that media consumption is too intense, addictive, and pervasive. Furthermore, they state that "anxiety around these technologies engages the notions of neuroplasticity" and the worry about fundamentally altering the teenage brain in a negative way is presumptuous because the empirical data is simply not yet strong enough to determine the long-term ramifications of media use. Burgeoning research on media use and the developing brain is already well underway and the next few years will undoubtedly produce a wealth of evidence from which to draw data-based conclusions.

Despite much speculation about the potentially unique effects of media on the adolescent brain, there is very little empirical research that has examined this question. However, one study developed a novel fMRI task to simulate Instagram, a popular social media tool in which users share photos. One draw to Instagram is the ability to receive "likes" for one's pictures. In the fMRI study, Sherman and colleagues measured adolescents' behavioral and neural responses to "likes" (Sherman, Payton, Hernandez, Greenfield, and Dapretto, 2016). Adolescents were more likely to endorse ("like") photos that had already been endorsed by other participants with many likes, which was associated with greater engagement of neural regions linked to reward processing (ventral striatum), social cognition (medial prefrontal cortex), imitation (parietal cortex), and attention (frontal cortex) (Figure 8.4). A particularly compelling finding of the study was that adolescents evinced decreased activation of the cognitive control network when viewing photos of individuals engaged in risky behaviors (e.g. smoking marijuana). The results from this study underscore the possible neural mechanisms that underlie the strong affinity adolescents have for social media and peer influence. Research in young adults has also found an association between ventral striatal activation and Facebook use (Meshi, Morawetz, and Heekeren, 2013). Interestingly, in the limited fMRI studies on media use in both adolescents and adults, a common thread is that regions implicated in non-media based social cognition, including TPJ, striatum, mPFC, and insula, which we reviewed in Chapter 7, are also relevant. This may suggest that, as far as the brain is concerned, the operative word in social media is the word "social"; the brain is going to treat the medium (whether it be on the internet or face-to-face) in much the same way. Chances are that vibrant interest in this topic will spur many more studies to address this question in upcoming years.

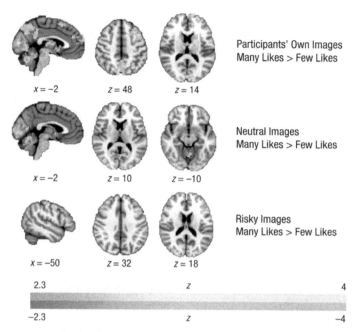

Participants' Own Images
Many Likes > Few Likes

$x = -2$ $z = 48$ $z = 14$

Neutral Images
Many Likes > Few Likes

$x = -2$ $z = 10$ $z = -10$

Risky Images
Many Likes > Few Likes

$x = -50$ $z = 32$ $z = 18$

2.3 z 4

−2.3 z −4

Figure 8.4 In a study aimed at examining neural responses to social media "likes," there was greater neural activation in response to participants' own photos that generated more versus fewer "likes" (*top* and *bottom*). When participants viewed neutral images (compared with risky images) ostensibly submitted by peers (*middle*), significantly greater activity was observed in the bilateral occipital cortex, the medial prefrontal cortex, and the inferior frontal gyrus. See color plate 16.

8.7 Sex Education

Sex education gained widespread public support in the 1970s and 1980s following the outbreak of HIV/AIDS and increasing rates of teenage pregnancy. The general topics covered in sex education, including sexual activity, reproductive health and pregnancy, reproductive rights and responsibility, sexual abstinence, birth control, and sexually transmitted infections, are controversial in that parents, teachers, policymakers and lawmakers, different religious groups, and society in general have drastically different opinions about the content, detail, and recommendations of sex education programs in public schools. Unfortunately the variability in sex education between different US states (and even between different school districts within a state) leaves many adolescents without comprehensive information.

Today, many states have a policy requiring sex education. Twenty-two states and the District of Columbia (DC) mandate sex education and 33 states and DC mandate HIV education (Guttmacher, 2014). The similarities end there, as the specific instruction and implementation of it vary greatly by state. For instance, only 13 states require that the instruction be medically accurate. Twenty-six states and DC require that the information be appropriate for the students' age, 8 states require that the program must provide instruction that is appropriate for a student's cultural background and not be biased against any race, sex, or ethnicity, and 2 states prohibit the program from promoting religion. There is also significant variability among states about the role of parents and parental consent. Twenty-two states and DC require parental notification that sex and HIV education will be provided, 3 states require parental consent for students to participate, and 35 states and DC allow parents to remove their children from sex education. Finally, the content of sex education varies greatly. Nineteen states require that instruction on the importance of engaging in sexual activity only within marriage be provided. Only 12 states require discussion of sexual orientation, and 3 of those require that the information on sexual orientation be negative. Thirteen states require the inclusion of information on the negative outcomes of teen sex and pregnancy. Eighteen states and DC require contraception information, 25 states require that abstinence be stressed, and 12 states require that it is included in the materials. From the time that abstinence-only sex education was added in 1996 through 2007, over 1.5 billion dollars in state and federal funds were spent to support the development and implementation of these programs. This includes the requirement that youth be taught to abstain from sex until marriage, and that, besides leading to disease and pregnancy, "sexual activity outside of the context of marriage is likely to have harmful psychological and physical effects" (510(b)(2)(E)) (Social Security Administration Act of 2010, 42 USC §710). This directive persists despite no clear research demonstrating positive social or emotional outcomes of abstaining from sexual activity until marriage (Suleiman, Johnson, Shirtcliff, and Galván, 2015).

Some researchers and sex education developers have begun inaccurately using neuroscience research to claim that it proves that "the healthiest behavior, both physically and emotionally, is for persons to abstain from sex until they can commit to one partner for the rest of their lives" (Bush and McIlhaney, 2008). This is an inappropriate use of neuroimaging research on love, sex, and desire as there are currently no studies that have examined the neural effects of sex outside the context of marriage.

However, there are some important messages to glean from neuroscience research we have reviewed in this book regarding adolescent sexuality. In Chapter 2 we discussed the pubertal changes that emerge at the onset of adolescence. The neural development associated with puberty leads to increased sensation-seeking and risk-taking behavior. Together, these hormonal and behavioral changes yield increases in romantic and sexual behavior. A review by Suleiman and colleagues suggests that, instead of ignoring this newly discovered sexual interest, it would be more beneficial for sex education to help adolescents learn how to direct these desires in positive ways to garner experience and to build social relationship skills (Suleiman et al., 2015). The notion of plasticity that we reviewed in Chapter 4 is a good reminder that a range of social, didactic, and environmental factors can have a huge influence on adolescent behavior. Within the context of sexual desires, teens can be guided to practice healthy relationships.

Research in animals suggests that intense sexual desires observed early in pair bonding are essential for forming long-term bonding behavior (Smeltzer, Curtis, Aragona, and Wang, 2006). The same is true in humans, and in adolescents in particular. The unique nature of adolescent romantic relationships, which often include passionate emotions and trial-and-error learning of how to regulate them, contributes to learning the skills necessary for healthy bonds in future relationships.

However, despite our increased understanding of neural mechanisms supporting factors associated with sex and love, there are significant limitations to the inferences we can draw from neuroscience research as related to policy implications. To date, there are no studies that specifically explore the neurobiological difference between romantic love and sex among adolescents (Suleiman et al., 2015). In addition, there are no longitudinal neuroimaging studies that measure differences in neural functioning or development between adolescents who experience sex and romantic love and those who do not. Even if such studies were conducted, the significant potential confounds, including the developmental history, family beliefs, and geographic location (which has implications for the type of sex education received) of the participants, would greatly limit the knowledge learned. Despite conceptual and empirical advances in adolescent brain development and romantic and sexual decision-making resulting from neuroscience, overstating our current understanding of these advances leads to recommendations that drift significantly from the evidence (Suleiman et al., 2015). Understanding the neuroscience related to adolescent brain development, love, sex, and marriage does not fully explain adolescent behavior nor provide a definitive answer to how to deal with sex education. It helps inform fresh policies and programs to best support adolescents as they navigate this critical developmental window to enhance their lifelong sexual health.

8.8 Health Decisions

8.8.1 The Mature Minor Doctrine

The question of maturity and competence regarding adolescent health decisions has long been a tricky subject. Before we dive into the implications of maturity (or immaturity) on health policy, we will review the **Mature Minor Doctrine**. This American term refers to the regulatory or common law policy accepting that adolescents may have the maturity to make health care treatment decisions for themselves. These decisions are permitted to occur without the knowledge or consent of parental guardians. Although historically not the case, it is now generally considered a basic patient right. The doctrine is sometimes used to enforce confidentiality of minor patients from their parents. It allows health care providers to treat youth as adults based upon an assessment and documentation of maturity and enables them to ask questions of young people in order to determine whether or not they have the maturity to provide their own consent for treatment.

History of the Mature Minor Doctrine

The circumstances that led to the Mature Minor Doctrine are interesting. Albert G. Smith, an 18-year-old married father in Washington State, suffered from a progressive disease. Smith worried that his wife would eventually have to bear the burden of caring for him and their existing child so he decided he did not want to have additional children. He thus requested a vasectomy, a surgical procedure that prevents sperm from entering the seminal stream and thereby prevents fertilization. Smith provided written consent for the procedure and the surgery was performed. When he turned 21, Washington's statutory age of majority at the time, Smith sued the doctor, who claimed he had been a minor and thus should not have been allowed to consent to the surgery. The Supreme Court of Washington tried and rejected the case, *Smith v. Seibly*, 72 Wn.2d 16, 431 P.2d 719 (1967), noting in its ruling that "Age, intelligence, maturity, training, experience, economic independence or lack thereof, general conduct as an adult and freedom from the control of parents are all factors to be considered in such a case [involving consent to surgery]." The court further quoted another case, *Grannum v. Berard*, 70 Wn.2d 304, 307, 422 P.2d 812 (1967): "The mental capacity necessary to consent to a surgical operation is a question of fact to be determined from the circumstances of each individual case." The Court explicitly stated that a minor may grant surgical consent even without formal emancipation.

8.8.2 Abortion

The Mature Minor Doctrine has been called into question on the controversial decision regarding a minor's right to obtain an abortion without parental notification. In a 1990 US Supreme Court case, *Hodgson v. Minnesota*, the Court ruled that pregnant adolescents were not required to notify their parents before terminating a pregnancy (American Psychological Association, 1989). This ruling was based on arguments from psychologists that adolescents had comparable decision-making skills to those of adults. This was incongruent with arguments made over a decade later regarding adolescent maturity and decision-making competence in the juvenile justice system (as detailed above). Following the juvenile justice ruling in 2005, opponents of adolescents' right to have an abortion without parental consent argued, in *Ayotte v. Planned Parenthood*, that, because the Court had endorsed the notion that adolescents are not as psychologically and neurobiologically as mature as adults, parental involvement is essential in cases of abortion.

Today, states differ on whether or not parental permission is required for an adolescent to have an abortion. Thirty-eight states require some type of parental involvement in a minor's. In most states that do require parental permission, there are some alternatives. First, a minor can ask a judge to grant a "judicial bypass," in which the adolescent is excused from getting parental permission. Second, a legal guardian can give permission in place of a parent. Third, if an adolescent meets legal requirements to show that she is independent of the care and control of her parents, she does not need to receive permission. Some states also excuse parental involvement if the adolescent is a victim of abuse or neglect.

Advocacy groups have made several arguments in favor of parental notification. First, they argue that because abortion is a medical procedure, it should require parental notification and/or consent as this is required for most other types of medical procedures. Second, a study from the Heritage Foundation, a conservative think tank in Washington, DC, reported that parental involvement laws reduce the number of teenage abortions. Third, pressure from an older boyfriend, so as to conceal the fact that he is guilty of statutory rape, might lead to an adolescent unwillingly getting an abortion. Finally, parental notification laws give parents the opportunity to counsel their daughters about the possible consequences of abortion.

There are also strong arguments from advocates who oppose parental notification/consent laws. First, they argue that these laws increase the number of unsafe, illegal abortions because adolescents who are afraid to tell their parents seek out abortions that are not conducted in medically safe environments. Second, minors who do not want to tell their parents sometimes travel to nearby states where parental notification is not required. This travel time may delay the abortion and thereby increase risks associated with performing an abortion later in the pregnancy, particularly if the abortion is delayed into the third trimester. This view is supported by the American Academy of Pediatrics, which issued the following statement in 1996: "Legislation mandating parental involvement does not achieve the intended benefit of promoting family communication, but it does increase the risk of harm to the adolescent by delaying access to appropriate medical care . . . [M]inors should not be compelled or required to involve their parents in their decisions to obtain abortions, although they should be encouraged to discuss their pregnancies with their parents and other responsible adults" (American Academy of Pediatrics, 1996). Third, other reproductive health issues, such as testing and treatment for sexually transmitted diseases, do not require parental consent. Finally, the last reason opponents provide is the most subjective: they posit that many minors of childbearing age are sufficiently mature to make abortion decisions themselves, as ruled in the US Supreme Court Case, *Bellotti v. Baird* (1979).

So are minors mature, or not mature, enough to decide whether to have an abortion? And if so, when are they too immature to receive the same punitive sanctions as adult criminals? A group of developmental psychologists reconciled these arguments by underscoring the temporal differences in the decisions that lead to abortion versus those that lead to criminal activity (Steinberg, Cauffman, Woolard, Graham, and Banich, 2009). Unlike adolescents' decisions to commit crimes, which are usually rash and made in the presence of peers, adolescents' decisions about terminating a pregnancy can be made in an unhurried fashion and in consultation with adults. Why does this matter? It matters because research suggests that, when making deliberative decisions, youth can perform comparably to adults. However, in matters of psychosocial capacity and "heat of the moment" decisions, adolescents lag behind adults. Steinberg and colleagues argue, therefore, that the legal treatment of

Figure 8.5 High school students engaged in a football tackle. See color plate 17.

adolescents regarding abortion and juvenile justice are not contradictory, and instead emphasize the different aspects of maturity that each taps into, "in accordance with the differing nature of the decision-making scenarios involved in each case. The skills and abilities necessary to make an informed decision about a medical procedure are likely in place several years before the capacities necessary to regulate one's behavior under conditions of emotional arousal or coercive pressure from peers." The reader is encouraged to read the original article for a more in-depth explanation of these issues (Steinberg et al., 2009). Once again, this rationale and the strong opinions of advocates on both sides of the issue bring into question how our society can and does define maturity and competence.

8.9 Future Directions

This chapter is only the tip of the iceberg regarding the role of adolescent brain research in policy. We have reviewed the areas that have directly drawn on this research to inform policies, but this is an exciting time for discovery of the adolescent brain, and inroads in other domains are inevitable. For instance, the growing conversation about the vulnerability of the teenage brain to aggressive sports, such as high school football (Figure 8.5), and the rapidly growing use of technology, has already begun to include research on the teen brain.

In recent years, youth advocates and scientists have begun to more deeply question the potentially deleterious effects of sports-related concussions on brain development. Between 2008 and 2011, there were over 200 sports-related deaths (www.nata.org) in the United States, and during the prior decade, an estimated 2,651,581 youth below 19 years old were treated annually for sports-related injuries (CDC, 2011a). Several events have been effective at highlighting this important discourse. First, the White House held the first ever "Healthy Kids and Safe Sports Concussion Summit" in 2014. Second, the National Football League is dealing with ongoing litigation after being sued by former players who blame the sport for life-long injuries, mental health issues, and problem behavior. Finally, Steve Tisch, co-owner of the New York Giants, donated a $10 million grant to the UCLA School of Medicine for the BrainSPORT Program. The purpose of the grant is to train pediatric neurologists specializing in sports concussions and research how to prevent, diagnose, and treat the injuries among young athletes. This clinically relevant research will undoubtedly benefit from basic neuroscience research on the adolescent brain, which has already demonstrated both its vulnerability and its resilience (Galván, 2014). A deeper understanding of the substantive neurobiological and psychological impact of sports-related injuries on the developing brain will help inform strategies to reduce, prevent, and treat avoidable tragedies.

In sum, scientists and policymakers are increasingly focused on leveraging the knowledge that changes in the adolescent brain are adaptive for the individual and beneficial for society. Nonscientists are working to connect with developmental cognitive neuroscience researchers to enact meaningful voices in shaping social policy and legal sanctions related to adolescents (Galván, 2014). The next few years will undoubtedly lead to new shifts in policy as based on adolescent brain research.

8.10 Chapter Summary

- Adolescent research is important for policy.
- Maturity and competence are challenging to define and vary based on the circumstances.
- Adolescent research was used to abolish the juvenile death penalty and life imprisonment without parole.
- Graduated driving laws help provide the maturity and experience teens need to practice safe driving.
- Adolescent sleep is necessary for healthy brain development.
- Delaying school start time is one way to improve adolescent sleep.

8.11 Review Questions

1 What have been the most influential Supreme Court cases with regards to juvenile justice?

2 Why has there been resistance to delaying school start time?

3 What is the Mature Minor Doctrine?

4 List two major concerns with current sex education.

Further Reading

Bonnie, R.J., and Scott, E.S. (2013). The teenage brain: adolescent brain research and the law. *Current Directions in Psychological Science*, 22, 158–163.

Galván, A. (2014). Insights about adolescent behavior, plasticity and policy from neuroscience research. *Neuron*, 83, 262–265.

Steinberg, L., Cauffman, E., Woolard, J., Graham, S., and Banich, M. (2009). Are adolescents less mature than adults? Minors' access to abortion, the juvenile death penalty and the alleged APA "Flip-Flop." *American Psychologist*, 64, 583–594.

Glossary of Key Terms

1 What Is Adolescence?

Early adolescence: the period from the middle school years, including most of the pubertal development that characterizes the early part of adolescence

Early adulthood: the late adolescent years and early 20s through the mid-30s

Early childhood: the developmental period that follows the end of infancy and extends through about 5–6 years of age

Infancy: the period from birth through approximately 18 months of age

Late adolescence: the period after the majority of the pubertal transition

Late adulthood: the developmental period from approximately 65 years of age until death

Middle adulthood: begins at approximately 35 to 40 years of age and ends at approximately 55 to 65 years of age

Middle and late childhood: the developmental period that extends from about kindergarten to right before adolescence

Neurons: nerve cells in the brain

Prenatal period: the period from the point of conception until birth

2 Puberty

Adrenarche: an early stage of sexual maturation during which the adrenal cortex secretes increased levels of androgens

Bone age: a measurement of biological age based on the fusion of bones rather than actual or chronological age

Constitutional delay of puberty: a condition in which individuals undergo puberty later than is typical of their peers

Cortisol: a steroid hormone released in response to stress

Early timing puberty: a condition in which individuals undergo puberty earlier than is typical of their peers

Epiphysis: the end component of bones that is elongated as children get older

Estradiol: a hormone that is secreted from ovaries in females

Functional resolution: refers to the temporal precision; images with higher functional resolution provide greater precision of timing of brain activation

Gonadarche: a stage in early puberty during which the gonads begin to grow and increase the production of estradiol and testosterone

Gonadotropin-releasing hormone (GnRH) neurons: neurons that release GnRH, a hormone that releases follicle-stimulating hormone and luteinizing hormone, which are involved in pubertal maturation

Gonadotropins: hormones that stimulate the activity of the gonads (testes in males and ovaries in females)

Gray matter: the darker tissue of the brain that consists mainly of neuron cell bodies

Hemodynamics: changes in blood flow and blood oxygenation

Hypothalamic-pituitary-gonadal (HPG) axis: a system in the brain responsible for the release of pubertal hormones

Hypothalamus: a brain region that is responsible for the production of many hormones

Maturational compression hypothesis: proposed to explain the relationship between tempo of puberty and psychosocial and behavioral problems

Menarche: a girl's first menstrual period

Metaphyses: the wide portion of long bones in the legs, arms, fingers, and toes

Off-time or maturational deviance hypothesis: proposes that adolescents who develop either earlier or later relative to their peers experience psychological distress and behavioral problems

Pituitary gland: an endocrine gland that secretes hormones, which help control growth, blood pressure, sex organs, thyroid glands, and metabolism

Spermarche: a boy's first ejaculation of semen

Testosterone: a hormone that is secreted from testes in males

Voxel (volume pixel):   the smallest perceptible box-shaped part of a three-dimensional image

White matter: the lighter tissue of the brain that consists of myelin wrapped around axon tracts

3 Cognitive Neuroscience Methods to Study the Adolescent Brain

Brain scan: an image of the brain that is taken using machines that operate like giant cameras

Coronal plane: the dimension that slices the brain lengthwise from front to back

Default mode network: a brain network that includes regions that collectively exhibit higher brain activation when the participant is "at rest" compared to when the participant is performing a computerized task

Diffusion tensor imaging: a type of brain imaging that provides visualization of white matter tracts

Electroencephalography (EEG): a tool used to measure electrical impulses in the brain

Functional connectivity map (fcMap): an estimation of the correlation in function between different brain regions

Functional imaging: a type of brain imaging that shows how the brain processes information

Magnetoencephalography (MEG): a tool used to measure brain activity

Resting state fMRI (rsfMRI): a method with which to evaluate the interactions between brain regions when the participant is not performing an explicit computerized task

Sagittal plane: the dimension that slices the brain lengthwise from side to side

Spatial resolution: refers to the number of pixels used in the construction of a digital image; images with higher spatial resolution provide greater anatomical detail of the brain

Structural imaging: a type of brain imaging that provides images of brain anatomy and structure

Tesla: a unit of magnetic strength used in brain imaging

Transverse plane: the dimension that slices the brain from top to bottom

4 Brain Plasticity

Allostasis: the process of achieving stability through physiological or behavioral change

Allostatic load: physiological, metabolic, physical, and psychological burden to an organism in response to chronic stress

Atrophy: neural degeneration

Critical period: a period of enhanced plasticity in neural circuits

Environmental complexity paradigm: a test used to measure the development of neural circuits in complex versus simple environments

Gap junctions: special channels that connect the presynaptic and postsynaptic cell membranes

Glucocorticoids: stress hormones in nonhuman animals

Homeostasis: the tendency toward a relatively stable equilibrium

Long-term depression (LTD): the decrease in synaptic strength following decreasing use or communication between two neurons

Long-term potentiation (LTP): the long-lasting increase in signal transmission (communication) between two neurons

Monocular deprivation: the process of depriving visual input to an animal, usually by suturing the eye shut

Neurogenesis: the birth of new neurons
Neuroplasticity: changes in the brain in response to experience
Sensitive period: a period of enhanced opportunity for learning
Synapses: structures that permit the passage of an electrical or chemical signal from one neuron to another
Synaptogenesis: the generation of new synapses

5 Neurocognitive Development

Attention-Deficit Hyperactive Disorder (ADHD): a brain disorder characterized by difficulty paying attention and by hyperactive behavior
Cognition: mental abilities that include memory, response inhibition, problem solving, and decision-making
Cognitive control: the ability to control behavior, suppress attention to irrelevant information, and exhibit flexibility according to current goals
Delayed shifts: a neurodevelopmental path in which children afflicted with a disorder exhibit the same pattern of neurodevelopment as typically developing children but at a delayed timing
Deviant trajectories: a neurodevelopmental path in which children afflicted with a disorder exhibit patterns that do not at all resemble typical development
Disrupted velocity: a neurodevelopmental path in which children afflicted with a disorder exhibit the same general pattern as typically developing children but at an aberrant speed
Prefrontal cortex: the most anterior region in the brain that is involved in cognition

6 Motivational Systems

Dopamine: a neurotransmitter that helps process rewarding information, regulate movement and emotional responses, and learn from the environment
Rescorla-Wagner Model: an explanation of classical conditioning in which the animal is said to learn from the discrepancy between what is expected to happen and what actually happens
Reward system: a network in the brain that is comprised of regions that process rewarding information
Reward tasks: computer games developed for use in the MRI scanner to study how humans process rewards
Risk-taking: engagement in a behavior without knowing the outcomes of that behavior

7 The Social Brain

Affect processing: the neural processing of emotions or feelings

Autism: characterized by difficulties in social interactions, verbal and non-verbal communication, and stereotyped patterns of behavior; also sometimes associated with intellectual disabilities, motor coordination impairments, and physical health issues

Configural processing: processing a face in its entirety, rather than focusing on its constituent parts

Face processing: the neural process of identifying and storing face information in the brain

Fusiform face area (FFA):   a region in the temporal lobe that processes faces

Joint attention: the process of looking in the direction of someone else's gaze, an indication of jointly attending to something

Prosocial behavior: any action intended to help others

Self-development: the development of one's sense of self-awareness, agency, self-esteem, and the self within the social context; identity exploration

Social anxiety disorder: characterized by an intense fear or distress in social situations that causes impairments in daily functioning

Theory of mind/mentalizing: the ability to assign mental states, including beliefs, intents, desires, pretending, knowledge, and sarcasm, to oneself and others

8 The Implications of Adolescent Neuroscience on Policy

Competence: the ability to do something successfully or efficiently; in the legal system, an individual's ability to stand trial and to understand charges against her

Juvenile justice: the primary legal system used to address and deal with youths who are convicted of crimes in the United States.

Mature Minor Doctrine: the regulatory or common law policy in the United States accepting that adolescents may have the maturity to make health care treatment decisions for themselves

Complete List of References

Abe, J., and Izard, C. (1999). The development functions of emotions: an analysis in terms of differential emotions theory. *Cognition and Emotion*, 13, 523–549.

Adolescent Sleep Working Group, Committee on Adolescence, and Council on School Health (2014). School start times for adolescents. *Pediatrics*, 134, 642–649.

Adolphs, R. (2002). Recognizing emotion from facial expressions: psychological and neurological mechanisms. *Behavioral and Cognitive Neuroscience Reviews*, 1, 21–62.

Adrien, J., Faure, M., Perrot, A., Hameury, L., Garreau, B., Barthelemy, C., and Sauvage, D. (1991). Autism and family home movies: preliminary findings. *Journal of Autism Developmental Disorder*, 21, 43–49.

Ahmed, M., Ong, K., Morrell, D., Cox, L., Drayer, N., Perry, L., and Dunger, D. (1999). Longitudinal study of leptin concentrations during puberty: sex differences and relationship to changes in body composition. *Journal of Clinical Endocrinology and Metabolism*, 84(3), 899–905.

Ainsworth, M. (1989). Attachments beyond infancy. *American Psychologist*, 44(4), 709–716.

Albert, D., Chein, J., and Steinberg, L. (2013). The teenage brain: peer influences on adolescent decision making. *Current Directions in Psychological Science*, 22, 114–119.

Alfano, C.A., Reynolds, K., Scott, N., Dahl, R.E., and Mellman, T.A. (2013). Polysomnographic sleep patterns of non-depressed, non-medicated children with generalized anxiety disorder. *Journal of Affective Disorders*, 147, 379–384.

Allen, J.P., Porter, M.R., McFarland, F.C., Marsh, P., and McElhaney, K.B. (2005). The two faces of adolescents' success with peers: adolescent popularity, social adaptation and deviant behavior. *Child Development*, 76, 747–760.

Allison, T., Ginter, H., McCarthy, G., Nobre, A., Puce, A., Luby, M., and Spencer, D. (1994). Face recognition in human extrastriate cortex. *Journal of Neurophysiology*, 71, 821–825.

Allison, T., Puce, A., and McCarthy, G. (2000). Social perception from visual cues: role of the STS region. *Trends in Cognitive Science*, 4, 267–278.

American Academy of Pediatrics, Committee on Adolescence (1996). The adolescent's right to confidential care when considering abortion. *Pediatrics*, 97, 746–751.

American Psychological Association (1989). Amicus curiae brief in *Hodgson v. Minnesota*, 497 U.S. 417 (1990).

Amodio, D., and Frith, C. (2006). Meeting of the minds: the medial frontal cortex and social cognition. *Nature Reviews Neuroscience*, 7, 268–277.

Andersen, S., Dumont, N., and Teicher, M. (1997). Developmental differences in dopamine synthesis inhibition by (+/−)-7-OH-DPAT. *Naunyn-Schmiedebergs Archives of Pharmacology*, 356, 173–181.

Andersen, S., and Gazzara, R. (1993). The ontogeny of apomorphine-induced alterations of neostriatal dopamine release: effects of spontaneous release. *Journal of Neurochemistry*, 61, 2247–2255.

Andersen, S., Thompson, A., Rutstein, M., Hostetter, J., and Teicher, M. (2000). Dopamine receptor pruning in prefrontal cortex during the periadolescent period in rats. *Synapse*, 37, 167–169.

Anderson, S., Dallal, G., and Must, A. (2003). Relative weight and race influence average age at menarche: results from two nationally representative surveys of US girls studied 25 years apart. *Pediatrics*, 111(4 Pt. 1), 844–850.

Arnett, J. (2011). Emerging adulthood(s): the cultural psychology of a new life stage. In L. Jensen (ed.), *Bridging cultural and developmental approaches to psychology: new synthesis in theory, research and policy* (pp. 255–275). Oxford: Oxford University Press.

Asarnow, L., McGlinchey, E., and Harvey, A. (2014). The effects of bedtime and sleep duration on academic and emotional outcomes in a nationally representative sample of adolescents. *Journal of Adolescent Health*, 54, 350–356.

Aylward, E., Park, J., Field, K., Parsons, A., Richards, T., Cramer, S., and Meltzoff, A. (2005). Brain activation during face perception: evidence of a developmental change. *Journal of Cognitive Neuroscience*, 17, 308–319.

Baenninger, M. (1994). The development of face recognition: featural or configurational processing? *Journal of Experimental Child Psychology*, 57, 377–396.

Baird, A., Gruber, S., Fein, D., Maas, L., Steingard, R., Renshaw, P., and Yurgelun-Todd, D. (1999). Functional magnetic resonance imaging of facial affect recognition in children and adolescents. *Journal of the American Academy of Child and Adolescent Psychiatry*, 38, 195–199.

Banks, S., Eddy, K., Angstadt, M., Nathan, P., and Phan, K. (2007). Amygdala–frontal connectivity during emotion regulation. *Social Cognitive and Affective Neuroscience*, 2, 303–312.

Barkley-Levenson, E., and Galván, A. (2014). Neural representation of expected value in the adolescent brain. *Proceedings of the National Academy of Sciences USA*, 111, 1646–1651.

  (2016). Eye blink rate predicts reward decisions in adolescents. *Developmental Science*.

Barnes, C. (1979). Memory deficits associated with senescence: a neurophysiological and behavioral study in the rat. *Journal of Comparative Physiology and Psychology*, 93, 74–104.

Baron-Cohen, S., Wheelwright, S., Cox, A., Baird, G., Charman, T., Swettenham, J., Drew, A., and Doehring, P. (2000). Early identification of autism by the Checklist for Autism in Toddlers (CHAT). *Journal of the Royal Society of Medicine*, 93, 521–525.

Barrera, M., and Maurer, D. (1981). The perception of facial expressions by the three-month-old. *Child Development*, 52, 203–206.

Basch, C., Basch, C., Ruggles, K., and Rajan, S. (2014). Prevalence of sleep duration on an average school night among 4 nationally representative successive samples of American high school students, 2007–2013. *Preventing Chronic Disease*, 11, E216.

Basser, P., Mattiello, J., and LeBihan, D. (1994). MR diffusion tensor spectroscopy and imaging. *Biophysical Journal*, 66, 259–267.

Basser, P., and Pierpaoli, C. (2011). Microstructural and physiological features of tissues elucidated by quantitative-diffusion-tensor MRI. 1996. *Journal of Magnetic Resonance*, 213, 560–570.

Baumeister, R., and Leary, M. (1995). The need to belong: desire for interpersonal attachments as a fundamental human motivation. *Psychological Bulletin*, 117, 497–529.

Bavelier, D., and Neville, H. (2002). Cross-modal plasticity: where and how? *Nature Reviews Neuroscience*, 3, 443–452.

Beard, J. (2003). Iron deficiency alters brain development and functioning. *Journal of Nutrition*, 133(5 Suppl. 1), 1468S–1472S.

Bell, M., and Sisk, C. (2013). Dopamine mediates testosterone-induced social reward in male Syrian hamsters. *Endocrinology*, 154, 1225–1234.

Belsky, J., and Jaffee, S. (2006). The multiple determinants of parenting. In D. Cicchetti and D. Cohen (eds.), *Developmental psychopathology* (2nd edn., vol. 3, pp. 38–85). Hoboken, NJ: Wiley and Sons.

Belsky, J., Steinberg, L., and Draper, P. (1991). Childhood experience, interpersonal development, and reproductive strategy: an evolutionary theory of socialization. *Child Development*, 62, 647–670.

Benedict, R. (1934). *Patterns of culture*. New York: Houghton Mifflin.

Berquin, P., Giedd, J., Jacobsen, L., Hamburger, S., Krain, A., Rapoport, J., and Castellanos F.X. (1998). Cerebellum in attention-deficit hyperactivity disorder: a morphometric MRI study. *Neurology*, 50, 1087–1093.

Berry, H., O'Grady, D., Perlmutter, L., and Bofinger, M. (1979). Intellectual development and achievement in children treated early for phenylketonuria. *Developmental Medicine and Child Neurology*, 21, 311–320.

Bertenthal, B., and Campos, J. (1990). A systems approach to the organizing effects of self-produced locomotion during infancy. In C. Rovee-Collier and L. Lipsitt (eds.), *Advances in infancy research* (pp. 134–156). Amsterdam: Elsevier.

Biswal, B., Yetkin, F., Haughton, V., and Hyde, J. (1995). Functional connectivity in the motor cortex of resting human brain using echo-planar MRI. *Magnetic Resonance Medicine*, 34, 537–541.

Bjork, J., Knutson, B., Fong, G., Caggiano, D., Bennett, S., and Hommer, D. (2004). Incentive-elicited brain activation in adolescents: similarities and differences from young adults. *Journal of Neuroscience*, 24, 1793–1802.

Bjork, J., Smith, A., Chen, G., and Hommer, D. (2010). Adolescents, adults and rewards: comparing motivational neurocircuitry recruitment using fMRI. *PLoS One*, 5, e11440.

(2011). Psychosocial problems and recruitment of incentive neurocircuitry: exploring individual differences in healthy adolescents. *Developmental Cognitive Neuroscience*, 1, 570–577.

Bjorklund, D., and Harnishfeger, K. (1990). The resources construct in cognitive development: diverse sources of evidence and a theory of inefficient inhibition. *Developmental Review*, 10, 48–71.

Blake, P., and McAuliffe, K. (2011). "I had so much it didn't seem fair": eight-year-olds reject two forms of inequity. *Cognition*, 120, 215–224.

Blakemore, S. (2008). The social brain in adolescence. *Nature Reviews Neuroscience*, 9, 267–277.

Blakemore, S., and Mills, K. (2014). Is adolescence a sensitive period for sociocultural processing? *Annual Review of Psychology*, 65, 187–207.

Blakemore, S.J., Burnett, S., and Dahl, R.E. (2010). The role of puberty in the developing adolescent brain. *Human Brain Mapping*, 31, 926–933.

Blum, K., Braverman, E., Holder, J., Lubar, J.F., Monastra, V., Miller, D., Lubar, J.O., Chen, T.J., Comings, D. (2000). Reward deficiency syndrome: a biogenetic model for the diagnosis and treatment of impulsive, addictive and compulsive behaviors. *Journal of Psychoactive Drugs*, 2, 1–112.

Blumenthal, H., Leen-Feldner, E., Babson, K., Gahr, J., Trainor, C., and Frala, J. (2011). Elevated social anxiety among early maturing girls. *Developmental Psychology*, 47, 1133–1140.

Boddaert, N., Chabane, N., Gervais, H., Good, C., Bourgeois, M., Plumet, M.H, Barthelemy, C., Mouren, M.C., Artiges, E., Samson, Y., Brunelle, F., Frackowiak, R.S., and Zilbovicius, M. (2004). Superior temporal sulcus anatomical abnormalities in childhood autism: a voxel-based morphometry MRI study. *Neuroimage*, 23, 364–369.

Bola, L., Zimmerman, M., Mostowski, P., Jednorog, K., Marchewka, A., Rotkowski, P., and Szwed, M. (2017). Task-specific reorganization of the auditory cortex in deaf humans. *Proceedings of the National Academy of Sciences USA*, 114, E600–E609.

Bolanos, C., Glatt, S., and Jackson, D. (1998). Subsensitivity to dopaminergic drugs in periadolescent rats: a behavioral and neurochemical analysis. *Developmental Brain Research*, 111, 25–33.

Bonnie, R. (1993). The competence of criminal defendants: beyond Dusky and Drope. *University of Miami Law Review*, 47, 539–601.

Bonnie, R., and Grisso, T. (2000). Adjudicative competence and youthful offenders. In T. Grisso and R. Schwartz (eds.), *Youth on trial: a developmental perspective on juvenile justice* (pp. 73–103). Chicago, IL: University of Chicago Press.

Bonnie, R., and Scott, E. (2013). The teenage brain: adolescent brain research and the law. *Current Directions in Psychological Science*, 22, 158–161.

Bos, P., van Honk, J., Ramsey, N., Stein, D., and Hermans, E. (2013). Testosterone administration in women increases amygdala responses to fearful and happy faces. *Psychoneuroendocrinology*, 38, 808–817.

Botvinick, M., Cohen, J., and Carter, C. (2004). Conflict monitoring and anterior cingulate cortex: an update. *Trends in Cognitive Neuroscience*, 8, 539–546.

Boucher, J., and Lewis, V. (1992). Unfamiliar face recognition in relatively able autistic children. *Journal of Child Psychology and Psychiatry*, 33, 843–859.

Braams, B., van Duijvenvoorde, A., Peper, J., and Crone, E. (2015). Longitudinal changes in adolescent risk-taking: a comprehensive study of neural responses to rewards, pubertal development, and risk-taking behavior. *Journal of Neuroscience*, 35, 7226–7238.

Bradford Cannon, W. (1929). *Bodily changes in pain, hunger, fear, and rage*. New York: Appleton-Century-Crofts.

Braitenberg, V. (2001). Brain size and number of neurons: an exercise in synthetic neuroanatomy. *Journal of Computational Neuroscience*, 10, 71–77.

Bramen, J.E., Hranilovich, J.A., Dahl, R.E., Chen, J., Rosso, C., Forbes, E.E., and Sowell, E.R. (2012). Sex matters during adolescence: testosterone-related cortical thickness maturation differs between boys and girls. *PLoS One*, 7, e33850.

Breiter, H., Etcoff, N., Whalen, P., Kennedy, W., Rauch, S., Buckner, R., Strauss, M.M., Hyman, S.E., and Rosen, B. (1996). Response and habituation of the human amygdala during visual processing of facial expression. *Neuron*, 17, 875–887.

Brenhouse, H., and Andersen, S. (2008). Delayed extinction and stronger reinstatement of cocaine conditioned place preference in adolescent rats, compared to adults. *Behavioral Neuroscience*, 122, 460–465.

Brenhouse, H., Sonntag, K., and Andersen, S. (2008). Transient D1 dopamine receptor expression on prefrontal cortex projection neurons: relationship to enhanced motivational salience of drug cues in adolescence. *Journal of Neuroscience*, 28, 2375–2382.

Brooks-Gunn, J., Warren, M.P., Rosso, J., and Gargiulo, J. (1987). Validity of self-report measures of girls' pubertal status. *Child Development*, 58, 829-841.

Brown, T., Lugar, H., Coalson, R., Miezin, F., Petersen, S., and Schlaggar, B. (2005). Developmental changes in human cerebral functional organization for word generation. *Cerebral Cortex*, 15(3), 275–290.

Bruner, J. (1972). Nature and uses of immaturity. *American Psychologist*, 27, 687–708.

Brunner, R., Berch, D., and Berry, H. (1987). Phenylketonuria and complex spatial visualization: an analysis of information processing. *Developmental Medicine and Child Neurology*, 29, 460–468.

Buckhalt, J. (2011). Insufficient sleep and the socioeconomic status achievement gap. *Child Development Perspectives*, 5, 59–65.

Bullock, M., and Russell, J. (1985). Further evidence on preschoolers' interpretation of facial expressions. *International Journal of Behavioral Development*, 8, 15–38.

Bunge, S.A., Dudukovic, N.M., Thomason, M.E., Vaidya, C.J., and Gabrieli, J.D.E. (2002). Immature frontal lobe contributions to cognitive control in children: evidence from fMRI. *Neuron*, 33, 301–311.

Burklund, L., Eisenberger, N., and Lieberman, M. (2007). The face of rejection: rejection sensitivity moderates dorsal anterior cingulate activity to disapproving facial expressions. *Social Neuroscience*, 2, 238–253.

Burnett, S., Bault, N., Coricelli, G., and Blakemore, S. (2010). Adolescents' heightened risk-seeking in a probabilistic gambling task. *Cognitive Development*, 25, 183–196.

Burnett, S., Bird, G., Moll, J., Frith, C., and Blakemore, S.-J. (2009). Development during adolescence of the neural processing of social emotion. *Journal of Cognitive Neuroscience*, 21, 1736–1750.

Burnett, S., Sebastian, C., Cohen Kadosh, K., and Blakemore, S.J. (2011). The social brain in adolescence: evidence from functional magnetic resonance imaging and behavioural studies. *Neuroscience Biobehavioral Review*, 35, 1654–1664.

Bush, F., and McIlhaney, J. (2008). *Hooked: new science on how casual sex is affecting our children*. Chicago, IL: Northfield.

Butterworth, G., and Hopkins, B. (1988). Hand–mouth coordination in the newborn baby. *British Journal of Developmental Psychology*, 6, 303–314.

Cain, N., and Gradisar, M. (2010). Electronic media use and sleep in school-aged children and adolescents: a review. *Sleep Medicine*, 11, 735–742.

Cappuccio, F., Taggart, F., Kandala, N., Currie, A., Peile, E., Stranges, S., and Miller, M. (2008). Meta-analysis of short sleep duration and obesity in children and adults. *Sleep*, 31, 619–626.

Capron, C., and Duyme, M. (1989). Assessment of effects of socioeconomic status on IQ in a full cross-fostering study. *Nature*, 340, 552–554.

Carey, S., and Diamond, R. (1977). From piecemeal to configurational representation of faces. *Science*, 195, 312–314.

Carey, S., Diamond, R., and Woods, B. (1980). Development of face recognition – a maturational component? *Developmental Psychology*, 16, 257–269.

Carlson, S., and Moses, L. (2001). Individual differences in inhibitory control and children's theory of mind. *Child Development*, 72, 1032–1053.

Carlson, S., Moses, L., and Claxton, L. (2004). Individual differences in executive functioning and theory of mind: an investigation of inhibitory control and planning ability. *Journal of Experimental Child Psychology*, 87, 299–319.

Carpendale, J., and Lewis, C. (2004). Constructing an understanding of mind. The development of children's social understanding within social interaction. *Behavioral and Brain Sciences*, 27, 79–96.

Carper, R., and Courchesne, E. (2005). Localized enlargement of the frontal cortex in early autism. *Biological Psychiatry*, 57, 126–133.

Carrell, S., Maghakian, T., and West, J. (2011). A's from Zzzz's? The causal effect of school start time on the academic achievement of adolescents. *American Economic Journal: Economic Policy*, 3, 62–81.

Carskadon, M. (2011). Sleep in adolescents: the perfect storm. *Pediatric Clinics of North America*, 58, 637–647.

Casey, B.J. (2015). Beyond simple models of self-control to circuit-based accounts of adolescent behaviour. *Annual Review of Psychology*, 66, 295–319.

Casey, B.J., and Caudle, K. (2013). The teenage brain: self control. *Current Directions in Psychological Science*, 22, 82–87.

Casey, B.J., Galván, A., and Hare, T. (2005). Changes in cerebral functional organization during cognitive development. *Current Opinion in Neurobiology*, 15, 239–244.

Casey, B.J., Galván, A., and Somerville, L. (2015). Beyond simple models of adolescence to an integrated circuit-based account: a commentary. *Developmental Cognitive Neuroscience*, 17, 128–130.

Casey, B.J., Getz, S., and Galván, A. (2008). The adolescent brain. *Developmental Review*, 28, 62–77.

Casey, B.J., Giedd, J., and Thomas, K. (2000). Structural and functional brain development and its relation to cognitive development. *Biological Psychology*, 54, 241–257.

Casey, B.J., Somerville, L., Gotlib, I., Ayduk, O., Franklin, N., Askren, M., Jonides, J., Berman, M.G., Wilson, N.L., Teslovich, T., Glover, G., Zayas, V., Mischel, W., and Shoda, Y. (2011). Behavioral and neural correlates of delay of gratification 40 years later. *Proceedings of the National Academy of Sciences USA*, 108, 14,998–15,003.

Casey, B.J., Tottenham, N., and Fossella, J. (2002). Clinical, imaging, lesion and genetic approaches toward a model of cognitive control. *Developmental Psychobiology*, 40, 237–254.

Casey, B.J., Trainor, R.J., Orendi, J.L., Schubert, A.B., Nystrom, L.E., Giedd, J.N., Castellanos, F.X., Haxby, J.V., Noll, D.C., Cohen, J.D. Forman S.D., Dahl, R.E., and Rapoport, J.L. (1997). A developmental functional MRI study of prefrontal activation during performance of a Go-No-Go task. *Journal of Cognitive Neuroscience*, 9, 835–847.

Castellano, J., Roa, J., Luque, R., Dieguez, C., Aguilar, E., Pinilla, L., and Tena-Sempere, M. (2009). KiSS-1/kisspeptins and the metabolic control of reproduction: physiologic roles and putative physiopathological implications. *Peptides*, 30, 139–145.

Castellanos, F., Lee, P., Sharp, W., Jeffries, N., Greenstein, D., and Clasen, L. (2002). Developmental trajectories of brain volume abnormalities in children and adolescents with attention-deficit/hyperactivity disorder. *Journal of the American Medical Association*, 288, 1740–1748.

Cavasos-Rehg, P., Krauss, M., and Spitznagel, E. (2012). Associations between selected state laws and teenagers' drinking and driving behaviors. *Alcohol and Clinical Experimental Research*, 36, 1647–1652.

CDC (2011a). Nonfatal traumatic brain injuries related to sports and recreation activities among persons aged ≤19 years – United States, 2001–2009. *Morbidity Mortality Weekly Report*, 60, 1337–1342.

(2011b). *Tobacco use: targeting the nation's leading killer*. Washington, DC: National Center for Chronic Disease Prevention and Health Promotion, Office of Smoking and Health.

(2012). Web-based Injury Statistics Query and Reporting System (WISQARS). Retrieved from www.cdc.gov/injury/wisqars/index.html.

Chambers, R., Taylor, J., and Potenza, M. (2003). Developmental neurocircuitry of motivation in adolescence: a critical period of addiction vulnerability. *American Journal of Psychiatry*, 160, 1041–1052.

Chein, J., Albert, D., O'Brien, L., Uckert, K., and Steinberg, L. (2011). Peers increase adolescent risk taking by enhancing activity in the brain's reward circuitry. *Developmental Science*, 14, F1–F10.

Chein, J., and Schneider, W. (2005). Neuroimaging studies of practice-related change: fMRI and meta-analytic evidence of a domain-general control network for learning. *Cognitive Brain Research*, 25, 607–623.

Chen, L., Baker, S., Braver, E., and Li, G. (2000). Carrying passengers as a risk factor for crashes fatal to 16- and 17-year-old drivers. *Journal of the American Medical Association*, 283, 1578–1582.

Cheng, G., Gerlach, S., Libuda, L., Kranz, S., Gunther, A., Karaolis-Danckert, N., Kroke, A., and Buyken, A. (2010). Diet quality in childhood is prospectively associated with the timing of puberty but not with body composition at puberty onset. *Journal of Nutrition*, 140, 95–102.

Cho, Y., Fromm, S., Guyer, A., Detloff, A., Pine, D., Fudge, J., and Ernst, M. (2013). Nucleus accumbens, thalamus and insula connectivity during incentive anticipation in typical adults and adolescents. *Neuroimage*, 66C, 508–521.

Choudhury, S., and McKinney, K. (2013). Digital media, the developing brain and the interpretive plasticity of neuroplasticity. *Transcultural Psychiatry*, 50, 192–215.

Christakou, A., Brammer, M., and Rubia, A. (2011). Maturation of limbic corticostriatal activation and connectivity associated with developmental changes in temporal discounting. *Neuroimage*, 54, 1344–1354.

Chumlea, W., Schubert, C., Roche, A., Kulin, H., Lee, P., Himes, J., and Sun, S. (2003). Age at menarche and racial comparisons in US girls. *Pediatrics*, 111, 110–113.

Church, J., Petersen, S., and Schlaggar, B. (2010). The "Task B problem" and other considerations in developmental functional neuroimaging. *Human Brain Mapping*, 31, 852–862.

Cohen, J., and Servan-Schreiber, D. (1992). Context, cortex and dopamine: a connectionist approach to behavior and biology in schizophrenia. *Psychological Review*, 99, 45–77.

Cohen, J.R., Asarnow, R.F., Sabb, F.W., Bilder, R.M., Bookheimer, S.Y., Knowlton, B.J., and Poldrack, R.A. (2010). A unique adolescent response to reward prediction errors. *Nature Neuroscience*, 13, 669–671.

Cohen-Gilbert, J., and Thomas, K. (2013). Inhibitory control during emotional distraction aross adolescence and early adulthood. *Child Development*, 84, 1954–1966.

Cohen Kadosh, K., Henson, R., Cohen Kadosh, R., Johnson, M., and Dick, F. (2010). Task-dependent activation of face-sensitive cortex: an fMRI adaptation study. *Journal of Cognitive Neuroscience*, 22, 903–917.

Cohen Kadosh, K., Johnson, M., Dick, F., Cohen Kadosh, R., and Blakemore, S. (2013). Effects of age, task performance, and structural brain development on face processing. *Cerebral Cortex*, 23, 1630–1642.

Constantinidis, C., and Klingberg, T. (2016). The neuroscience of working memory capacity and training. *Nature Reviews Neurosciences*, 17, 438–449.

Courchesne, E., Carper, R., and Akshoomoff, N. (2003). Evidence of brain outgrowth in the first year of life in autism. *Journal of the American Medical Association*, 290, 337–344.

Craig, A.D. (2009). How do you feel now? The anterior insula and human awareness. *Nature Reviews Neuroscience*, 10, 59–70.

Crone, E., and Dahl, R. (2012). Understanding adolescence as a period of social-affective engagement and goal flexibility. *Nature Reviews Neuroscience*, 13, 636–650.

Crone, E., Wendelken, C., Donohue, S., Van Leijenhorst, L., and Bunge, S. (2006). Neurocognitive development of the ability to manipulate information in working memory. *Proceedings of the National Academy of Sciences USA*, 103, 9315–9320.

Crowley, S., Acebo, C., and Carskadon, M. (2007). Sleep, circadian rhythms, and delayed phase in adolescence. *Sleep Medicine*, 8, 602–612.

Crowley, S., and Carskadon, M. (2010). Modifications to weekend recovery sleep delay circadian phase in older adolescents. *Chronobiology International*, 27, 1469–1492.

Csikszentmihalyi, M., Larson, R., and Prescott, S. (1977). The ecology of adolescent activity and experience. *Journal of Youth and Adolescence*, 6, 281–294.

Curcio, G., Ferrara, M., and De Gennaro, L. (2006). Sleep loss, learning capacity and academic performance. *Sleep Medicine Reviews*, 10, 323–337.

Curry, A., Hafetz, J., Kallan, M., Winston, F., and Durbin, D. (2011). Prevalence of teen driver errors leading to serious motor vehicle crashes. *Accident Analysis and Prevention*, 43, 1285–1290.

Curry, A., Mirman, J., Kallan, M., Winston, F., and Durbin, D. (2012). Peer passengers: how do they affect teen crashes? *Journal of Adolescent Health*, 50, 588–594.

Cynader, M., and Mitchell, D. (1977). Monocular astigmatism effects on kitten visual cortex development. *Nature*, 270(5633), 177–178.

Dahl, R.E. (2004). Adolescent brain development: a period of vulnerabilities and opportunities. *Annals of the New York Academy of Sciences*, 1021, 1–22.

Dalton, K., Nacewicz, B., Johnstone, T., Schaefer, H., Gernsbacher, M., Goldsmith, H., and Davidson, R. (2005). Gaze fixation and the neural circuitry of face processing in autism. *Nature Neuroscience*, 8, 519–526.

Danner, F., and Phillips, B. (2008). Adolescent sleep, school start times, and teen motor vehicle crashes. *Journal of Clinical Sleep Medicine*, 4, 533–535.

Dapretto, M., Davies, M., Pfeifer, J., Scott, A., Sigman, M., Bookheimer, S., and Iacoboni, M. (2006). Understanding emotions in others: mirror neuron dysfunction in children with autism spectrum disorder. *Nature Neuroscience*, 9, 28–30.

Darki, F., and Klingberg, T. (2014). The role of fronto-parietal and fronto-striatal networks in the development of working memory: a longitudinal study. *Cerebral Cortex*, 25, 1587–1595.

Davidow, J.Y., Foerde, K., Galván, A., and Shohamy, D. (2016). An upside to reward sensitivity: the hippocampus supports enhanced reinforcement learning in adolescence. *Neuron*, 92, 93–99.

Davidson, R., Kabat-Zinn, J., Schumacher, J., Rosenkranz, M., Muller, D., Santorelli, S., and Sheridan, J. (2003). Alterations in brain and immune function produced by mindfulness meditation. *Psychosomatic Medicine*, 65, 564–570.

Davidson, R., and McEwen, B. (2012). Social influences on neuroplasticity: stress and interventions to promote well-being. *Nature Neuroscience*, 15, 689–695.

Davis, T., LaRocque, K., Mumford, J., Norman, K., Wagner, A., and Poldrack, R. (2014). What do differences between multi-voxel and univariate analysis mean? How subject-, voxel-, and trial-level variance impact fMRI analysis. *Neuroimage*, 97, 271–283.

Decety, J., and Svetlova, M. (2012). Putting together phylogenetic and ontogenetic perspectives on empathy. *Developmental Cognitive Neuroscience*, 2, 1–24.

de Lange, F., Koers, A., Kalkman, J., Bleijenberg, G., Hagoort, P., van der Meer, J., and Toni, I. (2008). Increase in prefrontal cortical volume following cognitive behavioural therapy in patients with chronic fatigue syndrome. *Brain*, 131, 2172–2180.

De Leonibus, C., Marcovecchio, M., Chiavaroli, V., de Giorgis, T., Chiarelli, F., and Mohn, A. (2014). Timing of puberty and physical growth in obese children: a longitudinal study in boys and girls. *Pediatric Obesity*, 9, 292–299.

Delcher, C., Johnson, R., and Maldonado-Molina, M. (2013). Driving after drinking among young adults of different race/ethnicities in the United States: unique risk factors in early adolescence? *Journal of Adolescent Health*, 52, 584–591.

Delgado, M., Nearing, K., Ledoux, J., and Phelps, E. (2008). Neural circuitry underlying the regulation of conditioned fear and its relation to extinction. *Neuron*, 59, 829–838.

Demerath, E., Towne, B., Chumlea, W., Sun, S., Czerwinski, S., Remsberg, K., and Siervogel, R. (2004). Recent decline in age at menarche: the Fels Longitudinal Study. *American Journal of Human Biology*, 16, 453–457.

Demetriou, A., Christou, C., Spanoudis, G., and Platsidou, M. (2002). The development of mental processing: efficiency, working memory, and thinking. *Monographs of the Society for Research in Child Development*, 67, 1–155.

Demos, K., Heatherton, T., and Kelley, W. (2012). Individual differences in nucleus accumbens activity to food and sexual images predict weight gain and sexual behavior. *Journal of Neuroscience*, 32, 5549–5552.

Deutsch, G., Dougherty, R., Bammer, R., Siok, W., Gabrieli, J., and Wandell, B. (2005). Chidren's reading performance is correlated with white matter structure measured by diffusion tensor imaging. *Cortex*, 41, 354–363.

Devlin, M., Walsh, B., Katz, J., Roose, S., Linkie, D., Wright, L., and Glassman, A. (1989). Hypothalamic-pituitary-gonadal function in anorexia nervosa and bulimia. *Psychiatry Research*, 28, 11–24.

Diamond, A. (2002). Normal development of prefrontal cortex from birth to young adulthood: cognitive functions, anatomy, and biochemistry. In D. Stuss and R. Knight (eds.), *Principles of frontal lobe function* (pp. 466–503). Oxford: Oxford University Press.

(2012). Activities and programs that improve children's executive functions. *Current Directions in Psychological Science*, 21, 335–341.

Diamond, A., Barnett, W., Thomas, J., and Munro, S. (2007). Preschool program improves cognitive control. *Science*, 318, 1387–1388.

Diamond, A., and Goldman-Rakic, P. (1989). Comparison of human infants and rhesus monkeys on Piaget's AB task: evidence for dependence on dorsolateral prefrontal cortex. *Experimental Brain Research*, 74, 24–40.

Diamond, A., Prevor, M., Callender, G., and Druin, D. (1997). Prefrontal cortex cognitive deficits in children treated early and continuously for

PKU. *Monographs of the Society for Research in Child Development*, 62, 1–208.

Diamond, R., and Carey, S. (1977). Developmental changes in the representation of faces. *Journal of Experimental Child Psychology*, 23, 1–22.

Diamond, R., Carey, S., and Back, K. (1983). Genetic influences on the development of spatial skills during early adolescence. *Cognition*, 13, 167–185.

Dickinson, M., Chekaluk, E., and Irwin, J. (2013). Visual attention in novice drivers: a lack of situation awareness. In M. Regan, J. Lee, and T. Victor (eds.), *Driver distraction and inattention: advances in resarch and countermeasure* (pp. 277–292). Burlington, VT: Ashgate.

Dollaghan, C., Campbell, T., Paradise, J., Feldman, H., Janosky, J., Pitcairn, D., and Kurs-Lasky, M. (1999). Maternal education and measures of early speech and language. *Journal of Speech, Language and Hearing Research*, 42, 1432–1443.

Doremus-Fitzwater, T.L., Varlinskaya, E.I., and Spear, L.P. (2010). Motivational systems in adolescence: possible implications for age differences in substance abuse and other risk-taking behaviors. *Brain Cognition*, 72, 114–123.

Dorn, L.D., Dahl, R.E., Woodward, H.R., and Biro, G. (2006). Defining the boundaries of early adolescence: a user's guide to assessing pubertal status and pubertal timing in research with adolescents. *Applied Developmental Science*, 10, 30–56.

Dosenbach, N., Nardos, B., Cohen, A., Fair, D., Power, J., Church, J., Nelson, S.M., Wig, G.S., Vogel, A.C., Lessov-Schlaggar, C.N., Barnes, K.A., Dubis, J.W., Feczko, E., Coalson, R.S., Pruett, J.R., Barch, D.M., Petersen, S.E., and Schlaggar, B.L. (2010). Prediction of individual brain maturity using fMRI. *Science*, 329, 1358–1361.

Doucet, M., Guillemot, J., Lassonde, M., Gagne, J., Leclerc, C., and Lepore, F. (2005). Blind subjects process auditory spectral cues more efficiently than sighted individuals. *Experimental Brain Research*, 160, 194–202.

Douglas, L., Varlinskaya, E., and Spear, L. (2003). Novel-object place conditioning in adolescent and adult male and female rats: effects of social isolation. *Physiology and Behavior*, 80, 317–325.

(2004). Rewarding properties of social interactions in adolescent and adult male and female rats: impact of social versus isolate housing of subjects and partners. *Developmental Psychobiology*, 45, 153–162.

Doupe, A., and Kuhl, P. (2008). Birdsong and human speech: common themes and mechanisms. In H. Zeigler and P. Marler (eds.), *Neuroscience of birdsong*. Cambridge: Cambridge University Press.

Draganski, B., Gaser, C., Busch, V., Schuierer, G., Bogdahn, U., and May, A. (2004). Neuroplasticity: changes in grey matter induced by training. *Nature*, 427, 311–312.

Duncan, G., Brooks-Gunn, J., and Klebanov, P. (1994). Economic deprivation and early childhood development. *Child Development*, 65(2 Spec. No.), 296–318.

Dunlop, S., and Romer, D. (2010). Adolescent and young adult crash risk: sensation seeking, substance use propensity, and substance use behaviors. *Journal of Adolescent Health*, 46, 90–92.

Durston, S., Davidson, M., Tottenham, N., Galván, A., Spicer, J., Fossella, J., and Casey, B. (2006). A shift from diffuse to focal cortical activity with development. *Developmental Science*, 9, 1–8.

Durston, S., Mulder, M., Casey, B., Ziermans, T., and van Engeland, H. (2006). Activation in ventral prefrontal cortex is sensitive to genetic vulnerability for attention-deficit hyperactivity disorder. *Biological Psychiatry*, 60, 1062–1070.

Eaton, D., Kann, L., Kinchen, S., Shanklin, S., Flint, K., Hawkins, J., Harris, W.A., Lowry, R., McManus, T., Chyen, D., Whittle, L., Lim, C., and Wechsler, H. (2012). Youth risk behavior surveillance – United States, 2011. *MMWR Surveillance Summaries*, 61, 1–162.

Eisenberger, N., Lieberman, M., and Williams, K. (2003). Does rejection hurt? An fMRI study of social exclusion. *Science*, 302, 290–292.

Eisenberger, N.I., Taylor, S.E., Gable, S.L., Hilmert, C., and Lieberman, M. (2007). Neural pathways link social support to attenuated neuroendocrine stress responses. *Neuroimage*, 35, 1601–1612.

Elbert, T., Pantev, C., Wienbruch, C., Rockstroh, B., and Taub, E. (1995). Increased cortical representation of the fingers of the left hand in string players. *Science*, 270, 305–307.

Elias, C. (2012). Leptin action in pubertal development: recent advances and unanswered questions. *Trends in Endocrinology and Metabolism*, 23, 9–15.

Elkind, D., and Bowen, R. (1979). Imaginary audience behavior in children and adolescents. *Developmental Psychology*, 15, 38–44.

Ellis, B. (2004). Timing of pubertal maturation in girls: an integrated life history approach. *Psychological Bulletin*, 130, 920–958.

(2013). The hypothalamic-pituitary-gonadal axis: a switch-controlled, condition-sensitive system in the regulation of life history strategies. *Hormones and Behavior*, 64, 215–225.

Erickson, K., Voss, M., Prakash, R., Basak, C., Szabo, A., Chaddock, L., Kim, J.S., Heo, S., Alves, H., White, S.M., Wojcicki, T.R., Mailey, E., Vieira, V.J., Martin, S.A., Pence, B.D., Woods, J.A., McAuley, E., and Kramer, A.F. (2011). Exercise training increases size of hippocampus and improves memory. *Proceedings of the National Academy of Sciences USA*, 108, 3017–3022.

Eriksen, B., and Eriksen, C. (1974). Effects of noise letters upon identification of a target letter in a non-search task. *Perception and Psychophysics*, 16, 143–149.

Erikson, K., Jones, B., and Beard, J. (2000). Iron deficiency alters dopamine transporter functioning in rat striatum. *Journal of Nutrition*, 130, 2831–2837.

Ernst, M. (2014). The triadic model perspective for the study of adolescent motivated behavior. *Brain and Cognition*, 89, 104–111.

Ernst, M., Nelson, E., Jazbec, S., McClure, E., Monk, C., Leibenluft, E., Blair, J., and Pine, D. (2005). Amygdala and nucleus accumbens in responses to receipt and omission of gains in adults and adolescents. *Neuroimage*, 25, 1279–1291.

Ernst, M., Pine, D., and Hardin, M. (2006). Triadic model of the neurobiology of motivated behavior in adolescence. *Psychological Medicine*, 36, 299–312.

Escalona, A., Field, T., Nadel, J., and Lundy, B. (2002). Brief report: imitation effects on children with autism. *Journal of Autism Developmental Disorder*, 32, 141–144.

Esteban-Cornejo, I., Tejero-Gonzalez, C.M., Sallis, J.F., and Veiga, O.L. (2015). Physical activity and cognition in adolescents: a systematic review. *Journal of Science and Medicine in Sport*, 18, 534–539.

Everitt, B., and Robbins, T. (2005). Neural systems of reinforcement for drug addiction: from actions to habits to compulsion. *Nature Neuroscience*, 8, 1481–1489.

Fair, D., Cohen, A., Dosenbach, N., Church, J., Miezin, F., Barch, D., Raichle, M.E., Petersen, S.E., and Schlaggar, B.L. (2008). The maturing architecture of the brain's default network. *Proceedings of the National Academy of Sciences USA*, 105, 4028–4032.

Farooqi, I. (2002). Leptin and the onset of puberty: insights from rodent and human genetics. *Seminars in Reproductive Medicine*, 20, 139–144.

Fehr, E., and Fischbacher, U. (2003). The nature of human altruism. *Nature*, 425, 785–791.

Feinstein, J., Adolphs, R., Damasio, A., and Tranel, D. (2011). The human amygdala and the induction and experience of fear. *Current Biology*, 21, 34–38.

Fernandez-Fernandez, R., Martini, A., Navarro, V., Castellano, J., Dieguez, C., Aguilar, E., and Tena-Sempere, M. (2006). Novel signals for the integration of energy balance and reproduction. *Molecular Cell Endocrinology*, 254, 127–132.

Figner, B., Mackinlay, R., Wilkening, F., and Weber, E. (2009). Affective and deliberative processes in risky choice: age differences in risk taking in the Columbia Card Task. *Journal of Experimental Psychology: Learning, Memory and Cognition*, 35, 709–730.

Finney, E., Fine, I., and Dobkins, K. (2001). Visual stimuli activate auditory cortex in the deaf. *Nature Neuroscience*, 4, 1171–1173.

Fiorillo, C., Tobler, P., and Schultz, W. (2003). Discrete coding of reward probability and uncertainty by dopamine neurons. *Science*, 299, 1898–1902.

Flor, H., Elbert, T., Knecht, S., Wienbruch, C., Pantev, C., Birbaumer, N., and Taub, E. (1995). Phantom-limb pain as a perceptual correlate of cortical reorganization following arm amputation. *Nature*, 375, 482–484.

Forbes, E., and Dahl, R. (2010). Pubertal development and behavior: hormonal activation of social and motivational tendencies. *Brain and Cognition*, 72, 66–72.

Fox, M., Snyder, A., Vincent, J., Corbetta, M., Van Essen, D., and Raichle, M. (2005). The human brain is intrinsically organized into dynamic, anticorrelated functional networks. *Proceedings of the National Academy of Sciences USA*, 102, 9673–9678.

Fox, P., Raichle, M., Mintun, M., and Dence, C. (1988). Nonoxidative glucose consumption during focal physiologic neural activity. *Science*, 241, 462–464.

Fransson, P., Aden, U., Blennow, M., and Lagercrantz, H. (2011). The functional architecture of the infant brain as revealed by resting-state fMRI. *Cerebral Cortex*, 21, 145–154.

Fredriksen, K., Rhodes, J., Reddy, R., and Way, N. (2004). Sleepless in Chicago: tracking the effects of adolescent sleep loss during the middle school years. *Child Development*, 75, 84–95.

Freedman, D., Khan, L., Serdula, M., Dietz, W., Srinivasan, S., and Berenson, G. (2002). Relation of age at menarche to race, time period, and anthropometric dimensions: the Bogalusa Heart Study. *Pediatrics*, 110, e43.

Freud, A. (1966–1980). The writings of Anna Freud, 8 vols. New York: Indiana University of Pennsylvania: vol. 4, Indications for child analysis and other papers (1945–1956) (1946); vol. 5, Research at the Hampstead Child-Therapy Clinic and other papers (1956–1965) (1958); vol. 7, Problems of psychoanalytic training, diagnosis, and the technique of therapy (1966–1970) (1968).

Friedman, N., Haberstick, B., Willcutt, E., Miyake, A., Young, S., and Corley, R. (2007). Greater attention problems during childhood predict poorer executive functioning in late adolescence. *Psychological Science*, 18, 893–900.

Friemel, C., Spanagel, R., and Schneider, M. (2010). Reward sensitivity for a palatable food reward peaks during pubertal developmental in rats. *Frontiers in Behavioral Neuroscience*, 4, 1–10.

Frisch, R., and Revelle, R. (1970). Height and weight at menarche and a hypothesis of critical body weights and adolescent events. *Science*, 169, 397–399.

Friston, K., Worsley, K., Frackowiak, R., Mazziotta, J., and Evans, A. (1994). Assessing the significance of focal activations using their spatial extent. *Human Brain Mapping*, 1, 210–220.

Frith, C. (2008). Social cognition. *Philosophical Transactions of the Royal Society of London B Biological Sciences*, 363(1499), 2033–2039.

Fuster, J. (2001). The prefrontal cortex – an update: time is of the essence. *Neuron*, 30, 319–333.

Fuster, J., and Alexander, G. (1971). Neuron activity related to short-term memory. *Science*, 173, 652–654.

Galani, R., Coutureau, E., and Kelche, C. (1998). Effects of enriched postoperative housing conditions on spatial memory deficits in rats with selective lesions of either the hippocampus, subiculum or entorhinal cortex. *Restorative Neurology and Neurosciences*, 13, 173–184.

Galván A (2013a). Sensitivity to reward in adolescence. *Current Directions in Psychological Science*, 22, 100–105.

(2013b). The teenage brain: sensitivity to rewards. *Current Directions in Psychological Science*, 22, 88–93.

(2014). Insights about adolescent behavior, plasticity and policy from neuroscience research. *Neuron*, 83, 262–265.

Galván, A., Hare, T., Parra, C., Penn, J., Voss, H., Glover, G., and Casey, B. (2006). Earlier development of the accumbens relative to orbitofrontal cortex might underlie risk-taking behavior in adolescents. *Journal of Neuroscience*, 26, 6885–6892.

Galván, A., Hare, T., Voss, H., Glover, G., and Casey, B. (2007). Risk-taking and the adolescent brain: who is at risk? *Developmental Science*, 10, F8–F14.

Galván, A., and McGlennen, K. (2013). Enhanced striatal sensitivity to aversive reinforcement in adolescents versus adults. *Journal of Cognitive Neuroscience*, 25, 284–296.

Galván, A., Van Leijenhorst, L., and McGlennen, K. (2012). Considerations for imaging the adolescent brain. *Developmental Cognitive Neuroscience*, 2, 293–302.

Gardner, M., and Steinberg, L. (2005). Peer influence on risk-taking, risk preference, and risky decision-making in adolescence and adulthood: an experimental study. *Developmental Psychology*, 4, 625–635.

Gauthier, I., and Nelson, C.A. (2001). The development of face expertise. *Current Opinion in Neurobiology*, 11, 219–224.

Gee, D.G., Humphreys, K.L., Flannery, J., Goff, B., Telzer, E.H., Shapiro, M., Hare T.A., Bookheimer, S.Y., and Tottenham, N. (2013). A developmental shift from positive to negative connectivity in human amygdala-prefrontal circuitry. *Journal of Neuroscience*, 33, 4584–4593.

Geier, C., and Luna, B. (2009). The maturation of incentive processing and cognitive control. *Pharmacology, Biochemistry and Behavior*, 93, 212–221.

Geier, C., Terwilliger, R., Teslovich, T., Velanova, K., and Luna, B. (2010). Immaturities in reward processing and its influence on inhibitory control in adolescence. *Cerebral Cortex*, 20, 1613–1629.

Giedd, J., Castellanos, F., Casey, B., Kozuch, P., King, A.C., Hamburger, S.D., and Rapoport, J.L. (1994). Quantitative morphology of the corpus callosum in attention deficit hyperactivity disorder. *American Journal of Psychiatry*, 151, 665–669.

Giedd, J., Raznahan, A., Alexander-Bloch, A., Schmitt, E., Gogtay, N., and Rapoport, J. (2015). Child psychiatry branch of the National Institute of Mental Health longitudinal structural magnetic resonance imaging study of human brain development. *Neuropsychopharmacology*, 40, 43–49.

Gillen-O'Neel, C., Huynh, V., and Fuligni, A. (2013). To study or to sleep? The academic costs of extra studying and sleep loss. *Child Development*, 84, 133–142.

Goddings, A.L., Burnett Hayes, S., Bird, G., Viner, R.M., and Blakemore, S.J. (2012). The relationship between puberty and social emotion processing. *Developmental Science*, 15, 801–811.

Goddings, A.L., Mills, K.L., Clasen, L.S., Giedd, J.N., Viner, R.M., and Blakemore, S.J. (2014). The influence of puberty on subcortical brain development. *Neuroimage*, 88, 242–251.

Gogtay, N., and Rapoport, J. (2008). Childhood-onset schizophrenia: insights from neuroimaging studies. *Journal of the American Academy of Child and Adolescent Psychiatry*, 47, 1120–1124.

Gohlke, J., Griffith, W., and Faustman, E. (2007). Computational models of neocortical neuronogenesis and programmed cell death in the developing mouse, monkey, and human. *Cerebral Cortex*, 17, 2433–2442.

Golarai, G., Ghahremani, D.G., Whitfield-Gabrieli, S., Reiss, A., Eberhardt, J.L., Gabrieli, J.D., and Grill-Spector, K. (2007).

Differential development of high-level visual cortex correlates with category-specific recognition memory. *Nature Neuroscience*, 10, 512–522.

Golarai, G., Grill-Spector, K., and Reiss, A. (2006). Autism and the development of face processing. *Clinical Neuroscience Research*, 6, 145–160.

Golarai, G., Liberman, A., Yoon, J.M., and Grill-Spector, K. (2010). Differential development of the ventral visual cortex extends through adolescence. *Frontiers in Human Neuroscience*, 3, 80.

Goldman-Rakic, P. (1996). The prefrontal landscape: implications of functional architecture for understanding human mentation and the central executive. *Philosophical Transactions of the Royal Society B*, 351, 1445–1453.

Goldenberg, D., and Galván, A. (2015). The use of functional and effective connectivity techniques to understand the developing brain. *Developmental Cognitive Neuroscience*, 12, 155–164.

Goldman-Rakic, P. (1996). The prefrontal landscape: implications of functional architecture for understanding human mentation and the central executive. *Philosophical Transactions of the Royal Society B*, 351, 1445–1453.

Gomez, J., Barnett, M.A., Natu, V., Mezer, A., Palomero-Gallagher, N., Weiner, K.S., Amunts, K., Zilles, K., and Grill-Spector, K. (2017). Microstructural proliferation in human cortex is coupled with the development of face processing. *Science*, 355, 68–71.

Gopnik, A., and Wellman, H. (2012). Reconstructing constructivism: causal models, Bayesian learning mechanisms, and the theory theory. *Psychological Bulletin*, 138, 1085–1108.

Gordon, R. (1992). The simulation theory: objections and misconceptions. *Mind and Language*, 7, 11–34.

Gould, E., Reeves, A.J., Graziano, M.S., and Gross, C.G. (1999). Neurogenesis in the neocortex of adult primates. *Science*, 286, 548–552.

Goyal, M., Hawrylycz, M., Miller, J., Snyder, A., and Raichle, M. (2014). Aerobic glycolysis in the human brain is associated with development and neotenous gene expression. *Cell Metabolism*, 19, 49–57.

Graber, J. (2013). Pubertal timing and the development of psychopathology in adolescence and beyond. *Hormones and Behavior*, 64, 262–269.

Graber, J., Nichols, T., and Brooks-Gunn, J. (2010). Putting pubertal timing in developmental context: implications for prevention. *Developmental Psychobiology*, 52, 254–262.

Graber, J., Seeley, J., Brooks-Gunn, J., and Lewinsohn, P. (2004). Is pubertal timing associated with psychopathology in young adulthood?

Journal of the American Academy of Child and Adolescent Psychiatry, 43, 718–726.

Greenough, W., Black, J., and Wallace, C. (1987). Experience and brain development. *Child Development*, 58, 539–559.

Greenough, W., and Volkmar, F. (1973). Pattern of dendritic branching in occipital cortex of rats reared in complex environments. *Experimental Neurology*, 40, 491–504.

Greenough, W., Volkmar, F., and Juraska, J. (1973). Effects of rearing complexity on dendritic branching in frontolateral and temporal cortex of the rat. *Experimental Neurology*, 41, 371–378.

Greenough, W., Withers, G., and Anderson, B. (1992). Experience-dependent synaptogenesis as a plausible memory mechanism. In I. Gormezano and E. Vasserman (eds.), *Learning and memory: the behavioral and biological substrates* (pp. 209–229). Hillsdale, NJ: Lawrence Erlbaum Associates.

Gregersen, N., and Bjurulf, P. (1996). Young novice drivers: towards a model of their accident involvement. *Accident Analysis and Prevention*, 28, 229–241.

Gregory, A., and Sadeh, A. (2012). Sleep, emotional and behavioral difficulties in children and adolescents. *Sleep Medicine Reviews*, 16, 129–136.

Grelotti, D., Gauthier, I., and Schultz, R. (2001). Social interest and the development of cortical face specialization: what autism teaches us about face processing. *Developmental Psychobiology*, 40, 213–225.

Grisso, T., Steinberg, L., Woolard, J., Cauffman, E., Scott, E., Graham, S., Lexcen, F., Reppucci, N.D., and Schwartz, R. (2003). Juveniles' competence to stand trial: a comparison of adolescents' and adults' capacities as trial defendants. *Law and Human Behavior*, 27, 333–363.

Groman, S., James, A., Seu, E., Tran, S., Clark, T., Harpster, S., and Jentsch, J. (2014). In the blink of an eye: relating positive-feedback sensitivity to striatal dopamine D2-like receptors through blink rate. *Journal of Neuroscience*, 34, 14,443–14,454.

Grossmann, T., and Johnson, M. (2007). The development of the social brain in human infancy. *European Journal of Neuroscience*, 25, 909–919.

Guroglu, B., van den Bos, W., and Crone, E. (2014). Sharing and giving across adolescence: an experimental study examining the development of prosocial behavior. *Frontiers in Psychology*, 5, 291–297.

Guttmacher (2014). State policies in brief: sex and HIV education. Guttmacher Institute. Retrieved from www.guttmacher.org/statecenter/spibs/spib_SE.pdf.

Guye, M., Bartolomei, F., and Ranjeva, J. (2008). Imaging structural and functional connectivity: towards a unified definition of human brain organization? *Current Opinion in Neurology*, 21, 393–403.

Guyer, A., Choate, V., Pine, D., and Nelson, E. (2012). Neural circuitry underlying affective response to peer feedback in adolescence. *Social Cognitive and Affective Neuroscience*, 7, 81–92.

Guyer, A., McClure-Tone, E., Shiffrin, N.D., Pine, D., and Nelson, E. (2009). Probing the neural correlates of anticipated peer evaluation in adolescence. *Child Development*, 80, 1000–1015.

Guyer, A., Monk, C., McClure-Tone, E., Nelson, E., Roberson-Nay, R., Adler, A., Fromm, S.J., Leibenluft, E., Pine, D.S., and Ernst, M. (2008). A developmental examination of amygdala response to facial expressions. *Journal of Cognitive Neuroscience*, 20, 1565–1582.

Gweon, H., Dodell-Feder, D., Bedny, M., and Saxe, R. (2013). Theory of mind performance in children correlates with functional specialization of a brain region for thinking about thoughts. *Child Development*, 83, 1853–1868.

Haacke, E., Cheng, N., House, M., Liu, Q., Neelavalli, J., Ogg, R., and Obenaus, A. (2005). Imaging iron stores in the brain using magnetic resonance imaging. *Magnetic Resonance Imaging*, 23, 1–25.

Haber, S. (2011). Neuroanatomy of reward: a view from the ventral striatum. In J. Gottfried (ed.), *Neurobiology of sensation and reward* (pp. 235–262). Boca Raton, FL: CRC Press.

Haber, S., and Knutson, B. (2010). The reward circuit: linking primate anatomy and human imaging. *Neuropsychopharmacology*, 35, 4–26.

Hackman, D., Farah, M., and Meaney, M. (2010). Socioeconomic status and the brain: mechanistic insights from human and animal research. *Nature Reviews Neuroscience*, 11, 651–659.

Hadjikhani, N., Joseph, R., Snyder, J., and Tager-Flusberg, H. (2006). Anatomical differences in the mirror neuron system and social cognition network in autism. *Cerebral Cortex*, 16, 1276–1282.

Hagenauer, M., and Lee, T. (2013). Adolescent sleep patterns in humans and laboratory animals. *Hormones and Behavior*, 64, 270–279.

Hall, G.S. (1904). *Adolescence: its psychology and its relations to physiology, anthropology, sociology, sex, crime, religion, and education*, vols. I and II. New York: D. Appleton & Co.

Halverson, H. (1933). The acquisition of skill in infancy. *Journal of Genetic Psychology*, 43, 3–48.

Hare, T., Tottenham, N., Galván, A., Voss, H., Glover, G., and Casey, B. (2008). Biological substrates of emotional reactivity and regulation in adolescence during an emotional go-nogo task. *Biological Psychiatry*, 63, 927–934.

Hariri, A., Mattay, V., Tessitore, A., Fera, F., and Weinberger, D. (2003). Neocortical modulation of the amygdala response to fearful stimuli. *Biological Psychiatry*, 53, 494–501.

Harlan, W.R., Harlan, E.A., and Grillo, G.P. (1980). Secondary sex characteristics of girls 12 to 17 years of age: the U.S. Health Examination Survey. *Journal of Pediatrics*, 96, 1074–1078.

Harrison, E., and Fillmore, M. (2011). Alcohol and distraction interact to impair driving performance. *Drug and Alcohol Dependence*, 117, 31–37.

Hart, B., and Risley, T. (2003). The early catastrophe: the 30 million word gap by age 3. *American Educator*, Spring, 4–9.

Harter, S. (1999). *The construction of the self: a developmental perspective*. New York: The Guilford Press.

Hartley, C., Fischl, B., and Phelps, E. (2011). Brain structure correlates of individual differences in the acquisition and inhibition of conditioned fear. *Cerebral Cortex*, 21, 1954–1962.

Hartman, R., and Huestis, M. (2013). Cannabis effects on driving skills. *Clinical Chemistry*, 59, 478–492.

Haxby, J., Gobbini, M., Furey, M., Ishai, A., Schouten, J., and Pietrini, P. (2001). Distributed and overlapping representations of faces and objects in ventral temporal cortex. *Science*, 293, 2425–2430.

Haxby, J., Grady, C., Horwitz, B., Ungerleider, L., Mishkin, M., Carson, R., Herscovitch, P., Schapiro, M.B., and Rapoport, S.I. (1991). Dissociation of object and spatial visual processing pathways in human extrastriate cortex. *Proceedings of the National Academy of Sciences USA*, 88, 1621–1625.

Haxby, J., Hoffman, E., and Gobbini, M. (2000). The distributed human neural system for face perception. *Trends in Cognitive Science*, 4, 223–233.

Hebb, D. (ed.) (1949). *The organisation of behaviour: a neuropsychlogical theory*. New York: John Wiley and Sons.

Heimer, L., De Olmos, J., Alheid, G., Person, J., Sakamoto, N., Shinoda, K., Marksteiner, J., and Switzer, R.C. (1999). The human basal forebrain. Part II. In F. Bloom, A. Bjorkland and T. Hokfelt (eds.), *Handbook of chemical neuroanatomy* (pp. 57–226). Amsterdam: Elsevier.

Herculano-Houzel, S. (2009). The human brain in numbers: a linearly scaled-up primate brain: *Frontiers in Human Neuroscience*, 9, 31.

Herman-Giddens, M., Slora, E., Wasserman, R., Bourdony, C., Bhapkar, M., Koch, G., and Hasemeier, C. (1997). Secondary sexual characteristics and menses in young girls seen in office practice: a study from the Pediatric Research in Office Settings network. *Pediatrics*, 99, 505–512.

Herman-Giddens, M., Steffes, J., Harris, D., Slora, E., Hussey, M., Dowshen, S., and Reiter, E. (2012). Secondary sexual characteristics in boys: data from the Pediatric Research in Office Settings Network. *Pediatrics*, 130, e1058–e1068.

Herman-Giddens, M., Wang, L., and Koch, G. (2001). Secondary sexual characteristics in boys: estimates from the National Health and Nutrition Examination Survey III, 1988–1994. *Archives of Pediatrics and Adolescent Medicine*, 155, 1022–1028.

Herting, M.M., Gautam, P., Spielberg, J.M., Kan, E., Dahl, R.E., and Sowell, E.R. (2014). The role of testosterone and estradiol in brain volume changes across adolescence: a longitudinal structural MRI study. *Human Brain Mapping*, 35, 5633–5645.

Hillman, C., Erickson, K., and Kramer, A. (2008). Be smart, exercise your heart: exercise effects on brain and cognition. *Nature Reviews Neuroscience*, 9, 58–65.

Hoffman, E.A., and Haxby, J.V. (2000). Distinct representations of eye gaze and identity in the distributed human neural system for face perception. *Nature Neuroscience*, 3, 80–84.

Huttenlocher, P. (1990). Morphometric study of human cerebral cortex development. *Neuropsychologia*, 28, 517–527.

Huttenlocher, P., and Dabholkar, A. (1997). Regional difference in synaptogenesis in human cerebral cortex. *Journal of Comparative Neurology*, 387, 167–178.

Hwang, K., Velanova, K., and Luna, B. (2010). Strengthening of top-down frontal cognitive control networks underlying the development of inhibitory control: an fMRI effective connectivity study. *Journal of Neuroscience*, 30, 15,535–15,545.

Hyde, K., Lerch, J., Norton, A., Forgeard, M., Winner, E., Evans, A., and Schlaug, G. (2009). Musical training shapes structural brain development. *Journal of Neuroscience*, 29, 3019–3025.

Hymovitch, B. (1952). The effects of experimental variations on problem solving in the rat. *Journal of Comparative Physiology and Psychology*, 45, 313–321.

James, W. (1890). *The principles of psychology*. New York: Henry Holt and Company.

Jansons, K., and Alexander, D. (2003). Persistent Angular Structure: new insights from diffusion MRI data. Dummy version. *Information Processing in Medical Imaging*, 18, 672–683.

Jarcho, J., Benson, B., Plate, R., Guyer, A., Detloff, A., Pine, D., and Ernst, M. (2012). Developmental effects of decision-making on sensitivity to reward: an fMRI study. *Developmental Cognitive Neuroscience*, 2, 437–447.

Jensen, J., Helpern, J., Ramani, A., Lu, H., and Kaczynski, K. (2005). Diffusional kurtosis imaging: the quantification of non-Gaussian water diffusion by means of magnetic resonance imaging. *Magnetic Resonance Medicine*, 53, 1432–1440.

Johnson, M. (2005). Subcortical face processing. *Nature Reviews Neuroscience*, 6, 766–774.

(2011). Interactive specialization: a domain-general framework for human functional brain development? *Developmental Cognitive Neuroscience*, 1, 7–21.

Johnson, M., Dziurawiec, S., Ellis, H., and Morton, J. (1991). Newborns' preferential tracking of face-like stimuli and its subsequent decline. *Cognition*, 40, 1–19.

Johnson, S.B., Riis, J.L., and Noble, K.G. (2016). State of the art review: poverty and the developing brain. *Pediatrics*, 137, 1–16.

Johnston, M. (2009). Plasticity in the developing brain: implications for rehabilitation. *Developmental Disabilities Research Review*, 15, 94–101.

Juraska, J., Fitch, J., Henderson, C., and Rivers, N. (1985). Sex differences in the dendritic branching of dentate granule cells following differential experience. *Brain Research*, 333, 73–80.

Kang, H., Burgund, E., Lugar, H., Petersen, S., and Schlaggar, B. (2003). Comparison of functional activation foci in children and adults using a common stereotactic space. *Neuroimage*, 19, 16–28.

Kanold, P. (2009). Subplate neurons: crucial regulators of cortical development and plasticity. *Frontiers in Neuroanatomy*, 3, 1–9.

Kanwisher, N., McDermott, J., and Chun, M. (1997). The fusiform face area: a module in human extrastriate cortex specialized for face perception. *Journal of Neuroscience*, 17, 4302–4311.

Karni, A., Meyer, G., Jezzard, P., Adams, M., Turner, R., and Ungerleider, L. (1995). Functional MRI evidence for adult motor cortex plasticity during motor skill learning. *Nature*, 377, 155–158.

Karson, C. (1983). Spontaneous eye-blink rates and dopaminergic systems. *Brain*, 106, 643–653.

Kawashima, R., Sugiura, M., Kato, T., Nakamura, A., Hatano, K., Ito, K., Kukuda, H., Kojima, S., and Nakamura, K. (1999). The human amygdala plays an important role in gaze monitoring. A PET study. *Brain*, 122, 779–783.

Keating, D. (2007). Understanding adolescent development: implications for driving safety. *Journal of Safety Research*, 38, 147–157.

Kelly, A., Di Martino, A., Uddin, L., Shehzad, Z., Gee, D., Reiss, P., and Milham, M. (2009). Development of anterior cingulate functional connectivity from late childhood to early adulthood. *Cerebral Cortex*, 19, 640–657.

Kessler, R., Berglund, P., Demler, O., Jin, R., Merikangas, K., and Walters, E. (2005). Lifetime prevalence and age-of-onset distributions of DSM-IV disorders in the National Comorbidity Survey Replication. *Archives of General Psychiatry*, 62, 593–602.

Killgore, W., and Yurgelun-Todd, D. (2007). Unconscious processing of facial affect in children and adolescents. *Social Neuroscience*, 2, 28–47.

Kim, H., Somerville, L., Johnstone, T., Polis, S., Alexander, A.L., Shin, L.M., and Whalen, P.J. (2004). Contextual modulation of amygdala responsivity to surprised faces. *Journal of Cognitive Neuroscience*, 16, 1730–1745.

Kim, M., Loucks, R., Palmer, A., Brown, A., Solomon, K., Marchante, A., and Whalen, P. (2011). The structural and functional connectivity of the amygdala: from normal emotion to pathological anxiety. *Behavior Brain Research*, 223, 403–410.

Ki-moon, B. (2013). *Five-year action agenda: Office of the Secretary General's Envoy on Youth*. New York: United Nations.

Kirkham, N., Slemmer, J., and Johnson, S. (2002). Visual statistical learning in infancy: evidence for a domain general learning mechanism. *Cognition*, 83, B35–B42.

Kishiyama, M., Boyce, W., Jimenez, A., Perry, L., and Knight, R. (2009). Socioeconomic disparities affect prefrontal function in children. *Journal of Cognitive Neuroscience*, 21, 1106–1115.

Klapwijk, E., Goddings, A., Burnett Heyes, S., Bird, G., Viner, R., and Blakemore, S. (2013). Increased functional connectivity with puberty in the mentalising network involved in social emotion processing. *Hormones and Behavior*, 64, 314–322.

Klapwijk, E.T., Peters, S., Vermeiren, R.R., and Lelieveld, G.J. (2013). Emotional reactions of peers influence decisions about fairness in adolescence. *Frontiers in Human Neuroscience*, 7, 745.

Klingberg, T., Forssberg, H., and Westerberg, H. (2002). Increased brain activity in frontal and parietal cortex underlies the development of visuospatial working memory capacity during childhood. *Journal of Cognitive Neuroscience*, 14, 1–10.

Knutson, K., and Lauderdale, D. (2009). Sociodemographic and behavioral predictors of bed time and wake time among US adolescents aged 15 to 17 years. *Journal of Pediatrics*, 154, 426–430.

Koch, R., and Wenz, E. (1987). Phenylketonuria. *Annual Review of Nutrition*, 7, 117–135.

Koenderink, M., Ulyings, H., and Mrzljiak, L. (1994). Postnatal maturation of the layer III pyramidal neurons in the human prefrontal cortex: a quantitative Golgi analysis. *Brain Research*, 653, 173–182.

Koolschijn, P., Schel, M., de Rooij, M., Rombouts, S., and Crone, E. (2011). A three-year longitudinal functional magnetic resonance imaging study of performance monitoring and test–retest reliability from childhood to early adulthood. *Journal of Neuroscience*, 31, 4204–4212.

Krain, A., Gotimer, K., Hefton, S., Ernst, M., Castellanos, F., Pine, D., and Milham, M. (2008). A functional magnetic resonance imaging investigation of uncertainty in adolescents with anxiety disorders. *Biological Psychiatry*, 63, 563–568.

Krain, A., Hefton, S., Pine, D., Ernst, M., Castellanos, F., Klein, R., and Milham, M. (2006). An fMRI examination of developmental differences in the neural correlates of uncertainty and decision making. *Journal of Child Psychology and Psychiatry*, 47, 1023–1030.

Kuhnen, C., and Knutson, B. (2005). The neural basis of financial risk taking. *Neuron*, 47, 763–770.

Kwon, H., Reiss, A., and Menon, V. (2002). Neural basis of protracted developmental changes in visuo-spatial working memory. *Proceedings of the National Academy of Sciences USA*, 99, 13,336–13,341.

LaBar, K., and Cabeza, R. (2006). Cognitive neuroscience of emotional memory. *Nature Reviews Neuroscience*, 7, 54–64.

Ladouceur, C.D., Peper, J.S., Crone, E.A., and Dahl, R.E. (2012). White matter development in adolescence: the influence of puberty and implications for affective disorders. *Developmental Cognitive Neuroscience*, 2, 36–54.

Lakes, K., and Hoyt, W. (2004). Promoting self-regulation through school-based martial arts training. *Applied Developmental Psychology*, 25, 283–302.

Langdell, T. (1978). Recognition of faces: an approach to the study of autism. *Journal of Child Psychology and Psychiatry*, 19, 255–268.

Larsen, B., and Luna, B. (2015). In vivo evidence of neurophysiological maturation of the human adolescent striatum. *Developmental Cognitive Neuroscience*, 12, 74–85.

Larson, R., Richards, M., Moneta, G., Holmbeck, G., and Duckett, E. (1996). Changes in adolescents' daily interactions with their families from ages 10 to 18: disengagement and transformation. *Developmental Psychology*, 32, 744–754.

Laviola, G., Macri, S., Morley-Fletcher, S., and Adriani, W. (2003). Abstract risk-taking behavior in adolescent mice: psychobiological determinants and early epigenetic influence. *Neuroscience and Biobehavioral Reviews*, 27, 19–31.

Laviola, G., Pasucci, T., and Pieretti, S. (2001). Striatal dopamine sensitization to D-amphetamine in periadolescent but not in adult rats. *Pharmacology, Biochemistry and Behavior*, 68, 115–124.

Lawrence, N., Hinton, E., Parkinson, J., and Lawrence, A. (2012). Nucleus accumbens response to food cues predicts subsequent snack consumption in women and increased body mass index in those with reduced self-control. *Neuroimage*, 63, 415–422.

Lazarus, R.S. (1963). *Personality and adjustment*. Englewood Cliffs, NJ: Prentice Hall.

Leary, M., and Tangney, J. (eds.) (2003). The self as an organizing construct in the behavioral and social sciences. In *Handbook of self and identity* (pp. 3–14). New York: The Guilford Press.

Lebel, C., Gee, M., Carmicioli, R., Wieler, M., Martin, W., and Beaulieu, C. (2012). Diffusion tensor imaging of white matter tract evolution over the lifespan. *Neuroimage*, 60, 340–352.

Le Bihan, D. (1995). Diffusion, perfusion and functional magnetic resonance imaging. *Journal des maladies vasculaires*, 20, 209–214.

Lee, H.K., and Whitt, J.L. (2015). Cross-modal synaptic plasticity in adult primary sensory cortices. *Current Opinion in Neurobiology*, 35, 119–126.

Leggio, M., Mandolesi, L., Federico, F., Spirito, F., Ricci, B., Gelfo, F., and Petrosini, L. (2005). Environmental enrichment promotes improved spatial abilities and enhanced dendritic growth in the rat. *Behavior Brain Research*, 163, 78–90.

Le Grand, R., Mondloch, C., Maurer, D., and Brent, H. (2003). Expert face processing requires visual input to the right hemisphere during infancy. *Nature Neuroscience*, 6, 1108–1112.

Lenhart, A., Ling, R., Campbell, S., and Purcell, K. (2010). *Teens and mobile phones*. Retrieved from http://pewinternet.org/Reports/2010/Teens-and-Mobile-Phones.aspx.

Lenroot, R., Gogtay, N., Greenstein, D., Wells, E., Wallace, G., Clasen, L., and Giedd, J. (2007). Sexual dimorphism of brain developmental trajectories during childhood and adolescence. *Neuroimage*, 36, 1065–1073.

Leslie, A., Friedman, O., and German, T. (2004). Core mechanisms in "theory of mind." *Trends in Cognitive Sciences*, 8, 528–533.

Lessard, N., Pare, M., Lepore, F., and Lassonde, M. (1998). Early-blind human subjects localize sound sources better than sighted subjects. *Nature*, 395, 278–280.

LeVay, S., Wiesel, T., and Hubel, D. (1980). The development of ocular dominance columns in normal and visually deprived monkeys. *Journal of Comparative Neurology*, 191, 1–51.

Levelt, C., and Hübener, M. (2012). Critical-period plasticity in the visual cortex. *Annual Review of Neuroscience*, 35, 309–330.

Lewis, M., and Carmody, D. (2008). Self-representation and brain development. *Developmental Psychology*, 44, 1329–1334.

Lind, S., and Bowler, D. (2008). Episodic memory and autonoetic consciousness in autistic spectrum disorders: the roles of self-awareness, representational abilities and temporal cognition. *Memory in Autism: Theory and Evidence*, 48, 166–187.

Liston, C., McEwen, B.S., and Casey, B. (2009). Psychosocial stress reversibly dirupts prefrontal processing and attentional control. *Proceedings of the National Academy of Sciences USA*, 106, 912–917.

Liszkowski, U., Carpenter, M., Striano, T., and Tomasello, M. (2006). Twelve- and 18-month-olds point to provide information for others. *Journal of Cognitive Development*, 7, 173–187.

Liu, J., Harris, A., and Kanwisher, N. (2002). Stages of processing in face perception: an MEG study. *Nature Neuroscience*, 5, 910–916.

Logue, S., Chein, J., Gould, T., Holliday, E., and Steinberg, L. (2014). Adolescent mice, unlike adults, consume more alcohol in the presence of peers than alone. *Developmental Science*, 17, 79–85.

Lohmann, H., and Tomasello, M. (2003). The role of language in the development of false belief understanding: a training study. *Child Development*, 74, 1130–1144.

Lombardo, M., Chakrabarti, B., Bullmore, E., Sadek, S., Pasco, G., Wheelwright, S., and Baron-Cohen, S. (2010). Atypical neural representation in autism. *Brain*, 133, 611–624.

Lufi, D., Tzischinsky, O., and Hadar, S. (2011). Delaying school starting time by one hour: some effects on attention levels in adolescents. *Journal of Clinical Sleep Medicine*, 7, 137–143.

Luna, B., Garver, K., Urban, T., Lazar, N., and Sweeney, J. (2004). Maturation of cognitive processes from late childhood to adulthood. *Child Development*, 75, 1357–1372.

Luna, B., Marek, S., Larsen, B., Terro-Clemens, B., and Chahal, R. (2015). An integrative model of the maturation of cognitive control. *Annual Reviews in Neuroscience*, 38, 151–170.

Luna, B., Padmanabhan, A., and O'Hearn, K. (2010). What has fMRI told us about the development of cognitive control through adolescence? *Brain and Cognition*, 72, 101–113.

Luna, B., Thulborn, K.R., Munoz, D.P., Merriam, E.P., Garver, K.E., Minshew, N.J., and Sweeney, J.A. (2001). Maturation of widely distributed brain function subserves cognitive development. *Neuroimage*, 13, 786–793.

Lupien, S., McEwen, B. S., Gunnar, M., and Heim, C. (2009). Effects of stress throughout the lifespan on the brain, behavior and cognition. *Nature Reviews Neuroscience*, 10, 434–445.

Magarinos, A., McEwen, B., Flugge, G., and Fuchs, E. (1996). Chronic psychosocial stress causes apical dendritic atrophy of hippocampal CA3 pyramidal neurons in subordinate tree shrews. *Journal of Neuroscience*, 16, 3534–3540.

Maguire, E., Gadian, D., Johnsrude, I., Good, C., Ashburner, J., Frackowiak, R., and Frith, C. (2000). Navigation-related structural change in the hippocampi of taxi drivers. *Proceedings of the National Academy of Sciences USA*, 97, 4398–4403.

Mahy, C., Moses, L., and Pfeifer, J. (2014). How and where: theory-of-mind in the brain. *Developmental Cognitive Neuroscience*, 9, 68–81.

Manjunath, N., and Telles, S. (2001). Improved performance in the Tower of London test following yoga. *Indian Journal of Physiological Pharmacology*, 45, 351–354.

Mannuzza, S., Klein, R., Bonagura, N., Malloy, P., Giampino, T., and Addalli, K. (1991). Hyperactive boys almost grown up: replication of psychiatric status. *Archives of General Psychiatry*, 10, 4877–4883.

Mantzoros, C., Flier, J., and Rogol, A. (1997). A longitudinal assessment of hormonal and physical alterations during normal puberty in boys. V. Rising leptin levels may signal the onset of puberty. *Journal of Clinical Endocrinology and Metabolism*, 82, 1066–1070.

Marsh, R., Zhu, H., Schultz, R., Quackenbush, G., Royal, J., Skudlarski, P., and Peterson, B. (2006). A developmental fMRI study of self-regulatory control. *Human Brain Mapping*, 27, 848–863.

Marshall, W.A., and Tanner, J.M. (1969). Variations in pattern of pubertal changes in girls. *Archives of Disease in Childhood*, 44, 291–303.

(1970). Variations in pattern of pubertal changes in boys. *Archives of Disease in Childhood*, 45, 13–23.

Martiniuk, A., Senserrick, T., Lo, S., Williamson, A., Du, W., Grunstein, R., Woodward, M., Glozier, N., Stevenson, M., Norton, R., and Ivers, R. (2013). Sleep-deprived young drivers and the risk for crash: the DRIVE Prospective Cohort Study. *JAMA Pediatrics*, 167, 647–655.

Martos-Moreno, G., Chowen, J., and Argente, J. (2010). Metabolic signals in human puberty: effects of over and undernutrition. *Molecular Cell Endocrinology*, 324, 70–81.

Masten, C.L., Eisenberger, N.I., Pfeifer, J.H., and Dapretto, M. (2010). Witnessing peer rejection during early adolescence: neural correlates of empathy for experiences of social exclusion. *Social Neuroscience*, 5, 1–12.

Matsumoto, M., and Hikosaka, O. (2009). Representation of negative motivational value in the primate lateral habenula. *Nature Neuroscience*, 12, 77–84.

May, A., Hajak, G., Ganssbauer, S., Steffens, T., Langguth, B., Kleinjung, T., and Eichhammer, P. (2007). Structural brain alterations following 5 days of intervention: dynamic aspects of neuroplasticity. *Cerebral Cortex*, 17, 205–210.

McCandliss, B., and Noble, K. (2003). The development of reading impairment: a cognitive neuroscience model. *Mental Retardation and Developmental Disabilities Research Review*, 9, 196–204.

McCartt, A., Mayhew, D., Braitman, K., Ferguson, S., and Simpson, H. (2009). Effects of age and experience on young driver crashes: review of recent literature. *Traffic and Injury Prevention*, 10, 209–219.

McCartt, A., Teoh, E., Fields, M., Braitman, K., and Hellinga, L. (2010). Graduated licensing laws and fatal crashes of teenage drivers: a national study. *Traffic and Injury Prevention*, 11, 240–248.

McCutcheon, J., and Marinelli, M. (2009). Technical spotlight: age matters. *European Journal of Neuroscience*, 29, 997–1014.

McLoyd, V. (1998). Socioeconomic disadvantage and child development. *American Psychologist*, 53, 185–204.

McKnight, A., and McKnight, A. (2003). Young novice drivers: careless or clueless? *Accident Analysis and Prevention*, 35, 921–925.

Mead, M. (1928). *Coming of age in Samoa: a psychological study of primitive youth for western civilization*. New York: William Morrow.

Mendle, J., Harden, K., Brooks-Gunn, J., and Graber, J. (2010). Development's tortoise and hare: pubertal timing, pubertal tempo, and depressive symptoms in boys and girls. *Developmental Psychology*, 46, 1341–1353.

Mendle, J., Leve, L., Van Ryzin, M., Natsuaki, M., and Ge, X. (2011). Associations between early life stress, child maltreatment, and pubertal development among girls in foster care. *Journal of Research on Adolescence*, 21, 871–880.

Menzel, R., and Giurfa, M. (2001). Cognitive architecture of a mini-brain: the honeybee. *Trends in Cognitive Science*, 5, 62–71.

Meshi, D., Morawetz, C., and Heekeren, H. (2013). Nucleus accumbens response to gains in reputation for the self relative to gains for others predicts social media use. *Frontiers in Human Neuroscience*, 29, 439–445.

Miller, E.K., and Cohen, J.D. (2001). An integrative theory of prefrontal cortex function. *Annual Review of Neuroscience*, 24, 167–202.

Miller, E.K., and Desimone, R. (1994). Parallel neuronal mechanisms for short-term memory. *Science*, 263, 520–522.

Mills, K., Lalonde, F., Clasen, L., Giedd, J., and Blakemore, S. (2014). Developmental changes in the structure of the social brain in late childhood and adolescence. *Social Cognitive Affective Neuroscience*, 9, 123–131.

Milner, B. (1963). Effects of different brain lesions on card sorting. *Archives of Neurology*, 9, 90–97.

Mitchell, J.P., Macrae, C., and Banaji, M. (2006). Dissociable medial prefrontal contributions to judgments of similar and dissimilar others. *Neuron*, 50, 655–663.

Mohammed, A., Jonsson, G., and Archer, T. (1986). Selective lesioning of forebrain noradrenaline neurons at birth abolishes the improved maze learning performance induced by rearing in complex environment. *Brain Research*, 398, 6–10.

Monk, C., Weng, S., Wiggins, J., Kurapati, N., Louro, H., Carrasco, M., and Lord, C. (2010). Neural circuitry of emotional face processing in autism spectrum disorder. *Journal of Psychiatry and Neuroscience*, 35, 105–114.

Monteleone, P., Luisi, M., Colurcio, B., Casarosa, E., Monteleone, P., Ioime, R., and Maj, M. (2001). Plasma levels of neuroactive steroids are increased in untreated women with anorexia nervosa or bulimia nervosa. *Psychosomatic Medicine*, 63, 62–68.

Moore, C. (2009). Fairness in children's resource allocation depends on the recipient. *Psychological Science*, 20, 944–948.

Morris, D., Jones, M., Schoemaker, M., Ashworth, A., and Swerdlow, A. (2011). Familial concordance for age at menarche: analyses from the Breakthrough Generations Study. *Paediatric Perinatal Epidemiology*, 25, 306–311.

Morris, J., Frith, C., Perrett, D., Rowland, D., Young, A., Calder, A., and Dolan, R. (1996). A differential neural response in the human amygdala to fearful and happy facial expressions. *Nature*, 383, 812–815.

Mosconi, M., Mack, P., McCarthy, G., and Pelphrey, K. (2005). Taking an "intentional stance" on eye-gaze shifts: a functional neuroimaging study of social perception in children. *Neuroimage*, 27, 247–252.

Munakata, Y., and Pfaffly, J. (2004). Hebbian learning and development. *Developmental Science*, 7, 141–148.

Myers, C.A., Vandermusten, M., Farris, E.A., Hancock, R., Gimenez, P., Black, . . . Hoeft, F. (2014). White matter morphometric changes uniquely predict children's reading acquisition. *Psychological Science*, 25, 1870–1883.

Nagy, Z., Westerberg, H., and Klingberg, T. (2004). Maturation of white matter is associated with the development of cognitive functions during childhood. *Journal of Cognitive Neuroscience*, 16, 1227–1233.

Nakao, H., and Itakura, S. (2009). An integrated view of empathy: psychology, philosophy, and neuroscience. *Integrative Psychology and Behavioral Science*, 43, 42–52.

National Sleep Foundation (2011). *Sleep in America poll: teens and sleep*.Washington, DC: National Sleep Foundation.

Navarro, V., Fernandez-Fernandez, R., Castellano, J., Roa, J., Mayen, A., Barreiro, M., and Tena-Sempere, M. (2004). Advanced vaginal opening and precocious activation of the reproductive axis by KiSS-1 peptide, the endogenous ligand of GPR54. *Journal of Physiology*, 561, 379–386.

nces.ed.gov (2016). nces.ed.gov/pubs2005/2005016.pdf.

Needham, A., Barrett, T., and Peterman, K. (2002). A pick-me-up for infants' exploratory skills: early stimulated experiences reaching for objects using "sticky mittens" enhances young infants' object exploration skills. *Infant Behavior and Development*, 25, 279–295.

Negriff, S., Susman, E., and Trickett, P. (2011). The developmental pathway from pubertal timing to delinquency and sexual activity from early to late adolescence. *Journal of Youth and Adolescence*, 40, 1343–1356.

Nelson, E., Herman, K., Barrett, C., Noble, P., Wojteczko, K., Chisholm, K., Delaney, D., Ernst, M., Fox, N.A., Suomi, S.J., Winslow, J.T., and Pine, D.S. (2009). Adverse rearing experiences enhance responding to both aversive and rewarding stimuli in juvenile rhesus monkeys. *Biological Psychiatry*, 66, 702–704.

Nelson, E., Lieibenluft, E., McClure, E., and Pine, D.S. (2005). The social re-orientation of adolescence: a neuroscience perspective on the process and its relation to psychopathology. *Psychological Medicine*, 35, 163–174.

Nemmi, F., Helander, E., Helenius, O., Almeida, R., Hassler, M., Räsänen, P., and Klingberg, T. (2016). Behavior and neuroimaging at baseline predict individual response to combined mathematical and working memory training in children. *Developmental Cognitive Neuroscience*, 20, 43–51.

Nguyen, T., McCracken, J., Ducharme, S., Botteron, K., Mahabir, M., Johnson, W., Israel, M., Evans, A.C., Karama, S., and Brain Development Cooperative (2013). Testosterone-related cortical maturation across childhood and adolescence. *Cerebral Cortex*, 23, 1424–1432.

Nichols, T., Das, S., Eickhoff, S., Evans, A., Glatard, T., Hanke, M., Kriegeskorte, N., Milham, M.P., Podrack, R.A., Poline, J.-B., Proal, E., Thirion, B., Van Essen, D.C., White, T., and Yeo, B. (2015). Best practices in data analysis and sharing in neuroimaging using MRI. *bioRxiv*.

Nieuwenhuys, R., Donkelaar, H., and Nicholson, H. (1998). *The central nervous system of vertebrates*, vol. 3. Berlin: Springer.

Nishimura, H., Hashikawa, K., Doi, K., Iwaki, T., Watanabe, Y., Kusuoka, H., Nishimura, T., and Kubo, T. (1999). Sign language "heard" in the auditory cortex. *Nature*, 397, 116.

Noble, K., Houston, S., Brito, N., Bartsch, H., Kan, E., Kuperman, J., ... Sowell, E. (2015). Family income, parental education and brain structure in children and adolescents. *Nature Neuroscience*, 18, 773–778.

Noble, K., McCandliss, B., and Farah, M. (2007). Socioeconomic gradients predict individual differences in neurocognitive abilities. *Developmental Science*, 10, 464–480.

Nomi, J.S., and Uddin, L.Q. (2015). Face processing in autism spectrum disorders: from brain regions to brain networks. *Neuropsychology*, 71, 201–216.

Norman, K., Polyn, S., Detre, G., and Haxby, J. (2006). Beyond mind-reading: multi-voxel pattern analysis of fMRI data. *Trends in Cognitive Sciences*, 10, 424–430.

Nottelmann, E., Susman, E.J., Dorn, L., Inoff-Germain, G., Loriaux, D., Cutler, G., Jr., and Chrousos, G. (1987). Developmental processes in early adolescence. Relations among chronologic age, pubertal stage, height, weight, and serum levels of gonadotropins, sex steroids, and adrenal androgens. *Journal of Adolescent Health Care*, 8, 246–260.

Oberman, L., Hubbard, E., McCleery, J., Altschuler, E., Ramachandran, V., and Pineda, J. (2005). EEG evidence for mirror neuron dysfunction in autism spectrum disorders. *Cognition Brain Research*, 24, 190–198.

Oberman, L., and Pascual-Leone, A. (2013). Changes in plasticity across the lifespan: cause of disease and target for intervention. *Progress in Brain Research*, 207, 91–120.

Olds, J., and Milner, P. (1954). Positive reinforcement produced by electrical stimulation of septal area and other regions of rat brain. *Journal of Comparative Physiology and Psychology*, 47, 419–427.

Oleson, P., Macoveanu, J., Tegner, J., and Klingberg, T. (2007). Brain activity related to working memory and distraction in children and adults. *Cerebral Cortex*, 17, 1047–1054.

Olesen, P., Westerberg, H., and Klingberg, T. (2004). Increased prefrontal and parietal activity after training of working memory. *Nature Neuroscience*, 7, 75–79.

Onoda, K., Okamoto, Y., Nakashima, K., Nittono, H., Yoshimura, S., Yamawaki, S., and Ura, M. (2010). Does low self-esteem enhance social pain? The relationship between trait self-esteem and anterior cingulate cortex activation induced by ostracism. *Social Cognitive and Affective Neuroscience*, 5, 385–391.

Op de Macks, Z., Gunther Moor, B., Overgaauw, S., Guroglu, B., Dahl, R., and Crone, E. (2011). Testosterone levels correspond with increased ventral striatum activation in response to monetary rewards in adolescents. *Developmental Cognitive Neuroscience*, 1, 506–516.

Osterlund, M., Keller, E., and Hurd, Y. (1999). The human forebrain has discrete estrogen receptor messenger RNA expression: high levels in the amygdaloid complex. *Neuroscience*, 95, 333–342.

Ouimet, M., Simons-Morton, B., Zador, P., Lerner, N., Freedman, M., Duncan, G., and Wang, J. (2010). Using the U.S. National Household Travel Survey to estimate the impact of passenger characteristics on young drivers' relative risk of fatal crash involvement. *Accident Analysis and Prevention*, 42, 689–694.

Overgaauw, S., Guroglu, B., Rieffe, C., and Crone, E. (2014). Behavior and neural correlates of empathy in adolescents. *Developmental Neuroscience*, 36, 210–219.

Owens, J.; Adolescent Sleep Working Group; Committee on Adolescence (2014). Insufficient sleep in adolescents and young adults: an update on causes and consequences. *Pediatrics*, 134, e921–e932.

Owens, J., and Jones, C. (2011). Parental knowledge of healthy sleep in young children: results of a primary care clinic survey. *Journal of Developmental and Behavioral Pediatrics*, 32, 447–453.

Padmanabhan, A., Geier, C., Ordaz, S., Teslovich, T., and Luna, B. (2011). Developmental changes in brain function underlying the influence of reward processing on inhibitory control. *Developmental Cognitive Neuroscience*, 1, 517–529.

Papagiannopoulou, E., Chitty, K., Hermens, D., Hickie, I., and Lagopoulos, J. (2014). A systematic review and meta-analysis of eye-tracking studies in children with autism spectrum disorders. *Social Neuroscience*, 9, 610–632.

Pascalis, O., de Haan, M., and Nelson, C. (2002). Is face processing species-specific during the first year of life? *Science*, 296, 1321–1323.

Passarotti, A., Paul, B., Bussiere, J., Buxton, R., Wong, E., and Stiles, J. (2003). The development of face and location processing: an fMRI study. *Developmental Science*, 6, 100–117.

Passingham, R.E., Stephan, K.E., and Kotter, R. (2002). The anatomical basis of functional localization in the cortex. *Nature Reviews Neuroscience*, 3, 606–616.

Paus, T. (2013). How environment and genes shape the adolescent brain. *Hormones and Behavior*, 64, 195–202.

Paus, T., Keshavan, M., and Giedd, J. (2008). Why do many psychiatric disorders emerge during adolescence? *Nature Reviews Neuroscience*, 9, 947–957.

Pears, K., and Moses, L. (2003). Demographics, parenting, and theory of mind in preschool children. *Social Development*, 12, 1–20.

Peelen, M., Glaser, B., Vuilleumier, P., and Eliez, S. (2009). Differential development of selectivity for faces and bodies in the fusiform gyrus. *Developmental Science*, 12, F16–F25.

Pelphrey, K., Morris, J., and McCarthy, G. (2005). Here's looking at you, kid: neural systems underlying face and gaze processing in fragile X syndrome. *Archives of General Psychiatry*, 61, 281–288.

Pelphrey, K., Sasson, N., Reznick, J., Paul, G., Goldman, B., and Piven, J. (2002). Visual scanning of faces in autism. *Journal of Autism and Developmental Disorders*, 32, 249–261.

Pelphrey, K.A., Shultz, S., Hudac, C.M., and Vander Wyk, B.C. (2011). Research review: constraining heterogeneity: the social brain and its development in autism spectrum disorder. *Journal of Child Psychology and Psychiatry*, 52, 631–644.

Peper, J., Brouwer, R., Schnack, H., van Baal, G., van Leeuwen, M., van den Berg, S., and Hulshoff Pol, H. (2008). Cerebral white matter in early puberty is associated with luteinizing hormone concentrations. *Psychoneuroendocrinology*, 33, 909–915.

Peper, J., and Dahl, R. (2013). The teenage brain surging hormones – brain-behavior interactions during puberty. *Current Directions in Psychological Science*, 22, 134–139.

Peper, J., Koolschijn, P., and Crone, E. (2013). Development of risk taking: contributions from adolescent testosterone and the orbitofrontal cortex. *Journal of Cognitive Neuroscience*, 25, 2141–2150.

Peper, J., Schnack, H., Brouwer, R., Van Baal, G., Pjetri, E., Szekely, E., van Leeuwen, M., van den Berg, S.M., Collins, D.L., Evans, A.C., Boomsma, D.I., Kahn, R.S., and Hulshoff Pol, H. (2009). Heritability of regional and global brain structure at the onset of puberty: a magnetic resonance imaging study in 9-year-old twin pairs. *Human Brain Mapping*, 30, 2184–2196.

Perlman, S., and Pelphrey, K. (2011). Developing connections for affective regulation: age-related changes in emotional brain connectivity. *Journal of Experimental Child Psychology*, 108, 607–620.

Perrin, A. (2015). Social networking usage: 2005–2015. Pew Research Center.

Perrin, J., Leonard, G., Perron, M., Pike, G., Pitiot, A., Richer, L., Veillette, S., Pausova, Z., and Paus, T. (2009). Sex differences in the growth of white matter during adolescence. *Neuroimage*, 45, 1055–1066.

Petersen, A.C., Crockett, L., Richards, M., and Boxer, A. (1988). A self-report measure of pubertal status: reliability, validity, and initial norms. *Journal of Youth and Adolescence*, 17, 117–133.

Pew Research Center (2012). www.pewresearch.org/fact-tank/2016/05/24/in-the-u-s-and-abroad-more-young-adults-are-living-with-their-parents/.

Pezawas, L., Meyer-Lindenberg, A., Drabant, E., Verchinski, B., Munoz, K., Kolachana, B., Egan, M.F., Mattay, V.S., Hariri, A.R., and Weinberger, D. (2005). 5-HTTLPR polymorphism impacts human cingulate-amygdala interactions: a genetic susceptibility mechanism for depression. *Nature Neuroscience*, 8, 828–834.

Pfeifer, J., and Allen, N. (2012). Arrested development? Reconsidering dual-systems models of brain function in adolescence and disorders. *Trends in Cognitive Sciences*, 16, 322–329.

Pfeifer, J., Iacoboni, M., Mazziotta, J., and Dapretto, M, (2008). Mirroring others' emotions relates to empathy and social abilities during childhood. *Neuroimage*, 39, 2076–2085.

Pfeifer, J., Lieberman, M., and Dapretto, M. (2007). "I know you are but what am I?!": neural bases of self- and social knowledge retrieval in children and adults. *Journal of Cognitive Neuroscience*, 19, 1323–1337.

Pfeifer, J., and Peake, S. (2012). Self-development: integrating cognitive, socioemotional, and neuroimaging perspectives. *Developmental Cognitive Neuroscience*, 2, 55–69.

Pfeifer, J.H., Masten, C.L., Borofsky, L., Dapretto, M., Fuligni, A.S., and Lieberman, M. (2009). Neural correlates of direct and reflected self-appraisals in adolescents and adults: when social perspective-taking informs self-perception. *Child Development*, 80, 1016–1038.

Pfeifer, J., Masten, C., Moore, W.R., Oswald, T., Mazziotta, J., Iacoboni, M., and Dapretto, M. (2011). Entering adolescence: resistance to peer influence, risky behavior, and neural changes in emotion reactivity. *Neuron*, 69, 1029–1036.

Pickrell, T. (2006). *Driver alcohol involvement in fatal crashes by age group and vehicle type*. Washington, DC: National Highway Traffic Safety Administration.

Pierce, K., Haist, F., Sedaghat, F., and Courchesne, E. (2004). The brain response to personally familiar faces in autism: findings of fusiform activity and beyond. *Brain*, 127, 2703–2716.

Pierpaoli, C., Jezzard, P., Basser, P., Barnett, A., and Di Chiro, G. (1996). Diffusion tensor MR imaging of the human brain. *Radiology*, 201, 637–648.

Pine, D., Lissek, S., Klein, R., Mannuzza, S., Moulton, J., 3rd, Guardino, M., and Woldehawariat, G. (2004). Face-memory and emotion:

associations with major depression in children and adolescents. *Journal of Child Psychology and Psychiatry*, 45, 1199–1208.

Poldrack, R. (2015). Is "efficiency" a useful concept in cognitive neuroscience? *Developmental Cognitive Neuroscience*, 11, 12–17.

Pollak, S.D., Nelson, C., Schlaak, M., Roeber, B., Wewerka, S., Wiik, K., Frenn, K.A., Loman, M.M., and Gunnar, M. (2010). Neurodevelopmental effects of early deprivation in postinstitutionalized children. *Child Development*, 81, 224–236.

Post, G., and Kemper, H. (1993). Nutritional intake and biological maturation during adolescence. The Amsterdam growth and health longitudinal study. *European Journal of Clinical Nutrition*, 47, 400–408.

Power, J., Barnes, K., Snyder, A., Schlaggar, B., and Petersen, S. (2012). Spurious but systematic correlations in functional connectivity MRI networks arise from subject motion. *Neuroimage*, 59, 2142–2154.

Preuss, T.M. (2000). What's human about the human brain? In M. Gazzaniga (ed.), *The new cognitive neurosciences* (2nd edn.). Cambridge, MA: MIT Press.

Puce, A., Allison, T., Bentin, S., Gore, J., and McCarthy, G. (1998). Temporal cortex activation in humans viewing eye and mouth movements. *Journal of Neuroscience*, 18, 2188–2199.

Qu, Y., Galván, A., Fuligni, A., Lieberman, M., and Telzer, E. (2015). Longitudinal changes in prefrontal cortex activation underlie declines in adolescent risk taking. *Journal of Neuroscience*, 35, 11,308–11,314.

Radley, J., Rocher, A., Janssen, W., Hof, P., McEwen, B., and Morrison, J. (2005). Reversibility of apical dendritic retraction in the rat medial prefrontal cortex following repeated stress. *Experimental Neurology*, 196, 199–203.

Raichle, M., and Snyder, A. (2007). A default mode of brain function: a brief history of an evolving idea. *Neuroimage*, 37, 1083–1090; discussion 1097–1099.

Ramón y Cajal, S. (1899). *Textura del sistema nervioso del hombre y de los vertebrados*. Madrid: Imprenta y Librería de Nicolás Moya.

Rao, U., Sidhartha, T., Harker, K., Bidesi, A., Chen, L., and Ernst, M. (2011). Relationship between adolescent risk preferences on a laboratory task and behavioral measures of risk-taking. *Journal of Adolescent Health*, 48, 151–158.

Raschle, N., Lee, M., Buechler, R., Christodoulou, J., Chang, M., Vakil, M., and Gaab, N. (2009). Making MR imaging child's play – pediatric neuroimaging protocol, guidelines and procedure. *Journal of Visualized Experiments*, 29, 1309.

Rauschecker, J. (1995). Compensatory plasticity and sensory substitution in the cerebral cortex. *Trends in Neuroscience*, 18, 36–43.

Raznahan, A., Shaw, P., Lerch, J., Clasen, L., Greenstein, D., Berman, R., ... Giedd, J.N. (2014). Longitudinal four-dimensional mapping of subcortical anatomy in human development. *Proceedings of the National Academy of Sciences USA*, 111, 1592–1597.

Reyna, V., and Farley, F. (2006). Risk and rationality in adolescent decision making: implications for theory, practice, and public policy. *Psychological Science in the Public Interest*, 7, 1–44.

Rivers, S., Reyna, V., and Mills, B. (2008). Risk taking under the influence: a fuzzy-trace theory of emotion in adolescence. *Developmental Review*, 28, 107–144.

Roa, J., Garcia-Galiano, D., Castellano, J., Gaytan, F., Pinilla, L., and Tena-Sempere, M. (2010). Metabolic control of puberty onset: new players, new mechanisms. *Molecular Cell Endocrinology*, 324, 87–94.

Robinson, D., Heien, M., and Wightman, R. (2002). Frequency of dopamine concentration transients increases in dorsal and ventral striatum of male rats during introduction of conspecifics. *Journal of Neuroscience*, 22, 10,477–10,486.

Robinson, D., Zitzman, D., Smith, K., and Spear, L. (2011). Fast dopamine release events in the nucleus accumbens of early adolescent rats. *Neuroscience*, 176, 296–307.

Rogers, S., and Pennington, B. (1991). A theoretical approach to the deficits in infantile autism. *Developmental Psychology*, 3, 137–162.

Roitman, M., Wheeler, R., Wightman, R., and Carelli, R. (2008). Real-time chemical responses in the nucleus accumbens differentiate rewarding and aversive stimuli. *Nature Neuroscience*, 11, 1376–1377.

Romer, D., Lee, Y., McDonald, C., and Winston, F. (2014). Adolescence, attention allocation, and driving safety. *Journal of Adolescent Health*, 54, S6–S15.

Rosenfield, R., Lipton, R., and Drum, M. (2009). Thelarche, pubarche, and menarche attainment in children with normal and elevated body mass index. *Pediatrics*, 123, 84–88.

Rosenzweig, M., Krech, D., Bennett, E., and Diamond, M. (1962). Effects of environmental complexity and training on brain chemistry and anatomy: a replication and extension. *Journal of Comparative Physiology and Psychology*, 55, 429–437.

Rothmayr, C., Sodian, B., Hajak, G., Dohnel, K., Meinhardt, J., and Sommer, M. (2010). Common and distinct neural networks for false-belief reasoning and inhibitory control. *Neuroimage*, 56, 1705–1713.

Routtenberg, A. (1978). The reward system of the brain. *Scientific American*, 7, 154–164.

Rovee-Collier, C., and Hayne, H. (2000). Memory in infancy and early childhood. In E. Tulving and F. Craik (eds.), *The Oxford handbook of memory* (pp. 267–282). Oxford: Oxford University Press.

Rubia, K., Overmeyer, S., Taylor, E., Brammer, S., Williams, S.C., Simmons, A., et al. (2000). Functional frontalisation with age: mapping neurodevelopmental trajectories with fMRI. *Neuroscience and Biobehavioral Reviews*, 24, 13–19.

Rubia, K., Smith, A., Taylor, E., and Brammer, M. (2007). Linear age-correlated functional development of inferior fronto-striato-cerebellar networks during response inhibition and anterior cingulate during error-related processes. *Human Brain Mapping*, 28, 1163–1177.

Rubia, K., Smith, A., Woolley, J., Nosarti, C., Heyman, I., Taylor, E., and Brammer, M. (2006). Progressive increase of frontostriatal brain activation from childhood to adulthood during event-related tasks of cognitive control. *Human Brain Mapping*, 27, 973–993.

Sabbagh, M., Bowman, L., Evraire, L., and Ito, J. (2009). Neurodevelopmental correlates of theory of mind in preschool children. *Child Development*, 80, 1147–1162.

Salas, R., Baldwin, P., de Biasi, M., and Montague, P.R. (2010). BOLD responses to negative reward prediction errors in human habenula. *Frontiers in Human Neuroscience*, 11, 36–45.

Sallet, J., Mars, R., Noonan, M., Andersson, J., O'Reilly, J., Jbabdi, S., Croxson, P.L., Jenkinson, M., Miller, K.L., and Rushworth, M. (2011). Social network size affects neural circuits in macaques. *Science*, 334, 697–700.

Sanchez-Garrido, M., and Tena-Sempere, M. (2013). Metabolic control of puberty: roles of leptin and kisspeptins. *Hormones and Behavior*, 64, 187–194.

Sanfey, A.G., Rilling, J.K., Aronson, J., Nystrom, L.E., and Cohen, J.D. (2003). The neural basis of economic decision-making in the Ultimatum Game. *Science*, 300, 1755–1758.

Sato, S., Schulz, K., Sisk, C., and Wood, R. (2008). Adolescents and androgens, receptors and rewards. *Hormones and Behavior*, 53, 647–658.

Satterthwaite, T., Elliott, M., Gerraty, R., Ruparel, K., Loughead, J., Calkins, M., Eickhoff, S.B., Hakonarson, H., Gur, R.C., Gur, R.E., and Wolf, D. (2013). An improved framework for confound regression and filtering for control of motion artifact in the preprocessing of resting-state functional connectivity data. *Neuroimage*, 64, 240–256.

Satterthwaite, T., Wolf, D., Loughead, J., Ruparel, K., Elliott, M., Hakonarson, H., Gur R.C., and Gur, R. (2012). Impact of in-scanner head motion on multiple measures of functional connectivity: relevance for studies of neurodevelopment in youth. *Neuroimage*, 60, 623–632.

Saxe, R., and Kanwisher, N. (2003). People thinking about thinking people. The role of the temporo-parietal junction in "theory of mind." *Neuroimage*, 19, 1835–1842.

Schendan, H., Ganis, G., and Kutas, M. (1998). Neurophysiological evidence for visual perceptual categorization of words and faces within 150 ms. *Psychophysiology*, 35, 240–251.

Scherf, K.S., Behrmann, M., and Dahl, R.E. (2012). Facing changes and changing faces in adolescence: a new model for investigating adolescent-specific interactions between pubertal, brain and behavioral development. *Developmental Cognitive Neuroscience*, 2, 199–219.

Scherf, K. S., Behrmann, M., Humphreys, K., and Luna, B. (2007). Visual category-selectivity for faces, places and objects emerges along different developmental trajectories. *Developmental Science*, 10, F15–F30.

Scherf, K.S., Luna, B., Avidan, G., and Behrmann, M. (2011). "What" precedes "which": developmental neural tuning in face- and place-related cortex. *Cerebral Cortex*, 21, 1963–1980.

Scherf, K., Smyth, J., and Delgado, M. (2013). The amygdala: an agent of change in adolescent neural networks. *Hormones and Behavior*, 64(2), 298–313.

Schlaggar, B., Brown, T., Lugar, H., Visscher, K., Miezin, F., and Petersen, S. (2002). Functional neuroanatomical differences between adults and school-age children in the processing of single words. *Science*, 296, 1476–1479.

Schlaug, G., Forgeard, M., Zhu, L., Norton, A., Norton, A., and Winner, E. (2009). Training-induced neuroplasticity in young children. *Annals of the New York Academy of Sciences*, 1169, 205–208.

Schlegel, A. (2001). The global spread of adolescent culture. In L. Crocket and R. Silbereisen (eds.), *Negotiating adolescence in times of social change* (pp. 63–86). Cambridge: Cambridge University Press.

Schlund, M.W., Cataldo, M.F., Siegle, G.J., Ladouceur, C.D., Silk, J.S., Forbes, E.E., and Ryan, N.D. (2011). Pediatric functional magnetic resonance neuroimaging: tactics for encouraging task compliance. *Behavior Brain Function*, 7, 10.

Schultz, W., Dayan, P., and Montague, P.R. (1997). A neural substrate of prediction and reward. *Science*, 275, 1593–1599.

Schultz, J., Imamizu, H., Kawato, M., and Frith, C. (2004). Activation of the human superior temporal gyrus during observation of goal attribution by intentional objects. *Journal of Cognitive Neuroscience*, 16, 1695–1705.

Schultz, R., Gauthier, I., Klin, A., Fulbright, R., Anderson, A., Volkmar, F., and Gore, J. (2000). Abnormal ventral temporal cortical activity during face discrimination among individuals with autism and Asperger syndrome. *Archives of General Psychiatry*, 57, 331–340.

Schweren, L., de Zeeuw, P., and Durston, S. (2013). MR imaging of the effects of methylphenidate on brain structure and function in attention-deficit/hyperactivity disorder. *European Journal of Neuropsychopharmacology*, 23, 1151–1164.

Scott, E. (2000). The legal construction of adolescence. *Hofstra Law Review*, 29, 547–598.

Scott, E., and Steinberg, L. (2008). *Rethinking juvenile justice*. Cambridge, MA: Harvard University Press.

Seitz, V., Rosenbaum, L., and Apfel, N. (1985). Effects of family support intervention: a ten-year follow-up. *Child Development*, 56(2), 376–391.

Senju, A., Yaguchi, K., Tojo, Y., and Hasegawa, T. (2003). Eye contact does not facilitate detection in children with autism. *Cognition*, 89, B43–B51.

Shackman, A., Salomons, T., Slagter, H., Fox, A., Winter, J., and Davidson, R. (2011). The integration of negative affect, pain, and cognitive control in the cingulate cortex. *Nature Reviews Neuroscience*, 12, 154–167.

Shaw, P., Gogtay, N., and Rapoport, J. (2010). Childhood psychiatric disorders as anomalies in neurodevelopmental trajectories. *Human Brain Mapping*, 31, 917–925.

Shaw, P., Sharp, W., Morrison, M., Eckstrand, K., Greenstein, D., Clasen, L., and Rapoport, J. (2009). Psychostimulant treatment and the developing cortex in attention deficit hyperactivity disorder. *American Journal of Psychiatry*, 166, 58–63.

Shedler, J., and Block, J. (1990). Adolescent drug use and psychological health. A longitudinal inquiry. *American Psychologist*, 45, 612–630.

Shepherd, G. (1998). *The synaptic organization of the brain*. Oxford: Oxford University Press.

Sherman, L., Payton, A., Hernandez, L., Greenfield, P., and Dapretto, M. (2016). The power of the like in adolescence: effects of peer influence on neural and behavioral responses to social media. *Psychological Science*, 27, 1027–1035.

Sibson, N., Dhankhar, A., Mason, G., Rothman, D., Behar, K., and Shulman, R. (1998). Stoichiometric coupling of brain glucose metabolism and glutamatergic neuronal activity. *Proceedings of the National Academy of Sciences USA*, 95, 316–321.

Siebner, H., and Rothwell, J. (2003). Transcranial magnetic stimulation: new insights into representational cortical plasticity. *Experimental Brain Research*, 148, 1–16.

Simos, P., Fletcher, J., Bergman, E., Breier, J., Foorman, B., Castillo, E., Davis, R., Fitzgerald M., and Papanicolaou, A. (2002). Dyslexia-specific brain activation profile becomes normal following successful remedial training. *Neurology*, 58, 1203–1213.

Sisk, C., and Foster, D. (2004). The neural basis of puberty and adolescence. *Nature Neuroscience*, 7, 1040–1047.

Sisk, C., and Zehr, J. (2005). Pubertal hormones organize the adolescent brain and behavior. *Frontiers in Neuroendocrinology*, 26, 163–174.

Slee, P., Campbell, M., and Spears, B. (2012). *Child, adolescent and family development* (3rd edn.). Cambridge: Cambridge University Press.

Slovic, P., Finucane, M., Peters, E., and MacGregor, D. (2004). Risk as analysis and risk as feelings: some thoughts about affect, reason, risk and rationality. *Risk Analysis*, 24, 311–322.

Smeltzer, M., Curtis, J., Aragona, B., and Wang, Z. (2006). Dopamine, oxytocin, and vasopressin receptor binding in the medial prefrontal cortex of monogamous and promiscuous voles. *Neuroscience Letters*, 394, 146–151.

Smith, D., Xiao, L., and Bechara, A. (2012). Decision making in children and adolescents: impaired Iowa Gambling Task performance in early adolescence. *Developmental Psychology*, 48, 1180–1187.

Smith, I., and Beasley, M. (1989). Intelligence and behavior in children with early treated phenylketonuria. *European Journal of Clinical Nutrition*, 43, 1–5.

Smith, L., and Thelen, E. (2003). Development as a dynamic system. *Trends in Cognitive Sciences*, 7, 343–348.

Smith, L., Thelen, E., Titzer, R., and McLin, D. (1999). Knowing in the context of acting: the task dynamics of the A-not-B error. *Psychological Review*, 106, 235–260.

Snow, C., and Hoefnagel-Hohle, M. (1977). Age differences in the pronunciation of foreign sounds. *Language and Speech*, 20, 357–365.

Sokoloff, L. (1973). Metabolism of ketone bodies by the brain. *Annual Reviews of Medicine*, 24, 271–280.

Somerville, L.H. (2013). The teenage brain: sensitivity to social evaluation. *Current Directions in Psychological Science*, 22, 121–127.

Somerville, L., and Casey, B. (2010). Developmental neurobiology of cognitive control and motivational systems. *Current Opinion in Neurobiology*, 20, 236–241.

Somerville, L., Hare, T., and Casey, B.J. (2011). Frontostriatal maturation predicts cognitive control failure to appetitive cues in adolescents. *Journal of Cognitive Neuroscience*, 23, 2123–2134.

Somerville, L., Heatherton, T., and Kelley, A. (2006). Anterior cingulate cortex responds differentially to expectancy violation and social rejection. *Nature Neuroscience*, 9, 1007–1008.

Somerville, L., Jones, R., Ruberry, E., Dyke, J., Glover, G., and Casey, B.J. (2013). The medial prefrontal cortex and the emergence of self-conscious emotion. *Psychological Science*, 24, 1554–1562.

Sowell, E., Peterson, B., Thompson, P., Welcome, S., Henkenius, A., and Toga, A. (2003). Mapping cortical change across the human life span. *Nature Neuroscience*, 6, 309–315.

Sowell, E., Thompson, P., Holmes, C., Jernigan, T., and Toga, A. (1999). In vivo evidence for post-adolescent brain maturation in frontal and striatal regions. *Nature Neuroscience*, 2, 859–861.

Spear, L. (2000). The adolescent brain and age-related behavioral manifestations. *Neuroscience and Biobehavioral Reviews*, 24, 417–463.

(2011). Rewards, aversions and affect in adolescence: emerging convergences across laboratory animal and human data. *Developmental Cognitive Neuroscience*, 1, 392–400.

(2013). Adolescent neurodevelopment. *Journal of Adolescent Health*, 52, S7–S13.

Spencer, N., Bambang, S., Logan, S., and Gill, L. (1999). Socioeconomic status and birth weight: comparison of an area-based measure with the Registrar General's social class. *Journal of Epidemiology and Community Health*, 53, 495–498.

Spencer-Smith, M., and Klingberg, T. (2015). Benefits of a working memory training program for inattention in daily life: a systematic review and meta-analysis. *PLoS One*, 10, e0119522.

Spielberg, J., Jarcho, J., Dahl, R., Pine, D., Ernst, M., and Nelson, E. (2015). Anticipation of peer evaluation in anxious adolescents: divergence in neural activation and maturation. *Social Cognitive and Affective Neuroscience*, 10, 1084–1091.

Spielberg, J., Olino, T., Forbes, E., and Dahl, R. (2014). Exciting fear in adolescence: does pubertal development alter threat processing? *Developmental Cognitive Neuroscience*, 8, 86–95.

Stang, J., and Story, M. (2005). *Guidelines for adolescent nutrition services*. Center for Applied Research and Educational Improvement. St. Paul: University of Minnesota.

Steinberg, L. (2008). A social neuroscience perspective on adolescent risk-taking. *Developmental Review*, 28, 78–106.

(2010). A dual systems model of adolescent risk-taking. *Developmental Psychobiology*, 52, 216–224.

(2014). *Age of opportunity: lessons from the new science of adolescence.* New York: Mariner Books.

Steinberg, L., Albert, D., Cauffman, E., Banich, M., Graham, S., and Woolard, J. (2008). Age differences in sensation seeking and impulsivity as indexed by behavior and self-report: evidence for a dual systems model. *Developmental Psychology*, 44, 1764–1768.

Steinberg, L., Cauffman, E., Woolard, J., Graham, S., and Banich, M. (2009). Are adolescents less mature than adults? Minors' access to abortion, the juvenile death penalty and the alleged APA "Flip-Flop." *American Psychologist*, 64, 583–594.

Steinberg, L., Graham, S., O'Brien, L., Woolard, J., Cauffman, E., and Banich, M. (2009). Age differences in future orientation and delay discounting. *Child Development*, 80, 28–44.

Steinberg, L., and Morris, A. (2001). Adolescent development. *Annual Review of Psychology*, 52, 83–110.

Stevens, M., Kiehl, K., Pearlson, G., and Calhoun, V. (2007). Functional neural networks underlying response inhibition in adolescents and adults. *Behavioural Brain Research*, 181, 12–22.

Sturman, D., and Moghaddam, B. (2012). Striatum processes reward differently in adolescents versus adults. *Proceedings of the National Academy of Sciences USA*, 109, 1719–1724.

Sussman, S. (2002). Effects of sixty-six adolescent tobacco use cessation trials and seventeen prospective studies of self initiated quitting. *Tobacco Induced Diseases*, 1, 35–81.

Swartz, J., Carrasco, M., Wiggins, J., Thomason, M., and Monk, C. (2014). Age-related changes in the structure and function of prefrontal cortex–amygdala circuitry in children and adolescents: a multi-modal imaging approach. *Neuroimage*, 86, 212–220.

Swartz, J.R., Phan, K.L., Angstadt, M., Klumpp, H., Fitzgerald, K.D., and Monk, C.S. (2014). Altered activation of the rostral anterior cingulate cortex in the context of emotional face distractors in children and adolescents with anxiety disorders. *Depression and Anxiety*, 31, 870–879.

Sweeney, J., Mintun, M., Kwee, S., Wiseman, M., Brown, D., Rosenberg, D.R., and Carl, J. (1996). Positron emission tomography study of voluntary saccadic eye movements and spatial working memory. *Journal of Neurophysiology*, 75, 454–468.

Suleiman, A., Johnson, M., Shirtcliff, E., and Galván, A. (2015). School-based sex education and neuroscience: what we know about sex, romance, marriage, and adolescent brain development. *Journal of School Health*, 85, 567–574.

Takahashi, Y., Roesch, M., Stalnaker, T., Haney, R., Calu, D., Taylor, A., and Schoenbaum, G. (2009). The orbitofrontal cortex and ventral tegmental area are necessary for learning from unexpected outcomes. *Neuron*, 62, 269–280.

Tamm, L., Menon, V., and Reiss, A. L. (2002). Maturation of brain function associated with response inhibition. *Journal of the American Academy of Child and Adolescent Psychiatry*, 41, 1231–1238.

Tanaka, J., and Farah, M. (1993). Parts and wholes in face recognition. *Quarterly Journal of Experimental Psychology A*, 46, 225–245.

Tantam, D., Monaghan, L., Nicholson, H., and Stirling, J. (1989). Autistic children's ability to interpret faces: a research note. *Journal of Child Psychology and Psychiatry*, 30, 623–630.

Teicher, M., Andersen, S., and Hostetter, J.C. (1995). Evidence for dopamine receptor pruning between adolescence and adulthood in striatum but not nucleus accumbens. *Developmental Brain Research*, 89, 167–172.

Teles, M., Silveira, L., Tusset, C., and Latronico, A. (2011). New genetic factors implicated in human GnRH-dependent precocious puberty: the role of kisspeptin system. *Molecular Cell Endocrinology*, 346(1–2), 84–90.

Telzer, E., Fuligni, A., Lieberman, M., and Galván, A. (2014). Neural sensitivity to eudaimonic and hedonic rewards differentially predict adolescent depressive symptoms over time. *Proceedings of the National Academy of Sciences USA*, 111, 6600–6605.

Thomas, K.M., Drevets, W.C., Dahl, R.E., Ryan, N.D., Birmaher, B., Eccard, C.H., and Casey, B.J. (2001). Amygdala response to fearful faces in anxious and depressed children. *Archives of General Psychiatry*, 58, 1057–1063.

Thompson, P., Hayashi, K., Sowell, E., Gogtay, N., Giedd, J., Rapoport, J., de Zubicaray, G.I., Janke, A.L, Rose, S.E., Semple, J., Doddrell, D.M., Yang, Y., van Erp, T.G., Cannon, and Toga, A. (2004). Mapping cortical change in Alzheimer's disease, brain development, and schizophrenia. *Neuroimage*, 23, S2–S18.

Thompson, R.A., and Nelson, C.A. (2001). Developmental science and the media. Early brain development. *American Psychologist*, 56(1), 5–15.

Thorell, L., Lindqvist, S., Bergman Nutley, S., Bohlin, G., and Klingberg, T. (2009). Training and transfer effects of executive functions in preschool children. *Developmental Science*, 12, 106–113.

Todd, M., Nystrom, L., and Cohen, J. (2013). Confounds in multivariate pattern analysis: theory and rule representation case study. *Neuroimage*, 77, 157–165.

Toldi, J., Rojik, I., and Feher, O. (1994). Neonatal monocular enucleation-induced cross-modal effects observed in the cortex of adult rat. *Neuroscience*, 62, 105–114.

Tolson, K., and Chappell, P. (2012). The changes they are a-timed: metabolism, endogenous clocks, and the timing of puberty. *Frontiers in Endocrinology (Lausanne)*, 3, 45.

Torres, O., Tejeda, H., Natividad, L., and O'Dell, L. (2008). Enhanced vulnerability to the rewarding effects of nicotine during the adolescent period of development. *Pharmacology, Biochemistry and Behavior*, 90, 658–663.

Tottenham, N. (2014). The importance of early experiences for neuro-affective development. *Current Topics in Behavioral Neuroscience*, 16, 109–129.

Tottenham, N., Hare, T., and Casey, B. (2009). A developmental perspective on human amygdala function. In P. Whalen and E. Phelps (eds.), *The human amygdala* (pp. 107–117). New York: The Guilford Press.

Tottenham, N., Hare, T.A., Milner, A., Gilhooly, T., Zevin, J.D., and Casey, B.J. (2011). Elevated amygdala response to faces following early deprivation. *Developmental Science*, 1, 46–61.

Tottenham, N., Hare, T., Quinn, B., McCarry, T., Nurse, M., Gilhooly, T., Milner, A., Galván, A., Davidson, M.C., Eigsti, I.M., Thomas, K.M., Freed, P.J., Booma, E.S., Gunnar, M.R., Altemus, M., Aronson, J., and Casey, B. (2010). Prolonged institutional rearing is associated with atypically large amygdala volume and difficulties in emotion regulation. *Developmental Science*, 13, 46–61.

Treadway, M., Buckholtz, J., Cowan, R., Woodward, N., Li, R., Ansari, M., Baldwin, R.M., Schwartzmann, A.N., Kessler R.M., and Zald, D. (2012). Dopaminergic mechanisms of individual differences in human effort-based decision-making. *Journal of Neuroscience*, 32, 6170–6176.

Treit, S., Chen, Z., Rasmussen, C., and Beaulieu, C. (2014). White matter correlates of cognitive inhibition during development: a diffusion tensor imaging study. *Neuroscience*, 276, 87–97.

Turkheimer, E., Haley, A., Waldron, M., D'Onofrio, B., and Gottesman, I. (2003). Socioeconomic status modifies heritability of IQ in young children. *Psychological Science*, 14, 623–628.

Tymula, A., Rosenberg Belmaker, L., Roy, A., Ruderman, L., Manson, K., Glimcher, P., and Levy, I. (2012). Adolescents' risk-taking behavior is driven by tolerance to ambiguity. *Proceedings of the National Academy of Sciences USA*, 109, 17,135–17,140.

UN (2011). The state of the world's children 2011. Adolescence: an age of opportunity. New York, United Nations Children's Fund, 2011;

Emerging issues in adolescent health. *Journal of Adolescent Health*, 52, S1–S45.

(2012). The Lancet Series on Adolescent Health. *The Lancet*.

Urberg, K. (1992). Locus of peer influence: social crowd and best friend. *Journal of Youth and Adolescence*, 21, 439–450.

Urošević, S., Collins, P., Muetzel, R., Lim, K., and Luciana, M. (2012). Longitudinal changes in behavioral approach system sensitivity and brain structures involved in reward processing during adolescence. *Developmental Psychology*, 48, 1488–1500.

US Department of Education (2015). http://collegecost.ed.gov/catc/default .aspx.

van den Bos, W., Cohen, M., Kahnt, T., and Crone, E. (2012). Striatum-medial prefrontal cortex connectivity predicts developmental changes in reinforcement learning. *Cerebral Cortex*, 22, 1247–1255.

van der Geest, J., Kemner, C., Verbaten, M., and van Engeland, H. (2002). Gaze behavior of children with pervasive developmental disorder toward human faces: a fixation time study. *Journal of Psychology and Psychiatry*, 43, 669–678.

van der Meer, L., Groenewold, N., Nolen, W., Pijnenborg, M., and Aleman, A. (2011). Inhibit yourself and understand the other: neural basis of distinct processes underlying Theory of Mind. *Neuroimage*, 56(4), 2364–2374.

van Dijk, K., Sabuncu, M., and Buckner, R. (2012). The influence of head motion on intrinsic functional connectivity. *Neuroimage*, 59, 431–438.

van Duijvenvoorde, A., and Crone, E. (2013). The teenage brain: a neuroeconomic approach to adolescent decision making. *Current Directions in Psychological Science*, 22, 108–113.

van Duijvenvoorde, A., Jansen, B., Bredman, J., and Huizenga, H. (2012). Age-related changes in decision making: comparing informed and noninformed situations. *Developmental Psychology*, 48, 192–203.

van Duijvenvoorde, A.C., Op de Macks, Z.A., Overgaauw, S., Gunther Moor, B., Dahl, R.E., and Crone, E.A. (2014). A cross-sectional and longitudinal analysis of reward-related brain activation: effects of age, pubertal stage, and reward sensitivity. *Brain and Cognition*, 89, 3–14.

Van Leijenhorst, L., Crone, E., and van der Molen, M. (2007). Developmental trends for object and spatial working memory: a psychophysiological analysis. *Child Development*, 78, 987–1000.

van Leijenhorst, L., Moor, B., Op de Macks, Z., Rombouts, S., Westenberg, P., and Crone, E. (2010a). Adolescent risky decision-making:

neurocognitive development of reward and control regions. *Neuroimage*, 51, 345–355.

van Leijenhorst, L., Zanolie, K., van Meel, C., Westenberg, P., Rombouts, S., and Crone, E. (2010b). What motivates the adolescent? Brain regions mediating reward sensitivity across adolescents. *Cerebral Cortex*, 20, 61–69.

van Praag, H., Shubert, T., Zhao, C., and Gage, F. (2005). Exercise enhances learning and hippocampal neurogenesis in aged mice. *Journal of Neuroscience*, 25, 8680–8685.

Varlinskaya, E., and Spear, L. (2008). Social interactions in adolescent and adult Sprague-Dawley rats: impact of social deprivation and test context familiarity. *Behavioral Brain Research*, 188, 398–405.

Vasilyeva, M., Waterfall, H., and Huttenlocher, J. (2008). Emergence of syntax: commonalities and differences across children. *Developmental Science*, 11, 84–97.

Vidal, C., Rapoport, J., Hayashi, K., Geaga, J., Sui, Y., McLemore, L., Alaghband, Y., Giedd, J.N., Gochman, P., Blumenthal, J., Gogtay, N., Nicolson, R., Toga, A.W., and Thompson, P. (2006). Dynamically spreading frontal and cingulate deficits mapped in adolescents with schizophrenia. *Archives of General Psychiatry*, 63, 25–34.

Voas, R., Torres, P., Romano, E., and Lacey, J. (2012). Alcohol-related risk of driver fatalities: an update using 2007 data. *Journal of Studies on Alcohol and Drugs*, 73, 341–350.

Volgyi, B., Farkas, T., and Toldi, J. (1993). Compensation of a sensory deficit inflicted upon newborn and adult animals. A behavioural study. *Neuroreport*, 4, 827–829.

Volkow, N., Wang, G., Fowler, F., and Tomasi, D. (2012). Addiction circuitry in the human brain. *Annual Review of Pharmacology and Toxicology*, 52, 321–336.

Volman, I., Toni, I., Verhagen, L., and Roelofs, K. (2011). Endogenous testosterone modulates prefrontal–amygdala connectivity during social emotional behavior. *Cerebral Cortex*, 21, 2282–2290.

Vorona, R., Szklo-Coxe, M., Wu, A., Dubik, M., Zhao, Y., and Catesby Ware, J. (2011). Dissimilar teen crash rates in two neighboring southeastern Virginia cities with different high school start times. *Journal of Clinical Sleep Medicine*, 7, 145–151.

Voss, H., and Schiff, N. (2009). MRI of neuronal network structure, function, and plasticity. *Progress in Brain Research*, 175, 483–496.

Voss, P., Collignon, D., Lassonde, M., and Lepore, F. (2010). Adaptation to sensory loss. *Wiley Interdisciplinary Review of Cognitive Science*, 1, 308–328.

Vyas, A., Mitra, R., Shankaranarayana Rao, B., and Chattarji, S. (2002). Chronic stress induces contrasting patterns of dendritic remodeling in hippocampal and amygdaloid neurons. *Journal of Neuroscience*, 22, 6810–6818.

Wager, T., Davidson, M., Hughes, B., Lindquist, M., and Ochsner, K. (2008). Prefrontal-subcortical pathways mediating successful emotion regulation. *Neuron*, 59, 1037–1050.

Wahlstrohm, K. (2002). Changing times: findings from the first longitudinal study of later high school start times. *National Association of Secondary School Principles (NASSP) Bulletin*, 286, 3–21.

Wahlstrohm, K., Dretzke, B., Gordon, M., Peterson, K., Edwards, K., and Gdula, J. (2014). *Examining the impact of later school start times on the health and academic performance of high school students: a multi-site study. Center for Applied Research and Educational Improvement*. St. Paul: University of Minnesota.

Walden, T., and Field, T. (1982). Discrimination of facial expressions by preschool children. *Child Development*, 53, 1312–1319.

Wang, A., Dapretto, M., Hariri, A., Sigman, M., and Bookheimer, S. (2004). Neural correlates of facial affect processing in children and adolescents with autism spectrum disorder. *Journal of the American Academy of Child and Adolescent Psychiatry*, 43, 481–490.

Warneken, F., and Tomasello, M. (2006). Altruistic helping in human infants and young chimpanzees. *Science*, 311, 1301–1303.

(2008). Extrinsic rewards undermine altruistic tendencies in 20-month-olds. *Developmental Psychology*, 44, 1785–1788.

(2009). Varieties of altruism in children and chimpanzees. *Trends in Cognitive Neuroscience*, 13, 397–402.

(2013). The emergence of contingent reciprocity in young children. *Journal of Experimental Child Psychology*, 116, 338–350.

Warren, M., and Vu, C. (2003). Central causes of hypogonadism – functional and organic. *Endocrinology Metabolism Clinics of North America*, 32(3), 593–612.

Watanabe, Y., Gould, E., and McEwen, B. (1992). Stress induces atrophy of apical dendrites of hippocampal CA3 pyramidal neurons. *Brain Research*, 588, 341–345.

Waylen, A., and Wolke, D. (2004). Sex 'n' drugs 'n' rock 'n' roll: the meaning and social consequences of pubertal timing. *European Journal of Endocrinology*, 151 Suppl. 3, U151–U159.

Weeks, S., and Hobson, R. (1987). The salience of facial expression for autistic children. *Journal of Child Psychology and Psychiatry*, 28, 137–151.

Weisleder, A., and Fernald, A. (2013). Talking to children matters: early language experience strengthens processing and builds vocabulary. *Psychological Science*, 24, 2143–2152.

Wellman, H., Lopez-Duran, S., LaBounty, J., and Hamilton, B. (2008). Infant attention to intentional action predicts preschool theory of mind. *Developmental Psychology*, 44, 618–623.

Westerberg, H., and Klingberg, T. (2007). Changes in cortical activity after training of working memory – a single-subject analysis. *Physiology and Behavior*, 92, 186–192.

Westlake, E., and Boyle, L. (2012). Perceptions of driver distraction among teenage drivers. *Transportation Research, Part F*, 15, 644–653.

Whalen, P., Kagan, J., Cook, R., Davis, F., Kim, H., Polis, S., McLaren, D.G., Somerville, L.H., McLean, A.A., Maxwel, J.S., and Johnstone, T. (2004). Human amygdala responsivity to masked fearful eye whites. *Science*, 306, 2061.

Whalen, P., Rauch, S., Etcoff, N., McInerney, S., Lee, M., and Jenike, M. (1998). Masked presentations of emotional facial expressions modulate amygdala activity without explicit knowledge. *Journal of Neuroscience*, 18, 411–418.

Wiesel, T., and Hubel, D. (1963). Single cell responses in striate cortex of kittens deprived of vision in one eye. *Journal of Neurophysiology*, 26, 1003–1017.

Will, G., van Lier, P., Crone, E., and Guroglu, B. (2016). Chronic childhood peer rejection is associated with heightened neural responses to social exclusion during adolescence. *Journal of Abnormal Psychology*, 44, 43–55.

Williams, A. (2006). Young driver risk factors: successful and unsuccessful approaches for dealing with them and an agenda for the future. *Injury and Prevention*, 12, 4–8.

Williams, J., Waiter, G., Gilchrist, A., Perrett, D., Murray, A., and Whiten, A. (2006). Neural mechanisms of imitation and "mirror neuron" functioning in autism spectrum disorder. *Neuropsychologia*, 44, 610–621.

Wilmouth, C., and Spear, L. (2009). Hedonic sensitivity in adolescent and adult rats: taste reactivity and voluntary sucrose consumptio. *Pharmacology, Biochemistry and Behavior*, 92, 566–573.

Wong, W., Nicolson, M., Stuff, J., Butte, N., Ellis, K., Hergenroeder, A., and Smith, E. (1998). Serum leptin concentrations in Caucasian and African-American girls. *Journal of Clinical Endocrinology and Metabolism*, 83, 3574–3577.

Woolley, C., Gould, E., and McEwen, B. (1990). Exposure to excess glucocorticoids alters dendritic morphology of adult hippocampal pyramidal neurons. *Brain Research*, 531, 225–231.

Wu, T., Mendola, P., and Buck, G. (2002). Ethnic differences in the presence of secondary sex characteristics and menarche among US girls: the Third National Health and Nutrition Examination Survey, 1988–1994. *Pediatrics*, 110, 752–757.

Zatorre, R., Chen, J., and Penhune, V. (2007). When the brain plays music: auditory–motor interactions in music perception and production. *Nature Reviews Neuroscience*, 8, 547–558.

Zhang, Y., Proenca, R., Maffei, M., Barone, M., Leopold, L., and Friedman, J. (1994). Positional cloning of the mouse obese gene and its human homologue. *Nature*, 372, 425–432.

Index

Printed in the USA
CPSIA information can be obtained
at www.ICGtesting.com
LVHW021123290823
756611LV00003B/36

9 781107 461857